RELIGIOUS BROADCASTING
IN THE MIDDLE EAST

KHALED HROUB

Editor

Religious Broadcasting in the Middle East

HURST & COMPANY, LONDON

First published in the United Kingdom in 2012 by
C. Hurst & Co. (Publishers) Ltd.,
41 Great Russell Street, London, WC1B 3PL
© Khaled Hroub and the Contributors, 2012
All rights reserved.

Distributed in the United States, Canada and Latin America by
Oxford University Press, 198 Madison Avenue, New York, NY 10016,
United States of America.

The right of Khaled Hroub and the Contributors to be identified as
the authors of this publication is asserted by them in accordance with
the Copyright, Designs and Patents Act, 1988.

A Cataloguing-in-Publication data record for this book
is available from the British Library.

ISBN: 978-1-84904-132-4 *Hardback*
  978-1-84904-133-1 *Paperback*

This book is printed on paper from registered sustainable
and managed sources.

www.hurstpublishers.com

CONTENTS

ACKNOWLEDGEMENTS

This volume is the outcome of a research project which has benefitted from invaluable and wide-ranging individual and institutional contributions. I first need to thank Roula El-Rifai of the Middle East Unit at the Canadian International Development Research Centre (IDRC). Roula and her colleagues were the first to receive our proposal on the rise of religious broadcasting in the area and discussed it thoroughly with us. From IDRC approval of the funding of the project, right through to publication, she has been hugely helpful and supportive. Needless to say, without the generous grant made by the dedicated IDRC to fund the proposal, neither the project nor this book would ever have materialised. The IDRC deserves our sincerest gratitude, not only for supporting the project, but also for their impressively wide-ranging work over the years in supporting research on the Middle East.

Leading the project and editing this volume would have not been possible for me without the fantastic help of my colleagues at the Cambridge Arab Media Project (CAMP) and the Centre of Islamic Studies (CIS) at the Faculty of Asian and Middle Eastern Studies of the University of Cambridge. At the head of a long list is my friend and colleague Professor Yasir Suleiman, the Director of the CIS and the Head of the Middle East Department at the time the project was conducted, for which the concluding conference took place in December 2009. His overall professional supervision of the project was a model of academic management, giving space to individual initiatives, yet intervening at the right time and place. At the CIS I also thank my colleague Dr Paul Anderson who attended our conference before joining the CIS as its Assistant

Director, and marvellously compiled and edited a short monograph summarising the proceedings of the conference; Emma Wells and Kathy Oswald, at the time secretaries at the CIS, who worked tirelessly during the period of the project; Clare Bannister the current secretary of CIS; and Dr Saeko Yazaki, the outreach and project officer at the CIS, who took over and followed the detailed administration of the project impressively. My dearest friend and colleague Dr Abduallah Baabood, the Director of the Cambridge branch of the Gulf Research Centre (GRCC), has, as usual, been a source of inspiration and a rock throughout.

In Abu Dhabi, we are extremely grateful to the Emirates Centre for Strategic Studies and Research (ECSSR) and its Director Jamal Al-Suwaidi for the wonderful help and support they provided us. Dr Suwaidi made available to us the highly equipped multi-recording facilities of the media unit, where the staff led by the kind Mr Mohammad Al-Ali monitored and recoded material transmitted on dozens of channels over many weeks. Sincere thanks go also to Dr Ahmad Jamil Azm who helped in connecting CAMP and ECSSR and followed the process of communication. Also in the UAE, sincere thanks are due to Professor Mohammad Ayish, from Sharja University, and Dr Abeer Al-Najjar, from The American University of Sharja, for the preliminary and immaculate job of drafting the 'coding-categories' and tools for content analysis which have been used by our team of 'decoders.' Both colleagues have contributed two indispensible chapters to this volume. I also owe my friend Shatha Al-Juburi sincere thanks for her insightful remarks on Iraqi channels and their nuanced links with political parties.

In Ramallah and Birzeit, Palestine, Juman Qunies from the Media Department of Birzeit University led a team of energetic young media graduates who worked on transcribing and producing coded-categories of the televised recorded material. Besides the time and effort that she devoted in order to accomplish her other part of the project and write a chapter for this volume, she had to follow the demanding process of monitoring and transcribing, then guaranteeing that every contributor received their material ready for analysis. The Ramallah-based Palestinian media NGO, *Amin Network*, offered the venue and technical facilities for the team to undertake their job. The Director of Amin, Khalid Abu Aker, showed extraordinary kindness in hosting the team of young media researchers, always with a smile and with wonderful spirit. Michael Dwyer, Managing Director of Hurst & Co., our publisher in London, his Editor Jonathan de Peyer, and Kathleen May, the Marketing Director, and the rest of the team at Hurst have all done a wonderful job in following this volume step by step. Michael embraced the idea of publishing the findings and proceedings of the conference from the outset. I also thank my colleague Pam Manix, based in Oxford, who has helped in the preliminary editing of some of the chapters, polishing their style and language. Finally, the greatest gratitude goes to the contributors of this volume who have each and every one allocated significant time and effort to produce this book, which I hope will pioneer a new research area and advance discussion and debate on religious broadcasting in the Middle East.

Khaled Hroub

ABOUT THE CONTRIBUTORS

Gihan Abou Zeid is a veteran of the human rights movement and a specialist in female Islamist preachers in the Arab world. Since 2005 she has been an advisor for the United Nations Special Report on Disability in the Arab region, and is a Technical Advisor in the areas of women's political participation, youth polices and gender mainstreaming in the Arab world. In addition to writing two books, she has edited four others, and contributes to scholarly books and journals.

Dr Abeer Al-Najjar is the Dean of the Jordan Media Institute, Amman, Jordan and Assistant Professor of Journalism Studies at the American University of Sharjah in the UAE. She has a PhD in international journalism from Edinburgh and considerable professional media experience in both print journalism and television production.

Dr Atef Alshaer completed his PhD on the topic of 'Language and National Identity in Palestine' at the School of Oriental and African Studies (SOAS), where he now teaches. He has published several articles and book reviews in various academic journals, journalistic media and websites.

Professor Mohammad Ayish holds a doctorate in international broadcasting and public diplomacy from the University of Minnesota-Twin Cities, USA (1986). He had worked both as Dean of the College of Communication and Professor of Communication at the University of Sharjah, United Arab Emirates. Ayish is currently on leave in Ottawa, Canada.

Farah Dakhlallah is a communications specialist and researcher on Middle East affairs. She has worked with numerous international organisations including Reuters, Al Jazeera, Channel 4, France 24, PBS, News Xchange, the Arab Broadcast Forum, Relief International, the United Nations High Commissioner for Refugees and the International Labour Organization. She is a graduate of the Université Saint Joseph, the London School of Economics and the University of Cambridge.

Rafid Fadhil Ali is journalist, writer and reporter for the BBC World Service. Rafid is an expert in Iraqi politics and militant groups in the Middle East. He covered the Iraq war from the field. Rafid writes frequently in English and Arabic for publications such as the Jamestown Foundation's *Terrorism Monitor* and *Militant Leaders Monitor*, and the daily Arab newspaper *al-Hayat*.

Sameh Fawzy is a researcher in graduate studies at Sussex University, and holds a Masters degree in Governance and Development, and accountability in public administration. Fawzy is a writer, researcher and the Deputy Director of the Dialogue Forum at Bibliotheca Alexandrina. He has authored a number of books on Coptic concerns, minority freedom and good governance. He is a member of the Arab Muslim Christian Team for Dialogue.

Dr Ehab Galal is Assistant Professor at the Institute for Cross-Cultural and Regional Studies at the University of Copenhagen. He has studied Arab media. His current research project is a qualitative and comparative study of audience responses to Islamic TV, both in Europe and the Middle East, where he has undertaken several long-term ethnographic fieldwork projects.

Dr Ayla Göl is a lecturer on the international politics of the Middle East and a Research Associate at the Centre for the Study of Radicalisation and Contemporary Political Violence (CSRV) in the Department of International Politics, Aberystwyth University. She holds a PhD from the London School of Economics (LSE). Her recent publications include 'The Identity of Turkey: Muslim and Secular', *Third World Quarterly*, 30(4), 2009 and (as Guest Editor), Special Issue, 'The War on Terror: Perspectives from the Global South', *Critical Studies on Terrorism*, 2010.

Dr Khaled Hroub is the Director of the Cambridge Arab Media Project (CAMP) in association with the Centre for Islamic Studies, University of Cambridge. He is the author of *Hamas: A Beginner's Guide*, (Pluto Press, 2006) and *Hamas: Political Thought and Practice* (IPS: Washington DC, 2000); and has edited *Political Islam: Context vs Ideology* (Saqi, 2010). Hroub hosted a weekly book review show on Al Jazeera from 2000 to 2006 and is a writer and commentator for several Arab and Western media outlets.

Ilan Manor graduated from Tel Aviv University, where he studied media studies, communication and psychology. He is currently involved in a research group which examines the use of remote learning as a tool for increasing health literacy amongst adolescents. His writings, which deal with the portrayal of Israeli society in the mass media, have appeared in numerous publications and websites.

Dr Yonatan Mendel has a PhD from Cambridge University and is now a post-doctoral researcher at the Department of Politics and Government at the Ben Gurion University of the Negev. His current research deals with Zionist publications in Arabic in the pre-state period. Mendel previously worked as a journalist in Israel, and is a contributor to the *London Review of Books*.

Juman Quneis teaches broadcast media at Birzeit University, and holds a Masters in human rights and democracy from that university. She was the Project Manager for AMIN Network (2007–2009) and the Senior Announcer and Producer for Voice of Palestine (1996–2006). Quneis has edited three books on the media, published by the Media Development Center at Birzeit University.

Olfa Tantawi has a dual Master's degree in International Communication And Television Journalism from Tantawi and gained extensive experience working as a communicator in the field of development, advocating human rights and policy reform on a variety of issues, using social media among other tools. Currently, she is the Advocacy And Communication Officer at a UN joint programme sponsored by the MDG Achievement Fund. Tantawi is also a documentary filmmaker, her first film, 'No Choice', dealt with the personal life choices of young activists in Egypt.

PREFACE

When the idea of the research project that was the basis for this book was conceived three years ago there had been no Arab revolutions. The initial impulse of the project in 2008 had been to examine the significance of the rapidly increasing number of religious broadcasting channels in the Arab world. Religious media in various forms have always been a principal tool in the process of Islamising societies, a strategy adopted and promoted by Islamist parties, whether legal or outlawed. During and after the Arab Spring the role of Islamists and religion at large has become an immediate concern for many. In the cases where revolutions succeeded in overthrowing old regimes, as in Tunisia, Egypt and Libya, liberal and secular circles fear that post-revolution political systems could fall under the control of Islamist parties. The spectre of replacing police states with religious states is very worrying, to say the least.

In the successful revolutionary cases, as well as in those where revolutions are still in progress, Islamist parties have invested enormous effort and mobilised masses in order to gain control of the political system resulting from these revolutions. Opponents of the Islamists view any such control as an impediment that would block any space that may have emerged for evolving civil, secular and plural politics. Moderate and fanatical Islamists, in their pursuit of power and control, have joined forces to deploy all the resources at their disposal, including, of course, the media. If the media have always been widely and massively employed by Islamists to promote the 'Islam is the solution' mantra, TV broadcasting and modern means of communication have now become a central strategy in the 'imagined phase' of the implementation of that motto. Many Islamists are nervous about missing this historic opportunity, when Arab societies emerging from peaceful or bloody revolutions are at a crossroads: either they 'slip' into a form of 'un-Islamic polity', repeating previous cycles of secular governance, or they head in a direction in which Islam takes a leading position. The battle nowadays is in fact becoming very fierce between Islamist and secular forces, notwithstanding the remarkable imbalance of power favouring the former.

In the middle of this battle religious channels are gearing up. In this book contributors have examined religious channels which in pre-revolution times avoided covering politics and kept to their orthodox discourse of religion. Then, the purity of religion would have been tainted by politics and keeping a healthy distance was a must. This stance was promoted and strongly embraced by mainstream Salafi discourse, scholars, movements and channels. Salafi channels are the most influential, as the chapters in this volume demonstrate. After the revolutions, and the sharp rise of Islamist parties, Salafi and non-Salafi alike, this approach has dramatically changed. Salafi discourses and movements, particularly in Tunisia and Egypt, have not only become politicised at an astonishing speed, but have also taken the leap to form official parties which aim to compete in elections—practices that until recently were depicted as akin to sinning. The same applies to what used to be apoliticised religious channels, whose recent and enthusiastic engagement in politics and political debates has broken years of tradition and political indifference. At this juncture, this shift in Islamist politics and media, especially Salafi-oriented ones including religious broadcasting, is remarkable. Therefore this book, I hope, comes at no more appropriate a time.

Khaled Hroub
January 2012

1

INTRODUCTION

RELIGIOUS BROADCASTING: BEYOND THE INNOCENCE OF POLITICAL INDIFFERENCE

Khaled Hroub

Over the past decade and a half the influence of television broadcasting in the Middle East has become central to the shaping of public attitudes. It varies in form, substance, scale of operation, nature of ownership and outreach, and while the most influential mainstream television broadcasting has been news-focused, entertainment and religious broadcasting have been no less significant. Mostly functioning against a public backdrop marked by sustainable authoritarian governments, political instabilities, wars and pervasive foreign military interventions, this diverse broadcasting emerged as a somewhat unique platform for the expression of public views and opinions that would otherwise have been less articulated, if not totally disallowed. Numerous research approaches have analysed the various socio-political and cultural aspects of the impact of this broadcasting. Most research has focused, however, on the novelty of the phenomenon and the provision of venues for a Habermasian 'public sphere' within a Middle Eastern (and mainly Arabic) setting. The crossing of hitherto inflexible and narrow boundaries of expression and the breaking of taboos have been

1

acknowledged as some of the greatest achievements of news broadcasting in particular. The role and effect of Al Jazeera, in particular,
has been widely discussed, and the channel is credited with leading
a revolution not only in Arab media but, for some analysts, in Arab
politics as well.[1] The general scene and format of Middle Eastern,
and specifically Arab, media has thus dramatically changed.

Relatively less focus, however, has been given to the substance
and discursive content that has been emerging and occupying the
countless broadcasting outlets, large and small, that have mush-
roomed across the region. Or at least certain tendencies in this
broadcasting, including religious tendencies, have not attracted as
much attention and research as they really merit. In the midst of
this uncontrolled wave of expansion, due in part to the technical
ease and relative low cost of launching a satellite channel, a number of purely 'religious' channels have appeared.[2] Equally importantly, mainstream channels, such as Al Jazeera, Al Arabiya (and
its sister channel the MBC), and Dubai, have their own religious
programmes and talk shows. Each of the newly emergent religious channels or programmes promotes a particular interpretation
of the issues under discussion. Some insist on a non-political
approach, others have no such limitation. But taken as a whole
these channels and programmes comprise a truly new phenomenon in the area, given their number, capabilities, audiences and
outreach. The charged regional political and religious atmosphere
is certainly propitious for the messages and content delivered by
this kind of broadcasting. Given the fact that the 'Arab street' is
mostly dominated by movements and discourses which are shaped
or influenced by political Islam, religious broadcasting has been
playing a greater role than other kinds of broadcasting in communicating values and promoting certain social and cultural ideals
that correspond to the existing political and cultural projects advocated by political Islam movements.[3] Thus, there is a mutual 'feed-
in' process spiralling between the dominant 'religious atmosphere'
and religious broadcasting. Central to this process, as is shown in
most of the chapters in this volume, is the socio-political and cultural claim of ethical superiority and higher moral ground embedded in the discursive deliveries of these religious broadcasters.

Religious broadcasting in the Arab world is not limited to Islamic channels and broadcasting. Rather it expands to include Christian and Jewish broadcasting. Part of this broadcasting has evolved as a response to internal factors and changes that have taken place within their own particular settings. Yet other parts, especially Arabic-Christian broadcasting have, arguably, emerged in response to the dramatic rise of Islamic broadcasting (and Islamism at large).[4] Television channels (the focus of these contributions) and radio stations promoting Christian or Jewish ideals have been established in the past few years, again claiming a divine and superior value system that is second to none. The three types of broadcasting—Islamic, Christian and Jewish—offer a new phenomenon that is still as yet under-researched. The bulk of this volume will focus on the first type.

Religious Resurgence and the Media

Religious broadcasting is part of a global religious resurgence that has been taking place over the past few decades. The term 'Televangelists' goes beyond its Christian connotations and could be conveniently applied to preachers of all religions and creeds who vigorously use televised media to proselytise a religious message. In the Middle East, the same phenomenon has emerged within Muslim, Christian and Jewish communities. Clergymen (and women) in all faiths have long shared virtually the same diagnosis regarding the ills that have befallen their societies. Ignorance of religion and preoccupation with a materialistic life are the roots of all kinds of problems and misery at individual and collective levels. Whatever the religion, and across time and space, the basic message promulgated by the clergy has been simple and straightforward: a return to religion is the key to solving all problems. From this perspective the following discussion will attempt to contextualise the emergence and influence of religious broadcasting in the Arabic Middle East in particular, for this broadcasting is in fact the main focus of most of the chapters in this volume. A convenient starting point is to place this broadcasting within the broader phenomenon of Islamism and the rise of political Islam.

3

In the background of most forms of Islamism is a particular sense of Muslim weakness along with the nagging feeling of lagging behind 'advanced nations.' For contemporary Islamists, it all started amid the consequences of the historic Muslim defeat at the hands of the West which culminated in the collapse of the Ottoman Caliphate in the early 1920s. At the heart of the 'Islamist' diagnosis of the reasons behind the drastic fall of the Caliphate and its pan-Muslim system lies one single factor: the deviation of Muslims from the true path of Islam. The causal link between the chains of disasters that had befallen Muslims in the last two centuries and their divergence from 'pure Islamic teachings' is undoubtedly within Islamist thinking. For Muslims to regain the glorious position they enjoyed in the past they must embrace Islam and reinstate it at the top of their political and social system. Therefore, re-Islamisation of Muslims has thus far emerged as the major concern and strategy of Islamism. Islamisation, the Islamist argument goes, would bring back strong Muslim peoples and countries that would be able to defy domestic and foreign challenges and rid the *umma* of all signs of weakness and backwardness.

The Islamisation project assumes that Muslims the world over have to be re-Islamised, brought back to the course of religion that they have abandoned over time. How to implement this Islamisation in reality is an area over which the Islamists have differed, and in some cases, fought with each other fiercely. Some groups believe that Islamisation is a non-violent, reformist and slow bottom-up process starting from the basic unit of the individual. Gradual change would expand the 'Islamised' spheres horizontally and vertically, ultimately leading to the desired change at the top. Others advocate a revolutionary course of action believing that the incremental grassroots approach has run out of steam and proved to be a failure. Fighting, violently if needed, against the status quo to bring about radical change by revolution is the way to circumvent what would have otherwise been a long and endless process. These two main strands of understanding have of course many intellectual sub-divisions and organisational offshoots. Proponents of each approach to Islamism would propagate their vision of change and strive to implement specific mechanisms of Islamisation.

But all branches of Islamism focus greatly on the use of all sorts of media to reach out to more audiences and deliver their message. Trans-border televised media has proven in the past decade to be the genie that could generate wonders for Islamisation. A sermon that used to be given to a crowd of hundreds of people inside a mosque could be now transmitted across borders to hundreds of thousands of viewers. Reaching out to such disparate and distant audiences had until recently been unthinkable. Even ordinary religious teaching and reciting of the Quran and Sunnah (the sayings and deeds of the Prophet) has enjoyed the benefits offered by the new platform of transnational television. Instead of those small circles of individuals reciting Quranic versus in mosques or classes of religious schools for, say, an hour at a time, the same recitation is now followed and imitated by tens of thousands, and that hour of time becomes multiplied many times.

Religious Material on Arab TV

Broadcasting 'benign' religious material on Arab TV had in fact started with the introduction of the first TV transmission systems in the Arab world in the late 1950s and early 1960s. Over the years, religious features, such as starting the broadcasting day with verses of the Quran, relaying the *Azan* (call prayer), and covering Friday Prayer became common. On religious occasions and during seasons such as the holy month of Ramadan more religion-oriented material would be aired, including historical drama. Bearing in mind that these stations were then under the full control of the state, the religious dose in this official media, including TV, had been carefully injected and politically calculated, mostly to furnish an Islamic image to the eyes of the public of secular and corrupt regimes.

The greatest push that religious broadcasting had enjoyed came about in the late 1990s with the rapid rise of Arab broadcasting stations such as Al Jazeera which, in 1996 started to transmit a weekly religious life show, 'Sharia and Life' (*Al Sharia wa al Hayat*), led and delivered by the charismatic scholar Yousuf Al Qardawi, as detailed by Mohammad Ayish in chapter two in this volume. Al Jazeera changed the face of Arab media, and politics to a certain extent, forever. Among other things, it introduced into the Arab media three new, major and dramatic changes all at once: trans-border broadcasting, trans-ceiling coverage and modern technology. Trans-border TV broadcasting meant that a channel based at one end of the Arab world, could beam out to audiences at the other end, or beyond the Arab world altogether. Trans-ceiling coverage meant that imposed limitations with low ceilings of expression were broken. Modern technology meant the introduction of a state of the art TV industry, which includes all stages of production.

Al Jazeera became a pioneering role model for hundreds of channels that would emerge in the following years, with various colourings and interests across the whole spectrum. In 1998 Iqraa Channel was set up in Saudi Arabia as the first exclusive religious trans-border TV station. Established by a Saudi businessman, Iqraa represented a real turning point in Islamic media, shifting resources and focus from traditional press media airwaves, as explained by Ehab Galal in chapter four.[5] Since then Arab skies have become crowded with dozens of religious stations with a wide range of leanings, all competing to win more followers. After the fall of Saddam Hussein and with the new political system in Iraq, another group of dozens of Sunni and Shia channels entered the fray, most of them with clear political connections to this party or that, and again fiercely competing with one another.

In terms of outlets and platforms, religious broadcasting could be categorised into four groups. The first category is state-controlled television systems which continue to transmit 'light' religious material. Cultivating legitimacy for their control, ruling elites in Arab countries have anxiously claimed to speak in the name of Islam and compete with other rising (Islamist) forces over the issue of Islamic representation. The second group is the semi-official religious broadcasting channels such as Al-Majd, Iqraa and Al-Risaleh (see separate chapters). These channels would claim independence and no state-control over them. This is true in a way but misleading in another. Mostly based in Saudi Arabia, these channels function according to a 'gentleman's agreement' by which they avoid any state-sensitive material. They focus on proselytising a strict interpretation of Islam stripped of any political dimension that could disturb the status quo. The third group is what we could call 'resistance channels' including Al-Aqsa of Hamas, Al-Manar of

Hizbullah and Al-Zawra' of the 'Iraqi resistance.' As the function of these channels is self-explanatory, they devote their airtime to promoting and supporting the resistance cause that relates to each of them. The discourse they employ is a blend of Islamist and nationalist, and of course is highly politicised, unlike the first two groups. The fourth group is the aggregation of religious broadcast material on mainstream broadcasting channels such as Al Jazeera, Al Arabiya, Abu Dhabi and others. These channels transmit weekly religious shows that have been highly popular, as with Al Jazeera's *Al Sharia wa al Hayat*. Apart from Al Jazeera shows which tend to turn highly politicised, shows on these mainstream TV stations avoid politics almost entirely, unless it is in accordance with respect to the official line.

Religious broadcasting in the Arab world could be seen as both a distinctive media but also as one embedded into mainstream broadcasting with significant influence and great outreach. In certain ways this conflation of religious and mainstream media reflects the status quo with regard to the infusion of religion into society and politics. Cases of blurred or well-defined boundaries between distinctive religious media and mainstream media translate the relative status of religion in society and polity. Maybe some comparative research is needed to examine the role and pervasive presence of religious media in different societies in order to establish the extent to which this media, with its focus on religion, corresponds to the reality of separation or entanglement between religion and the public and political spheres.

Apolitical Broadcasting?

Leading religious channels such as Iqraa, Al-Majd and Al-Risaleh claim that they are apolitical, an assertion that is mostly accurate, at least superficially. Many of these channels, especially Salafi-oriented ones, consciously and deliberately avoid tackling politics and keep their distance from sensitive issues. This policy emanates from the wider conviction within the Salafi school of thought that politics are by definition corrupt and would corrupt religion if brought into it. Yet, despite this belief in and practice of being apolitical, the outcome of their political passivity is in fact actively political. Their declared neutrality acts squarely in favour of governments which have been more than happy with these channels and their pacifying effect on people. By preoccupying the public with religious, social and other issues, away from scrutinizing the practices of the ruling elites, the policy of avoiding politics is anything but apolitical.

Furthermore, the outcome of the apolitical religious process can't be separated from the exploitation of a political religious process. In fact there has been strong complementarity between the two processes. In the realm of Islamism, mainstream Salafi movements have for a long time been apolitical, focusing on bringing Muslims back to what they perceived as the 'pure' (Salafi) path of Islam. Their work lies at the heart of the 'Islamisation' endeavour. They had shown no interest in challenging corrupt political systems in their countries. On the other hand, Islamist political parties such as the Muslim Brotherhood organisations have long functioned directly in politics, opposing governments, facing oppression and running for elections where possible. Yet at the same time they have combined with all political activism processes of Islamisation, bringing them to meet with non-political religious movements at the middle ground. The achievements of the Islamisation process, whether realised by political or non-political movements, would eventually greatly benefit the project of the politicised movement. It is the ordinary people, influenced by the Islamisation process, at mosques, media platforms, social networks and elsewhere, who cast their votes on the day of the elections. On that day the rivalry would become reduced to those who hold Islamist slogans, *Islam is the solution*, against all 'others' who don't.

'Fatwa Institution', Religious Legitimacy and the Public Sphere

The nature of teachings delivered on Middle Eastern religious channels is conservative, promoting stricter interpretation and understanding of religion as perceived and practiced by the average man in the street. This is one clear conclusion, among others, that has been shown in the material and programmes transmitted by these channels and examined in the chapters of this volume. The core message is almost the same: individuals should adhere to a certain preached version of religion in order for them to save their souls and for society at large to become better. Marginalisation of religion and deviation from the religious 'true path' is the root of all social illnesses and shortcomings at both the individual or collective level, including backwardness and defeat by external enemies. In Islamic broadcasting, echoing Islamist activism, the remedy for individual and societal ills is crystal clear and all summed up in the powerful mantra 'Islam is the solution.'

The preaching of this 'solution' in Islamist discourses as expressed in religious broadcasting transcends the form of promoting a certain choice to the people. Rather, it is delivered in a patriarchal format based on religious argumentation legitimising or delegitimising social practices and behaviour—the *halal* versus *haram* binary. This process has expanded astonishingly over the past two decades where small or large issues now have to go through this 'legitimisation' machinery. Best manifested by the mushrooming of *fatwas* (religious decrees), the process of Islamic legitimisation has left no aspect of personal or collective life untouched. Given the high illiteracy rates in the Arab world, the media have always been perceived as the source of knowledge and authority for mass audiences. Religious broadcasting has taken this knowledge-authority further ahead to unprecedented points. Hundreds of preachers and clergymen on TV screens assume the moral high ground and assert teachings and directions onto ordinary people on almost all aspects of living.

Issuing *fatwas* has become the backbone of (Islamic) religious broadcasting, pointing out to Muslims which matters are religiously permissible *halal* or impermissible *haram*. The *fatwa* is a well-known classical tool in Islam as well as in other religions where it may have a slightly different form or mechanism. When uncertain about a matter on which no clear religious position is stated in the Quran or Prophet's Sayings, ordinary people would ask religious scholars whether they should be permitted to do this or that and in what ways. In issuing *fatwas* that direct people's lives preachers would obtain great authority. The more *fatwas* issued, the more control these preachers would exercise over individuals and groups. *Fatwas* delivered by TV preachers over the past few years have spared no aspect of private and public life, mostly widening the circle of forbidden matters. There have been *fatwas* issued forbidding many things including Internet surfing by women without a male companion, organ donation, watching Mickey Mouse cartoons, car-driving by women and wearing shorts for footballers. The *'fatwa* institution' would come to cover all areas of public life including financial transactions, political decisions, social behaviour and cultural activities.[6]

Religious broadcasting (with the influence of its *fatwas* and programmes) offers very interesting challenges in relation to the understanding of free media, civil society and the public sphere. It is true, of course, that not all people follow religious broadcasting and/or listen to and implement every issued *fatwa*. But there are important societal processes and phenomena resulting from the spread of religious broadcasting along with the increasingly imposing status of the *fatwa* institution in society. One of these processes is the creation of public religious authority (physical and virtual) that invents and controls a process of legitimisation of all aspects of life. From the perspective of the public sphere of understanding, we know that free media would create spaces for civic social agents to function away from the full control of the state and/or higher authorities. The main idea is to make available to ordinary people spaces and mechanisms in which to function and express their desires and needs, free from structured channels of authority. The state tends, by definition, to extend its control and coercion over society, leaving no corner free from the imposition of its own authority. The public sphere is a process against that tendency, and is where 'civil society' emerges as opposed to 'state society', with less authority imposed on individuals.

Religious broadcasting, as part of the wider phenomenon of Islamism and Islamisation, exploits the space created by a relatively free media and ease of access to guaranteed public outreach. In the same way that Islamism in general functions, religious broadcasting occupies territories in the spaces liberated from the control of the state and higher authorities. But it fills them with a new 'religious' authority, which launches its own impositions and diktats on people. This leads to a situation in which the individual faces rising and new multiple authorities with various legitimacies: political (the state) and moral (religious/political institution). The traditional religious institutions attached to the state and seen as official organs in the service of ruling elites have had little legitimacy and power over the people. The 'new' rising state-free religiosity with its agents, however, enjoys such power and credibility, and wants to exercise that power over people. Thus, the clash between authoritarian regimes and Islamist parties over power and occupying more territories of public space would not necessarily end in favour of the individual and a freer public sphere.

Profit-making Channels

Religious broadcasting channels are mostly profit-making enterprises. Most of these channels, however, give the impression of being charitable and doing good, but the economics of the religious broadcasting industry deserves a full study on its own. As the chapters in this volume show, many of these channels were established because their owners banked on the notion that 'the market wants religion.' Another set of channels belong to the broader group of channels run by networks that are profit-making companies. These networks transmit on the same band of frequencies channels that cover all interests: entertainment, sport, religion, pop music, reality TV and news. Covering such a spectrum of interests is tailored to market demand and specific audiences. Programmes on a religious channel would keep attacking the decadence and immorality of 'westernised' programmes, e.g. songs and music of the kind that are transmitted on channels belonging to the same network.

Within the profit-making environment of these channels a 'celebrity' culture has been cultivated. Many preachers, male and female, have become fully-fledged celebrities who compete with one another over who is paid the highest fees, and who maintains more popularity. Religious channels engage in dirty tricks to woo these celebrities as they guarantee more viewership rates and more money. When reports revealed that the annual income of some of these religious preachers exceeds a million dollars audiences were shocked, as the followers of these preachers come mostly from middle and poorer classes.[7]

Religious Screens: No Modesty in Cutting Edge Technologies

Among the many challenges that religious broadcasting has faced is the form and limits of using what could be seen by their followers as 'tainting', westernising technologies. Surrounded by entertainment and music channels of numerous tastes that attract young people at the expense of 'boring' religious channels, the latter ones felt the heat of unequal rivalry. In order to counterbalance the lack of the attractiveness that entertainment channels easily offer without conservative limitations, religious channels have embraced the highest state of the art technology. The screen presence of leading Islamic channels, such as Iqraa and Al-Risaleh, looks sleek and professional. Female presenters, all in *hijab*, are beautiful and carefully presented. They are allowed to wear makeup and are well trained.

Religious broadcasting channels also try to be creative with the format of their shows. The days of having bearded preachers lecturing on screen for an hour have passed. The traditional preacher is still there, but side by side with modern shaven and western-looking young preachers. The programming contains Islamic song (*nasheed*), alongside quiz shows, competitions and variety of short and medium-length light documentaries, with noticeable focus on children. Not only this but a religious 'reality TV' was also produced, interestingly by the Algerian national television, The Holy Quran Caravan, to rival other reality TV shows that swept Arab audiences in the past years which were considered as immoral and Westernising. The Algerian 'Islamic reality TV' show offers sixteen contestants competing in reciting the Quran and the audience is left to vote for who is the best.[8]

2

RELIGIOUS BROADCASTING ON MAINSTREAM CHANNELS

AL JAZEERA, MBC AND DUBAI

Mohammad Ayish

Introduction

Since the mid-1950s, religion has been a central feature of television programming in the Arab world. In the 1960s and 1970s, terrestrial state-operated Arab television channels carried religious programmes ranging from direct talk shows, to religious sermons, to Qur'anic recitations, to Friday prayer transmissions, to historical dramas dealing with specific issues and values in Islamic culture.[1] In many ways, those shows echoed government-sanctioned views on religion and were concerned more with the ritualistic and spiritual aspects of Islam than with its political and social facets. In the age of terrestrial transmissions and single-channel broadcast systems, religious television broadcasting had limited effects, and was often eclipsed by the more effective and pervasive radio broadcasting operations. By the early 1990s, however, new information and communication transitions around the world were beginning to leave highly enduring marks on the Arab region, as marked by the advent of satellite television and the Internet.[2] Parallel to that technological revolution, a new wave of sweeping political, social and cultural transformations, mostly defined by democratisation, socio-demographic transitions, and a remarkable resurgence in Islamic consciousness, was taking shape.[3]

On the eve of the tragic events of 9/11, the dominant worldwide view about the region was that of a breeding ground for religious fanaticism and terror, and when the horrendous attacks took place, convictions were deepening that anti-Western sentiment in the region was not only politically-motivated, but also had significant religious ingredients, perpetuated by both regressive educational systems and a religiously-informed, anti-Western media discourse. It was at that time that satellite television programmes, including those with visible religious orientations, were brought under the spotlight to ensure their conformity with the moderate and centrist view of Islam as a religion of peace and tolerance.[4] In reaction to emerging criticism of how satellite television channels are faring in the religious domain, state-affiliated mainstream satellite channels in the Middle East have come to embrace an accommodating religious discourse that dodges politics and intercultural and interfaith tensions through promoting spiritual religiosity, a dialogue of civilisations and global coexistence.

This chapter looks at the new face of religious discourse on three mainstream television channels in the Middle East: the Al Jazeera Satellite Channel (JSC), the Middle East Broadcasting Center (MBC1), and Dubai Television (DTV). The programmes are *Al Sharia wa al Hayat* ('Sharia and Life') (JSC), *Al Haya Kalima* ('Life is a Word') (MBC), and *Al Boyout Al Amena* ('Safe Homes') (DTV). I will argue that because the three shows have been associated with specific Muslim scholars since their inception, their discourse is a function not only of declared state policies on religious issues in the post 9/11 era, but also of the peculiar theological and ideological views of their guests and/or presenters. This point is highly significant since it suggests that any commentary on the content of the three programmes is essentially about the religious perspectives of the scholars who appear on them. Hence, my argument is that the three programmes would be better addressed in the wider context of their key figures' views and orientations. It follows from this point that the programmes' value would be rendered rather useless if the analysis is carried out within the peculiar context of the sample episodes. This point might provoke another question about the nature of the analysis conducted in this paper: is it about a religious discourse that is peculiar to the television channel carrying the show, or is it about a religious discourse that reflects the unique ideas and perspectives espoused by the guest? I suggest that the discourse of the three shows actually reflects a 'negotiated convergence' of both states' and guests' orientations and perspectives on religious issues and developments.

The Broadcasters

Though the history of television broadcasting in the Arab World dates back to the mid-1950s, it was only in the early 1990s that the region came to have its fullest experience with freer, more diverse, and higher quality television.[5] In 1991, the then London-based Middle East Broadcasting Centre (MBC) kicked off its transmissions as the first private television service with Western-style programming, the first of its kind to be experienced in the region. From then on, government television channels started going international, including Dubai Television (DTV), which had its first direct satellite transmissions in 1992. But the most dramatic development in the recent history of satellite television in the Arab world took place in 1996, when the Qatar-based Al Jazeera Satellite Channel (JSC) began transmissions from studio facilities in Doha of Western-style programming with highly-critical and investigative content. The three channels, rated as among the most watched in the Middle East, carry wide-ranging content that combines entertainment with cultural and social material (in the cases of DTV and MBC1) and draws on news and current affairs (in the JSC case). This section provides an overview for each one of the three channels.

Al Jazeera Satellite Channel (JSC)

Al Jazeera Satellite Channel (JSC) was launched in 1996 from Qatar, in the aftermath of the discontinuation of the BBC Arabic Satellite Channel's joint venture with Saudi-owned Orbit Television and Radio Network. Over the past twelve years, JSC has presented itself as a forum for 'the Opinion and the Other Opinion.' Funded by both advertising revenue and subsidies from the Government of Qatar, JSC has marked a major transition in the Arab world's broadcasting landscape with its scathing talk shows and live coverage of regional and global events. The channel's critical reporting of domestic, political and religious affairs in several Arab countries has triggered diplomatic incidents, as well as closures of some of its offices abroad.[6] But regardless of the debates over the circumstances giving rise to Al Jazeera, or to conspiratorial thoughts about its connections with global and regional powers and groups, it has undeniably brought about a dramatic transformation in the long-stagnant Arab World media sphere. Lynch[7] notes that Al Jazeera has presented itself as an alternative to state-run television, providing a forum for political views that are not likely to be positively received by government-operated media in the Arab World. Such comments about JSC's groundbreaking broadcast journalism contributions in the region have been echoed by other researchers.[8]

Middle East Broadcasting Center (MBC1)

The Middle East Broadcasting Center (MBC) was launched from studio facilities in London on 18 September 1991 as the region's first private satellite television channel with mostly Western-style programming.[9] Owned by the Saudi ARA Group of Waleed Al Ibrahim, MBC has, in the recent past, turned into a six-channel television network with headquarters in the Dubai Media City. As a commercially-orientated network, MBC has sought to present mostly Western-style entertainment content, in addition to Arab World-produced programming with a mixed social, cultural, and drama output. MBC network's channels include MBC1, MBC2, MBC3, MBC4, MBC Persian, and Action Channel. The MBC channel covered by this study is MBC1, the first station in the group to be launched, in 1991. The channel offers both Arabic entertainment (with a mix of in-house productions and a carefully crafted acquisitions policy) and news content. MBC2 is the first free-to-air 24 hour movie channel in the world, featuring both top-rated Hollywood blockbusters and an array of B-movies. MBC3 was one of the first to broadcast a programming schedule devoted entirely to children.

The recently reformatted MBC4 is now completely dedicated to women's programming, through top-rated programmes across a variety of TV genres, including comedy, talk shows, drama and reality TV.

Dubai TV Channel (DTV)

Dubai Television was initially launched in 1974 as a terrestrial monochrome service with a variety of locally produced and imported programmes. Dubai Television is the state-owned network of the Emirate of Dubai, and the official broadcaster of events and activities taking place in Dubai. Targeting Arabs and Arabic-speaking viewers worldwide, Dubai TV achieved a distinctive presence for a large segment of the Arab audience, and became one of the most prominent and pioneering TV channels, broadcasting balanced and credible content that respects the local and Arab heritage. In early 2003, Dubai Television was operating as part of the newly established Dubai Media Inc. (DMI), an umbrella organisation housing several radio services, publications, and five television channels. DMI seeks to reach viewers around the Arab World with creative and meaningful television content that respects social, cultural, and family values in the UAE, the Gulf and the Arab world.

The Shows and Presenters

The following section highlights the main features of the three programmes analysed by this study.

Al Sharia Wal Hayat ('Shari'a and Life') (JSC)

This is one of the few programmes that has existed since the launch of the Al Jazeera Arabic Channel in 1996. Currently presented by Othman Othman, and previously by Ahmad Mansour, the show hosts an Islamic scholar, normally Yousuf Al Qaradawi, and takes calls from viewers on the theme of the episode. The programme is broadcast live on Sunday evenings, from a studio set decorated with Islamic motifs, re-broadcast later in the week and made available on the Internet. Over the past few years, the show has been reputed to have promoted rather progressive Islamic visions of society and the state, though its guest Sheikh Yousuf Al Qaradawi continues to be viewed as a controversial figure in contemporary Islamic jurisprudence. Credited with the evolution of what has been termed as *Fiqh Al Waqei* or 'Jurisprudence of Reality', Sheikh Al Qaradawi has sought to ground his *fatwas* and religious views in both the past and the present, without compromising the core theological tenets of the Islamic faith. In recent years, he has found himself in the eye of numerous storms over what some people see as his covert 'fundamentalist inclinations.'

JSC, MBC and DTV Episodes Covered by this Study

N	JSC	MBC	DTV
1.	Open Meeting (about the show)	Historical accounts in the Qur'an	First Year of Marriage
2.	Epidemic	Divine Principles or Sunan	Being Kind to Women
3.	Water Wars	The World of Jin	Arabic Language
4.	Turkey	Marriage Problems	Dealing with the Wife
5.	Meetings	Dress Code for Muslim Women	Proposing for Engagement
6.	Partnership	Psychological Diseases	Ethics of Gallantry
7.	The Environment	Youth and Religiosity	The Honest
8.	Feedback (Numerous Subjects)	Islamic Preaching	
9.	Daring Attitudes	Jurisprudence of Expectation	
10.	Regular Religious Prayers	Function of the Jurisprudent	
11.	Jerusalem	Being Swayed by the Self	
12.	The Visit		
13.	Differences		

Al Boyout Al Amena ('Safe Homes') (DTV)

This is one of the most popular television shows in the Middle East. Presented by the Egyptian-born Islamic scholar Omar Abdul Kafi, the programme is a direct-address show moderated by Abdul Kafi himself with occasional guest speakers from related fields. The show addresses wide-ranging issues pertaining to family security, children's upbringing, youth behaviour, women's rights, parental guidance and others. Typically, each episode addresses a family problem for which Sheikh Abdul Kafi offers 'Islamic solutions.' The programme frequently also airs the views of some non-religious specialists in psychology and sociology. Viewers are also encouraged to call the programme for Islamic answers to emerging social and psychological questions. Sheikh Abdul Kafi's website[10] includes archives of his lectures, media contributions and articles. In general, he is much more focused in this show on spiritual and individual behavioural matters with a bearing on community life, and has nothing to do with critical political and social issues, as is the case with the two other shows. He also presents another programme entitled 'Call of Faith' on Al Risala Channel.

Al Haya Kalima ('Life is a Word') (MBC)

This programme is aired weekly and addresses issues relating to family life, social relations, and community ethics. Moderated by Fahd Saawi, the programme hosts Saudi preacher Sulieman Al Oudeh and is broadcast on Fridays after *Jumaa* prayers (Mecca local time) and on MBC FM Panorama Radio from 2 to 3pm on the same day. Al Oudeh, currently the General Supervisor of the *Islam Today Group Establishment*,[11] holds a doctorate in *Sunna* studies and is a member of the World Islamic Scholars Federation. In a book entitled *The 500 Most Influential Muslims in the World—2009*, Sheikh Al Oudeh was ranked nineteenth.[12] In that book, he is described as an 'advocate of peaceful coexistence' and 'ambassador of non-violence' who 'is outspoken about the importance of inculcating love and mercy as opposed to violence in the daily life of Muslims.'[13] In an article against Al-Qaeda ideology, Sheikh Al Oudeh wrote:

Today, I must stress how important it is for us to condemn the abominable and criminal acts being perpetrated around the world in Islam's name and which are being misrepresented as 'jihād.' We must expose those acts and the people who carry them out by calling them what they really are, whether their perpetrators refer to themselves as al-Qaeda, or a jihad organization, or a militant organization or an 'Islamic state.' It is not enough to give vague indications and make ambiguous general statements. Al-Qaeda is not what it was before September 11. It has turned into a media phenomenon with many people claiming the name merely for its symbolic value, mobilizing the youth under its umbrella. In this way, the strategy has changed, the evil has shaken loose from its reins and become like shrapnel all over the place, possessing a regional character but making a global noise. Al-Qaeda has become like a trademark that anyone can get hold of and carry out their activities in its name. It is no longer a cohesive organization with strong ties between its leaders and followers.[14]

Quantitative Data Analysis

Quantitative data for the three programmes show that they addressed topics relating to ethics, historical events and contemporary issues. Both JSC and MBC programmes discussed *fatwas* and interpretations of the Qu'ran and *Sunna*. Values promoted by the three shows ranged from tolerance, to piety, to religiosity and peaceful coexistence. This suggests, among other things, that these programmes are serving as platforms for the diffusion of values that deal with aspects of contemporary life for their audience, even when historical traditions are invoked. The interesting thing is that the three programmes adopt moderate, centrist and accommodating approaches to the promotion of those values, something that bodes well for the future contributions of this broadcasting genre to the development of Arab societies in the context of globalisation. It was quite heartening to see none of the three shows carrying any fundamentalist messages, nor holding any elements of religious or sectarian hate.

Qualitative Analysis

The following section presents an analysis of the three programmes centring on five major themes: knowledge, reason, centrism, freedom, and coexistence.

JSC Data

Topic	No.	%	Value	No.	%	Approach	No.	%
Ethics	4	14.8	Piety	3	15.7	Extremist	1	11.1
Historical	3	11.1	Religiosity	5	26.3	Centrist	6	66.6
Contemporary	7	25.9	Integrity	1	05.2	Accommodating	1	11.1
Fatwas	8	29.6	Mercy	3	15.7	Inclusive	1	11.1
Qu'ran & Sunna	5	18.5	Spirituality	1	05.2	Total	9	100
Total	27	100	Others	6	31.5			
			Total	19	100			

MBC Data

Topic	No.	%	Value	No.	%	Approach	No.	%
Ethics	6	46.1	Tolerance	1	11.1	Accommodating	13	100
Historical	1	07.6	Religiosity	1	11.1	Total	13	100
Contemporary	4	30.7	Distinction	3	33.3			
Fatwas	1	07.6	Coexistence	1	11.1			
Qu'ran & Sunna	1	07.6	Others	2	22.2			
Total	13	100	Total	9	100			

DTV Data

Topic	No.	%	Value	No.	%	Approach	No.	%
Ethics	6	75.0	Piety	1	11.1	Centrist	7	100
Historical	1	12.5	Religiosity	6	66.6	Total	7	100
Contemporary	1	12.5	Tolerance	1	11.1			
Total	8	100	Coexistence	1	11.1			
			Total	9	100			

Knowledge

Knowledge in the three programmes is presented on the basis of both revelation and real-world experiences. Faith is the pillar of this revealed knowledge that sets the conceptual parameters for how both the metaphysical and existential worlds should be comprehended. The three programmes take religious faith not only as a matter of spirituality, but as the anchoring point for understanding all issues and events taking place in this world. Revealed knowledge is presented here as the prism through which human values and behaviours are framed and legitimised or de-legitimised. It is the centre-point in a comprehensive world-view that harnesses shari'a perspectives, historical traditions and contemporary theological views, to define wide-ranging temporal and transcendental facets of our lives. Of course, this is natural in programmes with a declared mission to bolster religious attitudes and spiritual orientations among individuals and communities in the region. It actually fits quite closely with the dominant view of 'Islam as offering solutions in all times and places', voiced by mainstream Islamist movements.

The way contemporary phenomena and issues are contextualised and rationalised within revelation-based conceptual frameworks is a defining feature of the three programmes. The explanatory power of Islamic shari'a has been evident in the three programmes, as presenters and guests sought to contextualise the details of our contemporary life within the Islamic principles of human life on this planet. In *Sharia wal Hayah*, Sheikh Al Qaradawi was keen on making this contextualisation in the strongest of terms. For Al Qaradawi, human life is an inseparable part of the broader universal phenomenon created by Allah. In order to furnish the most compelling understanding of human actions, attitudes and relations, we need to ground them in a broader framework of analysis, fully informed by an Islamic world-view. In this case, Man is no more than a player in a very broad universal arena with physical and metaphysical manifestations. In one episode, Al Qaradawi talked about marriage in the broader, binary view of the universe that started with the creation of Adam and Eve. 'He was not alone and could not survive on his own. So Allah created a mate for him to perpetuate his existence', Al Qaradawi noted. The binary nature of the universe was applied to plants, insects, animals and even to the nucleus of the atom (again here we see the reference to science to support religious premises) where we have protons and neutrons. By locating marriage relationships in a universal framework of understanding, Al Qaradawi seems to tell viewers that this relationship is sacred, and is indispensable for the survival of human species and for the immortalisation of the noble values embedded in the Islamic faith.

In another episode, about the true nature of the world of Jin (something from the metaphysical world) and how it relates to humans, Al Qaradawi contextualised the world of Jin in the universal views of creation where there are two worlds: the transcendental and the existential. He invoked scientific theories about invisible worlds or black holes, and drew on the Holy Qur'an to answer the question by noting three categories of creation: human, Jin and angels (built to be obedient worshippers). Commenting on a video clip about exorcism sessions in Morocco, Al Qaradawi described it as a form of epilepsy or psychological disease, rather than a form of Jin haunting. The interplay between theology and science in Al Qaradawi's discourse is impressive.

In *Al Haya Kalima*, Sheikh Al Oudeh draws on shari'a-based values and conventions to make sense of our contemporary realities. His repeated references to Qur'anic teachings and the Prophet's traditions to explain temporal issues and developments are outstanding features of the programme. His main focus is on social relations in Muslim families and communities, which he seeks to codify within the confines of revealed knowledge. He uses those traditions to explain issues like women's relationships with men in the context of marriage, devotion to religious principles and practices, social problems and relations with others in the age of globalisation. By contextualising all discussions in the essentially revealed shari'a, Al Oudeh seems to furnish viewers with the spiritual and intellectual world-view that they need to understand the realities around them in the twenty-first century. But in one episode, he came to quote the 'I have a dream' speech of Martin Luther King to show that dreams are legitimate forms of our living experiences, though we should not dwell much on their interpretations while overlooking the realities around us. He also quoted King, saying that he wanted to plant an apple tree, even if tomorrow was the end of the world. He equated this quotation with one of the Prophet's instructions, that even if the end of the world comes, a Muslim with a seedling in his hand should go ahead and plant it.

Sheikh Omar Abdul Kafi, in *Al Boyout Al Amena*, demonstrated this more visibly by stressing the centrality of Islamic shari'a as an anchoring point for our contemporary attitudes and behaviours.

Because his show is entirely devoted to family relations and values, he makes frequent references to Islamic jurisprudence relating to women. His many references to Qur'anic verses and the Prophet's sayings demonstrate his keenness to contextualise Muslim community ethics within the notion of faith. As in the other two programmes, *Al Boyout Al Amena* presents a view of Islamic ethics that derives from the different aspects of Shari'a. In the programme about the value of manliness and gallantry (*Morou'aa*) in Muslim societies, he began by wondering about the expected view of 'the Prophet or His Companions should they enter Muslim homes in these times, would they be happy or disappointed when they see how children are raised, and how family and community relations are conducted?'[15] Even when he refers to family problems and divorce in modern Muslim societies, he seems to demonstrate more adherence to the spirit and substance of Islamic traditions on these matters. In the many calls he used to receive from viewers, he always grounded their concerns about travelling, raising children, fostering intimacy, taking decisions and sharing views in the family, in Islamic shari'a.

Reason

It is interesting to see how the three programmes seem to draw heavily on reason in their religious discourse. Reason is a God-endowed capacity, that underscores the centrality of Man's responsibility and accountability in this life, and therefore it has to be used to its full capacity. The three presenters or guests promote the Islamic notion of Man as created by Allah with a rational capacity that does not seem to be possessed by Angels. The three shows appear to adopt a highly rational approach in the discussion of different issues, and their appeal to human reason takes numerous forms. Sheikh Al Qaradawi has written a book about scientific miracles in the Qur'an, in which he related modern life breakthroughs to specific Qur'anic citations regarding earth, creation and other physical phenomena. His basic thesis is that religion and science are in full harmony, and both maintain some symbiotic relationship that can be empowering for both spheres. The use of scientific innovations and discoveries to beef up religious beliefs, has been quite evident in the programme. In early 2009, media in the region circulated a *fatwa* by Sheikh Al Qaradawi, in which he claimed that Muslims may drink beverages with low alcohol ratios. The *fatwa* stirred up widespread debates across the region, most of them critical of Al Qaradawi and his views that, for many, contravened the basic principles of Islam on intoxicating materials. In one episode of 'Shari'a and Life', Sheikh Al Qaradawi rebutted those charges by noting that he was terribly misunderstood, and his ideas were awfully misrepresented in the media, for what he had advocated was a meagre 0.05 per cent rather than 5.0 per cent alcohol ratio to be permitted. He noted that the whole idea had started when he was approached by a local measurements and specifications authority in Qatar, regarding the presence of a very low alcoholic amount in some energy drinks. He said that Muslims may have those drinks because the very low level of alcohol was too meagre to stir up worries, and it was not caused by the addition of alcohol but rather by some chemical processes related to the beverage itself. He invoked some scientific theories regarding such matters, including some views of the Islamic Medical Association in Kuwait, who made energy drinks with low levels of alcohol permissible. His references to science and technology were quite vital in enabling him to justify his *fatwa* and insist on its righteousness. He also invoked scientific explanations of contemporary phenomena when he talked about epileptic fits, which many people attributed to a Jin haunting humans. He noted that while Jin do exist within Islamic theological views, the idea of them haunting humans remains rather shaky. He talked of epilepsy as a psychological disease with physical symptoms that can be cured through medicine or counselling.

In an episode on human organ donation, stem cells, and organ transplantation and transfer, Sheikh Al Qaradawi was quite forceful in stressing the scientific aspects of the issue, as long as the outcome has some redeeming human and social value. He noted that organ donation or transfer for the purpose of saving lives and securing human survival is permissible in certain conditions: if it is meant to help others and save a human life. It is one of the greatest religious feats to relieve others and to save human life, he noted. For Al Qaradawi, the strings attached to organ donation include the availability of healthy organs and the personal consent of the donor. For him, it is permissible for Muslims to use organs from non-Muslims and even from pigs.

In *Al Haya Kalima*, the tone of Sheikh Al Oudeh has the full features of a rational discourse. The centrality of reason in the show also implies a call for harnessing rational human potential to bring about concrete changes to individual and community life. In an episode on lessons from *Hejra*, or the migration of the Prophet from Mecca to Medina, Salman talks about his visit to Ireland and how some students were committed Muslims while others were less devout. But while calling on them not to discard their Islamic values and piety, he seemed to be cognisant of the peculiarities of social and cultural life in that part of the world that have a bearing on students' behaviour. He calls on students to acquire knowledge and positive values in their host societies, to benefit their mother countries. In another episode, on female circumcision, Sheikh Al Oudeh talked about social traditions, calling for the handling of the issue with care since there is no consensus. Concerning man's supremacy over women (*Quwama*), he pointed out that the concept describes the husband over wife, not the brother over sister. He noted that since there is no agreement on the concept of supremacy or *Quwama*, it is clear that man should be fair and consultative, and the whole thing is part of the mandate that men command to make women happy. For him, women are smart and should not be handled like remote-controlled toys.

While *Al Boyout Al Amena* has a strong rational appeal in its discourse, it draws more on intuition and faith-based arguments than on reason to promote Islamic values. The presenter does not take the same trouble taken by Sheikh Al Qaradawi and Sheikh Al Oudeh in highlighting human potential to be free and rational as a basis for determining the merits of Islamic teachings in the twenty-first century. Whatever he says is grounded in the traditions of the Prophet or in Qur'anic principles, and viewers have to abide by them. Even when he tries to rationalise some commandments and conducts, he justifies them more on faith-based traditions. For example, he talks about the deterioration of the Arabic language in our age, and calls for rectifying problems in language usage by stressing that Arabic is the language of the Qur'an and *Sunna* and we should keep it afloat out of cultural pride and religious zeal. When the issue of marriage problems is raised, Sheikh Abdul Kafi also seems to position this issue within Islamic ideals of men and women forging the sacred marriage relationship. During the phonecalls he received on-air from viewers in the Middle East, Sheikh Abdul Kafi presented himself as a counsellor who has the power to address all audience concerns from an Islamic perspective. In one call, a woman asked about her rights as a second wife when it comes to receiving certain benefits. He was clear in highlighting Allah's command for men to be just and fair among their wives. He called for men to consult their wives and be kind to them, but when it comes to making final decisions on matters pertaining to the family, he insisted that men rather than women have the upper hand.

Centrism

The notion of centrism is used here to denote middle-of-the-road views and perspectives, as opposed to fundamentalist or liberal ones. Generally speaking, the three shows represent a centrist, Islamic world-view with no tendency to any type of extremism or fundamentalism in their discourse. When compared to the highly-charged messages embedded in fundamentalist or liberal discourse, the three programmes carry moderate and highly accommodating views that are neither detached from the basic roots of shari'a, nor influenced by the core premises of Western liberalism. In many of their writings, the three scholars make references to the assimilative power of Islam throughout history to interact with other cultures and civilisations, and integrate them into its universal mission. The notion of centrism suggests that Muslims should always balance between competing interests when it comes to making choices concerning critical issues in their lives, and should choose the most moderate ones without compromising the essential components of their religious *Aqida* or ideology. In one of the episodes of *Sharia wal Haya*, Sheikh Al Qaradawi commented on the notion of *Takfir* (accusing others of apostasy or heresy) by condemning the idea and viewing it as a reaction to the persecution experienced by Islamists in government prisons in the

Muslim world. He notes that Salafi, Sunna, and Shi'a, all engage in *Takfir* and asks why that should be. According to Al Qaradawi, *Takfir* started in Egypt in military prisons as a result of state torture, reminding viewers that the Muslim Brotherhood does not see others as *Kuffar* (infidels).

For Al Qaradawi, many of the tensions arising in contemporary Muslim societies are a function of the failure to harmonise the past with the present, by taking each extreme as the defining framework for addressing social and political woes. In one episode, he cited an enlightened contemporary Islamic author who speaks of Muslims being caught between two dismal realties: fourteenth-century traditions and twentieth-century lifestyles. He also refers to examples from the Traditions of the Prophet concerning the necessity for men to see women in person before they make up their minds about possible marriages. But some families make it difficult for men and women to become more familiarised with each other, thus creating chances for surprises that might not be positive for both individuals. For Al Qaradawi, this example shows how engaged couples may fall victim to traditional taboos that inhibit interpersonal communications between them, as well as to modern Western-style views of unfettered meetings and outings.

Freedom

If the three scholars believe that Man is a rational being, then he commands freedom of choice, something that is vital for other competing values: responsibility or accountability. Unlike many television preachers in the Arab World, Al Qaradawi seems to advocate freedom of choice as a natural feature of the rational human being. He appears to have profound faith in reason as a central force, defining how we make sense of reality around us. Of course, he also advocates faith as another important tool for dealing with reality, especially when it derives from the Holy Qur'an and the honourable *Sunna*. But when it comes to making choices in real life, reason seems to have an edge over faith. In one episode analysed for the study about the choice of a partner in marriage, he addressed common conceptions of the issue as subject to fate or *Qisma*, noting that while the whole issue in the broader analysis is a pre-determined, divine fate that is allotted by Allah, its intricate details have to be worked out through rational choices. In marriage, though, the issue is conceived as subject to *Qisma*, that does not negate the chain of causality, 'because Allah has created this universe on the basis of certain principles rather than chaos. Everything has a reason or cause. A person has responsibility to ensure the best choice of his/ her mate', he notes.[16] Al Qaradawi cites one of the Prophet's sayings about choosing a wife on the basis of beauty, prestige or wealth, and that one should choose a wife with religion. But one has to see the other partner before a choice is made.

The notion of freedom was also evident in *Al Hayah Kalima* when Sheikh Al Oudeh called for more participation from the community in running their own affairs. He also referred to a new generation of youths who seem to diverge from mainstream traditions under the sway of the global information revolution, and stated that the best way to deal with this phenomenon is not through repression, but through accommodation and respect for the choices they have made. There is a sense of determinism concerning freedom as a social value that needs to be instituted to empower individuals to shoulder responsibility in serving their communities. Freedom, for Sheikh Al Oudeh, is not about political choices, but social ones as well. It goes down to the basic level of human relations in the contexts of marriage partner choice, careers, and interests. In one episode, Sheikh Al Oudeh noted that 'freedom' also suggests freedom to participate and contribute to community welfare in a broad context. In this context, he calls for freedom of expression within national consensus. In an episode on changes in the life of *Duaa* like Salman Al Oudeh, he replied that we always work for change, as we all tell people that we seek change. Discussion of the past and the present should be made available and criticism should be encouraged. As I criticise others, why do I feel offended when they criticise me? There is no need to always call on the past to understand the present. Many new generations may not be interested in the past discourse as they look to the future.

In *Al Boyout Al Mena*, the power of scripture to define our choices remains highly visible. For Sheikh Abdul Kafi, traditions constitute what might be described as a roadmap for community members to follow. In fact, the way he addresses issues like family relations, children's upbringing, and education seems to suggest a vision of an ideal community that can be realised only through the application of inherited principles and practices. There was no sign of Sheikh Abdul Kafi venturing into the realm of *fatwas*, to empower individuals to undertake certain activities that might eventually lead to the construction of new living experiences. Freedom, for him, means the ability of individuals to follow the path of the Qur'an and the *Sunna*, with little room left for new visions.

Coexistence

Muslims' relations with other cultures and denominations were recurring topics in *Al Sharia wa Al Hayat* and *Al Hayat Kalima*, while *Al Boyout Al Amena* was mostly focused on the internal Muslim family, and community affairs in the context of ethical righteousness and religiosity. Sheikh Al Oudeh spoke favourably about education in UK institutions as he visited Saudi Arabian students there.

The basic ingredient in *Sharia* is *tayseer*, or making things more convenient, as according to Sheikh Al Oudeh hardship brings convenience. He believes that the more transparent and clear a society, the more engaged and cognisant of existing problems it will be. He calls for harmony between the political establishment and religious authority because:

political despotism hurts society and so do close-minded jurisprudence and also the weak civil society movement. We should realise that we are in a state of change. It is better that we have a say in how this change goes on ... we should not exaggerate talking about peculiarity. What is this? We are part of the world, barriers have been eroded and you can read signs of change in young faces, their words, conducts, dresses, and web sites.

He comments on a letter about scholarships for women to study abroad, noting that it is natural that females also make use of such learning opportunities outside their countries.

Al Oudeh rejects any coexistence that would mean that Muslims would have to compromise their identity or religion to cope with others.[17] For him, coexistence suggests some reconciliation in this world through agreement on a set of human ethical values that enable dialogue and persuasion. Coexistence seeks to help people to interact constructively with each other for the sake of human development, and the diffusion of genuine Islamic values and beliefs. But he has taken to calling on Muslims not to take part in Christmas celebrations.

Al Qaradawi, on the other hand, while calling for peaceful coexistence based on justice and mutual respect, was not hesitant about condemning Islamophobic acts in the West, whether in the form of Danish cartoons, Dutch films, or pontifical statements. In the UK, the House of Commons Media Select Committee called on Al Jazeera to stop broadcasting Al Qaradawi's programme, because it claimed he was celebrating the Holocaust and calling for the killing of Jews. It was revealed later that the whole controversy was stirred up by The Middle East Media Research Institute, a pro-Israeli, right-wing organisation that has become notorious for its distorted coverage of Middle Eastern politics. Al Qaradawi argues:

The Quran states that [religious] disagreement exists because God [himself] wills it ... that people will have different religions. After all, if God had wanted everyone to have the same religion and the same path, he would have created Man differently ... the [believing Muslim] does not try to pass judgment upon those who disagree [with his religion] in this world. God is the one who will pass judgment on the day of resurrection...[18]

He highlights the Universalist and progressive message of the Prophet Muhammad that all are equal in the eyes of God:

Islam honours Man as such, regardless of gender, religion, colour, language, geographic region, or status ... [People] said to God's Messenger: 'This is the funeral of a Jew. That coffin belongs to a Jew, not a Muslim.' He answered: 'Is this not a soul [too]? Is the Jew not a human soul?'[19]

Perhaps what infuriates some Western opinion about Al Qaradawi is that he pins the blame for modern anti-Semitism on Europe's long history of intolerance:

We did not invent this hostility [towards the Jews]. Jews lived among Muslims for centuries, even when Europe persecuted them and expelled them... They found a safe haven in Muslim territory and Muslim homelands. This is because Islam considers the Jews to be People of the Book ... This is how the Koran views the Jews, and this is how they lived in the countries of the Muslims. They have the protection [dhimma] of Allah, His Messenger, and of all the Muslims.[20]

Conclusions

It is clear that the three shows aired by Al Jazeera Satellite Channel, the Middle East Broadcasting Center, and the Dubai Channel reflect fairly enlightened views of Islam as a religion that respects tolerance, moderation and dignity. Of course, it would be odd to expect mainstream television channels associated with what are described as moderate Arab states in the Middle East to propagate *Salafi* or fundamentalist religious rhetoric simply because that would go against their stated political orientations, particularly in the post-9/11 era. Likewise, it would be hard to see those channels giving voice to liberal religious views that advocate explicit alignment with Western lifestyles and values. By promoting such rational and moderate views of Islam, the Arab government backers wanted to demonstrate their detachment from fundamentalist Islam as the defining feature of their religious discourse. The airing of the three shows represents some sort of negotiated discourse between politicians and religious scholars: the former would promote new religious thinking that both copes with political realities and marks a departure from fundamentalist perspectives. The latter, on the other hand, would find state patronage an opportunity to promote their unique religious perspectives that they have sought to popularise in books and other non-broadcast forums.

From critical Western intellectual perspectives, the description of the religious discourse promoted by the three programmes as moderate, centrist and accommodating, would seem highly flawed. The three scholars appearing on the programmes are basing their arguments on pre-determined principles and tenets associated with revealed knowledge and historical traditions. In most of the cases, the discourse is informed more by normative knowledge than experiential evidence, something that may not enable us to forcefully stave off counter arguments based on pure human reason and real-world experience. Hence, the three programmes have not generated what might amount to what we call 'liberal Islam' as opposed to Salafi Islam, simply because the three scholars featured in the programmes are limiting their views by mainstream Sunni Islamic traditions. This suggests that the parameters of debate are grounded in both existential and metaphysical premises and principles, as was evident on the issues of freedom, family life, and co-existence. The notions of interfaith dialogue and women's rights are always addressed within historical religious views that have not been carried forward to the same progressive levels reached by Al Azhar in Egypt, for example. It is for this reason that Western intellectuals may not find the religious discourse promoted in the three shows comparable to the traditional standards of media debates carried out in Western media. But the three shows also mark a departure from *Salafi* or fundamentalist discourse, though some analysts with profound investigative techniques might see the three shows converging with some features of *Salafi* discourse, particularly on the issues of women's rights and relations with the West. It is for this reason that this author believes that religious discourse carried by the three programmes should be investigated in the peculiar context of Muslim cultural traditions, which continue to be informed by revealed knowledge. The numerous intellectual attempts by the three scholars to confer harmony between religious and secular discourse, I believe, are worthy future scholarly pursuits.

3

'PURE' SALAFI BROADCASTING

AL-MAJD CHANNEL (SAUDI ARABIA)

Abeer Al-Najjar

The *'ulama'* [in the twenty-first century] have become agents of the state; their fortunes and religious project are directly linked to the continuation of Al-Saud rule in Arabia. They have developed the original Wahhabi insights, which were politically revolutionary (particularly in the religious sanction they give to acts of war against fellow Muslims) into a status quo doctrine that gives the Saudi rulers maximum discretion in the realm of foreign policy, while maintaining for themselves control (or substantial influence) over the interpretation and implementation of Islam at home. When Salafi opponents attack the regime for its relations with the United States (and Great Britain earlier), the *ulama* provide the rulers with a religious sanction of their right to rule. That sanction has helped the Al-Saud prevent the Salafi opposition from being able to mobilize a widespread support in Saudi society.[1]

Background

Broadly speaking, Salafism, or *Salafiyya*, is a boundary-blurred school of Islamic thinking that calls upon Muslims to emulate the 'pure' belief and righteous way of Islamic life as it had been practiced by the Prophet Muhammad and his *Salaf Saleh*—or pious

35

companions. Because of the powerful legitimacy that the notion of Salafism embodies, and the proclamation it entails of being a strict follower of the Prophet Muhammad, numerous parties within Muslim society including governments, Islamist groups, institutions, individuals, thinkers, militants and many others, would claim allegiance to the Salafi way of embracing Islam. In situations where the rivalry over who speaks in the name of Islam is fierce, to announce one's own self or party as 'purely Salafi' would empower one over other rivals. At the same time Salafism has been prone to various and contradictory interpretations. 'Radical' as well as 'moderate' voices within Islam would claim that they are the 'true Salafi' because their way is closer to the Prophet Muhammad's. Many jihadists and violent Islamists think of themselves as Salafis. Their opponents, both non-violent and accommodators, think about themselves in the same way.[2]

Wahhabism is historically linked to its founder Muhammad bin Abd Al-Wahhab (1703–1792),[3] who is known for his historic coalition with Al-Saud and his fundamental role in the establishment of the first Saudi emirate and its later expansion.[4] Wahhabis prefer the name *al-muwahhidun* or *ahl al-tawheed* (monotheists) over Wahhabis or Wahhabiyeen.[5] The movement is viewed and represented as both religious and nomadic. The latter attribute seems to be popular among non-Wahhabi writers who view it as being 'nomadic in its social affiliation and political orientation. The driving force here is not primarily religion but *assabiyyah* (the feeling of tribal affinity), hence the movement's objective is assumed to be to impose the political dominance of a certain *assabiyyah*: the Al-Saud vis-à-vis the others.'[6]

Salafism equals Wahhabism in much of the literature on Salafism in Saudi Arabia.[7] Wiktorowicz classifies Salafis or Wahhabis as purists, politicos and jihadis.[8] He acknowledges that Salafis represent a highly diverse group, but considers Salafism as an umbrella that accommodates both Osama bin Laden and the *mufti* of Saudi Arabia. Okruhlik emphasises the various meanings of the name Salafism based on one's religious environment (believers vs. non-believers) or geographical location (inside versus outside Saudi Arabia).[9] Furthermore, the use of the term has changed in the post 9/11 era. Although all Salafis agree on the centrality of the religious text and *aqida* (beliefs), they have different views on politics, particularly concerning their relationship with the Saudi regime.

This chapter looks at the Salafi Al-Majd network and its programming. It is an exploratory reading and mapping of the main themes and questions tackled by the channel, and the ways in which Islam and important Muslim questions are constructed and reproduced by leading influential *ulama* (Islamic scholars) addressing Al-Majd audiences. Special attention is paid to the socio-political discourse in the network. As part of the research into religious media broadcasting, this chapter is intended to be a careful examination—without preconceptions—of the meaning and content that is communicated by the network's channels. The content studied here is limited to the programmes broadcast on the general open-air Al-Majd. The study does not include programmes and material broadcast on other encrypted and free-to-air channels, into which further research needs to be conducted. However, it sketches an outline of the religious priorities and ideals presented by the Al-Majd *ulama* or preachers, to their audiences mainly in the Kingdom of Saudi Arabia (KSA) and Arab countries. It is important to point out here that many of these preachers are appointed in the Council of Senior *Ulama* in KSA; this decision is made by the highest political authority in the country, the King. This indicates a strong alliance between the Al-Majd *ulama* and the Saudi regime. Many of the members of the Council of Senior *Ulama* have access to the Al-Majd audience, as they are frequently invited to appear on the channel's shows. Consequently, many of these *ulama* enjoy the endorsement of the Saudi King himself, which gives a political weight to their interpretation of Islam and their religious authority on society. This official relationship between the state and the so-called 'state *"ulama"'* has been recognised and examined by many scholars.[10]

The channel's programming is under the control of a committee of *ulama* or shari'a experts, many of whom are members of *Hay'at Kibar al-Ulama*, the Council of Senior *Ulama* (CSU).[11] The *ulama* who have established the channel's media policy and supervise its implementation include Saleh bin 'Abd AlRahman AlHussein, 'Abd Allah bin Maneia, 'Abd Al'Aziz AlMisnad, 'Abd Allah AlMutlag, and Ibrahim Abu Abah.[12] Saleh bin 'Abd Rahman AlHussein is the General Director of the Grand Mosque (*alMasjid alHarām*) and the Prophet's Mosque. He is also one of the co-founders of the King Abdulaziz University endowment.[13]

Apparently, Al-Majd is the product of the Saudi Wahhabi movement, which coexisted and co-operated with the political structure in the kingdom and benefited from it. The political power in Saudi Arabia is concentrated in the royal family, Al-Saud, with no political participation and a highly restricted and segregated social environment. This chapter examines the adherence of the way in which Islam is constructed on the Al-Majd network to the 'strict code of behaviour in faith, morals, rituals and social affairs' that the Salafis have.

In this chapter, religion is analysed as it is communicated and constructed by the Al-Majd channel, particularly as an organising force among Salafi Muslims in Saudi Arabia. Salafis in general are purists who place more emphasis on religious text and pay more attention to the quality and correctness of the *aqida* (beliefs) held by individual Muslims. The study takes into consideration that the oneness of the correct interpretation of Islam is at the centre of Salafi belief. Islam and Muslims are defined by and directed to follow a very strict interpretation of the religious text that, according to the regime and *ulama* in the kingdom, centres on the permissible and forbidden (*halal* and *haram*). Okruhlik stress that:

Islam, as mediated and propagated by the regime in Saudi Arabia, is exclusive and bounded, official and static, orthodox and state-centric, with clearly defined rules about what is permissible and what is prohibited. The message that emanates from official orthodoxy is mostly about a narrow reading of the text. It insists on a strict conformity in belief and behaviour, and it is the state's responsibility to enforce proper behaviour. It does not welcome local interpretations that vary across time or space. There is only a single religious truth, and the religious establishment claims it.[14]

Context

The increase in the politicisation of Islam, technological development and the satellite revolution, and the commercial opportunities brought by oil and the advent of a mass market, among other factors, have been used to explain the conditions which have led to the steep increase in the number or religious channels and religious publications or media outlets in the Arab nations. Undoubtedly, one cannot look at the proliferation of religious media channels and publications, including Al-Majd TV, without pinpointing the dominance of the Islamic social and political discourse during the past few decades, particularly after the Six-Day War of 1967, as noted in Khaled Hroub's introduction to this book. The defeat experienced by the Arabs went beyond the borders of the countries defeated, namely Egypt, Syria and Jordan. Its effect was, and still is, dominant not only on the street in Arab nations, but also within the Arab elite.[15] Arab Nationalism lead by the then Egyptian President Gamal Abd Al-Nasser was crushed too. Islamists viewed this defeat in the war as 'punishment for misplaced trust in the promise of alien ideologies that had been fostered as a means of mobilising for modernisation and development. The defeat was devastating because the margin of deviance from the faith was great.'[16]

In an interview with former Al-Majd News Editor Ahmad Fahmi, he stated that the network was a response to a market need. It was intended to satisfy hundreds of thousands of families in the KSA and the Gulf region who had retained the belief that watching television, including religious Islamic channels, was *haram* (forbidden in Islam). Thus, *telfezyoun natheef* (pure television) has been their target. For these families, it is *haram* to see any woman on TV, even when covered from head to toe; all types of music and all musical instruments are forbidden too. Al-Majd conducted a survey before they launched and found that there were more than 200,000 families in the KSA alone who preferred their homes to be without a TV set for this reason.[17] One of these families was that of the founder of Al-Majd network, Fahd Al-Shmaimri.

Al-Majd Shows

The following two prime-time talk shows have been chosen for the study: *Sa'at Hawar* ('Dialogue Time') and *AlJawab AlKafi* ('The Adequate Answer'). Both are weekly programmes on the general free-to-air Al-Majd channel, and are moderator-guest talk shows with audience participation, in which prominent Saudi religious figures are repeatedly invited to address the audience. These talk shows are read as social texts, and religion is regarded as a social and political organising force. To some extent they demonstrate the priorities and the world-views of the Al-Majd network, its present-ers and prominent guests. The fact that many of these guests have been given a platform on Al-Majd as a result of repeated appear-ances on the programmes indicates how highly they are viewed by the network.

Al-Majd is known within specialised circles in the United States and the international English-speaking media for its many infa-mous *fatwas*, including the high-profile 'Mickey Mouse Must Die', issued by Sheikh Muhammad Saleh AlMunjid on Al-Majd televi-sion.[18] On the other hand, Al-Majd, with its alleged socially and religiously constructive role is greatly appreciated by the Saudi media.[19] Sheikh Muhammad AlHabdan issued a *fatwa* on Al-Majd television concerning the face veil (*niqāb*). He maintained that it was permitted for a woman to show only one eye, the other eye being hidden beneath the *niqāb*.[20] The woman could, however, decide which eye to show.

Al-Majd is not the only channel known for its *fatwa* programmes, for they are also broadcast on many other religious channels. A '*fatwa* war' has been waged among these channels over audience ratings rather than the *fatwas* themselves.[21] Moreover, 'Abd AlHa-mid AlAnsari, a professor of Islamic Studies at Qatar University, was quoted in the Dubai Media Forum as stating, 'In addition to fame and stardom, *fatwas* have turned into a lucrative business', indicating the high income of the *ulama* from religious broadcast-ing.[22] Al-Majd has several competitors in the *fatwa* 'market' includ-ing AlNas, Al-Rrisala and other channels. When it comes to audience ratings, Al-Majd occupies fifth place on the list of the most viewed channels in Saudi Arabia.[23] Media experts confirm that Saudi Arabia continues to be the most important market in the region.[24] This is why much of the media produced in Arabic targets the Saudi audience.

A Saudi Channel

Al-Majd is stated to have the fourth highest income of all the televi-sion networks in the Arab world after Orbit, ART and Showtime. It has grown over six years to have twelve working channels with studios in Dubai, Riyadh, Cairo and Rabat. The capital of the Ola

Al-Majd Company, the owner of the Al-Majd network, reached US$34 million at the end of 2008 according to Al-Majd sources. The ownership of the Ola Al-Majd Company is believed to be spread among many shareholders, although most of the shares were held by the Chairman of the Board of Directors, Fahd AlShamamri. However, in May 2009, some of these shares were transferred to the new Chairman, Sheikh Hamad AlGamas, who owns 55.4 per cent of the network's assets. Some inside sources were quoted in the Saudi Press as asserting that some of the network's shares had been transferred to Sheikh Salman AlUdeh.[25]

The content of the Al-Majd general channel and the public statements issued by the Al-Majd network's decision-makers indicate that the network is, first and foremost, a Saudi Salafi channel. Nevertheless, this does not mean that other nationalities, in particular Egyptians, Jordanians, Kuwaitis and Yemenis, are excluded from the audience. However, this study looks at the target audience and the nature of the topics and programmes offered by the channel. In 'Dialogue Time', for instance, although many of the episodes, such as 'The Truth about Victory' and 'The Westernisation of Arab Countries', take a pan-Arab/Islamic view of the topics, their treatment tends to have a Saudi focus. All the examples and references quoted relate to Saudi Arabia, such as Saudi society and Saudi education in 'The Westernisation of Arab Countries.' In both 'Dialogue Time' and 'The Adequate Answer', the majority of the callers come from places within Saudi Arabia, for example, Ta'if, Riyad, Jiddah and Dammam. Furthermore, Dīratī ('My Home') is a quiz show about the geography and history of Saudi Arabia on the Al-Majd Children's Channel.

An IPSOS study of the audience share of various television networks in 2009, shows that Al-Majd holds tenth place on the list, with 3.6 per cent of the Saudi audience reporting that they watched the channel. The same study also shows that the network is not among those with the top audience ratings in any other Arab country.[26]

'Adel bin Ahmad AlMajid, the deputy program manager of the network, emphasised in an interview with alWatan newspaper, that the Al-Majd network was committed to the 'media policy' of the Kingdom of Saudi Arabia:

It attempts to enhance and empower the Saudi citizen in all areas in the Kingdom of Saudi Arabia, the Arab and Muslim worlds ... The network is depicting and enhancing a positive image of Saudis, and it also focuses on the social dynamism and development of the country.[27]

Al-Majd is also a nationalised television network. Rubai'an bin Fahd AlRubai'an, the former Production Manager of the network, emphasised this point, asserting that more than 40 per cent of its employees are Saudi. He took pride in the network's training centre, where young Saudis trained in media production were destined for employment in the Al-Majd networks.

On 16 May 2009, Hamad AlGamas took over the Al-Majd network by buying AlShamamri's share for 50 million SR (Saudi Riyal), resulting in a dramatic change in the ownership and management of the company. Saudi media reported disagreement between AlShamamri and other board members over management matters, especially relating to budgeting and finance. One of the major changes brought about by the new administration was the business orientation of the network. This is described in the various news reports covering the company's important deals with leading regional names, including the Saudi Telecommunications Company (STC) and the Emirati Du communications company. The STC was reported to have sponsored an evening show that began broadcasting on Al-Majd in December 2009.[28] During Ramadan 2009, Al-Majd had a deal with the Emirati integrated telecommunications company Du (EITC), offering a range of Islamic mobile content.[29]

Having outlined these concerns and priorities, it could be asked which social, cultural and political matters are raised and addressed by the Al-Majd Network. Which aspects of Saudi government and society are highlighted and emphasised? What are the duties of members of the public and what should be their relationship with the political and religious authorities or anyone else of a similar status?

Al-Majd Programming

Al-Majd has twelve channels that apparently represent the comprehensiveness (*shumuliyah*) of Islam as an everyday religion. Four channels are free-to-air and eight are encrypted. There are conflicting reports about plans for creating more free-to-air channels. The science channel, for instance, was reported to have been encrypted only in January 2008. Three of the network's channels target children: *Basmah* ('Smile'), *Fakkar wa Ila'ab* ('Think and Play'), and the *Rawdah* ('Kindergarten'). The network has special equipment that blocks the reception of other channels, even those that broadcast religious topics, such as Iqra' and alNas, among others.[30] This technical blocking of others is attached to the receivers sold to subscribers, in effect monopolising their viewing.

The network produces more than 7,000 hours of broadcasting time annually. In addition to its four main production sites in

Table 1: Al-Majd Network FTR and encrypted channels

Al-Majd Network Channels	
FTR Channels	*Encrypted*
Al-Majd, Main General	*Khidmat AlAkhbar* (News Service)
Al-Majd, Hadīth	Al-Majd, *AlWathaqiyah* (First Arabic Language Documentary Channel)
Al-Majd, Holy Qur'an	Al-Majd, *AlTabiyah* (Second Documentary Channel)
Al-Majd, *'Ilmiyah* (Religious Sciences)	Al-Majd (Children's Channel)
	Al-Majd, *Basmah* (Cartoon Channel for Children)
	Fakkar wa Ila'ab (Think and Play—interactive games for children)
	Al-Majd, *Ramadaniyah* (Special Channel during the holy month of Ramadan)
	Al-Majd, Promo Channel (A multi-view of the 9 main channels of the Al-Majd bouquet)
	Shada TV
	Radio *Dal* for Children (Live SMS Chat on the Channel round the clock)

Dubai, Riyad and Cairo, it has many representative offices in other Arab capitals, including Rabat in Morocco. With more than 250,000 subscribers, it is rated the fourth largest subscription-based Arab television network. Al-Majd's Open Islamic Academy is an online educational institution that teaches shari'a sciences (al'ulūm alshari'ah) to more than 17,000 registered students. Many of the lectures are delivered on one of the encrypted channels.

The comprehensiveness of the channels provided by Al-Majd and the exclusiveness of its reception highlights the particular audience for which the network is catering. It is the only source of media for that audience, and it acts as a barrier between its viewers and other media content in keeping with its ideology of religious exclusiveness. The network offers a range of channels for the whole family, covering science, documentary, news, the Qur'an, Hadīth and health. This practise of offering the audience all the content that they would possibly need or demand fits very well with the network's stated view of the media as a major source of social and religious ills and problems. Its views are discussed below.

By implementing this policy, Al-Majd is apparently attempting to create for its audience a specially designed world that is woman-free, music-free, and sin-free. In its programmes, much attention is given to thought and abstract topics. The programmes are based on the view that Muslims' faith and beliefs have suffered from distortion and that matters need to be put right. In the opinion of the Al-Majd interviewees and audiences, much of the damage to the Islamic faith aqida is caused by various social institutions and bodies including the media, education and advocates of the Westernisation of the Arab countries. There has been significant supporting evidence in the polls and in the framing of social and religious questions on Al-Majd's show 'Dialogue Time.' On a global level, typically, even among other religious groups, '[m]ovies, television and the Internet, for example, are often seen as threats to religious identity when they present alternative ways of expressing faith.'[31]

'Dialogue Time'

This is a weekly prime-time show on the Al-Majd general channel and is the first live programme on Al-Majd from Riyad. In each episode, their titles indicating their content, a new guest is invited to discuss questions of importance to Muslims, especially in Saudi Arabia. The show's host, Fahd bin 'Abd Al'Aziz AlSnaidi, has the appearance of a very mainstream young Saudi. He is also a Professor of Islamic Studies at King Saud University.[32] Previously, he was employed in the Department of Religious Affairs at the Ministry of Defense. Besides hosting 'Dialogue Time' at Al-Majd, AlSnaidi is employed at the Qur'an alKarīm radio station and supervises the website of the Islamic Magazine.[33]

AlSnaidi states that 'Dialogue Time' was originally conceived of by Al-Majd Television at the outbreak of the war on Iraq in April 2003. He adds: 'The network envisioned a talk show to host Saudi thinkers and media people who did not have access to the audience through other channels.'[34] The questions addressed in 'Dialogue Time' are mostly abstract, and there is a focus on the ways of thinking about certain topics. Themes covered in the show have included the 'Islamic Renaissance', 'Liberal Islam', 'Atheism', 'Redefining Victory', 'The Westernisation of Arab Countries' and alda'wah. The 'Islamic Renaissance' was explained by equating it to advancement (taqadum), development (tatawur), and civilisation (hadarah).

The show has a non-traditional Salafi appearance that is manifested in the glossy background and huge modern screens. AlSnaidi has no beard and he wears a white robe (thaūb) and a traditional head covering (ghatrah).[35] He is well prepared for his show, supplying books for his guests, using their quotations from earlier conferences, published works or news items, and asking them to clarify their previous positions or opinions. He speaks traditional, classical Arabic, emphasising the pronunciation of his words as if he were reciting the Qur'an. Most of the guests that have been invited to take part in this show have been university Professors, including Muhammad bin 'Abd Al'Aziz Muhammad Qasim, Professor Sabir Tuaimah, and Sheikh Nasser Ibn Suleiman Al'Umur, among others.[36]

When compiling the titles of the episodes, it is customary to include the expression 'The Phenomenon of' this or that, particularly where the topic for discussion is considered a negative societal change. In this context, the use of 'phenomenon' is twofold; on the one hand, it is indicative of the newness of the behaviour or way of thinking at hand, which is seen in a negative light, and on the other hand, 'phenomenon' emphasises the academic and scientific accuracy of the opinions of (predominantly) academics interviewed on the show. Much of the discourse is against new ideas and practices. These are labelled as *bid'a* (heresy). In one particular episode, the talk show host AlSnaidi and guest Professor Sabir Tuaimah criticised the 'Phenomenon of Dishonouring the Sacred' (*Tadnīs alMuqadasāt*). The 'Sacred', as they defined it, referred to the Islamic texts, especially the Qur'an and the *Hadīth*. Tuaimah explained that a lack of respect for the sacred (*muqadasāt*) was the main reason for the nurturing of terrorism in the world (*al-Ard*). One example, he continued, was a story from AlHurra Television, in which a woman was cursing the rule that a wife must ask her husband's permission if she wished to go out or that woman was originally created from a crooked rib (*urradelaq a'wajwaj*). In Tuaimah's view, similar statements and what he described as the culture of a lack of respect for, and repeated offences against, the sacred which were published in texts and broadcast on radio and television, were the real cause of the growth in anti-social thinking (*fikr*) and hence, fanaticism (*asabiyah*) and violence. In another episode, entitled 'The Westernisation of Arab Countries', one's way of thinking (*fikr*) was of major concern and an important means of judging people and classifying them. Also expressed frequently on the show is the speakers' concern regarding accusations that the *ulama* are being Westernised, or that they are advocating a Western agenda and values and promoting secularism.

Writers, film directors, novelists, journalists, and other media professionals are considered the real agents of Westernisation and colonisation, even if they call themselves reformists. In one episode, the guest (AlGhamidi) argued that agency toward Westernisation could come from party affiliation, country citizenship, or the mere adoption and advocacy of these ideas and trends. According to AlGhamidi, the most dangerous aspect of Westernisation (*taghrīb*) was the new liberalism. Al-Majd *ulama* use strong language against these public figures and describe them as collaborators paid by American politicians. Prominent Arab scholars such as Sadiq Jalal AlAzem, Sa'ad AlDīn Ibrahim, Hassan Hanafi,

Shaker AlNabulsi and other writers are among those alleged agents, because of their liberal beliefs.

AlJawab AlKaf ('The Adequate Answer')

This is a *fatwa* program on Al-Majd, presented by Muhammad AlMagran. It is broadcast every Friday and Sunday on the general and science channels. Although a few of the episodes are of general interest, the majority are based on particular themes. The host receives questions by telephone from members of the audience, who can be women, children or men. The show has an online forum,[37] on which members of the audience can post questions, suggestions, and comments. These are answered every week by AlMagran, the show's host, as stated on the forum's home page.

On examining the episodes of 'The Adequate Answer', the same themes were found to recur, particularly women, the media, Islamic purity, and Westernisation. However, a new theme that is currently dominating many of the episodes is finance, with discussions on aspects such as banking, investment, *zakat* and insurance.[38] In one of the episodes analysed, it was brought to the audience's attention that the episode was devoted to answering all the accusations made by secularists against Islam—surprisingly, most of the episode revolved around the veil (both *hijāb* and *niqāb*).

Members of the phone-in audience frequently ask detailed questions about Islamic rituals such as *ibadāt*. Other topics include the giving of presents, the playing of drums by women during wedding celebrations, and whether it is permitted (*halāl*) in Islam to read novels on the Internet.[39] Some of the questions are about the use of language, such as whether the inclusion of 'Great' (*al'azīm*), as in *astaghfiru Allah al'Azīm*, is a heresy (*bid'a*) or a Tradition of the Prophet (*Sunnah*), and whether it is *halāl* for a Muslim to say 'What a shame!' (*wa khazyah!*).

An examination of Al-Majd shows indicates that they tend to focus on four main recurrent topics: the media, women, the West and its secular (*alalmaniyīn*) advocates and collaborators, and the correctness of Islamic doctrine (*aqida*). Notably, criticism of the media is not limited to the question of morality and the threat posed by the deterioration in the ethics of young Muslims. It frequently extends to the disapproval and condemnation of the 'deviations' of the other 'unorthodox' (*mubtada'īn*) Islamic religious channels and Sheikhs, emphasising the ramifications of giving them a platform to reach Muslims through the media. Similarly, questions and concerns are also raised regarding the fact that many of these other religious channels are reluctant to invite the 'wise' *ulama* of Al-Majd and their associate Salafis (although they do not usually refer to them as Salafis).

In the shows examined, political events and issues are rarely discussed, if at all. Unlike most of the other media, terrorism is not a major theme, nor a recurring frame in Al-Majd. If mentioned at all, it is called violence and attributed to the four recurrent afore-mentioned topics: the media, women, the West, and the threat of unorthodox scholars on Muslim society and the real understanding of Islam. Therefore violence is a product of evil deeds (*almafāsid*), Westernisation, and secularists (*alalmaniyīn*), rather than a result of the lack of political participation, oppression, social, political and economic injustices or a problem that needs to be addressed in itself. In the opinion of Al-Majd, young men are exposed to these threats by the media and the collaborators of the West who wish to Westernise and secularise the Arab countries. Moreover, all the problems in the Arab/Muslim world are the result of a conspiracy hatched by the West or its collaborators.

According to Al-Majd *ulama*, there is only one surviving group and only one truthful understanding of Islamic doctrine (*aqida*)—and that is their group. It is comprised of those who are close to the accurate interpretation of the Qur'an and the *Hadīth*, who are committed to that interpretation, who also have a sound understanding of the West and its conspiracies against Islam, and who avoid those media that corrupt ethics, ruin families and spoil women's behaviour. Consequently, those who watch only Al-Majd programmes endorsed by the *ulama* are the righteous group. The in-group/out-group classifications are based on alignment with the Islamic texts and a particular understanding of them, in addition to approval by certain *ulama*, who are in turn endorsed by the political establishment. Any media content is regarded as a threat to them and their audiences except that which they have filtered, censored and approved.[40]

The contents of Al-Majd programmes were analysed to identify the most recurrent questions and values, for it is these items that represent the agenda of individual Muslims and Muslim society, especially in Saudi Arabia. Moral and ethical questions came at the top of the list and were also given priority for treatment by Al-Majd over *fatwas*, present-day issues and challenges in that order (see Table 2). More solid moral questions such as equality and social justice are ignored due to the 'trivialisation' of morality practised by Wahhabi *ulama* in Saudi Arabia. Okruhlik asserts that:

[T]he problem is not with conservative morality but that the very idea of morality has been trivialized. It is conflated with the codification of social absurdities, demonstrated by religious rulings that regulate the plucking of eyebrows, the use of nail polish, and the length of gowns rather than grapple with explicitly political issues that revolve around distributive fairness, governmental accountability, and social justice.[41]

Table 2: Issues addressed by Al-Majd's programs

Questions	*Dialogue Time*	*Adequate Answer*	*Total*	*Per cent*
Moral/ethical dilemmas	9	5	14	29.8
Historical experiences and narratives	6	0	6	12.8
Present-day issues and challenges	7	1	8	17.1
Fatwas	5	4	9	19.1
Qur'anic and *Hadīth* Interpretations	1	4	5	10.6
Transcendental issues	1	1	2	4.2
Other	1	2	3	6.3
Total	30	17	47	99.9

A qualitative analysis confirmed these results, especially in relation to moral and ethical questions. Most of the accusations levelled against the media, the West, or even education in many episodes, are based on the perceived effectiveness of these forces in undermining the morality of young people and thus causing chaos in society.

The values highly appreciated by Al-Majd are decency of women (*ihtisham*), which comprises almost 20 per cent of the total instances of the promotion of values, followed by integrity (*istiqama*). Both of these fit well with the channel's interest in morality and ethical questions. Religiosity comprises 15 per cent and is followed by harmony (*tamāsuk/insijām ma'a alnafs*). On the other hand, the broader aspects of morality, such as honesty, mercy, and co-existence, comprised less than 8 per cent of the total. This result raises a question about Al-Majd's definition of morality and ethics. Bearing in mind that women and their effect on morality have been most important in Al-Majd programmes, it is clear that the channel's definition of morality and ethics is very narrow.[42] Al-Majd's debate about women has been limited to discussing their presence in public places and interaction with men. The broader understanding of morality, which includes other important Islamic principles, is considered less important and thus is less frequently

Table 3: Values promoted by Al-Majd programs

Values	Dialogue Time	Adequate Answer	Total	Per cent
Decency (of women) (*ihtishām/ layqah/tahthīb*)	8	7	15	19.20
Honesty (*amānah*)	1	1	2	2.50
Piety (*taqwā*)	4	1	5	6.40
Religiosity (*tadayūn*)	8	4	12	15.38
Integrity (*istiqāmah*)	8	5	13	16.66
Mercy (*rahmah*)	1	1	2	2.50
Harmony (*tamāsuk/insijām ma'a alnafs*)	6	3	9	11.80
Tolerance (*tasāmuh*)	2	3	5	6.40
Distinction (*tafāwuq/sumūwi*)	3	1	4	5.10
Spirituality (*rūhānīyah*)	0	1	1	1.30
Coexistence (*ta'āyush*)	1	1	2	2.50
Other	1	2	3	3.80
Consensus (*ijmā'*)	1	1	2	2.50
Diversity (*tannawu'*)	2	1	3	3.80
Total	46	32	78	99.99

mentioned (see Table 3). According to the Al-Majd programmes women are always seen as a physical attraction, and even their appearance on television, wearing colourful clothes and make-up, is regarded by many of the Al-Majd Sheikhs as an open invitation to sin (*ma'asy*) and sedition (*fitnah*).

As the only major provider of media available to a certain segment of the Saudi population and different religious groups in the Gulf region, Egypt, Jordan and Libya,[43] Al-Majd has an unusually strong influence over its audience in following a particular way of life. The broadcasting of restricted sources of information to a conservative Saudi audience could raise questions about its effect on the viewers' ideas of life and the outside world. The type and level of participation resulting from this exposure, the opportunities available to, and choices made by their children, their experiences and the type of family relations created, the future position of women, and their envisioned roles, are all worth further research.

Media

The religious scholars of Al-Majd apportion a generous share of the blame to the media for the deterioration in ethics, the immoral behaviour and the Westernised values that are currently found among young people. Sheikh AlLehidan, Head of the Kingdom's highest committee, the Supreme Judiciary Council, was quoted as saying that media channels have caused the 'deviance of thousands of people.' He added: 'Those calling for corrupt beliefs, certainly it's permissible to kill them ... Those calling for sedition, those who are able to prevent it but don't, it is permissible to kill them.'[44] This *fatwa* was strongly criticised by journalists and writers in the Arab media. In support of Sheikh AlLihedan's *fatwa*, Sheikh 'Abd Allah bin Jabrīn, a former member of the Saudi Establishment of Fatwas, told Al-Majd Television that journalists and writers who dared to criticise Sheikhs should be penalised. He is quoted on the website of the Committee to Protect Journalists as having said:

Those [writers] and journalists and satellite TVs who attack scholars, and particularly well-known sheikhs, and publish bad bulletins about them— they must be punished ... even by lengthy imprisonment ... or by dismissing them from their jobs, and flogging and rebuking.[45]

In 'Dialogue Time', as in 'The Adequate Answer', the media are regarded as one of the major agencies of guilt and blame. They are the cause of the increase in the phenomenon of desecrating the sacred (*tadnis almuqadasāt*) and corrupting the audience's Islamic ideals.[46]

New media technology and the relative openness of the marketplace of media production and consumption have been a challenge to the hegemony of the Saudi regime as well as to the influence of *ulama*. The availability of various ideas, values and lifestyles to the Saudi audience has broken the monopoly of the Saudi state on media content. The Saudi government since the 1990s has been constantly trying to censor and limit the access of its citizens to these sources: by limiting access to the Internet through proxy and other means, and by making satellite dishes illegal in the country.[47]

Women

Focusing on women is a common trend among all religious channels. Female preachers, mostly from Egypt but who serve on various channels such as Abla Al-Kahlawy, Neveen Al-Guindy, Soad Saleh and others, have even started having their own shows on Iqra', Al-Risalah, Dream and other religious and mainstream TV channels.[48] All of this is condemned by the Al-Majd *ulama*, and viewed as a deviance from the right path and from the 'teachings of the Prophet Muhammad' (*sunna*).

Debating women's issues, status and rights is never an exclusively social or religious endeavour. For many in the Kingdom, the late King Fahd's decision to allow coalition forces and the US military to have bases in the country in the early 1990s caused an unnecessary exposure to western culture and values. According to the Salafi *ulama*, women were particularly vulnerable to this cultural invasion. Likewise, the deterioration of women's ethics is due to the media and Westernisation, and is one of the most serious threats having fatal effects on society.

In the opinion of Al-Majd, women themselves can be a serious threat to society if not restricted to the home and to the right dress code and behaviour. Furthermore, morality and ethical standards are jeopardised by the presence of women, unless they are veiled from top to toe (*munāqabāt*). The appearance of women—even when veiled—on television programmes is also condemned as deviant and risky. On 'Dialogue Time', an episode entitled 'The Phenomenon of Evading Religious Commitment' turned into a programme aimed entirely at women and their appearance. The speaker, Dr. Muhammad Musa AlSharif, criticised religious channels for allowing women to appear on television programmes (meaning, to be present in the public sphere). The Sheikh reported that he had received complaints from members of the public about those women who wore make-up and colourful clothing, because their attractive appearance charmed and seduced religious viewers.

Saudi women in particular, are seen to be strongly influenced by the media, especially regarding the *hijāb* and the *niqāb*. *Ulama* who appear on other religious channels have been criticised for being in the same studio with women, which, according to the Al-Majd programmes, will have a bad influence on them. Even poetry is condemned by Al-Majd because it does not promote sacred values but, instead, flatters women, which is a great sin.[49]

'Abd Allah bin Muhammad AlDa'ūd, a researcher in women's issues, was the guest speaker on the episode entitled 'Women between Westernisation and Alienation' (*alMar'a bayna al Taghiyīb wa alTaghrīb*). According to him, the aim of encouraging women to go out to work was to provide sexual pleasure for the men in the workplace (the women's colleagues). AlDa'ud declared: 'All women who have called-in to this show have fully and positively participated in social change for the betterment of society', although they were neither seen nor present in the studio. The point of his statement was that although women should stay at home, it did not mean that they would be less active than working women.

Obviously, in Al-Majd's religious interpretation, Islam obliges women to stay within the private space—home. Furthermore, any public activity for women and any social or political roles are not allowed, since women would have to leave the private space and would be seen by other men, even if veiled. Women were not even allowed to be heard on the Al-Majd network when the network was first launched—it was not until a few years later that women could call-in to Al-Majd programmes.[50]

The West

Ethics distinguish between 'us' (Muslims) and 'them' (the West). In an episode about the Gaza War in 2009, Nasser Ibn Suleiman Al'Umur envisioned that the US and Israel would disintegrate from within, due to what he calls their 'ethical deterioration.'

In both of the shows examined here the media are also blamed as the major source of Westernisation in the Arab countries and the greatest facilitator of this invasion since Napoleon Bonaparte's various interactions at the end of the eighteenth century. AlGhamidi suggested that AlHurra TV transmitted in Arabic from Washington DC, acting on behalf of President George W. Bush and having the same aims as Napoleon two centuries earlier.[51] This common aim was to occupy Arab and Muslim land and Westernise their societies.

One of the poll options in each episode concerns the 'West.' These polls describe the causes of the problems discussed during the programme and include much rhetoric about Islam and the Arab countries being targeted by the West. For instance, in the episode on the 'Victory in Gaza War', the poll asks the audience's opinion on who was the winner in the Gaza War. In the episode concerning the antagonism between Islamists and the United States, the question was on the causes of these difficulties.

One particular episode of 'Dialogue Time' was dedicated to discussing the hostile relationship between Islamists and the United States,[52] with Awad Al-Qarni as the guest. The poll dealt with the main reasons for this hostility. The results were as follows: out of 477 respondents, more than 50 per cent (255) thought that the US position on the Palestinian-Israeli conflict was the main cause of hostility; 56 thought it was the US invasion of Iraq; 138 believed the cause was due to the country's control over many powerful international bodies and organisations; and only 4 thought that conspiracy theory amongst Islamists was the reason.

Conclusion

Al-Majd preachers and their version of correct Islam or the surviving group is very socially and religiously specific and focused.

These preachers provide very orthodox and traditional (Saudi) views. It is remarkable, if not surprising, that the Al-Majd programmes under examination did not indicate any type of political disagreement or contestation whatsoever with the political system in Saudi Arabia. Very little attention, if any at all, was given to internal politics. Al-Majd *ulama* and its programmes, to a large extent, drew away the attention of their audience to social order and morality of the Saudi/Muslim society on the one hand, and to the external political challenges facing Muslims such as the occupation of Iraq and the 'Westernisation' of Muslim society on the other. In doing so, Al-Majd programmes can be seen as a deflection of their audience's attention from internal political issues. In this respect, Al-Majd and their interpretation of Islam are reinforcing the current political system within the kingdom and the authority of the King and royal family. This is done through the concentration on an individualised version of Islam that focuses on social issues, and through the emphasis of the Al-Majd *ulama* on the necessity of obeying the rulers, *ta'at waley al amar*, as a major issue in the lives of Muslims and as equally important to *ta'at allah*, to obey God. On the social level, there appears to be more contestation regarding their emphasis on women's issues and the *ulama* encounter with the Westernisation of Muslim society that is the embodiment of all evil in their eyes.

Whereas the *ulama* on Al-Majd TV do not necessarily condemn *jihad*, they do not encourage it. When discussed, *jihad* is viewed as a reaction to aggression and Westernisation and the deterioration of ethics. All this leads young Muslims to mistakenly take the application of shari'a into their own hands, and thus to violence.

4

'MODERN' SALAFI BROADCASTING

IQRA' CHANNEL (SAUDI ARABIA)

Ehab Galal

After the first Arab satellite channel was launched in 1990 (the Saudi-owned Middle East Broadcasting Centre [MBC] in London), approximately eight years went by until the first Islamic-defined satellite channel in Arabic, Iqra', was established on 21 October 1998. The channel's choice of name was not a coincidence. The word 'Iqra' is the imperative mood of the verb 'to read.' 'Iqra' was the first word that was revealed to the Prophet Muhammad by the angel Gabriel. Historically, the word Iqra' has been frequently used among Muslims to recall the importance of education.

Iqra' is a part of Arab Radio & Television's satellite TV-package (ART). The package consists of twenty-one thematic channels, amongst which Iqra' stands out by being defined as religious. The ART network is owned by the Saudi billionaire Sheikh Saleh Kamel and was established in 1993, with its headquarters in Italy. ART started off with a few thematic channels, including a movie channel, a music channel and a sports channel. The idea of establishing a religious channel in 1998 stuck to the thematic concept to which ART was already accustomed and in which it had expertise. One can argue that religion is a somewhat different topic than the previous purely entertainment-based channels that ART had operated for some years, but the choice of promoting a religious channel can also be understood as an expression of an increasing trend that presents religion, including Islam, as a consumer and entertainment product that is financially beneficial to produce. Religion can be brilliant entertainment while complying with the need for identity among people in a globalised world.[1] However, entertaining or not, market orientated or not, the channel's programmes do mediate religious values and identities through a differentiated and varied programme schedule. The questions to ask are: What values does Iqra' promote? How are the values related to the different religious identities that are promoted by Iqra'? And what kind of religious space does Iqra' offer its audience?

In order to answer these questions, the chapter proceeds as follows. First, I will give an account of the channel's defined goals, its position within the broader satellite landscape, and the varied programming that Iqra' is offering its audience. Secondly, in order to get a deeper understanding of the values promoted, I will examine the general outline of two programmes that were broadcast in 2009: *Al-Bayynah* ('Evidence') and *Mauadah wa Rahma* ('Affection and Mercy'). The general outline will be followed by a comparison between the two chosen programmes' content. Finally, I will particularly look into how the two different kinds of programmes support different relationships with their audience and thereby offer different kinds of religious spaces. The discussion will be followed by short conclusive remarks.

Iqra's Goals

Like other popular[2] Islamic channels such as Al-Resalah, Al-Majd and Al-Nas, Iqra' defines its purpose with very general statements about Islam as a universal value that unites all Muslims. Iqra' writes on the channel's website under 'Our Mission':

Iqra' Channel seeks to build a modern Muslim society that truly believes in and loves God and His Prophet Muhammad, acts upon the Qur'an and the Prophetic Tradition and follows in the righteous Muslim ancestors' lead. Iqra' Channel aims to help Muslims apply the teachings of Islam that call for tolerance and for addressing others mildly; a Muslim society whose members will be able to positively interact both on the local and international levels. Iqra' Channel also aims at presenting the true moderate face of Islam to people in the West where media does not present an objective view of Islamic Law.[3]

According to this statement, the channel considers itself to be a facilitator of knowledge about religious, cultural, social, educational, economic and political issues based on the Qur'an and the Prophet Muhammad's *Sunna*. Iqra''s goal is to strengthen the Muslims' belonging to 'the Arab-Islamic nation and culture.' Thus, Iqra' refers to an idea of an imagined Arab community defined by a common Arab culture and a common religious identity as Muslims. With the intention of strengthening this identity, the channel will disseminate knowledge of the Arabic language and the Arab-Islamic civilisation's contribution to history.

By highlighting words like tolerance, moderate Islam and positive interaction, nationally and internationally, Iqra' expresses a desire to correct the image of the Muslims in the West. While building bridges between different Muslim countries and other cultures, the channel supports the idea of a moderate course (*al-Wasatiya*) of Islam. Nonetheless, a more specific definition of 'a moderate course of Islam' is not presented. Consequently, in order to identify how the channel ascribes meaning to its claim of 'a moderate course' in practice, it is necessary to analyse the content of the channel's programmes. The concept of a moderate course of Islam seems rather diffuse and open for interpretation, but does at the same time signal openness to change and dialogue. The question is, though, how is this implemented in practice?

According to Iqra''s self presentation and programme schedule, the Muslim community is characterised by a specific Muslim behaviour rather than by a specific way of organising a political society. The channel claims to promote behaviour that defines Muslims as those who 'believe in and love God, act in accordance with the Qu'ranic tradition, are tolerant and meet others with kindness, interact positively, and show the true picture of Islam.' On Iqra''s website under the heading 'Our Vision', the emphasis on the individual Muslim's behaviour is reinforced:

Iqra' Channel seeks to meet the viewers' needs through presenting a number of serious programmes on the viewers' everyday life problems, serving their spiritual, cultural, social and economic interests, from an Islamic perspective with a modern vision.

By stressing the everyday life problems, the focus on Islam as related to the individual is further emphasised. Thus, the questions about the individual's needs, spiritual interests and salvation are accentuated, rather than focusing on political questions requiring specific community changes. The tendency to highlight lifestyle issues is further supported by the programming.[4]

Iqra' in the Wider Phenomenon of Religious Broadcasting

Iqra' is like most other Islamic satellite channels funded and launched by Arab businessmen, business consortiums, or finance companies. This means that Iqra', in common with other Islamic satellite channels, is not derived largely from religious groups or organisations, as is often the case for websites and various forms of Islamic pamphlet literature which have more explicit membership or attachment to different groups. While many Christian-Arab channels are launched by churches or religious groups,[5] the Islamic channels are usually not identified with a specific interpretation or Islamic school. Instead, they identify themselves with Islam as a declared common and universal value claiming to represent a universal and global Islam.

The rapid growth of Islamic channels may, among other reasons, be seen in the context of the large increase in the number of Arab satellite channels in general. As mentioned in the introduction, Iqra' is part of a Saudi business empire which also contains several other media and forms of investment. Iqra' can therefore be seen as a business among other business interests. To invest in an Islamic channel is to invest in yet another audience. Frequently, the Islamic channel is the only one among other non-Islamic, general or thematic channels in a media empire. Thus, the ART network today has twenty-one thematic channels,[6] among them a movie channel, a sports channel, a channel with cartoons, etc. Naomi Sakr argues that the establishment of satellite television may be seen as a result of both political and economic interests.[7] She has not dealt specifically with religious channels, but with the various businessmen who are behind Arab satellite TV. The channels, she argues, were

at first incorporated as tools in the businessmen's empires to advertise other products and to advertise for the businessmen themselves. By launching a satellite channel, they introduce themselves
as reliable business partners—no less powerful when it turns out
to be an Islamic channel. Secondly, the satellite channels are one
area of interaction between the economic and political elite in the
Arab countries.[8] To launch a satellite channel is thus a means to
earn money as well as political influence. Moreover, it cannot be
denied that the launch of an Islamic channel may be associated
with the promotion of the owner's own religious values.

Hence, the first step towards a general characterisation of Iqra'
is that like other Islamic channels it is the result of strong financial
interests, which also means that it is expected to provide some kind
of economic return. However, looking into the channels' defined
goals as presented on their websites or in their programmes, the
goal is to produce television with an Islamic frame of reference.
This overall similar goal does not mean, though, that the channels
do not differ in religious interpretation and ideology, and it does
not mean that they cannot have a political as well as a more specific
religious goal. While the channels' religious interpretations can be
different, they all stress the existence of an Islamic perspective on
all aspects of life. Most of the channels are Sunni Muslim, some of
them have Sufi connections, and others are Salafi with close connections to the Saudi religious establishment. A minority of the
channels is Shiite (e.g. Al-Kawthar TV, al-Anwar TV and Ahl Al-
Bayt TV),[9] but they do also formulate a strategy of universal Islam
similar to the Sunni Muslim channels.

Despite the emphasis on a universal Islam, it is necessary to
notice that the owners behind Iqra', Al-Resalah and Al-Majd all
have good relations with the Saudi royal family. There is a kind of
arrangement between the Saudi government wanting to promote a
conservative re-Islamisation, and a private and economically liberal media, which according to the channels' descriptions of themselves can be said to be largely focussed on the individual, and
what Roy describes as the privatisation of re-Islamisation.[10] On the
one hand, the channels represent a political-religious strategy for
the Islamic Mission (da'wa) dominated by a Saudi traditionalistic
Salafi tradition; on the other hand they represent the privatisation

of religion through economic liberalism which emphasises individual re-Islamisation with dignitaries as models.[11] In contrast to Al-Majd, the Salafism promoted by Iqra' could be categorised as a *Wahhabi-light* Salafism. As Salafism in general, the idea is to go back to the early tradition of the Prophet Muhammad and his followers and to the authentic texts (Qur'an and *Hadith*) as the basis for interpretation. Thus, in the programmes on Iqra', the references to the texts and the *Sunna* are a recurrent and prevalent basis for discussion. However, as will be demonstrated, the textual references are given different weight and perspectives depending on the topic of the programme.

The two trends of Islamisation seem to agree in rejecting a political and radical Islam, meaning Islamism. Al-Majd does, for instance, emphasise that the channel wants to get young people away from extremism. Comparing the two trends of Islamisation, Al-Majd leans toward state loyalty promoting a regional (Gulf countries), conservative re-Islamisation, while Iqra' and Al-Resalah to a higher degree can be placed within the category of the privatisation of re-Islamisation due to their programming and their focus on social and religious dignitaries and prominent Muslim celebrities. At Iqra' and Al-Resalah, the emphasis on the individuality of a Muslim lifestyle is further supported by the channels' websites where several programmes are promoted and identified with the programme host presented as a prominent and pious Muslim. As I will argue later, the religious figures on Iqra' are popular figures who function as a way of attracting audiences. At the same time Iqra', like Al-Resalah, is more global in its programming. Al-Majd meanwhile, only broadcasts through Arab satellites and today mostly as pay channels, Iqra' broadcasts through Arabsat 4B and 2B, Nilesat, Hotbird, Asiasat2. Not only is the reach global, but the Muslim community is also presented in a more global perspective by Iqra.' The programmes encourage Muslims from all over the world to participate and the Muslim figures presented are from different parts of the world.[12] The channels are, in this way, reflecting the change in Islamisation which Roy characterises as a development towards a more universalistic and less political interpretation of Islam.[13]

Major Lines of Programming

When a channel claims to be Islamic, one expects that the programmes and the content should reflect this categorisation. The question is what characterises Iqra''s programmes and what it means for the channel's frame of reference and perspective to be allegedly Islamic. A glance at the programme schedule reveals a line of programming that includes a wide range of programmes from news to entertainment.

Iqra' has, from the very beginning, broadcast different types of programmes that address different audiences and different needs. At the same time they draw on genre types known from secular television. There are children's programmes, quiz programmes, question programmes, recitation competitions, educational programmes, debates, talk shows, historical films, drama series, etc. By dividing the programmes into three types (which transgress traditional programme genres), it is possible to get a general understanding of how the Islamic perspective is translated into the programme schedule. At Iqra' the three types of programming are:

1. Programmes that explicitly present interpretations and recitations of the Qur'an, *Hadith* and *Sunna*, thereby mediating the scriptural tradition.
2. Programmes that explicitly or implicitly disseminate ideals of Islamic lifestyle emphasising the religious morally encoded practices of modern life and consumption.
3. Programmes that present aspects of society without any particular Islamic frame of reference.

1. Islamic Interpretation

The most widespread application of this type is the so-called '*fatwa* programme' which to varying degrees focuses on religious scholars' interpretations of the Muslim tradition. Iqra' has multiple *fatwa* programmes with quite different scholars who may be more or less conservative and may focus on various themes in relation to Islam. However, the focal point is the question of permitted and forbidden Islamic behaviour in relation to the individual Muslim's daily life. The Islamic perspective is explicit as the scholars extract the authorised evidence directly from the texts and tradition.

There are also programmes presenting Qur'anic interpretation, recitation and teaching.[14]

2. Islamic Lifestyle

The vast majority of programmes at Iqra' focus on how the individual Muslim lives everyday life and solves everyday problems in accordance with Islam. Instead of being a text corpus of knowledge, as in the *fatwa* programmes, Islam becomes a moral and practical frame of reference. The lifestyle programming includes a diversity of different programme genres. What they have in common is that they offer the viewer an identity as a 'proper' or 'real' Muslim.[15] Among them are entertaining talk shows about how to find a spouse in the proper Islamic way or how Muslim women are wearing their headscarf (*hijab*) in a fashionable way.[16] Another variant is the historical *musalsal* (soap or drama serial)[17] which typically deals with a specific historical event or person that has been significant for the development of Islam or the Muslim community. In these rather different types of programmes, the lifestyle and identity are explicitly presented as being Muslim.

A more implicit positioning of the Islamic identity is in programmes about economics,[18] health[19] and sex,[20] which sometimes involve examples of what the Prophet Mohammad said and did, but in which the focus of attention is the knowledge of contemporary economics and health. The implicit positioning is also recurrent in sitcoms and *musalsalat* which are broadcast by the channel. One example is the Jordanian serial *Ĥakāya al-Nas* ('People's History') which was broadcast on Iqra' in September 2006 and describes the family's daily life and problems. The overriding moral of the serial was presented repeatedly with reference to Islam.

Likewise, some of the historical *musalsalat* could to some extent be categorised as implicitly positioning the Islamic identity as they present events which are essential for Islamic Arab history but without underlining more than the intriguing story.[21]

3. Not Particularly Islamic

The programmes falling under this category are few, and represent only a small proportion of the total programme schedule. Though not focusing on Islam or religious themes, due to simply being broadcast the programmes are included as a legitimate element of Islamic identity and politics. From the point of view of the producers, these programmes are of course in accordance with Islam, and therefore are not non-Islamic. Islam is conceived as embracing all aspects of life. Another reason for Iqra' to broadcast these programmes might be the influence of and co-operation with other ART channels. Regularly, the same drama serials are transmitted by different ART channels, including Iqra.'

Examples of this kind of programme are, for instance, sports programmes and TV news. Iqra' broadcasts the daily news programme *Ahdath al-Youm* ('Today's Events') which is repeated several times daily. But also socially orientated programmes are available on Iqra.' The programme *al-Hayatu Amal* ('Life Is Hope') presents the life of disabled persons. It highlights, through examples, how the disabled person can be an active participant in different aspects of life by working, car driving, swimming, painting, and so on. In the same genre is a programme about how to become an entrepreneur and start your own business, called *al-Dunia bi Khair* ('Life Is Good'). There are also documentaries without any explicit references to Islam such as *Bahth 'an Knuz* ('Treasure Hunt'), which was broadcast on Iqra' in 2005 and revealed the story of treasure hunters finding and raising sunken ships with hidden treasures.

One final genre of programmes worth mentioning in this category are programmes like *Iktishāfāt 'arabiya* ('Arab Inventions') and *al-'ulūm 'ind al-'arab* ('Science with Arabs'), both broadcast by Iqra.' They tell the story of how Arabs have contributed to science through innovations in chemistry, mathematics, and so on, and through the continuation of others' work. Here it seems to be the Arab rather than Islamic identity which is the frame of reference. The same applies to a programme on 'Arabic grammar' on Iqra.' Even some of the broadcast *musalsalat* can be placed under this category, in which morals are strongly held but without reference to Islam. One example is the Egyptian *musalsal*, *'Ilet 'Abdīn* ('"Abdin's Family') which through the story of 'Abdin's family highlights a number of everyday problems and dilemmas. The *musalsal* was broadcast in October 2006 on Iqra.'[22]

The largest group of programmes fall under the category of 'Islamic lifestyle' but frequently there is overlap or mismatch between programme types. One example is *Mushkilāt min al-Hayat* ('Problems from Life') on Iqra' in which members of the audience submit by letter, email or phone, information about their problems. A religious scholar, who either sits alone or as a guest in the studio, gives advice on how to solve the problem, drawing on a range of sources as a frame of reference: the Qur'an, *Hadith*, traditions, logic, and so on. Though this format has a lot in common with a *fatwa* programme, it might be more accurate to categorise it as 'lifestyle'-related. Despite this analytical distinction between the dogmatic interpretation of *fatwa* programmes and the advice of the lifestyle genre, the difference is not automatically made in the viewer's mind. It is pertinent, then, to ask how the various programme genres position themselves as Islamic.

What distinguishes Iqra' as an Islamic channel from other satellite channels such as *Al Jazeera*, which broadcasts a religious programme like *al-Sharia wa al-Hayat* ('Sharia and Life')? The first difference is in the number of programmes which relate to Islam. While an Islamic frame of reference dominates most of the programme schedule on Iqra', it represents only a minimum of the total programming of non-Islamic channels like Al Jazeera.[23]

The second difference is the staging of the programmes on Iqra', in that they are positioned explicitly as Islamic. On Iqra', music and religious songs are regularly played between programmes, and whatever the degree of explicit reference to Islam in the various lifestyle programmes, the use of religious symbols and expressions is omnipresent. In a way, Iqra' is signalling that everything should be looked at from an Islamic perspective. The daily life of the handicapped is framed within Islam, just as entrepreneurship is presented as a specific and positive Islamic strategy. But again, the focus is on the individual and individual accomplishment, regardless of the implicit or explicit reference to Islam.

To sum up, what characterises 'an Islamic satellite channel' like Iqra' is a combination of self-identification with Islam as a universal frame of reference and programming in which Islam is involved implicitly or explicitly. By focusing on individual lifestyles, Iqra' might at the same time be thought of as a potential expression of the 'mainstreaming' or popularisation of Islam which may partially explain why the Arab states apparently—despite a tradition of secular television—seem not to identify an Islamic channel like Iqra' as a political problem. Also, the focus on individual lifestyle might explain the Saudi acceptance of programming presenting women without *hijab*, in contrast to the public politics in Saudi. As long as the focus is on the achievement of the individual, the principle of wearing the *hijab* is not challenged. The idea of inviting all Muslims to participate regardless of their dress is seen as *da'wa* (preaching) rather than as a submission to non-Muslim ideas.

At this stage of the discussion it is important to note that very little is known about the reception of Islamic satellite television. To my knowledge, no thorough reception analyses have been conducted. Therefore, when talking about audience practices, my point of departure is how the channel and the programmes position the audience and offer the viewer specific Muslim identities with which to identify themselves. However, until now, I have no systematic knowledge about how the audience receives and negotiates these offered identities. According to other studies, there are reasons to believe that the audience, in their constructions of religious identity, make use of a variety of different and also mainstream media and certainly not only self-defined religious media.[24] In the same way that mainstream commercial media can be used to negotiate religious identity, a religious channel such as Iqra' can be used to negotiate or practice other aspects of one's identity. For instance, people might watch Iqra' to practice the Arabic language, pass the time or be entertained.

This still leaves the question of how this general line of programming affects the Islamic values and ideas being promoted. To which role is Islam assigned beyond just being a frame of reference? To analyse these issues, the second part of this paper will analyse two selected programmes.

Two Programmes, Two Approaches: The Muslim Society and the Individual Muslim

In order to come closer to an understanding of the different values and identities that Iqra' promotes, two different programmes have been chosen for analysis. As previously introduced, the two programmes are *al-Bayynah* ('Evidence') and *Mauadah wa Rahma* ('Affection and Mercy'). From each programme, seven episodes from 2009 have been chosen as a sample. The two programmes differ in focus and topic: *al-Bayynah* ('Evidence') concentrates on issues related to society in a broader sense, while *Mauadah wa Rahma* ('Affection and Mercy') gives attention to the individual problems of Muslims. Thus, whereas *al-Bayynah* deals with Islamic issues at a macro level, *Mauadah wa Rahma* deals with Islamic issues at a micro level. By using a comparative approach, the objective is not only to present a variety of programmes transmitted by Iqra', but also to explore the connection between the genre and the religious discourses promoted by different programmes. Thus, the comparison makes it possible to discuss and differentiate between the identities on offer.

Al-Bayynah is a weekly programme. The host of the programme is Abdullah Al-Harthi, a Saudi Salafi thinker who had been presenter and host at Iqra' for several years. In each episode, an expert is invited to talk about and discuss particular topics with Al-Harthi in the studio. If the topic is specifically Islamic, the invited guest is often a Saudi scholar. Hence, the choice of guests underlines the Salafi stance of the programme. Often, the programme is introduced by a short two to three minute prologue including an *Ayah* (verse) from the Qur'an presented by Al-Harthi. Next, Al-Harthi gives an introduction to the topic that includes 'different perspectives' on and 'opinions' about the topic in question. After the introduction, Al-Harthi poses questions to his guest about the topic. During the programme, members of the listening audience are invited to call in to ask a few questions or comment on the issue. The length of the episode is fifty minutes. The topics of the seven programmes examined fall within three subjects. One recurrent and dominant issue is the Muslim *ummah*'s (world 'community' of Muslim believers) international relationships. The relationship with the United States is particularly prevalent.[25] Another major issue is the position and role of Islam concerning public order and disorder.[26] And finally, the third issue revolves around the relationship between citizens and their Government.[27] Of the seven chosen episodes, three fall within the first two issues and one within the last. While these divisions refer to the overall topic of the episodes, all three topics converge more or less in the different episodes. Cutting across the seven examples, some sub-issues are more frequent than others. These issues reflect the general interests of the programme:

- First, a common field of interest is Islam's relation to powerful institutions and institutionalised ideas such as the State, nationalism, human rights, law and the international community. Hence, 'institutional development' seems to be a vital concern for the programme. However, this development is, above all, a normative matter of the Islamisation of any societal institution.

- Second, another regular focal point is the position and identity of the individual Muslim *within* an institutional framework. Values such as duties, rights, and history/tradition are highlighted as significant for the 'development of the community' through the strengthening of the individual Muslim's relationship with the wider Muslim community. Yet again, community development is identical to the Islamisation of the community.

- Third, a recurrent subject is the Muslim community's coexistence with other religions and secularist movements and not least the challenges presented by this. By defining guidelines for living in a pluralist and global society on the basis of Islam, the programme suggests an Islamisation of coexistence.

Al-Bayynah ('Evidence') raises questions on a macro level of society while framing these questions as a key matter of the Muslim *ummah*. The chosen topic is presented as important due to its influence on Muslims as a group. If the issue of Muslim identity is discussed, it is with a focus on the collective identity. In contrast to the title of the programme which refers to 'something that is evident, obvious and clear', 'something that is well and convincingly argued' or 'something that has been given evidence for', the discussion is primarily abstract and avoids dealing with problems or suggesting solutions on a more concrete level. By and large, the programme avoids confrontational solutions. Two sidestepping strategies are continually employed, not least by the programme's host. The first is the assertion that all the problems facing Muslims are caused by the West, and particularly the United States. The second is the idealising of Muslim history, and the claim that the Prophet Mohammed solved all the problems of the Muslim community. An example bridging both strategies can be found in 'The Relationship Between Heads of State and the Citizens and Human Rights' (30 April 2009). Al-Harthi introduces the programme by stating that more than a thousand years before the French Declaration of the Rights of Man, Islam had established something much better. Much earlier, Islam had declared rights for orphans, economic distribution among all Muslims, and social security; all things that according to Al-Harthi provide 'pleasure in life and victory on the day of judgement.' By referring to the ideal principles of the Prophet Mohammed, Al-Harthi avoids confronting current problems, and at the same time rejects the relevance of positive influence by Western countries. Further, this strategy of talking in the abstract is supported by dramatised narratives and fantasies about persecuted Muslims, and weak Muslim leaders who have sold-out to satisfy the Western leaders, particularly the Americans. Thus, Al-Harthi repeats a widespread and popular narrative amongst Arab Muslims that positions the Muslims as the unfairly treated victims dominated by the Western world powers. Besides, by addressing Muslims all over the world with the phrase 'brothers in the East and brothers in the West', Al-Harthi constructs this position as shared by all Muslims regardless of where they live. Not only is Islam universalised in the programme, so is the Muslim *ummah*.

While *al-Bayynah* concentrates on the collective identity of Muslims, the other chosen programme, *Mauadah wa Rahma*, directs its attention to the individual Muslim.

Mauadah wa Rahma ('Affection and Mercy') is a talk show that discusses Muslims' problems in a modern Muslim society by looking into the problems of the individual, with Muslim women particularly in focus. Like an agony column, the programme receives letters from a primarily female audience and the questions raised in the letters are discussed and answered by the programme's host, Nivin Al-Gindi, and her guest, usually Abla Al-Kahlawi. Nivin Al-Gindi is a former programme hostess in the field of culture and tourism on the Egyptian channel 3 and represents a common trend

among female programme hostesses at Iqra.' Several female programme presenters at Iqra' are known from national TV and the
film industry for being former actresses or, like Al-Gindi, programme presenters. They personify the repentant and re-converted
Muslim and thus become role models for the audience.[28] The guest,
Al-Kahlawi, has a traditional education in Islam and is attached to
Al-Azhar University. She is one of several religious scholars who
have won fame due to her appearances on many different television channels. Amr Khafagah is Director of the Egyptian secular,
privately owned satellite channel 'Dream TV.' He explains that
Dream TV invites a person like Abla Al-Kahlawi to the channel's
religious shows, because she has become a star who attracts the
audience:

'It's a social trend, not a religious trend. It's something like a mania, with
fans and stars', said Dream TV's Khafaga. 'There's no difference between
the behaviour of the fans of Abla Al-Khalawy and Amr Khaled and the
fans of Amr Diab', he said, comparing the two preachers to Egypt's leading pop singers. 'Just like it's good for some people to say they were at a
party with Amr Diab, they want to go to a lecture with Amr Khaled or
Abla Al-Khalawy.'[29]

Thus, *Mauadah wa Rahma* represents a prevalent kind of programme on Iqra', marketed with the help of a specific popular
religious figure while the host's role is mainly to prompt the programme's star on the subject of the episode's subject. As an introduction to the programme, Nivin Al-Gindi presents the problem of
the episode. Next, excerpts of a letter might be read out by an
anonymous woman's voice or by the hostess herself. What follows
then is a dialogue between Al-Gindi and Al-Kahlawi about the
specific problem and how to solve it, the programme lasting for
thirty minutes.

The topics of the seven examined episodes are all about family
relations and, to a lesser degree, about friendships and other social
relations. In particular, the focus is on the challenges related to
transitions and personal conflicts in life, such as marriage, adultery
and divorce.[30] The title of the programme, 'Affection and Mercy',
is in accordance with the values and solutions it puts forward.
Thus, the values highlighted are mainly universal ethical and
moral points, though they are presented as being specifically

Islamic. These values are: honesty, integrity, honour (*Al Afaf*), decency (*Ehtesham*), tolerance, commitment, love (*al-Mahaba*), obedience (*Ta'a*) and repentance (*Tawbah*). Moreover, a catalogue of much coveted characteristics of the righteous Muslim is emphasised during the programmes. These characteristics are: independence, intelligence, creativity, family appreciation, spirituality, knowledge and success. Once again, these are very close to being universal values, but the programme presents them as being Islamic. And, though being universally positive signifiers, these values are, in the programme, framed within very conservative ideas about social relations. Just as these values seem indisputable, the outcome of the programme is consensus. Despite the format being a dialogue between the host and the guest, the predominant role of the host throughout the programme is to confirm the opinion of the guest. Thus, they both agree that Islam is the solution to everyone's problems.

Obviously, *al-Bayynah* and *Mauadah wa Rahma* differ in how they convey the importance and influence of Islam. As mentioned, *al-Bayynah* concentrates on the challenges for the Muslim community, while *Mauadah wa Rahma* focuses on the problems of the individual Muslim. Looking back at this chapter's earlier division of three programme types at Iqra', it is possible to place *al-Bayynah* as a mixture of the first and second type. During the programme, the scriptural tradition is used as a frame of reference in the Qur'an recitation of the introduction, and throughout the programme as the basis for argument. Still, part of the programme is much more loosely connected to scripture and religious interpretations. Instead, the centre of attention is a normative and populist interpretation of world politics, placing Islam in the background as a mere symbol of global injustice to Muslims. *Mauadah wa Rahma* can be placed within the second category of 'Islamic lifestyle' programmes. By using a mixture of common sense, Qur'an and *Hadith* citations, traditional conservative values and logic, the Islamic perspective is a mix of implicit and explicit references to religion.

The question is how these different focal points affect the Islamic aspects endorsed by the programmes. What kind of Muslim identity is constructed in these programmes? In order to come closer to answering this question, it is relevant to look in greater detail at the kind of religious spaces the two programmes offer their audience. By introducing an analytical perspective of space, I would suggest that the media have other functions than mediating information, ideas and values.

What Kind of Religious Space?

A widespread idea is that Iqra' as an Islamic channel can be ana-lysed as a space for change and the rethinking of Islamic interpreta-tion and values. However, the question is whether the programme's importance to the audience is only linked to the interpretation of and information about Islam. The two chosen programmes illus-trate that the aspect of interpretation is a rather limited part of the content. Moreover, when interpretation seems to be in focus, the articulation of the specific interpretation is often vague, abstract or ambivalent. On the one hand, the programming underlines the influence of the Qur'an and *Hadith* as the basis for interpretation of Islam, in as much as the programmes, to a certain degree, appear to have the aim of establishing legal conclusions, meaning and infor-mation. On the other hand, the diversity of the programmes, with different religious authorities and interpretations, indicates that other things are at stake as well. As a given interpretation in one programme is challenged by other scholars in other programmes, the authority and truth of each interpretation loses its weight. In *al-Bayynah*, this paradox becomes obvious, as Sheikh Abdallah ben Jabril in the programme about satellite TV *fatwas* is not able to clarify to the audience how to distinguish between different and opposite interpretations. The following extract from the pro-gramme illustrates his typical way of arguing:

Jabril: 'We can say that they have their *ijtihaad* and we have ours. And the disagreement among religious schools is a known fact. They each make an effort to do *ijtihaad*. However, as soon as we notice that something is right and something is wrong, we have to follow the right. Simultaneously, we should not talk badly about the others due to disagreements.'[31]

Thus, instead of focusing only on the interpretation, I suggest examining the function of the programme as linked to the audi-ence's modern use of media, rather than as a channel for unidir-ectional information. The audience uses Islamic TV as well as

other media as an instrument to practice and reflexively negotiate their own religious, cultural and personal identity. Thus,
though Islamic satellite television is proposing specific Islamic
values, the question is: how does this affect the space offered to
the audience by the channels and how is this space becoming a
morally defined space?

Time and again, television has been analysed as a mediator of
representations, pictures and ideas. As such, it may be examined
as 'the domain of representations and image.'[32] Compared to the
empirically measurable phenomena of place, this space is subjec-
tive and imagined. This distinction between a more material concept of 'place' and a more abstract concept of 'space' has been
reconstructed in many cultural geographic studies according to
Cresswell. He argues for a concept of place which, in some ways,
combines the measurable place with the imagined place. By introducing the notion of practical knowledge, he argues that place is
acquiring meaning and importance as 'practiced and lived', 'rather
than simply being material (conceived) or mental (perceived).'[33]
The practical knowledge is not only embodied, it is also 'placed' in
the world. The relationship between body and world is thus continuously reproduced and potentially transgressed, and place
becomes a stage for performance while place is performed. According to Cresswell, we need to think of place 'in a constant sense of
becoming through practice and practical knowledge.'[34] The
approach to media as a place of practice is further supported by the
development within media research, emphasising that the media
output is not to be evaluated by the ideology of the producer only,
or by the message of the programme. The audience is not a passive
receiver of media messages, ideology and products. Rather, the
audience is taking part in different media practices such as the
'interpretive' activity of constructing meanings from, and within,
media messages and like the practice of being 'participants' in, for
instance, reality shows, in phone-in programmes or as experts. This
interactivity between audience and media is an increasing aspect
of the current media.[35] In order to be a participant in the programmes, one needs to have practical knowledge about the practice of the programme. The participant is expected to practice or
embody the subject position offered by the programme. In continu-

ation of Cresswell's focus on practice theory, it is possible to talk about an embodied knowledge being practised, but also negotiated, confirmed or rejected by the participants in the programme and by the audience of the programmes. Hence, both kinds of activities can be analysed as part of the audience's identity formation, through meaning constructions and through socially embedded cultural and religious identifications.[36]

In addition, the practice perspective on media and place is, at the same time, in accordance with the development within the study of religious identities. As Hoover argues, instead of understanding religion as 'ascribed', it is more meaningful to understand religion as 'achieved.'[37] Religious identity is, like place, a result of a never-ending process of practices and identifications conceptualised as 'lived religion.'[38] Finally, an empirical argument may add further support to a perspective of space. In general Iqra', like other Islamic channels, presents itself as promoting a universal Islam. However, they do not specify which kind of Islam they are promoting, except for very general statements about a moderate and tolerant Islam. Obviously, Islam becomes the normative framework, but as the channels do not specify their theological or ideological position, it becomes an inevitable necessity to look at the practice of the programmes. Even Iqra' itself seems to find it more important to offer a space for practicing and identifying with Islam than to offer a clear definition of what it means to be Muslim. The particularity of the mediated space is constructed in practice, not in theory. In order to find out how Iqra' complies with Islam, one must therefore explore how the religious spaces of the programmes are brought into being.

By looking at the selected broadcast programmes, this analytical perspective of space draws attention to several points. First, the two programmes offer different religious spaces. While *al-Bayynah* offers a space to come into being as a politically aware Muslim citizen of an opposing global public, *Mauadah wa Rahma* offers a space which is semi-private and wherein the audience is expected to perform in line with conventional, conservative, and certainly not in any way counteractive ideas. Regarding *al-Bayynah*, the episode 'Neo-Conservatives and the End of Arrogance' (23 April 2009) illustrated the opposing public voice of the programme. Al-Harthi, the host of the programme, introduces the programme by giving a dramatic account of the Bush era in American politics: how people have died, children have become orphans and women have become widows. Al-Harthi blames the Americans for all evil. In contrast with the biased introduction, the guest of the episode, Aziz Fahmi, takes a more nuanced stance, and tries to explain that it is not the entire American population who hate Muslims. Rather, he explains, according to studies, most Americans know very little about the Middle East and do not have any particular interests or emotions towards Arabs. During the programme, members of the audience call in, with most of them criticising the Bush administration and what happened during his presidency. Fahmi suggests developing a modern Islamic political discourse that makes it possible to talk to the West in a new language, while focusing on peace-making and the rights of the nation. The episode exemplifies the kind of space that *al-Bayynah* offers its audience. The Muslim public is constructed as a political space in opposition to Western countries and particularly the United States and Israel. Islam is given a double role. First, Islam has become the signifier for the binary opposition between the Western and Islamic world. Hence, Islam is above all an identity. Second, Islam is not only the solution to the unworthy position that the Muslims are placed in by the Western countries, but also to the internal problems of the Muslim countries. Thus, Islam is not only an identity but also a political discourse.

Mauadah wa Rahma has a rather different perspective. Although the programme, as a general rule, promotes the idea of moral decay due to modernity, the religious space is not constructed as an opposing place but as a space for identifying with true and authentic Islamic values. In the episode 'Does Friendship Prevent Betrayal?' (24 February 2009) a conversation about friendship and adultery was conveyed:

The hostess: 'To reveal the secrets of others is a modern phenomenon, just like a good friendship?'

Abla Al-Kahlawi: 'It is a catastrophe. We are talking about a sick tendency. All this is *Haram* and a sin. I am against it. We need to behave Islamically. That shall be our path. Ali (the fourth Caliph after Prophet Mohammad) tells us: "You have to be cultured." The home has to be a safe and forbidden place. It has to be impossible for a thief to get access. We have to be aware of what a thief could do to our women and our daughters. Thus, you cannot trust anyone to go into the house. If it is unavoidable, then let him only into the guest room and not the living room.'

The conversation goes on, with a warning to the audience not to tell their private secrets to their friends and to never share any facts about their private life with anyone who is not their true friend. The idea is to prevent intruders from harming the family. As a result, one needs to create limits for friendship. This example illustrates the general discourse of the programme as it promotes conservative ideas about family life, protecting sexual morals from disintegration and social chaos. The space being offered is a space for discussing the lifestyle of modern Muslims, without compromising these conservative values that are framed as Islamic. Accordingly, the Islamic performance of the two programmes is closely related to the respective spaces created. Hence, different places need different ideas of Islamic performance. At the same time, the focus of *Mauadah wa Rahma* on correct Islamic behaviour in the private sphere emphasises the paradox for talk shows regarding private problems. By presenting one's private problems in the programme, they become entirely public, though the person behind the query might be anonymous. Thus, the private and public spaces seem to conflate and converge in the Islamic programming, by which the private space is performed publicly. The private space becomes a place to perform and confirm Muslim identity, and therefore simultaneously a place to watch over and evaluate in public. From a critical viewpoint, one could claim, the Islamic discourse encouraged by Iqra' is not only colonising the public and private space, but also colonising the individual by promoting a morally defined, embodied and practical knowledge.

Secondly, the examples from the two programmes illustrate how the religious spaces that are offered intersect with aspects such as gender and age. As such, religious identities are mixed in with gender identity, and religious practices become gendered on satellite television. What is essential is that not only religious but also gendered practices are defined by the place coming into being through the programming. While Islam offers an oppositional identity in the public space of *al-Bayynah* for both men and women,

women in particular should not be in opposition when it comes to social relations and family matters according to *Mauadah wa Rahma*.

Thirdly, as argued previously, the interpretations given are vague and ambivalent, which tell us that other aspects of the programme are more important than a once-and-for-all answer. Consequently, in asking questions of the scholar, it may not be the scholar's answer as such that is most important. Rather, it is the viewer's ability to raise questions and thus demonstrate a desire to be always looking for and striving for truth within academic discourse. This is also very much the case when looking at the *fatwa* programme in general. As mentioned, on Iqra' there are several *fatwa* programmes with quite different scholars and still the same kind of questions are asked repeatedly. By calling in or by sending a letter to ask these questions, the believer is not only demonstrating that he or she is taking Islam seriously; the person in question is actually practising and performing Islam by participating in the programme, regardless of whether the call is made in person or by a substitute. The *fatwa* programme becomes what Cresswell calls 'an unstable stage for performance.'[39] By the repetition of the act—passing on questions—the meaning is never finally fixed, as Cresswell writes.[40] Rather, it is the repetition of the act itself that brings the religious identity and space into being and not a once-and-for-all definition.

Conclusion

On the grounds of ownership and the channel's self-identification, general programming, and target group, it is possible to conclude that Iqra' is not explicitly or openly supporting any state or political movement. Instead it emphasises devotion, a moral and religious lifestyle and promotes an Islamic identity in politics. Focus is on the individual Muslim lifestyle, and the moral and ethical ideals of the Islamic community. When discussing issues (e.g. economics or foreign policy), this is done from a specifically Islamic perspective, but the channel does not go so far as to identify this Islamic perspective with any particular political institutions. Thus, it obviously appears that Iqra' generally supports a process of re-

Islamisation which most of all is a matter of symbolic politics and conservative moral values.

In relation to the comparison between *al-Bayynah* and *Mauadah wa Rahma*, one might remark in conclusion that while both programmes seem to argue for a modern way of life by including all kinds of modern topics, *Mauadah wa Rahma* succeeds to a higher degree than *al-Bayynah* in answering the question of how to live morally in accordance with modernity. To *Mauadah wa Rahma*, a modern Muslim life is an individualistic life but without compromising strictly conservative family values that are legitimised as being Muslim rather than an issue of mere tradition. To *al-Bayynah*, a modern Muslim life is connected to a politicised public sphere, wherein any Muslim is welcome to take an active part, but where the Salafi tradition does not help much in creating the modern means for navigating in a global, social, political, and economic field. Therefore, the modern Muslim according to *al-Bayynah* is defined by his opposition to the Western countries and their politics.

Finally, in my characterisation of Iqra', I categorised it as 'wahhabi-light.' Nevertheless, it seems that the channel has become more conservative over the years than it was in its early days. More conservative figures seem to have overtaken the progressive voices, and programmes raising more controversial issues seem to be fewer than in the beginning. One reason is the fierce competition with other, mostly Salafi, channels. Another reason is that many of Iqra''s more liberal hosts and scholars have moved to Al-Resalah and left Iqra' to define a new identity. How it will develop, only the future will tell.

5

AL NAS SATELLITE CHANNEL

OVERVIEW, CONTENT ANALYSIS, PREACHERS

Juman Quneis

The Beginnings

Al Nas TV started transmission from Egypt in January 2006 by broadcasting entertainment content including music, dream interpretations, wedding recordings, male and female acquaintance requests (whereby information is submitted in order to match potential marriage partners) and election broadcasts. The channel slogan at that time was 'Al Nas likul In-Nas' ('Al Nas for Everyone').

A year later, the channel hadn't achieved any considerable revenue. The administration had to either change its policy, or cease to exist. The channel, therefore, moved into the religious sphere and attracted the very popular religious leaders (Sheikhs) in Egyptian society, who did not appear on other Arab satellite channels.

Al Nas selected its preachers from progenitors (those that profess Salafi ideology) who refrained from tackling political issues. The influence of such preachers was instantly recognisable; songs were replaced with Islamic hymns, the slogan was changed to 'A Screen to take you to Heaven—Paradise.', and female announcers were forced to wear a full veil. Soon after the channel was saved, in response to calls from the Salafi preachers.

What is Al Nas?

Al Nas characterises itself as a social, cultural channel with religious traits. The name (Al Nas) indicates that it is 'for and from people, to lead them through the correct way in a moderate manner.' As stated on its website, Al Nas' aims to transport people to Paradise 'through beneficial knowledge, good deeds, and calling for Allah through the light of knowledge and insights derived from the holy Qu'ran, from the Prophet Mohammad's conversations and rubrics (*Sunna*), and from the sayings of the good progenitors (*Salaf*).'[1] Its goal is to 'give a hand to all Arabs and Muslims around the world, to think better and act differently.'

Source of Finance

Al Nas is owned by the Saudi businessman Mansour bin Kadasa.[2] As stated on its website, it depends on commercials, sponsorship and phonecalls and accepts no donations.[3]

Programmes

Programmes on the channel include debates, children's programmes, *fatwa* and contests, and its schedules have something aimed at all members of the Muslim family. Al Nas broadcasts twenty-seven programmes per week, eight of those programmes are daily or semi-daily, and the remaining are weekly. It is noted that the daily programmes are characterised by the generality of the questions posed, diversity in the issues raised, a significant amount of interaction with the audience and a large number of various casuistries (*fatwa*). As for the weekly programmes, they are characterised by their specific focus on serious subject matter, advanced preparation, and, rarely, phone calls from viewers. The episodes take the form of religious lessons or sermons presented by the preacher, with no audience interference.

Content Analysis (*Fadfadah* and *Han'ishha Sah*)

Fadfadah ('Heart to Heart') and *Han'ishha Sah* ('We'll Live it Right!') are the two programmes chosen for a sample analysis of the Al Nas channel and the values it promotes. Thirteen episodes of the *Fadfa-dah* daily show and seven episodes of the *Han'ishha Sah* weekly show were analysed, with the episodes randomly chosen. I ensured that the analysed episodes of *Fadfadah* were presented by preachers representing either the (Salafi) progenitors or Azhar doctrine. As for *Han'ishha Sah*, this programme had a completely different characteristic, as it was presented by a young man from the new school of preachers, and addressed its young audience in a completely different style.

Fadfadah—'Heart to Heart'

Al Nas describes this programme on its website as its flagship show. It is a daily live show, aired at 10 pm Cairo time, excluding Thursdays, and each episode is hosted by one of the channel's preachers. It is noticeable that the programme, as Al Nas states on its website, is about a 'preacher opening his heart to the viewers', not the viewers opening their hearts to a preacher, as many people would assume. Atif Abdirasheed, the general manager of the Al Nas Satellite Channel, describes *Fadfadah* as being their most popular show.[4]

Fadfadah is presented alternately by a 'number of scholars like Mohammad Hussein Yaqoub, Mohammad Hassan, Salem Abulfutuoh and Abu Ishaq Alhuweini.'[5] Since it has more than one presenter, this show doesn't have a specific identity or a general framework. It is not focused on any one specific issue and it has no particular style or plan that the preacher follows. It is entirely focused on the preacher hosting the show, with his style of presentation reflecting his own concerns, views and priorities.

Figure 5.1 below indicates that a considerable percentage of the thirteen episodes (21.2 per cent) is dedicated to issues related to particular subjects, often chosen by the presenting preacher. Such sections are usually outside of the main content of the programme, and are dictated by the preacher's personal experience in particular areas, or by his opinions concerning specific persons or practices. Some preachers also dedicate time to addressing and responding to preachers from other satellite channels and programmes. One example of this is Abu Ishaq Huweini, who dedicated a great deal of time in one of the *Fadfadah* episodes to reacting to Khalid Jundi's statements on an Egyptian TV channel concerning an article published in an unknown paper, where he denied that Ai'sha married the Prophet at a very young age.

Fadfadah, as shown in figure 5.1 below, is often centred on the recitation of historical stories and experiences, such as the stories of the companions of the Prophet, his followers and the progenitors (Salaf); this accounts for 27.3 per cent of the total programme running time. Naturally, such sections usually lead the preachers to talk about the morals and values learned from such stories (18.2 per cent). Often these morals are discussed in an abstract manner, with connections not being made between the lessons given, and the challenges of contemporary society. The programme encourages viewers to be pious as individuals, to withdraw and seclude themselves from society, and not to become involved in contemporary issues. This is because the central message of the programme is that imitating the progenitors (Salaf) and adopting their morals is the ultimate form of religious commitment, and will undoubtedly lead to Paradise. Because of this, the sections of the programme that deal with contemporary challenges in society are not allocated more than 9.1 per cent of the total programme content.

Fatwa occupies 18.2 per cent of the total programme content. The subjects addressed during *fatwa* are influenced by the viewers' calls and questions. The same *fatwa* may recur in one show, due to the viewers' repeated questions about the same issues.

The show greatly promotes piety through one's appearance (the veil and beard for example) and in one's practice, by promoting worship. It also urges viewers to obey Allah and to be decent and polite, particularly illustrated when the preacher addresses a woman, inviting her to 'obey her husband' and 'respect her mother in law.' The audience is encouraged to integrate themselves, so as to see the challenges facing their faith, and to act in accordance with the Islamic spirit. It is noted that tolerance, whether with those following different faiths or with different Islamic groups, is a topic rarely discussed in the programme. The statements that call for tolerance are restricted to common phrases and expressions such as, 'Muslims are brothers', and 'Muslims must support each other.' Topics such as mercy and peaceful coexistence, along with

Fig. 5.1: Relative distribution of the broadcasted religious content of *Fadfadah*

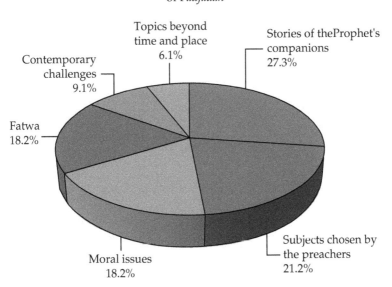

examples of their contemporary successes, are completely absent from the programme.

Han'ishha Sah—'Let Us Live it Right!'

This weekly live youth show, aired on Tuesdays at 7pm, Cairo time, is hosted by the young preacher Shereef Shahata, named 'the youngest preacher' on the Arab satellite channels. On his website, Shahata promotes his show with the following statement:

Don't you think that you need to think? Don't you think that you need a change? Don't you think that you want to rearrange your life? Don't you wish to succeed socially, religiously and in your life? Come on young fellows ... let us reform our defects and improve our manners ... and live our life ... this way, we'll certainly live it right ...[6]

The name of this show, *Han'ishha Sah*, is composed of two words in the Egyptian spoken dialect that convey future action (We will live right). On the programme, Shahata wears modern and elegant clothing, such as jeans and coloured cotton t-shirts, with his hair

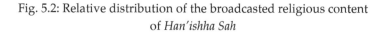

Fig. 5.2: Relative distribution of the broadcasted religious content
of *Han'ishha Sah*

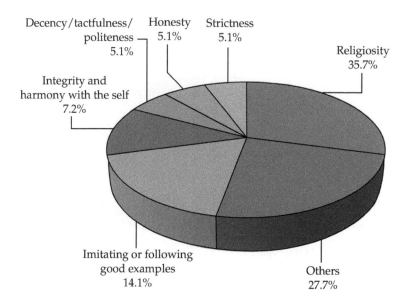

styled well and his beard trimmed. He is lively in his presenting
and he speaks the Egyptian dialect using contemporary expressions, sometimes using English expressions. He directly addresses
the younger generation, and he constantly repeats his calls to them,
saying, 'come on young fellows—*yallah ya shabab.*'

The show adopts an interactive format, with the viewers participating through phone calls, e-mails, SMS and forums. It also uses
segments filmed on the street, including vox pops and caricatures.
The discussion of contemporary problems occupies the greatest
proportion of the programme (42.9 per cent), with such topics usually dealing with social and psychological concerns, as well as family matters, and one's relations with the community. The presenter
of *Han'ishha Sah* seeks to face such challenges by changing young
people's ingrained manners and habits. This is done, he believes,
by holding to the Islamic ideal of character, as stated in the holy
Qur'an and rubrics of the Prophet (Sunna). Therefore, the moral
issues, Qur'an interpretations, *Sunna* and biographies, hold similar

percentages after the contemporary challenges (14.3 per cent each). *Han'ishha Sah* also dedicates a considerable amount of space to discussion over how to create a better future in places where Islam has a strong influence, this being the main theme of the programme. The show calls primarily for piety and returning to Allah, to assure a better life for the individual and community. Therefore this topic holds the highest percentage of the total programme content (35.7 per cent). But the piety promoted in this show is not completely divorced from a contemporary lifestyle, and thus covers aspects of young life at university, clubs, and cafés.

During his programme, therefore, Shahata suggests particular acts and initiatives that could change one's behaviour and habits. Such acts and initiatives do not demand seclusion from society or family, rather they require an active social life, looking for a better tomorrow and benefiting from modern societal developments. The programme professes the opinion that all this can be achieved by following the good examples of the progenitors (Salaf), adhering to and being in accordance with the Islamic ideal of character, and by furthering one's involvement with the community.

Characteristics of Al Nas

Based on the aforementioned analysis, and on interviews and readings, it appears that Al Nas can be distinguished by the following features.

The Salafi prevailing tone

Al Nas is an Islamic, Sunni and Egyptian channel, broadcasting several topical trends ranging from strictness to modernity. The Salafi preachers represent the strictest end of the spectrum on Al Nas, and they are the most prominent on the channel, as many of them present shows that are aired at peak times, with the channel hosting such preachers as Abu Ishaq Alhuweini, Mohammad Hussein Yaqoub and Mohammad Hassan.

The harmony between the Salafi preachers is obvious. They often appear on one another's programmes, or praise one another during their live shows where each lauds the other as being more informed than himself. A good deal of time is allocated to such preachers, as they are the main focus of the daily live programmes, giving Al Nas a Salafi character, causing some people to name it the 'Salafi trend channel.'

The role of the Salafi preachers has greatly increased since the channel's conception. They prevented female announcers from appearing on screen, even when veiled, and also forbade showing any female personalities on the programme, even in vox pops. The use of music was also curtailed, even in the programme jingles. The preachers Abu Ishaq Alhuweini, Mohammad Hussein Yaqoub and Mohammad Hassan soon appeared, with their long untrimmed beards, wearing loose smocks and head covers (turbans), adopting an intimidating approach rather than persuading, and speaking Arabic eloquently. In most of their programmes, they recount Salafi stories and attitudes, but do not make much effort to connect such stories with reality, or discuss the method of applying their recitations to society. Their programmes take the form of religious preaching, in which the preacher talks for long periods of time with no audience interaction.

These three preachers are known for their strict opinions with regards to women, moderate Islamic trends, Azhar, new preachers, Shi'a, Sufism, the West, Christians and Jews. They call for the audience to keep to the Salafi approach, to stay away from reprehensible innovation (*bida'*), and avoid criticising political groups and regimes, but often bring up controversial issues such as polygamy, circumcision and Shi'a. They do not call for participation in national politics, and instead encourage individual salvation and religiosity.

These three preachers requested to form a reference committee composed of Salafi preachers for the channel, to impose their complete control. This request was made when the channel Manager, Atif Abdirasheed, decided to broadcast the young preacher, Amr Khaled, to discuss a campaign launched against drugs. They blamed Khaled for 'associating too much with toilet women, and that he holds his lectures in clubs and public halls.'[7] The request was also made as a result of a decision to host the Sufi Sheik, Ahmad Awad, whom they denounced for resorting to reprehensible innovation and 'being fond of lieges (*awlia'*) and graves.'[8] When the channel rejected their request, they decided to withdraw unanimously from the channel in protest, to put pressure on the channel's bosses to reconsider.

An opposing trend to the dominant Salafi school of thought is one which is represented by the moderate young preachers who tackle public issues. They call on young people to join in with public life and to change their lifestyle through discarding bad behaviour, learning new skills, improving their personalities, promoting their self-confidence, and contributing to the community. But this trend has the smallest presence, and is represented by only one show, the aforementioned *Han'ishha Sah*.

In between these two opposing trends lies the Azhari trend, with their preachers forming the largest proportion of Al Nas preachers. They tend to discuss Islamic ethics and social solidarity in public life, and approach the political affairs of Muslims in more detail, particularly non-controversial issues such as the Israeli occupation, the anti-Islam campaigns, and colonialism. They might dare to confront neighbouring political regimes, such as the Palestinian Authority, but they would not tackle any Egyptian political issues. These preachers appear either wearing Azhar clothing (smocks and turbans) or in modern clothing with trimmed beards, and speak a simple language that is a mix of eloquent and spoken Arabic. However, they follow a traditional style of oration, much closer to the Islamic lessons, and they adopt a strict *fatwa* with regards to women.

The disagreement between Al Nas preachers who represent the Salafi trend on the one hand, and the preachers who represent the Azhar trend on the other, is very obvious. This disagreement reached its peak when Salem Abulfutouh, who belongs to the Azhar school, criticised some Salafi preachers such as Mohammad Hussein Yaqoub and Muhammad Hassan, for personal matters, in an article published in a local paper. 'The Salafi preachers did not wait long to defend themselves using the live transmission in a special feature on Al Nas channel', Abdullah Khalid said.

Removing the presence of women

A number of female announcers had worked on Al Nas programmes before it became an Islamic channel, and retained their positions after this shift. Alhuweini stipulated to employees that a condition for working on any of the channel's output was that female staff could not appear on any programmes. A big debate raged in the Egyptian media at that time, particularly as some of those presenters did not receive their full due salaries.[9] However, they were eventually let go in August 2006. The channel manager, Atif Abdirasheed, stated that removing the female presenters came in response to viewers requests, and that the decision to remove them was made during a meeting of a consulting committee composed of the preachers in charge of the channel. The explanation offered, according to Abdirasheed, was that the female presenters were not professionals, and thus they made many mistakes.[10]

When a fully-veiled announcer (with *niqab*) appeared once on Alhafez TV, a rival of the Al Nas channel, Alhuweini attacked her, stating that 'the full-veiled presenter is not less attractive than the other veiled ones.' He attempted to justify this by arguing that they were unaware of Shari'a and reading principles. He argued that the presence of women in the media should only occur when necessary, and if there is no necessity 'there is no need for a veiled presenter, dressed in black to appear in front of viewers', and went on to describe them as devils.[11]

Dispensing with Music

The channel dispensed with music at about the same time as it did female presenters in response to requests by the Salafi preachers. Music in programme jingles was replaced by special Islamic songs, and natural sound effects and echoes.

Avoiding Politics and All Related Struggles

It was a declared strategy to keep away from politics, said Atif Abdirasheed in an interview with Islam online:

We deliberately intended to be completely far from everything that has to do with politics. We never impeach any government, university, corporation, or individual. We are not interested in conflict, unlike the prevailing media that utilise conflict to attract viewers.[12]

He said, in the same interview, that:

We have a balanced policy that has no intention to oppose any Arab government. We support the trends adopted by states and formal institutions because we offer preachers that help to control young people's behaviour, and this is what states and governments need. The formal reactions to the channel are promising.

Whilst Al Nas programmes avoid attacking any political regime and do not call for social change, some independent Egyptian newspapers have linked Al Nas' strict programming to acts of violence against Christians in Egypt, such as the Alhussein explosions on 27 February 2009, and the murder of a Christian jeweller in the Zaiton neighbourhood of Cairo on 28 May 2008. One of the perpetrators, Mustafa Sayyed, confessed that his actions were inspired by the 'Islamic speeches of prominent progenitors (Salaf) like Abu Ishak Alhuweini, Sheikh Mohammad Hassan and Sheikh Mohammad Hussein Yaqoub', and that he used to attend prayers and sermons at Aljam'ia Ashar'ya mosque (mosque of the Shari'a community) and at Al-Aziz Billah mosque in Zaiton.[13]

In December 2009, a campaign was launched on Facebook to stop those channels known as 'the Islamic extremist channels', with the justification that they 'broadcast extreme Islamic messages that call for discrimination against women and hatred against the non-Muslims.'

Some Al Nas preachers discuss political issues related to the Palestinian question, and general political issues that criticise 'Western colonialism', and its 'greediness to control Muslim countries.' The channel has allocated some live programmes for the discussion of Gaza and its suffering, during and after the Gaza War (2008–2009). In such programmes, blame is not directed at any particular political regime, and there is no request for any action to be taken beyond preaching and donation. This issue is dealt with on an Islamic ideological basis rather than on a national basis, with the 'Jews' not the 'Israelis' being seen as responsible for the war against Gaza.

Strictness in Tackling Women's Issues

Strictness is the prevailing tone of Al Nas' programming concerning women. In addition to the absence of female presenters, women do not appear on any programmes to discuss any topic, even as guests or interviewees. Women's issues are greatly incorporated into the programming, but with women portrayed as less competent, less informed and less capable than men.

For example, Abu Ishak Alhuwieni states frankly that knowledge is 'for men only.' Mazen Sirsawi claims that a woman can't lead her household or even drive a car:

It's impossible to have a house in which the woman is the boss ... this is a failing house ... media and TV and the nonsense things ... want to deepen this principle ... they want to upturn and shift the leadership in the house from man to woman and they succeeded in doing this in many houses. The woman became the man who controls the house and directs the house, the woman tells him to do this ... He says "yes sir" ... the woman is not good to drive a car, not a house or bigger things because women deal with their emotions and have less religiosity and brains ... the real woman is the weak woman ... It's not possible for a woman to lead a house.[14]

This stereotypical image of a woman as a wife and a housewife, with no-one in her life beyond her husband and children, is frequently promoted on Al Nas. There is almost no reference to educated women, working women or female students, and instead women are called on to quit education if asked to unveil their faces. This is what Alhuweini asserted in a *fatwa* to a female student in her sixth year at a medical college. She was instructed to remove her veil to be able to finish her exams, after Cairo University issued a rule dictating it so, but he told her to cling on to her veil and to abandon her study:

...in the end, the girl obtains the certificate and stays in her house ... She enters the kitchen ... how many female doctors, engineers, pharmacists, and others from those holding higher colleges certificates are sitting in their houses ... not working ... Sitting in the kitchens and they hold the highest academic degrees ... and sitting in the kitchens. What a waste of money and years spent in obtaining a paper that ceased to have any value.[15]

All of these programmes invite women to stay under their husbands' wings and to preserve their marriage and family at all costs, even if it involves having to endure abuse and humiliation. Preacher Salem Abulfutouh, close to the Azhar, instructed a wife who had complained that her husband spat on her, not to spit back, and to retain her morality and shyness: 'No sister... Don't treat your husband this way ... Even if he is mistaken you must not treat him like this ... always retain your good manners, shyness and morals.'[16]

Mazen Sirsawi also advised the woman's family not to co-operate with her if she came to them complaining that her husband was mistreating her, and that they should not consider the husband to be responsible. Instead, he instructed, they must please him, and apologise to him for what their daughter had done:

... If the wife can't bear this situation due to a defect in the way she was brought up ... when she goes back to her father ... her father must fix her ... tell her no ... Go back to your house ... go back to your house ... you have no house in here with us ... you left it ... don't come back again ... if you're not content with this go to the street. Go ... you have nothing but your husband's house. She will then find everything shut down in front of her and she will survive ... she'll be able to endure and bear and live. Not all houses are built on love and romance.

Conversely, Shareef Shahata in *Han'ishha Sah*, refers to women in terms other than as the ideal of the housewife and he addresses female students and young women, but he is unable to make up the deficit of this group's interests in other programmes on the channel. However, this programme cannot be counted as being in opposition to the stereotypical views of women in the other daily programmes, for in the programmes observed during the viewing hours allocated for the purposes of this chapter, no preacher had ever asked a man to treat a woman nicely, or to respect her feelings or rights. Rather, Salem Abulfutouh ignored the case of a husband who had committed adultery with his female servants, and instead instructed the wife to employ men or ugly women instead, as will be discussed below.

The Trend of Consumption

Al Nas has been accused of going overboard in its expenditure and money-making activities. This is illustrated by the broadcasting of many long commercials, sometimes exceeding fifteen minutes in length, in addition to mobile ringtones, economic consultancies, and pre-paid *fatwa*. Such exaggerated practices are contrary to the Salafi preachers' calls for austerity and the giving up of possessions, and are also in contrast with the educational experts' views, and thus have been widely criticised. In addition, these advertisements are contrary to the belief in the important need to restrict the access of wealthy people to such information, since the good progenitors (Salaf) dedicated themselves to disseminating Islam but did not do so as a means to earn a living.

Al Nas airs Islamic spots between its scheduled items. These spots are entitled *Qabasat Wa Nasamat*, and they last around 3–5 minutes each. They urge people to engage in pious activities including praying, fasting and giving to charity, and they emphasise the need to have good morals. Each spot is concerned with one subject, and is composed of assembled quotations from previously aired programmes hosted by Al Nas preachers. These parts are linked by sound effects rather than any music, and the spot opens with four photographs of Al Nas preachers, to prepare the viewers for what the preachers are about to say on a related topic. The spots are also uploaded onto the Al Nas website, and are changed nearly every day. On religious occasions such as Hajj and Ramadan, the channel broadcasts spots related to the occasion. Normally, the focus of the content— such as the companions of the Prophet, the veil and the devil's plots—is suitable for all times of the year.

Al Nas Preachers

Shereef Shahata

Shahata was born in 1982. He majored in Physics and is now studying for his diploma in Shari'a at the Islamic Studies Institute in the Dar El-Uloum Faculty. He did not attend Azhar, nor did he learn the Holy Qur'an by heart. He worked as a teacher of Islamic education at Al-Jeel Al-Jadeed international school in Cairo, and at present he is hosting programmes on Islamic satellite channels such as Al Nas. It is said that Shahata is the youngest among the preachers, and he belongs to the school of Amr Khaled, Mustafa Husni and Almu'ez Mas'oud. Concerning his relaxed appearance (mentioned above), he said in an interview published on his site:

I am a young man and this is the style of clothing and talking that suits my age. I am free to wear my clothes everywhere, as long as they are decent and respectable. Does Islam necessitate certain clothes to be worn by Muslims only? I don't think so.[17]

In another interview with the *Alarabi* newspaper, Shahata wondered:

… why can't the preacher be elegant or styled? In other domains where people deal with other than Islamic subjects, we see them elegant and drive luxurious cars. Who is the foremost to be good-looking and own cars: those who call for anything, or those calling for Allah? Why do we always presume that the preacher must be poor, miserable and going on foot? Let us not forget that prophet Muhammad (peace upon him), the greatest preacher, was himself a rich man.[18]

As discussed above, he addresses the young generation, and tackles a number of daily life problems such as pornographic websites, clothing, false imitation of the West, good deeds, and morals, taking advantage of his position as a member of this young generation. He states that, 'Being young, playing, eating, drinking, and dressing in the same manner, we can closely see their problems and behaviour and work to reform their hearts ... this is innovation in Islam.'

In his programmes, Shahata promotes the modern image of a Muslim, rather than that of an eccentric or secluded personality. The Muslim woman in his programmes appears to be stylish in her veiled and loose dress. She goes out with her friends and goes shopping in malls, without going against the stipulations of Islam. The same applies for young men, dressing fashionably, practicing sports in clubs and meeting friends at cafés, without doing anything that would come into conflict with Islam. Throughout his shows, Shahata motivates and initiates various campaigns in support of the ideas he puts forth. Those campaigns do not end at the close of the episode; rather, they are actively continued on his Facebook page and website.

Shahata is accused of oversimplifying Islam by focusing on superficial matters and daily practices, being shallow with his judgments, and for not addressing the real challenges facing the nation. He doesn't deny these accusations, and admits that he's focusing on the form, manner and means of preaching (da'wa), more than on Islam itself. When asked about the position in society of young preachers such as himself, Ahmad Qaradawi, Ghazali, Jad el Haq and Naser Fareed, he said, 'Those people have specialised in many Islamic sciences and God accepted their efforts. But we focus on the art of preaching from the spiritual perspective of worship.' He sees such perspectives as 'things that help man to be more beautiful and more kind-hearted.'

When talking about his programme *Han'ishha Sah*, he said:

... to live it right in our morals, the content here is morals and going back to the good deeds of Prophet Mohammad (may peace be upon him). Our goal is to discard vices and bad manners from our streets, universities, clubs and all aspects of life in a practical manner, in order to reform our worship and strengthen our relation with God by obeying him and contenting our Prophet in the hereafter, knowing that the prophet's message emphasises good deeds and morals.

Abu Ishaq Alhuweini

Alhuweini was born in 1956 in the Kafr Sheikh Directorate to a rural, religious, middle-class family, and graduated from the Spanish Department at Alson College, Ain Shams University in Cairo with an excellent average. His dream was to be a member of the Spanish Language Assembly, so he obtained a scholarship to go to Spain, but returned because he did not like the country.[19] He started studying Hadith (Prophet's Mohammad's sayings) by reading for Albani and joining seminars for Mutee'i and other Sheikhs (Islamic scholars) of Azhar. He travelled to meet Albani in Jordan and then went on to Saudi Arabia, where he became a student of Abdelaziz bin Qaou'd, Abdelaziz bin Baz and Ibn Othaimeen.[20] He became one of the most informed people in Prophet rubrics (Hadith science), causing Albani to certify him as one of his students. He then became one of the most prominent and strict (Salafi) progenitors, and one of its figure-heads in Egypt.

Some in the Egyptian media labelled him as the 'king of inhibiting', after he issued strict statements (fatwa) on female circumcision, polygamy, veiling, Shi'a groups and Christians. Alhuweini's name, amongst other preaching progenitors, appeared in articles and papers that investigated the case of the Egyptian youths who carried out bloody acts of violence, such as the Al-Hussein explosions and the aforementioned murder of a Christian jeweller in the Azzayt town of Cairo.

The Azhar scholar Ahmad Sayeh, said in an interview with the Alyoum Asabe' Egyptian newspaper, published on 29 October 2009 that, 'this is a Salafi, Wahabi and terrorist invasion. Its danger on Muslims is more than the danger coming from the nation's enemies, because it wants to draw Muslims apart from Islamic principles.'[21] He added in the same interview, that:

... the Salafi ideology uses the good progenitors as a façade to alienate people from Islam and shift them away from its tolerant spirit so they will see nothing of Islam except terror, strictness and rejecting others. If the good progenitors were like those people, no one would ever have joined Islam.

Alhuweini is very strict concerning women, as mentioned above. He stated, in one episode, that 'illiteracy is widely spread amongst women', and when discussing women television presenters, he argued:

... one veiled woman sitting in front of the camera to address millions ... it is crazy ... This is the craziness we are living through nowadays ... what is the evidence that allows a woman to appear on a satellite channel, facing camera to address millions around the world! What does such a woman have to tell ... knowledge is for men ... Knowledge is for men only ... any woman, with all my respect for her ... I don't want any woman to think that I am humiliating her ... any woman, regardless of her high status, is an imitator and illiterate. No woman has studied the original principles, no woman can correctly classify, subdivide, devise, or tell whether a conversation [*Hadith*] is good or weak ... and so on. There is no single woman, at least as far as I know. And I know nearly most of the women teachers working in Egypt from the questions they ask and so on ... I know their level.

In one episode of *Fadfadah*, Alhuweini undermined the importance of education for women, and called upon those veiled women who had been prevented from entering their university campus' not to choose their education over the veil, as discussed above, because the outcome of their scientific certificates will inevitably be 'the kitchen.'

The relationship between Alhuweini and the Azhar school has often been tense. He criticised Azhar scholars (*Muftis*) several times for their casuistries (*fatwa*) on topics such as female circumcision or the veil, and on many occasions he accused them of illiteracy, taking sides with the official party and of issuing casuistries of which they did not have sufficient knowledge. In one of his speeches, he asserted that:

Azhar Sheik was asked to issue a *fatwa* that circumcision is inviolable (*haram*), when the case of girl circumcision came up and he was asked to issue a *fatwa* that it is inviolable ... I repeat ... He was asked to ... (Directly or indirectly).

He was smart in this area. He knew that they want to inhibit a controversial matter ... a matter that conveys many disagreements ... if he felt that they want to inhibit it ... he would say it is wrongdoing (haram), if he felt they want to legitimize it, he would say it's permitted (halal).[22]

Alhuweini has also criticised other preachers and has accused Amr Khaled of unjustified tolerance of Jews, and for being too lenient in his fatwa with issues such as legitimising acting and practising other kinds of art. He says in one of his speeches:

... when I was checking the questions, I saw three papers. Those three papers are for a man who is said to be a great, famous preacher and a famous star on [the scandalous channels] ... and the Mufti of the female artists ... Mufti of actors and actresses etc. The headlines were "I am against artist retirement." Mr. Amr Khaled is this star and he is the speaker ... it is impossible that these words come out from any man who has ever read a book in Islamic law (shari'a) ... for example, when he was told that women artists will retire, he said ... no, no, absolutely not. I am not asking for this, on the contrary, I want them to stay where they are ... we want an art that originate from our own environment ... arts must not be imported from other environments ... Jazz music for example, should not be imported to have people skipping and hopping to it, but Abdelwahab's music is beautiful ... why? Because it is ours ... and a product of our environment.

Alhuweini criticises the Egyptian Ministry of Islamic Affairs for advocating tolerance. He said, in an interview with the *Alfurqan* paper, also published on his website, that:

It is sad that there are recommendations issued by our Ministry of Islamic affairs that call for the necessity of considering the peaceful preaching ... And that Islam is the religion of tolerance, not of terrorism. This is a right statement that conveys evil intention. It is not problematic ... Islam can be tolerant and still be empowered by might. It is not imaginable that calling for Allah is restricted to means of wisdom and good preaching as if this is the only verse in Qu'ran! ... In my country Egypt, for example, preachers are told not to speak about the grave torture or scenes of Resurrection Day. The justification is that people will panic and become very depressed.[23]

Like the other Salafi preachers, Alhuweini refrains from discussing politics or state governing systems, sharing in the public life, or tackling the current societal challenges. He prefers to focus on faithfulness and individual salvation, and to be connected with

Islam and its symbols, regardless of what is occurring in one's sur-roundings. This is illustrated in an interview he gave with the *Alfurqan* newspaper:

I think that attacking Sahih Albukhari and Sahih Muslim (master books containing the correct rubrics [*Sunna*] of Prophet Mohammed) is more dangerous to the nation than the American invasion of Iraq, or the ene-mies taking the Muslim lands.[24]

Abulfutouh Salem

Abulfutouh Salem was born in Zaqazeeq in 1956 and grew up as a poor orphan. He was cared for by his mother, and sent to Azhar, where he learned the Qur'an by heart at a young age. He wanted to become a doctor, but turned to preaching at the request of his mother after graduating from Da'wa College.

Abulfutouh Salem is close to the Muslim Brotherhood, and says that he is influenced by several schools of thought such as Salafi (progenitors), Ansar Assuna (*Sunna* advocates) and Tableegh Dawa (Disseminating Islam), and states that he prefers the holistic school that studies all aspects of Islam as a comprehensive lifestyle, and is not restricted to prayer only.[25]

Abulfutouh stated that he was prone to harm by the state 'who hates the Muslim brothers', and the state gave freedom to other groups (meaning the Salafi), in order to fight them.[26] When he inquired about this, he was physically hurt and part of his salary was discounted.

His relationship with the Salafi preachers has always been tense, particularly with those who work on the satellite channels. This tension reached its peak when he wrote an article in one of the Egyptian newspapers entitled, 'Barbers, Tuk-tuk Drivers and Iron-ers are Preaching on Satellites Now.' Two photos of Mohammad Hassan and Mohammad Hussein Yaquob appeared beside the article. In this article, Abulfutouh accused the Salafi preachers of cultivating an aggressive ideology that aimed at spreading vices and damaging the minds of the younger generation. In doing this, Abulfutouh Salem was recreating the tense atmosphere and improper competitions that occurred as a result of the strained relationships between the Al Nas preachers, which he himself criti-cised in an interview on an Islamic group website:

... unfortunately, when a successful preacher appears, he faces strikes from everywhere while he is still new and tender. He surrenders because he is left hopeless and helpless. In addition to the external shocks, sometimes they attack in the studio using [direction, lighting, and sound]. Similar things happened to me during Rawdat Al-Firdaws show. There was a war waged against me but I endured ... till someone came to me and said, 'please forgive me; I was forced to do this by so and so.'[27]

Salem's opinions concerning women are very strict. He asserts that a woman should always be subordinate to a man, particularly her husband, and says that she should remain under the protection of the family umbrella at all costs. Any injustice or oppression the woman endures, he interprets as a test from God, so she must be patient and wait for God's reward. On his Al Nas programme *Aba' Wa Abna'* (Fathers and Sons), he received a letter from a woman, stating that her husband had committed adultery with the servants that she brought home to help with the housework, although her husband prayed, followed all the good practices and was otherwise benevolent. Abulfutouh instructed the woman to endure such treatment, even though her husband had committed adultery whilst married, and he did not address a single word to the man, knowing that in Islam, the adulterous are punished by being stoned to death:

Don't employ servants and that's it ... Comfort yourself, employ a man, wear your veil and let one of your sons watch over him as he cleans. Keep them away from your house I mean ... Or employ a shapeless servant ... I mean that the way she looks will make him goes out ... escape I mean ... Her shape with that body, so when he sees her, he flees, not to bring a nice woman wailing and swaying.

He advised a veiled woman who suffered from her husband's pathological jealousy, to endure it, and to avoid doing anything that might provoke his jealousy:

Dear sister, I ask you to calm down a little with him. His jealousy means that he loves you. But there is a favourable and unfavourable kind of jealousy. He suffers from the unfavourable one. Try not to provoke him, try not to open the window and stand by it, don't stand on the balcony, don't go out wearing make-up, don't do anything that would disturb him, don't talk to your cousins, don't sit cross–legged and laugh with your relative.[28]

Unlike the Salafi preachers, Abulfutouh Salem tackles public and non-controversial political issues. He adopts obvious attitudes, supports them and attempts to justify them, utilising emotion-provoking techniques, sometimes resorting to exaggeration, fabrication and falsity.

In one episode of *Fadfadah*, he adopted a stance against the Palestinian Authority, the Palestinian security forces, and some of the Authority officials and Oslo's engineers, whom he called 'traitors' and 'mercenaries.' While doing this, he showed some old pictures of the uprising (*intifada*) dating from more than eight years ago. He then expressed his opinions concerning a statement by a Palestinian official, Mahmoud Abbas, about negotiating with Israel (he did not mention the name directly):

'It was said that he is about to negotiate with the Israelis.' I heard the Palestinian official saying in Lebanon that we have no other way except negotiation. They told him that the Zionists do not want to negotiate, he said but I will negotiate. I am asking a question brothers ... negotiate about what ... for the past seventeen years following Oslo till now, settlement building raised by a very high rate (48%), and this fact is admitted by both Palestinians of the West Bank and by Israel.

Conclusion

The programmes of Al Nas are dominated by extremist views. The level of extremism varies according to the background of the preachers, with the majority of preachers belonging to the Salafi school, and some being Al-Azhar scholars, who hold very conservative opinions and *fatwa* regarding social issues, particularly women. The small voice of young, 'open minded' preachers is given very little space, but is overpowered by the extremist identity of the channel. The Salafi preachers of Al Nas are seen on many new religious channels, which inevitably means that they are constantly pumping more extremist religious content onto the Arab television networks.

6

'MODERN' PREACHERS

STRATEGIES AND MIXED DISCOURSES

Olfa Tantawi

Television preaching in the Middle East was, for a long time, mostly limited to elderly scholars in robes, reading holy texts and emphasising the importance of the afterlife over this life. But as TV has evolved from one or two tightly-controlled, state-owned channels to hundreds of private satellite offerings, a number of young televangelists, dressed in modern suits and with shaven faces, have emerged as increasingly popular alternatives. They started presenting themselves as the new voice of a tolerant brand of Islam: humane and compassionate. Their discourse, which preaches social reform through the integration of religion in all aspects of life, is markedly apolitical. However, their increasing popularity and influence among the Arab youth has turned some of them into either a potential political threat to autocratic rules, or a tool for legitimising the ruling regimes.

This chapter is concerned with comparing and contrasting the religious discourses of four prominent, competing, and controversial modern Muslim preachers within the Egyptian context: Amr Khaled, Khaled El Gondy, Moez Massoud and Tareq Suwaidan. However, they are not dealt with as individuals, but as reflections of complex structures that involve political or social elitist groups, target audiences, and business and commercial interests.

The chapter will first explore the historical background of the Piety discourse in Egypt, and outline the theoretical framework and methodology. It will then proceed to examine the role and influence of a religious TV preacher (da'yah). The third part of the article will attempt to outline the different structures of power and dominion in the media, the different religious texts that these preachers are carefully intertwining, and will then explore the political implications and under-structures of the different religious discourses.

Media, Religion and the State

In the mid-1990s, an Islamic revival movement that had been evolving in Egypt since the 1970s[1] started morphing into a media phenomenon. An increasing number of new religious leaders reached the heights of stardom, in a bustling and burgeoning media context. Since then and throughout the past decade, increasing numbers of private, religious satellite channels have emerged with different formats, ideologies and messages. This chapter, which is based on a content analysis of four religious programmes aired on three different satellite channels, attempts to explore the struggle for dominion between the different players: the various elite groups, the state, the media channels, the religious leaders and the audiences. It also aims to observe, identify, and map the religious discourses in broadcast media, which meant that religion was not dealt with in the context of received wisdom but in the context of observing people's interpretation and often manipulation of religion. Within this context, it is convenient to take up Clifford Geertz's commonly used yet controversial definition of religion as a cultural institution: a symbolic system that is active in integrating people's everyday routines and struggle within an implicit world-view.[2]

When inspected closely, media and religion both seem to occupy the same space: exchanging roles, interacting, sometimes wrangling and clashing, and at other times, teaming up and blending. Both media and religion are active in offering people presentations, interpretations and a comprehensible world-view. Typically it was media in its primal form, i.e., Gutenberg's printing press, that challenged the Christian Church or the institutional monopoly of knowledge, and was celebrated later in the Catholic Encyclopaedia in 1910 because it 'brought about an internal revolution in the intellectual world in the direction of what is profane [secular] and free from restraint [church control].'[3] James Beniger demonstrates at length this twofold trait of knowledge as power, and at the same time as the power to challenge power. He explains that the contemporary world that is made up of information societies has a basic need to develop new technologies, to manage and control a revolutionary information expansion that is prompted by the very same new technologies that are meant to tighten the control.[4] The recent developments in the media scene worldwide, with the Internet revolution and the seemingly wild expansion of satellite television, match up closely to Beniger's premise.

More importantly, both institutes play a substantial role in either validating or challenging state power. According to international law, the definition of a sovereign state necessarily entails the Jeffersonian notion of 'habitual obedience', that legitimates any ruling system as it constitutes a form of popular consent.[5] This habitual obedience is a dynamic process of negotiations that involve different, often conflicting, parties. Media and religion are at the core of these processes.

Ayubi uses the Sadat example to illustrate this point concerning the role of religion. In the mid-seventies, the late Egyptian president employed religion as a tool for hegemony, to counter the prevailing nationalist sentiment and socialist movements that opposed his economic 'open door', capitalist policies. Sadat's subsequent assassination is the most astounding testimony to the ensuing loss of control, where religion can be used 'as a tool for preserving the status quo... [and] can also work as a catalyst for change.'[6]

The Rise of an Apolitical Piety Discourse: A Historical Background

Following the assassination of Egyptian President Anwar Sadat at the hands of extremist Islamists, the state imposed tight controls and limitations on religious programming. A study dealing with religious programming on Egyptian television outlined an established policy that limited the broadcast hours of religious programming, and a heavy censorship practice that lead, in many instances, to the removal of episodes and programmes from the air. The study revealed a conflict between the communicators, that is the body of producers, editors and directors of the religious programmes on the one hand, and the higher management on the other, who had been constantly ignoring their suggestions to improve religious programming, and resisting the implementation of any concrete changes in the format or style of these programmes.[7] This tight restriction also coincided with the phasing-out of traditional Azhar Islamic preachers, such as Mohammed al-Ghazali, Sheikh Abdel Hameed Keshk, Sheikh Mohammed Motwale al-Shaarawe and others.[8] Notably, the 'new preachers phenomenon' crept onto the Egyptian scene as a result of the people's need to assert and reinforce their own set of values—in contrast to an official religious establishment that had lost its lustre due to being subject to tight control—and in response to media and educational systems that buttress the secular and undermine the religious.[9] The new preachers received further support and empowerment from the country's shift towards economic neo-liberal reforms,[10] and the advent of the booming satellite channels business.

Thus, in their rebellion over the liberal, secular values of the elite, the subordinate classes in Egypt succeeded in constructing their own opinion of the veil, for example, as a symbol of 'modesty and resistance.'[11] Field and Hamam quote sociologist Rafiq Habib as saying that 'people do not embrace rigid ideas because they read them in a book or hear them on TV. Rather, their social environment [relates to] how they interpret the words of the Qur'an, perhaps rigidly, to come to grips with the realities they experience on a daily basis.'[12] Ismail highlights the popular dimension of contemporary Islamism, and describes at length the role of the socio-economic setting in the grounding of the Islamist movement in the urban space of popular Cairo and its peripheries. She notes that this conservative Islamist discourse is further 'appropriated for tactical purposes by the dominant power block which comprises various class factions [including] state bourgeoisie and parasitic private capital.'[13] Subsequently, these conservative Islamist values gradually became prevalent, hegemonic common sense. They found their full expression in the pronounced discourse of the new modern preachers *Al-Do'ah al gudud*, whose expressed intention to avoid politics and focus on piety, well-matched the state's established public morality trend. The advent of the booming Gulf-financed satellite channels business, by the mid-1990s, played an important role in accentuating their impact.

Hegemony, as originally devised by Gramsci, is a process of struggle for dominion.[14] This mechanism of struggle between the micro-choices of social groups and the macro, commonsensical general attitude, works efficiently when the struggling groups succeed in producing their own outspoken intellectuals.[15] These new religious advocates reflect and elaborate Gramsci's hegemony theory, where a struggling group with a certain world-view and set of beliefs and values succeeded in conquering and ideologically replacing the hitherto dominant traditional world-view.

Hence, the new religious preacher's advocacy of the veil, for example, often seen as the cause behind the proliferation of this kind of dress in the Egyptian community, would not have had such an impact if it were not an expression of some prevalent, already existing, alternative common sense that had not been allowed to take expression in the government-controlled media. Several studies conducted amongst university students in the 1980s have indicated that the prevalence of this religious trend, and the Islamic veil for women, was fuelled by social and economic factors.[16] Since then, the social practices and world-view that appeared, at the time, to be unconventional and extreme, underwent a process of normalisation. *Hijab* for instance, became a social fashion item rather than the symbol of an Islamic movement.[17]

The fact that there is a media body, and more specifically Gulf media investors who are willing to sponsor and even profit from the proliferation of such a world-view, is in part due to the fact that these values have become part of an elitist common sense. Further, a ruling regime that is permissive of what is perceived as an apolitical discourse has also played a role in reinforcing these values. The process involves both cultural trends and thoughts making an upward journey, from micro (individual choices of media consumption) to macro (the institutional dissemination of media products to the largest possible number of people). It also involves the political elite and media organisations that have decided to profit from diffusing these values through satellite broadcasting to an already receptive audience, which suggests a cyclical process of interaction and influence.

Objective

This comparative study is concerned with comparing and contrasting the religious discourse of four prominent and competing modern Muslim preachers within the Egyptian social and political context. In this study the religious TV preacher or *Da'yah* is dealt with as a reflection of a complex structure that involves political and social elitist groups, target audiences and business commercial interests, where 'specific discourse structures are deployed in the reproduction of social dominance.'[18]

The study makes use of critical discourse analysis, which is most relevant to the subject of this research, since the specific notion of a religious programme implies 'a privileged access to a scarce social resource of power.'[19] This kind of tool for analysis is most useful when comparing different parties who might all share a certain basic ideology, but ultimately use varied arguments to serve differing interests within a constantly changing context. Hence there is a need to go beyond the immediate text, to unveil the dynamics of this process.[20]

The Trilogy of Interdependency: The Preacher, the Channel and the Audiences

The Preacher

The logic advanced hitherto should not lead to the assumption that the preachers of the new media age are representatives of the same social group as the subordinate classes at large, or that their moral stance is a simple reiteration of the ethos of a marginalised social group. The very fact that a particular TV channel has chosen to make a specific preacher responsible for the interpretation of the Islamic teachings to broadcast to the viewers, is also significant. In part, this means that the media channel has granted this person or preacher the privilege not only to speak and influence the masses, but also to speak to them of religion, that is 'God-talk.'

This notion of religion as 'God-talk' in the context of Islam is more expressive than to speak of the sacred as opposed to the profane. Instead, the religious sacred makes up an integral part of the practice of everyday life, in a generative fusion that is responsible for the formation of a 'collective consciousness, a moral order, and ultimately society itself.'[21] The potency of the religious discourse as 'God-talk', and its ability to restructure reality involves, according to Geertz, a prior acceptance of authority, which partly lies in the persuasive power of traditional imagery.[22]

Abou Al Fadl argues that the traditions of the Islamist juristic interpretive community have this element of authoritarian persuasiveness. The simple reference to the juristic symbolism of the forbidden *al haram*, the permissible *al halal* and the *sunnah* and *hadith*, acquires, by default, an authoritarian potency, regardless of the speaker's own standing in the juristic community.[23] The degree and amount of trust that the person enjoys from his listeners and followers is a crucial factor. This trust means that the listeners must willingly choose to suspend their own judgment, in order to be persuaded by the views and logic advanced by the speaker or *Da'yah*. However, this deferment of judgment is conditioned by the speaker's own charismatic presence, and relies on the fact that he does not disconcert his listeners with uncommon views that sternly drift away from the generally accepted rationale.[24] To summarise, the media preacher is located mid-way between the elitist common sense of the media as a business and as a tool of control, and the perceived common sense of the target audience. He employs a historical accumulation of juridical tradition to reinforce the values of the one or the other, the elitist's common sense at one point of time, or the audience's norms at another, or both, when and where they run in accord.

Al-Resalah Satellite Channel: Amr Khaled Vs. Tarek Suwaidan

Both Amr Khaled, Egyptian, and Tarek Suwaidan, Kuwaiti, belong to the category of what one can refer to as 'modern preachers.' They try to project an open-minded, centrist, friendly, non-violent and peaceful version of Islam. They take careful steps to deliver soft discourse that attempts to attract mainstream Muslims, but at the same time avoids antagonising governments. Yet their approach is always faced with the agenda and complexities that are tied up with the capital invested in the channels where they operate.

In the cases of Khaled and Suwaidan, Saudi capital plays an important role in backing the media religion project of each. Al-Resalah TV, launched in March 2006, was designed along the MBC model to attract secular viewers by offering them appealing yet 'Islam-friendly' programming.[25] The channel received its funding from Saudi billionaire Al-Waleed bin Talal, who owns Rotana group, which comprises several entertainment, variety, movie and music channels.

Suwaidan's early success on Al-Resalah TV faced a serious setback. His biggest mistake, according to Ahmed Abu Heiba, who worked closely with him in the early days of Al-Resalah, was to say that Al-Resalah programming was meant to represent a modern Islam. Although Talal was already the owner of the highly criticised and condemned music and entertainment channel Rotana, he could afford to simply ignore all the accusations regarding the presentation of 'improper' commercial entertainment content. However, according to Abu Heiba, Talal could not stand up to the accusation that he played a role in modernising Islam, which denoted introducing some unorthodox changes to the religious beliefs.[26] The attack was so fervent that it forced Al Walid bin Talal to demand a change in the channel's policy and style of programming. Plans by reformist and liberal presenters to air certain programmes had to be cancelled, female presenters were taken off air, and some Salafi preachers were invited onto Al-Resalah. Accordingly, the forceful pressure of capital in relation to the media programming, in this instance, was closely linked to the sensibilities of a certain religious elite, a Gulf Wahabi elite that was imposing its own set of values through the media and on the media.

Unlike Suwaidan, Amr Khaled has been able to counterbalance the pressure caused by capital, by maintaining flexibility by moving from one media outlet to another, from Iqra', to Orbit and El Rai, whenever there has been a clash of interests.[27] Often, when there is no media sponsor, Khaled goes on to produce his own talk show while waiting for the right media outlet.

Azhari Channel: the Preacher, the Institute and the State

Al Azhari is perhaps the only Islamic channel that is not being financed by Saudi Gulf money. Libyan businessman Hassan Tatanaki, an Egyptian doctor, and an Azhari preacher Khaled el Gondy, provided the seed money for the channel, and declared it to be a religious endowment, a *Waqf*. This *Waqf* status implies that the channel was meant to be a non-profit initiative. However, the channel has a paid phone services policy, which means that people sharing in its different talk shows pay for their contributions. The channel's website actively propagates a paid Islamic mobile service, with this paid service including downloads of religious rhymes, Qur'anic verse, and a calling service for customers to ask about *fatwas* and get the answer delivered to their mobile phones. This implies that the channel, despite its *Waqf* status, has also an embedded for-profit business plan.

Despite reports of governmental objections to the channel Azhari, which had its launch in June 2009 just one month before the advent of the holy month of Ramadan, it has its broadcast slot on both ArabSat and NileSat, the latter owned and run by the Egyptian government. Hence, it can be concluded that although Azhari is carefully portrayed as an independent, privately owned channel, it enjoys a no-objection position, if not full support, from the Egyptian government.

Moez Massoud, the Business Elite Choice

What makes the American University in Cairo (AUC) graduate Moez Massoud very different from all the other modern preachers is the fact that aside from his stardom as a religious talk show host, Massoud is an e-commerce entrepreneur, whose commercial guide to the Internet, *The Net Guide*, grossed LE 100,000 with its debut issue in 2003.

Massoud had a Westernised upbringing and education. Until the age of eighteen he was a Muslim only by name, and did not speak the Arabic language. A near-death experience in 1996 led him to a religious awakening, to give up the life of pleasure and enjoyment that he was immersed in, and to start praying regularly and respecting his parents.

In late 2002, Massoud was asked by friends to give a talk at AUC during the university's Global Injustice Week. He drew on examples from the Bible, the Torah and the Qur'an and ended the talk by singing Bob Dylan's 'Masters of War.' His presentation continued to be the talk of attendees for months later. This was the start of his career as a *Da'yah*. In 2003, he became the host of two English-speaking talk shows, 'Parables from the Qu'ran' and 'Stairway to Paradise', which were produced and aired by the Saudi-owned ART satellite network.[28] In 2006, in an attempt to replicate the success of Amr Khaled in the Arabic speaking world, ART chose the twenty-eight year old Massoud to reach out to the Arab youth through a programme entitled *El Tariq el Sah* ('The Right Path').

Later the young preacher was chosen to have a weekly presence on El Mehwar's main talk show '90 Minutes.' El Mehwar TV is a privately owned Egyptian Satellite channel, and like other private Egyptian satellite television stations, it is partly owned by the government through the compulsory shares bought by ERTU, NileSat and EMC. The station is, however, editorially independent. Hassan Rateb, a prominent Egyptian businessman, created and financed the media venture. He explained that the TV channel was meant to provide the private sector with a voice, to counter what he felt were the repeated and systematic media attacks on the business sector in Egypt. According to Rateb, 'the socialist way of thinking that was the reason for the collapse of the former Soviet Union is still very evident in this region. Many of our journalists, critics, and intellectuals are a product of the socialist legacy. One of the important missions of this station is to legitimise the private sector in Egypt.'[29] This is perhaps why AUC graduate Massoud was the natural choice to be the channel's liberal religious youth representative. Notably, the rise and fame of Massoud relies mainly on an upper-middle class viewership, that sees him as representative of the modern cultured Muslim youth. His discourse advances a mixture of concepts that bring to light the spirituality of Islam, a notion that appeals more to the West, and Western-minded Egyptian youth.

The Branding Processes for an Imaginary Audience

'Amr Khaled's audience is mostly the youth. I appeal more to the man in the street, those who live in the popular crowded neighbourhoods all around old Cairo' said El Gondy in response to a question about the difference between him and Amr Khaled.[30] El Gondy's expectation of who is his imaginary audience is reflected in the way he brands himself in contrast to Amr Khaled, Suwaidan, or Massoud. He sees himself as a preacher who has the talent to address the masses because he is one of them, born and educated in an old populated Cairien neighbourhood; therefore he understands their language and mindset.

His dress code and its significance and implications for the masses, is one tool that El Gondy uses for impact. From his point of view 'wearing *Al Azhary Emah* (the Egyptian head cover) is like wearing a crown.' This headdress sets the preacher wearing it on a higher level than the usual ordinary standard of the general public, because it signifies religious sacred power; this is why he usually wears his *Azhari* headdress in the mosque and at any other official event. On the other hand, he is also aware of the public's need to feel that the preacher is one of them. He is also someone who is like them in appearance and speaks their language. This is why, as a media presenter, he is usually dressed in an elegant modern suit.[31]

In one of El Gondy's early live programmes that was aired on 29 June, he had a heated discussion with his guest, the Salafi preacher Mahmud El Masry regarding dress codes and the significance of dress. El Gondy asked El Masry bluntly why he dressed in a Gulf-style *Galabya* and head cover (*Ghutrah*), while he, as his name clearly reflects, is an Egyptian preacher. The discussion revealed that El Masry, who is not a graduate of Al Azhar, resorted to this dress to brand himself as a Sheikh and a Muslim scholar, 'This gives me the appearance of a scholar.' Notably, El Masry and many others, especially in Salafi channels, use this kind of dress to signal to their viewership that they belong to Saudi Arabia, which to many is the cradle of Islam in its purest form.[32]

In contrast, when Suwaidan puts on his Gulf-style *Ghutrah* and *Galabya* dress, it does not specifically have any symbolic connotations since it is, in fact, part of his own culture and tradition as a

Kuwaiti national. Nevertheless, Suwaidan is more interested in branding himself as a Professor and a lecturer—a man of science who is keen to pass his acquired knowledge and life experience on to younger generations. Suwaidan studied engineering and management in the US, where he lived for seventeen years. Before starting his life project in the Al-Resalah network, he had established around sixty-eight companies and organisations.[33] Suwaidan and his sponsor, Al Waleed bin Talal, agreed on creating a channel that would 'serve Islam and change the ideas of the youth about terrorism.' This is done by offering programmes such as *Akadimyyat I'dad el qada* ('The Leaders Training Academy') that offers Muslim youths an understanding of their role in life. Like Amr Khaled, Suwaidan's goal is 'to change humans [by means of changing] their ideologies... and role models.'[34] The programme format is more like a university lecture, with the audience of young men and women receiving paper material, writing and following the lecturer who is preaching to them about life rather than religion. Suwaidan's image is thus a combination of a man of religion and a man of science; he has the insight and in-depth knowledge of both worlds. This image gives him a higher status and a deeper impact.

Although his dress code is designed along the lines of a casual, elegant, middle-class youth, forty year old Amr Khaled is careful to position himself as an idol for the younger generation to follow. His latest show *Al Mujadedoon* ('The Innovators'), that hit Arab TV screens for the first time on 8 January 2010, is formatted along the same lines as the American reality show 'The Apprentice.' In the first episode, the young competitors, whose goal is to design the best development plan to help those in need in different places, are gathered together, waiting for Khaled to show up. After a while he arrives, surrounded by his advisors, to address the youths. Throughout the show Khaled, like Donald Trump, is seen in fancy cars, talking on his mobile, watching the youthful competitors' videos and critiquing their plans and vision. Hence, he is no longer one of them, rather he is the mentor, the judge, and ultimately the idol whose wisdom and vision is the ultimate reference guide.

Massoud, like Khaled, maintains the modern look of an average youth. Massoud's dress is rather conservative, elegant but modest, and he often wears a suit but does not wear a neck-tie. Yet unlike

Khaled, Massoud is modestly elegant but there are no glitzy colours or fancy surroundings. His look is in accordance with his general ethos of paying more attention to the core principles and ideals, rather than form and appearances.

The four preachers have neatly shaven faces, and are careful to dress elegantly. This attention to elegance on their part denotes the characteristics of their target audiences. Bayatt notes that Islamic discourse with the advent of these new preachers has made a shift 'from constituencies centred around impoverished middle–classes, into more fragmented adherents including the privileged groups.'[35]

The Politics of the Piety Discourse

When seen in action within the Egyptian context, the new preachers, *Al Du'ah al Gudud*, made a dramatic shift 'from the earlier emphasis on Islamist polity to one on personal piety and ethics.'[36] Nevertheless, this kind of apolitical discourse did play a political role through channelling the social and political conflict with an authoritarian state, to other forms of struggle that are mostly identity-based. The ultimate impact is inducing more confusion in an already fragmented religious media space.

This process of channelling conflicts can be seen in the way that the discourse qualifies and portrays the dialectical conflict between man and the irreconcilable forces and contradictions of life. The key element in this discourse is how each of them identifies these conflicting forces of life, the types of problems and pressures that man has to handle in daily life, and finally the world-view put forth by each to a particular audience.

Qualifying the struggle

Suwaidan: the Supremacy of the State

In his programme *A'lamatny Al-Hayat* ('Life Lessons'), which was aired during the holy month of Ramadan 2009, Suwaidan deals, in the twenty-third episode, with the issue of poverty and individual finances (*Al Rizk*). At the beginning of the programme, he stressed the universality of poverty through a group of statistics, noting, for instance, that the poorest 40 per cent of the world's population accounts for 5 per cent of global income. Suwaidan then proceeded towards a conclusion that qualified poverty as 'an individual choice': this is because it is the people's choice not to make the necessary effort to make their lives better. To substantiate this view, Suwaidan used a statement by the former British Prime Minister Margaret Thatcher, as well as several stories from the Islamic literary cultural heritage *Al Turath*.[37]

Thus poverty, he asserted, as a universal reality and an individual choice, is not a consequence of the immediate social and political context. Poverty is about one's own life management, and the political and economic system of the state by which the wealth in this specific political and social entity is being managed or mismanaged was not in any way discussed, scrutinised or critiqued.

Similarly, in his attempt to develop a world-view of the role of Islamic *shari'ah*, and Islamic laws, Suwaidan, in the twenty-ninth and final episode of the programme, stressed the notion of civilisation as being an identity that needs protection. Religion, according to him, is a system of protection to protect Man's mind, soul, money and family, and this is done through the application of the Islamic *shari'ah*.

Suwaidan proceeded to note that the state is responsible for the defence and proper application of its own system and ideology amongst those who follow Islam. Part of the state's duty is to make sure that people obey its rules and laws (*foroudh*), whether through prayer, fasting or being ethically and morally committed.[38]

Accordingly, by aligning the state with religion and identity, the conflict is illustrated, in Suwaidan's world-view, as one of identity and identity-protection from intruding moral corruption, and the state's role and supreme right to dominate and protect is, more importantly, a religious duty.

Amr Khaled: The Systematic Processes of Obedience

In his programme *Bel Qu'ran Nahya* ('We Will Live By the Qur'a'n'), aired in late August 2009 during Ramadan, Amr Khaled related to his audience the story of the Prophet Moses. Khaled's account of Moses' birth, his conflict with the pharaoh and his personal dilemma, was designed so the audience could draw from these experiences and examples a number of ethical and moral values that the Muslim individual should refer to and apply in his daily life.[39] Often a Muslim's quandary in life is about re-adjusting attitude and good planning to achieve material success in life, and at the same time score points with God to be sure of a heavenly reward.

Moses, although he was the messenger of God, is not a sacred, unattainable, historical character. His story as a human being, who went from sufferance to success, is a prototype that can be replicated on an individual level. Like Suwaidan, Khaled also has a focus on the individual being responsible for his own happiness or misery.

Although the format of the different TV programmes hosted by Khaled vary from one to another, all of them directly and overtly pronounce his goal of reconstructing the moral fibre and behavioural system of the individual in a Muslim society. The notion of value, in Khaled's discourse, extends moral value to the sphere of practical life and decision-making. Aiming towards success, planning, and having stamina and perseverance are all life virtues that can be observed and learned from different Qur'anic examples.

'I'm serious when I said I'm going to do *Nahda* (social revival)' says Khaled.[40] His goal-orientated, action-plan style is manifest in the way that he deals with the title of his programme, which he turns into a slogan. He calls on his viewers to follow the slogan of *Bel Quran Nahya*, that is, to live their lives by the guidance of the Holy Book. Then, he invites them to log on to his website to download, print and distribute the slogan stickers that he and his team designed.

Khaled then proceeded to form another concrete plan of action, urging them to complete the reading of the Holy Book in the thirty days of the Holy month of Ramadan, a common practice known as *khatmah*. 'We want 10 million *khatmah*', he insisted, adding that there would be a counter on his website to calculate how many had succeeded in achieving this goal, which people could sign up to.[41] This behavioural, individualistic, goal defining, result-orientated religious discourse echoes Suwaidan's rationale whereby self-development is the key to a better life, with no reference to the immediate social and political context. In episode ten of the programme, Khaled recounted in detail, with his passionate style, the moment when Moses had to face the Pharaoh, calling on him to believe in the One and only God and also demanding that he let the people of Israel travel with him from Egypt. Although the connotations of such an encounter are political, Khaled emphasised instead the principle of dialogue and the notion of civility in managing differences. According to him, the Moses encounter 'is meant to teach Muslims that dialogue and not violence is the best way to solve differences.'[42] He then noted that in dealing with young children, parents must let them express their thoughts freely, and not impose their own will on the young, as this is the only way to bring them up with a strong and free will. Repeatedly, as he relates the encounter, Khaled draws from it lessons on family relations, polity in dealing with authority, and dialogue. This kind of analysis and reflection discharges the story from its political connotations, and draws the attention of the listeners to the sphere of family relationships and human daily exchanges.

Khaled El Gondy: Defending the Supremacy of Al Azhar

In introducing his newly established channel Azhari, which unmistakably identifies the Al Azhar institute as the initial reference of ideology and methodology, El Gondy, in a statement written on the channel's website, underscored the fact that the channel would not offend any 'pronounced political policies of any country.'[43]

El Gondy's first encounters with TV viewers were through satellite channel talk shows on Orbit and ART. However, according to El Gondy himself, he earned a great deal of popularity among the Egyptian masses when he had the opportunity to present his teachings through one of Egypt's state-owned television's most prominent talk shows, *El Beit Beitak*, which sought to provide an attractive, government-controlled alternative to compete with the rising popularity of satellite talk shows.

El Gondy presents himself to his audiences as a modern Azhar preacher, who is not as traditional as Egypt's Mufti Sheikh Ali Gomaa. Still, El Gondy as an Azhar scholar can issue *fatwa*, unlike Amr Khaled. This highlights his role as someone who has the authority to offer religious legitimacy, an authority that El Gondy is aware of possessing and keen to assert. However, this authority is mainly institutional, and it is by virtue of being educated and trained at Al Azhar that he is a certified preacher. He explains this by saying, 'One can read lots of books about medicine, but he will be punished for practising medicine and cannot perform surgery if he is not a university graduate with a certificate in medicine.' Similarly, a preacher who has the power to address and mobilise the masses has a vested authority, according to El Gondy, that should not be granted to just any one, regardless of the number of books he has read, and the depth and breadth of knowledge that he has accumulated.

The pronounced end goal of El Azhari is to re-instate the institutional power of Al Azhar as the supreme religious authority in Egypt and the Arab world. In one episode aired in October 2009, he and his guest heavily attacked Al Jazeera for its criticism of the institute, and its Head, at that time the late Sheikh Mohamed Hussein Tantawi, noting that the attack was directed at the Egyptian role in the region, especially the fact that El Azhar's wide influence is an integral part of Egypt's soft power.[44]

El Gondy's strategy to achieve this end is to engage in current debates as a commentator who reflects, sometimes evaluates, and at other times advises and guides. His live programme *Ma'a El Gondy* ('With El Gondy') usually starts with a collection of short news items, which he relates to his viewers along with comments and *fatwas*, asserting in the process his position as an authorised source of information as an Azhar preacher.

El Gondy also resorts to a confrontation and engagement strategy, inviting friends and foes onto his programme to engage in heated discussions. The widely varied list of guests includes: Azhar scholars, scientists, government officials and ministers, journalists, famous talk show presenters, liberal thinkers, secular writers and even Salafi preachers. Throughout, El Gondy understands perfectly that being the host means that he is the one who will have the last word. Although he is usually very careful not to attract attention to this particular point, one of his guests—a competing popular *da'yah* of Yemeni origin, Al Habib al Jafry—actually pointed out this fact when he commented rather sarcastically, 'It is left to you [now] to end your show with your word, since you are the owner of the channel.'[45]

The conflict within the Azhari world is thus of a regional nature, and arises from the intruding influence of other, mostly extremist, Islamic movements and the diffusion of superstition and misconceptions on a more local level.

Moez Massoud: Religion and the Veiling of the Truth

The marketing entrepreneur and TV preacher Moez Massoud, on the other hand, is careful to distance himself from El Gondy and Amr Khaled, whom he sees as offering some kind of Islamic televangelism. According to Massoud, this kind of televised preaching is all about making money.[46]

Ethics and morality are central in Massoud's discourse; to him, rituals are only one part of an overall world-view of Islam, yet in real life there is a separation between ethics and rituals that is class based; 'there are the poor who indulge in committing themselves to rituals but do not think much about moralities and ethics, and the rich who do not care for rituals and prefer to think of themselves as ethically correct.'[47] In the fourth episode of his programme *Al Tarik el Sah* ('The Right Path') that was aired in September 2008, Massoud used the title of his show as a metaphor that explained the meaning of religion from his point of view. To him, religion is a continuous process of learning and development, where rituals are a training tool that helps man in his fight against worldly desires and lust.[48]

Massoud's opinion about the veil illustrates that he does not support the strict application of the laws of *shari'ah*. 'If a woman is wearing a decent dress covering her body but not her hair, then we could simply say that she is 90 per cent veiled.'[49] Massoud's discourse diverges widely, not only from the Salafi trend of thought but also from the discourse of preachers such as Khaled El Gondy, who believes that he is offering a moderate and liberal Islam. El Gondy's Azhari channel uses music and often invites artists and liberal thinkers on to his programme. But he insists that there are rules and regulations, and red lines: 'of course, there are restrictions and limitations', El Gondy said, 'why is it that in the West if someone steps out of line, or goes against orders, this is unacceptable to them. Similarly, religion is a structured system with its own restrictions and orders to regulate society.' Thus, in contrast to Massoud, it does not matter if a woman is decent or modest, her ethical conduct does not relieve her from the duty of wearing a veil, El Gondy insists. The institutional element in El Gondy's world-view is thus not exclusively concerning Al Azhar's role in society, and instead, religion is an institution with a rather rigid, systematic structure of rituals. 'Ethics and morality are not religion; an infidel can have high morals and act ethically.'[50] The stress on meaning rather than form for Massoud extends to politics, where he stresses the need not to politicise religion. This is another use of religion that turns religiosity into a veil that keeps the rulers from listening to the advice of men of religion. Religion and its men become a threat rather than a guide, and thus meaning and guidance are lost when religion is a tool for politics.[51]

Moreover, like Amr Khaled, Suwaidan and El Gondy, Massoud is pronouncedly saying that religious wisdom orders Muslims to obey the ruler, even if one was religiously incorrect or disobedient. Thus the problem is not about politics, but the conduct that has serious political consequences and causes the suffering of believers.[52]

'Us' and 'Them'

All four preachers are busy engaging their viewers in an identity discourse. The conflict is not with the state, but with Western civilisation and other beliefs and religious sects, whether Shia, Sufi or Salafi. Suwaidan defines the role of the state as the protector of religion against any intruding foreign beliefs, by observing and imposing on its Muslim citizens the laws of religion or *foroudh*. In his programme 'Life Lessons', Suwaidan said, 'One principle I learned is that there is no social advancement, no civilisation without identity.'[53] Similarly, El Gondy's style, as detailed above, is to engage with representatives of other sects, religions and movements to highlight their weaknesses, and to prove the supremacy of Al Azhar's interpretation of Islam and its methodology. Although the notion of Islam as an identity that has to be defended against the attack of a materialistic West is a shared concern between all four preachers, there is an under-structure in their discourses of a continuous process of channelling the ideologies and behaviour models of Western culture to their Muslim audiences. To further expand his arguments, Massoud often uses many characters drawn from Western culture, such as Pinocchio or Mr. Miyagi in the film 'The Karate Kid', for instance, but his references to Western culture often go beyond popular culture. His occasional mention of Western philosophy, reveals an avid reader who is up to date with Western literature in general, and with what is being written about Islam and Muslim societies in particular.

Similarly, Massoud, Suwaidan and Amr Khaled frequently refer to the latest discoveries and scientific methodologies of Western civilisation as a guide and a model to follow when planning a project or even in planning one's own future development and career. Amr Khaled's adoption of Donald Trump's 'The Apprentice' show is a striking example, where Khaled uses the format of a show that is itself an embodiment of the materialist and individualist ethos of the West, that he and the others are constantly critiquing. In the programme, the losers are ruthlessly removed from the game and winning is the ultimate goal; the mentor and idol, whether Trump in the American version or Khaled in the Egyptian one, both are shown in luxurious surroundings with money, wealth and power. Although Amr Khaled's show is a competition to offer charity and benevolence to the needy and the underprivileged, in the final analysis, the basic notions of modesty and humility are largely absent and ignored.

The Underlying Subversive Structures of Meaning

It is notable that the emphasis on the apolitical nature of every channel and each preacher has led to the creation of a virtual media space in which there is a call to integrate religion in all aspects of life as a tool of social reform. To what extent can this depoliticised Islamic discourse on the religious media achieve *Nahda* (societal reform and revival) which is the pronounced goal of Khaled's preaching for instance, and which is the implied goal of the discourse of the other preachers as well? Can there be *Nahda* in the absence of political engagement? Can there be *Nahda* in the absence of a project that involves political and social restructuring?

According to Abu Heiba, who produced Khaled's shows at Al-Resalah TV and whose newly established channel 4Shabab has also sponsored many of Khaled's TV shows including *Bel Quran Nahya*, Khaled is a social reformer who uses religion as a tool to affect change and to reform society.' He added, 'Religion is very much like a train that needs tracks or it will hit a wall.'[54] Planning and channelling the energy and powers of youth believers towards concrete action is a means to provide this train with tracks to guide its journey.

However, Khaled's train does hit a wall quite frequently. He is often asked to leave the country to live in Lebanon or London, and his shows are mostly produced abroad.[55] Hence and specifically because piety in Amr Khaled's discourse overlaps with a mobilising social plan to combat poverty and to engage religious belief in social development,[56] the political aspect is latent in the basic structure. The fact remains that Khaled himself is reluctant to bring forth the political aspect, and unlike Moses, he prefers not to create any confrontation with the ruling authority. Notably, standing up to injustice and giving support to the oppressed was never the focus of Khaled's discourse. Yet, audiences seem to be more willing to read Khaled's subtext differently. This is reflected in their comments and reactions to the story of Moses and his confrontation with the Pharaoh—*el Masry el Yom* newspaper reported, for instance, that there were 400 comments on Khaled's website, and many of these comments were directly relating the story to Egypt in modern times which infuriated the authorities, and was one of the reasons why Kahlid was ordered to leave Egypt for London.[57]

Often, the potential under-structures and under-currents that are evoked by different preachers are not the result of absolute intent on their part. The different interpretations and connotations would exist because any text, by the virtue of being a text, has the power to evoke other readings and understandings, which were not immediately intended nor perceived by the author.

The fact that this kind of religious discourse is taking place within a specific geopolitical space also has to be closely considered. Within the imposed limitations of the state, the discourse of the new preachers has made use of religion as an alternative space to political participation, by offering an individualistic rather then communal approach. However, this kind of discourse, which is constantly making use of religion to offer the youth hope that they can achieve success in daily life—as a counter to political and social stagnation—eventually exposes the fragility of a ruling regime that bases its legitimacy on promises to serve the people and improve standards of life, yet fails to do so.[58]

Another concrete societal example of the political implications of a piety discourse that claims to be apolitical in nature, is the increasing number of upper-middle class Muslim youth organisations in Egypt that are engaged in voluntary social welfare activities, and who are seen as the new agents of reform.[59] According to Sparre, the youths' upper-middle class upbringing is not particularly religious, yet in response to a growing Islamisation of society 'they tend to combine Islamic texts and practices with contemporary Western ideas and concepts from fields such as business and management.'[60] The profile of these new social reformers reflects, in part, the profile of AUC graduate preacher Moez Massoud. They also mainly prefer the religious discourse of Amr Khaled to the more politicised discourse of the Muslim Brotherhood.[61] The question is: are these burgeoning new agents of change the result of a prevalent Islamic media discourse? Or is the tendency of Khaled, and lately of Massoud, to address development and voluntarism a reflection of a growing trend among the youth? Is Moez Massoud an exception amongst his generation of upper-middle class youth? Or is he the intellectual spokesman of a growing group of youths whose views have been systematically ignored and marginalised by the different social forces of society?

Other questions to ask concern the political significance of this social movement. Can reform be only social? Could this growing force of youth turn into a political movement at some point in time? Can social activism become political activism? Clark notes that part of the Islamist movement's struggle against the dominion of the state throughout history has been to establish alternative social institutes 'to demonstrate the viability and superiority of Islamism in the face of a struggling secular state', and to challenge 'the state's ability to do its job.'[62] Clark notes that the very concept of an Islamic call or *da'wa* is, in essence, a political concept—it is 'the act of activating Islam through deeds in all spheres of life.' As such, Islam becomes the solution to the socioeconomic ills of society.[63]

Conclusion

To sum up, when viewed within the social and political context, religious media discourse, in the light of the examples discussed above, reveals a Gramscian process of negotiation between different social groups struggling to enforce their values and dominion. The phenomenon of the new preachers illustrates such a process where the modern preachers' discourse reflects the conflicting values of a hegemonic business and political elite, yet at the same time they also reflect, on a deeper level, the values of different social groups in society. The way they brand themselves vis-à-vis their target audience, the fact that they, as individuals with certain features and characteristics, have gained prominence and influence, implies a receptive social medium that accepts the logic of these individuals as part of its own common sense and structure of values. The subtle differences between the different preachers reflect the different social groups to which they individually belong. Their impact, however, is not solely defined by what they actually preach or intend to say. There is a need to observe closely how the different audiences interpret and react to these discourses. For too long, media studies have been focused on observing the impact of the media discourse on the public; however, there is a dire need to reverse the focus and to observe more closely the impact of the audiences and different social groups on the media. There is a need to walk into Habermas's public-sphere coffee shops, to stroll down the streets and alleys to observe closely and to outline Gramsci's struggle for dominion processes from a micro-perspective lens, in order to see the mosaic of the different patterns and trends.

7

WOMEN PREACHERS

BROADCASTING PLATFORMS AND EVOLVING AGENDAS

Gihan Abou Zeid

A decade ago, Egyptian society started to witness a new phenomenon concerning the introduction of female preachers who began to preach to women in their homes.

My very first experience with mosques occurred during my first day in a sports gym, close to my home in Cairo. A middle-aged lady approached me after the workouts and asked if she could use my cellphone to make a call to a mosque. I was so curious that I began to ask her about her role at the mosque. From her answer, I realised that I was talking to a leading female preacher who was in charge of overseeing the preaching activities in a mosque in one of Cairo's modern neighbourhoods. She sounded optimistic, which encouraged me to carry on the conversation.

She was a university graduate, married with two daughters and one son, and had quit her job as an accountant at a foreign bank to take care of her family. After attending some religious classes at the mosque in the company of one of her neighbours, she began to attend those classes regularly. Next, she completed a two-year diploma from a preaching institute, had been promoted to the level of a chief preacher in her mosque, and was able to find a job for her retired husband.[1]

It was clear that the mosque had drastically changed her life. She spent long hours lecturing and interacting with her students. Sometimes she felt as though she acted like a problem solver or trouble-shooter, as she told me. In as much as the mosque had changed her life, it also highlighted many dark areas that guided my research journey.

This chapter attempts to explore the communication aspects of the rising phenomenon of female preachers in Egypt, a phenomenon that was born almost a decade ago with expanding groups of female preachers reaching out to fellow women in their homes. At that point, female preachers were not yet accepted to operate in mosques, and domestic preaching appeared to be a convenient means of communicating religious messages to women from both the middle and upper classes. Challenging the decrees from the Ministry of Waqfs and Islamic Affairs (Ministry of Religious Endowments) that prohibited those women from preaching in mosques, they have steadily expanded their scope of action to include social and outreach activities.

Their *de facto* success compelled a change in regulations, to the point that female preachers can be found nowadays in most urban mosques and in some rural mosques in Egypt. Their messages vary, but mainly they seek to strengthen the role of women within the family, and to encourage not only their commitment to Islamic traditions, but their resistance to Western culture, particularly their perception of the West's less formalised structure of the family and lack of commitment to societal values.

The messages of the female preachers are usually delivered through direct communication, by speaking to the female audience in mosques, in venues and spaces that are allocated for this purpose, or during meetings at someone's home. Female preachers tend to build immediate or even personal relationships with their audience. By contrast, male preachers rely on mass media, along with other means, to reach out to their audience on a larger scale.

It is of special interest in this chapter to examine whether female preachers are a part of Islamic politics or whether they contribute to and strengthen what is known as 'social Islam'—a less politicised version of Islamism. It also attempts to define the relationship between Islamic preachers and the media, and determine whether this relationship alters in response to gender dynamics. The analysis will seek to understand how women preachers employ the media in spreading and disseminating their content messages as compared to their male counterparts.

Background

Since the dawn of Islam, the preacher has been held in high esteem in Islamic Arab society. His calling is that of a religious man who must also practice politics within the realm of the mosque. The preacher has various roles within the mosque and its community, including religious instruction and practice, social services and economic aid. In modern days, he must fulfil his traditional role and responsibilities, despite the complexity of the modern civil state, whilst maintaining his high-profile position in the community.

It should be noted that there is neither a single class or group of preachers, nor a single oratory approach that is common to all of them. Male preachers are as diverse as politicians in how they interact with the public. According to Gaffney, 'Islamic preachers in Egypt fall into a number of significant categories rather than a single status group.'[2]As the Egyptian government sought to control da'wa (religious preaching), individuals and groups responded by offering their own versions, often framed in opposition to the 'official' discourse. Tellingly, Al-Da'wa was the name of the Egyptian Muslim Brotherhood's monthly magazine that was officially banned.[3]

The mosque is a space that brings together supporters and followers of Islam. The call to prayer could be seen as the oldest example in Islam of a media platform. Since the call is essentially a sound that comes from the heart of the mosque, audible and even visible to the public, the person making the call is also at the heart of the Muslim followers and supporters. This fact might have prevented women from using the same platform, and has also limited women's attendance in mosques, where they can only participate in prayer from the back rows. This has impeded women's ability to perform the call for prayer from inside the mosque in the same way as men. However, during the days of the Prophet Mohammed, some women opted to engage in home-based preaching, and among those were some of the wives and companions of the Prophet.

Mosques were a male-specific sanctum dedicated for prayers and/or religious speeches and classes. Today, according to Ahmed Abu Seif, Manager of the Islamic Call and Preaching Department at the Ministry of Religious Endowments (WAQF) in Egypt, the 'situation has changed and women have been allowed to preach in mosques for the past ten years.'[4]

There are two types of mosques in Egypt, public and state-owned. According to figures available in 2009, a total of 24,056 mosques are public mosques endowed and supported by private citizens, which the Ministry of Religious Endowments (WAQF) has neither control nor oversight over. At the same time, the Ministry of Religious Endowments (WAQF) administers a total of 80,333 mosques, spread all over the country,[5] while ensuring that they are supplied with Imams (a total of 50,000 preachers), who are vetted, certified and accredited by the Ministry.[6]

The Ministry of Religious Endowment (WAQF) recruits and employs women with relevant certificates or degrees in two different positions at mosques: as religious mentors for women and as women preachers (da'eyat).

Centres and institutes for training male and female preachers exist in twenty-one of Egypt's twenty-eight governorates. These began to accept female students more than ten years ago,[7] and the last five years have witnessed an unprecedented rise in the number of female graduates from these institutes. According to the Dean of Cairo's Nour Institute, which is responsible for the training of Islamic preachers, the number of female students noticeably surpasses that of male students. In fact, data for year 2008/09 show that female students outnumber their male peers by a ratio of 2:1. Further, female students tend to outperform their male peers in their academic studies.[8]

In November 2003, the London-based *Al-Sharq Al-Awsat* newspaper reported that the Egyptian Ministry of Religious Endowment (WAQF) had decided to recruit and appoint a total of fifty women in a number of leading mosques in Cairo, Giza and Alexandria, thus increasing one's access to Egyptian women, and enabling them to contribute significantly to the Islamic preaching and missionary efforts nationwide.[9] This was intended to rectify any misconceptions regarding women's ability to engage in preaching endeavours, with an emphasis placed on the need to avoid bigotry and immoderation. It was felt that it was sometimes embarrassing and uncomfortable for congregations of women to ask male preachers questions about certain issues related to their personal life. Female preachers are better positioned to respond exhaustively to such questions. More critically, the availability of female preachers would lift the burden from the shoulders of women who are sometimes denied the opportunity by their fathers or spouses to approach a stranger to receive advice or insight on a specific religious matter. Another advantage of the recruitment of female preachers is that it provides the congregation of women with access to the religion-orientated classes offered at the mosque, which are in most cases offered by men. This increase in the involvement of women in religious activities has been well received at the societal and governmental levels. It is also acknowledged that this growth in women's access to religious activities has been made possible as a result of the endeavours of Muslim female activists, who played an effective role during the 'Population and Development Conference' that took place in Cairo in 1994, as well as the UN Conference for Women in Beijing in 1995.

Muslim female activists in Egypt were driven by the slogan 'I have a point of view as a Muslim woman' that was established at the UN conference for women in Beijing in 1995. These early activists, operating within the Islamic revival movement, became prominent activists, teachers of religion, and preachers. Within ten years they had posed a conspicuous challenge to the male domination over these fields.[10]

Amongst the *da'eyat's* (women preachers) more salient achievements, are the addition and/or allocation of expanded mosque space devoted to women's Islamic studies and the right for women to preach in the mosque itself. Now the feminist Islamist movement uses thousands of mosques to reach women and their families. The Egyptian *da'eyats* are a part of the wider circle of Islamic activism in the Arab world. In 2009, Saudi Arabia's Ministry of Islamic Affairs, for the first time in its history, approved two lists of 189 and 200 women preachers respectively, who were qualified to lecture and preach to congregations of women in designated spaces within the mosques throughout the Kingdom. The Saudi Minister of Waqfs, Islamic Affairs, and Islamic Guidance, Sheikh Saleh Al Al-Sheikh said that within the framework of developing the female preaching discourse, the ministry is planning to establish a new 'department of female preaching.'[11] This is also intended to better prepare women as instructors in different branches of Islamic jurisprudence and other disciplines, and to qualify them to answer questions from their female audiences.

Already, the Dar Al-Fatah Institute, south of Riyadh, offers night courses to prepare female preachers. Applicants need to be at least seventeen years old, have learned five parts of the Qu'ran by heart, and pass an interview.[12]

Thus, *da'eyats* seem to have been flourishing in Saudi Arabia. They lecture in educational institutions, charity societies and in social centres. Websites are teeming with their presence, and some female preachers are calling for a co-ordinating or supervisory council to support their efforts. The first conference of *da'eyats* was organised by the World Forum of Islamic Youth in Saudi Arabia in 2007.

Saudi Arabia is not the only country in which considerable numbers of women have contributed to religious activities that were once confined to men. In Mauritania, many have fast become teachers and leaders; some creating names for themselves and enjoying sharing the limelight with well-known men. Although the first seeds of female Islamic activism date back to the late 1970s, the current call for revival began with the establishment of the Aisha Club. The Club, licensed in the early 1980s, is affiliated with the Islamic Cultural Society, and has a powerful influence on female activism in the country concerning preaching, charity, women and youth affairs.[13]

In Morocco, *da'eyats* moved from addressing study classes and sessions in homes, to organised civil societies, the most prominent of which is the Organisation for Renewing Women's Awareness, established in 1995. The organisation focuses on using Islamic law (*shari'a*) to defend the rights of Muslim women, and raises social awareness of cultural and historical issues related to the rights and duties of women within and outside of the family in Islamic society.[14] The Moroccan Islamic activist Malika Al-bu Anani, representative of the Unification and Reformation Movement, said:

Moroccan female activists have contributed one way or another to raising the level of awareness of women through combating illiteracy in general and in the religious sphere. Then they expanded their interest from mere preaching to individual women, to taking more interest in their religion, to attempting to engage women in large numbers in issues of development and serving society and country based on the principle of the true religion. Generally, the Moroccan female activist has presented a model for freeing women from traditions and superstitions. She was able to interact with the new developments of her time without dissolving in the Westernization attempts or losing sight of her religious identity.[15]

It should be noted that female Islamic activism in political life in the Arab world exists most visibly in Morocco, where female activist members of Islamic political parties have run for election to parliament. Also, in Jordan, the West Bank and the Gaza Strip, there were Islamist female activists who ran for elections and won seats at the Jordanian Parliament and the Palestinian Legislative Council in the years 2003 and 2006 respectively. In contrast, while some *da'eyats* belong to the Muslim Brotherhood organisation in Egypt, they are not active politically. In Syria, the Minister of Waqfs personally supervises the *da'eyats*. In a statement on the ministry's website he said:

Women's activism is so powerful in Syria, more so than in any other Arab or Islamic country. The ministry has adopted this call and allocated a department for women activism for the first time in the ministry. I appointed a woman counsellor specialised in the different Qu'ranic recitations. We have a special system for women preachers and 3,000 *da'eyat*. The woman who wants to teach religion has to do that in the right way, that is to say, should be qualified, so we arranged for unified tests and syllabi.[16] Bases for choosing such activists were set, and we conducted tests for appointing mosque preachers and Imams. Consequently, the *da'eyat* in Syria are under the supervision and control of the Ministry of Waqfs.[17]

While only a few examples are cited here, the *da'eyat* movement is flourishing, albeit at different levels of intensity, throughout the Middle East.

Da'eyat: Part of the Women's Movement?

Women's movements are defined as agents of society, and a part of civil society that functions outside state controls with the purpose of improving women's conditions. According to such a notion, and although the exact beginning and end of each stage cannot be determined by dates and does not occur in the same manner in all Arab countries, general stages in the history of Arab women's movements can be identified.

The first stage can be dated to the first thirty years of the twentieth century. The two forces at play, liberals and Islamists, focused on demanding women's rights to education and work, and addressed issues such as the wearing of the *hijab* (head scarf), the limitation on women's rights to leave home for work and education, and culturally appropriate jobs for women.

The second stage, in the 1940s and 1950s, established women's rights to education and employment. During this period, the discourse of the women's movement went beyond social demands to political rights. Women began participating in political action, particularly national liberation in Egypt, Palestine and Morocco. Consequently, voices were raised demanding women's rights to vote and be elected to parliament. While secular liberals called for political participation, the Islamists did not, despite women's powerful contribution to resistance and national liberation movements against the European colonial occupation of their countries.

The third stage occurred during the rise of state nationalism, where states dominated and controlled women's activism by promulgating labour and family laws that addressed some of its issues. Overshadowed by the intensified conflict with the Zionist state in Israel, women's demands retreated into the background.

In the 1980s, the fourth stage saw the influence of the state dwindling in relation to the effects of global changes. Perhaps as a reaction to the threat of globalisation to indigenous culture and values and to state-launched modernisation efforts, there was a significant rise in Islamic awareness. Whatever the reasons may be, the Islamist movement in the Arab world was concomitant with the rise of globalisation and, as a result of this rise in Islamic sensibility, a newly inspired women's Islamist movement took shape during the 1990s and acquired increased momentum in the post-Beijing 1995 period.

In 'Towards an Islamic Perspective of Feminist Epistemology',[18] Amani Saleh refers to two issues in Islamic feminist epistemology. The first addresses the rejection of Western feminism, which is seen by their non-Western counterparts as being bent on destroying old structures, while they actually prefer to work on reforming these structures. The second addresses the unique reality of Muslim women and their attempts to redress the formal, informal, cultural and religious matrices within social institutions that claim to represent religious truth, but that in fact mistreat women. Because these matrices are so complex, the attempts to achieve justice for women require indigenous Islamic knowledge.

Saleh concludes that Islamic feminism cannot defend women's rights until it adopts an epistemological component that distinguishes between the realities of human history and the sacred writings of Islamic texts. In other words, she talks of returning to the Qur'anic scripture and the Prophet's traditions, and excluding extraneous human additions that come in the form of interpretations based on social mores, opinions and prejudices.

Western feminism is not only criticised by the Islamists; it is also objected to by feminist thinkers in the Arab World and other developing countries for imposing a culturally Western hegemonic perspective on the Third World and ignoring their perspectives and specific experiences.

Some feminist thinkers, such as Gayatri Chakravorty Spivak, Chandra Talpade Mohanty and Sheila Sandoval, criticise Western feminists for interfering in cultural issues that should be beyond their scope. For instance, Mohanty in her book *Under Western Eyes*, attacks the manner in which feminist discourse portrays the ordinary woman in the Third World. While the Western woman is portrayed as 'educated, modern, in control of her body and sexuality, and enjoys the freedom of making her own decision', the ordinary Third World woman is depicted as 'living a divided life because of her gender.' She references the tendency to employ undertones of ignorance, poverty, lack of education, abiding by traditions, involvement in family life, becoming a victim, and so on. The feminist writer, Spivak, offers the concept of the 'follower' used by the First World to describe non-Western women as dejected and tending to be silently passive when receiving Western thought (with implied gratitude). She points out that, in doing so, they ignore the strategies that Third World women have invented to handle the repression that they face.

An informative study conducted in 2007 by the Carnegie Endowment on the rising role of Islamist Women, deals with the issue of defending women's rights within an Islamic context.[19] The study showed that some Islamist activists who support women's rights display reservations concerning the expression 'Islamic feminism.' The *da'eyat* seek solutions to the problems women face within an Islamic frame of reference. While acknowledging the questions raised by feminist groups worldwide, they avoid answers based on imitating Western models. According to the study, the *da'eyat* consider it important to position feminist demands within a wider context of the religion, and believe that defending women's rights is part and parcel of defending Islam itself. The argument is based on the belief that original Islamic teachings have been distorted by cultural and social traditions.

The Carnegie study also found evidence that the *da'eyat* have a history of activism, with their various organisations demanding and supporting a wide range of activities to foster political participation. As expected, the women harboured reservations about adopting a Western feminist agenda, and focused instead on positions that preserve the basic values of Islam. The study also found that many women refused to confine their role to charity and women's activities, and wished to be seen as qualified to occupy leading positions in their communities. The report included the statement that:

It is very rare when the Western commentators express a positive viewpoint on the relation of Islam, as an ideology or a religion, to women. The prevalent viewpoint in the West portrays women in the East as suffering under repression in patriarchal societies, chained with cultural and religious shackles.

Subscribers to this opinion base their belief on the rising numbers of women donning the *hijab* in different social stratifications. They jump to the conclusion that political Islam, which started to proliferate in the 1970s, uses religion as a pretext for passing and justifying discriminatory laws and practices.

All in all, for a Western research agency, the Carnegie report demonstrated admirable perceptiveness in distinguishing between prevailing cultural mores and Islam as a religion. It said, 'It is not simply the theory' since there are, for instance, programmes for educating women about their rights. The women's branches of the Islamist movements have also undergone a rapid change whereby they have become more critical of social traditions and incorrect interpretations—as they see them—of religious texts. They have not simply required a better representation of women; they have demanded a total integration of women into the principal Islamic movements.

Furthermore, simply walking down an Arab street illustrates the success of the Islamic movement in the unprecedented widespread practice of donning the Islamic *hijab* by all social classes and age groups. While those in the Islamist movement consider this a sign of the success of their religious educational programmes, others see the donning of the *hijab* as partially a reaction to Western hegemony. Antonio Gramsci, for example, believes that in their struggle for power, groups pass through a number of stages before they reach the last one, i.e. control. The counter-hegemony stage is the penultimate one, in which people find their place in centres of influence. Applying this to Egypt, we can consider the spread of the *hijab* among women from all social strata to be a declaration of counter-hegemony.

Another study of Islamist activists entitled 'Forms of Empowerment'[20] by Sherin Hafez, points out that the *da'eyat* are finding a role for themselves within today's surging religious revival. Assuming the positions of activists, preachers, and religious teachers, they are presenting a clear challenge to male dominance in these fields. Some have gained powerful pivotal positions in their societies and helped improve the status of women through combating illiteracy and offering free services in mosques and religious societies to address the lack of health care and high rates of poverty. Their work is distinctive because of their view that, rather than being independent entities seeking to unburden women from the unjust control of men, they are working on God's behalf as an integral part of a whole that includes husbands and families.

The research study notes that this more pronounced presence of women in mosques represents a form of empowerment that has long been pursued by the feminist movements allegedly supported by Western countries. Nevertheless, Muslim women preachers have denied this notion, and its western connotations. Many female preachers decline to refer to their activity as a type of empowerment, noting that empowerment is a means to an end: to reach religious integrity. At the same time, the respective female preachers operate within a paradigm framework that advocates the recognition of men's authority over women, although they can still empower themselves within the same framework.[21] These women are bonded and united together by their religious zeal, which aims to achieve greater religiosity and self-improvement. Even more, they act fervently to bring about changes in societal conditions through the services they deliver, at no cost, in mosques and faith-based associations. This has given rise to the phenomenon of 'Social Islam.'

Social Islam in Egypt, for example, is defined by scholars of Islamism, such as Dyaa' Rashwan, as a 'general trend in Egyptian society, especially among most segments in the middle class and some segments in the upper class, as well as the top segments of the lower class, that attempts to perceive religiosity in a worshipful sense and from a behavioural and phenotypic perspective.'[22] Rashwan also emphasises that this phenomenon of Social Islam has been coupled with other factors. The interplay of those factors has led to the growth of religiosity across society, which is now permeating into new social classes, brackets and categories, particularly the top rungs. This had been spearheaded by the so-called 'Neo Islamic Preachers.' Rashwan indicates that this growing societal religiosity has not necessarily been related to the overall move for increased political support toward politicised Islamic movements; neither does it reflect its popularity in the society. Moreover, social Islamists are not necessarily interested in politics; neither do they unavoidably back the most notable political Islamic groups in Egypt, namely the Muslim Brotherhood. The relationship between social Islamists and the political process is mostly similar to the relationship maintained by most Egyptians and politics; they tend to avoid or refrain from engaging in any political activities, actions and/or practices, including joining political parties, running for public elections, casting their ballots, and so on.

Saba Mahmoud concurs with the hypothesis offered by Rashwan, in his attempt to explain and elaborate on the phenomenon of Muslim female preachers, from a societal perspective. Saba concludes in her research that women preachers are not politically-orientated, but rather are morally-driven and religiously-sensitive. In her book *Activism of Women Preachers in Mosques*, Saba describes this phenomenon as a movement, classifying the increased presence of women in mosques as unparalleled and that which merits reflection. It is the first time in the history of Egypt that women have organised public gatherings in mosques to study and deliberate on Islamic tenets and doctrines; thus changing the masculine character of mosques and the art of Islamic education. It is worth noting that these issues, which used to be monopolised by the clergy, are now discussed by women in mosque-based classes, and in an open fashion. What is more, women are now able to raise questions regarding the finest details of their everyday life, in pursuit of Islamic piety.

Women Preachers and Media: A Relationship Deferred

The term 'Islamic Call' is known as 'the process of informing people about Islam, and sharing with them Islamic teachings and their applications in real life.'[23] In addition, the Islamic Call is also defined as the 'process of communicating to the public the teaching of Islam, in all ages and places, and inviting them to revert to Islam by all means.'[24] Abdel Aziz explains the mission of the Islamic Preachers as one that concerns itself with communicating to the people the teaching of Islam, while guiding and leading them through the way taken by God's prophets and messengers. Preaching is therefore about providing the congregation of Muslims with insight into the matters of their religion, while urging them to engage in good deeds.[25]

In recent years, the term 'Neo Preachers' has gained more popularity, describing the new group of young preachers who conduct preaching in un-traditional ways. Wael Latif describes 'Neo-Preachers' as those individuals who completed their education outside official religious institutions such as Al-Azhar, and who maintain a successful professional career, aside from being preachers. According to Latif, these preachers are individuals who concern themselves with the delivery of simple speeches that establish a connection between religion and life, religion and social problems, and so on. For the most part, this pool of neo-preachers includes young men and women who belong to higher social strata. It is worth noting that this definition encompasses both men and women alike. While the new male preachers wear modern and fashionable clothing, female preachers are expected to comply with the traditional Islamic outfit or dress code that covers the whole body from head to foot, and which shows the face only. Nevertheless, some women preachers opt to not uncover their faces either.[26]

The definition of both 'preaching' and 'preachers', involves the process of 'transferring a message.' Nevertheless, to communicate a message effectively, it is imperative to have an effective mediator, i.e. a strong mode of mass communication, which would differ depending on the age and time factor. Irrespective of the different types of communication, this mediator has been instrumental in introducing the preacher to his or her audience, as well as for helping him or her gain popularity. With the advent of radio broadcasting in most Arab countries, the radio became the most prominent and significant mediator or mode of communication. Nevertheless, radio continued to be a state-owned mode of communication that only transmits or transfers the government vision and insight, through the pool of preachers who are widely recognised by the government. It was only after a few years that the markets opened their doors to cassette tapes. This was a good omen for the opposition movements, as it offered a venue for numerous religious voices.

The process of Islamic preaching has employed the media from the onset of Islam. Oratory played a major role in communicating Islamic teachings and preaching messages for many centuries. For a long time, the preacher was the most talented orator, the one more likely to attract new devotees. Historically, oratory that depended on the charismatic presence of the orator had, generally, been the sole preserve of men. Nevertheless, with modernity and the evolution of publishing techniques and methods, newspapers and magazines became a prominent mode of communication for preachers, to communicate with, and reach out to their readers. However, needless to say, this type of communication, because of its literary nature, remained relatively limited to an educated audience. Newspapers served as the major pulpit for keynote preachers, including Sheikh Gamal Al-Din Al-Afghany and Imam Mohamed Abdu, in their *Al-Erwa Al-Wothqa'* Newspaper.[27]

On the other hand, in Egypt for instance, cassette recordings should take credit for the greater popularity that was gained by Sheikh Mohamed Keshk, who depended solely on this mode to communicate with his audience. In as much as the radio did not generate any value-added benefits to women Islamists as a potential forum or platform for communication, neither did cassette recordings bolster or contribute significantly to their presence in terms of the act of Islamic preaching. In Saudi Arabia, cassette recordings played a prominent role in terms of giving rise to a number of preachers in the early 1980s and 1990s. This was evident in the fact that both Sheikh Safer El-Hawaly and Sheikh Salman Bin Fahd Al-Ouda were able to engrave their names upon the world of preaching in the Kingdom of Saudi Arabia.[28]

The 1970s and 1980s had witnessed what one could describe as the first 'TV star preacher', in the form of Sheikh Mohamed Metwali Sha'rawi, a populist preacher whose religious shows swept through Egypt, Saudi Arabia and other Arabic countries. He was first hosted as a guest on a weekly talk show, before he initiated his own weekly televised programme, which was initially bought by local TV stations before the age of trans-border transmission. However, television had not provided female Islamic activists with any comparative advantage or assets for expanding their outreach and mass communication potentials, with the exception of a handful of female specialists who had been affiliated to Al-Azhar, and who were hosted as keynote guests on social and religious televised programmes.

With the more recent leaps in modern media and technology, satellite and cable channels have played an instrumental role in the emergence of preachers. The new satellite era, from as early as the 1990s, has raised the level of recognition, popularity and influence of these preachers, providing them with an unprecedented plat-form. The mushrooming of satellite channels, including religious ones as the chapters of this book demonstrate, has indeed brought about a completely new landscape for preaching, with sophistica-tion, actors, vested interests and outreach, that has changed the face of traditional practices in this field, perhaps forever. The criti-cal issue that this chapter attempts to tackle is to locate Islamist women activists and preachers within this new religious broadcast-ing, and study their role and influence.

The faith-based religious channels tend to serve a dual purpose: attracting a larger base audience and generating greater revenue. Initially it was realised by the owners of these channels that intro-ducing female preachers on screen would not help them to achieve this two-fold purpose. Consequently, the utilisation of satellite chan-nels by women preachers became restricted or restrained by these limitations, as well as others. Some of the limitations are created by the female Islamist activists themselves, while other limitations are more substantive and are imposed by the nature of the 'religious broadcasting industry', and its profit-making orientation, in addition to the cultural reality and rigid religious interpretations.

Despite what has been achieved by the satellite channels in terms of their overwhelming outreach and mass communication, the Internet has presented quite distinctive potentials as a well-devel-oped, effective mode of communication. Early on, and ahead of many other political forces, the religious movements and various splinter groups became more cognisant of the value and utility of the Internet as an effective and widely used mode of communica-tion across borders. Dyaa' Rashwan underscores the fact that the Islamic Group (*Al-Jamaah Al-Islamiah*) was the only organisation, and a hardliner at that, who owned a website in the early 1990s.[29]

Notably, the fewer the number of opportunities for increased outreach made available to the more extreme religious movements, whether these belong to the Shiite or Sunni sects, the more likely they have been to recourse to online sources of communication. This, for example, caused a delay in the emergence of websites belonging to the more moderate Islamic groups, including the Muslim Brotherhood in Egypt, whose website was not launched until 2003, which was then followed by the website of the Moder-ate Islamic Party.[30]

Later additional Islamic websites poured forth, and presently there are roughly 13,000 Islamic websites. Islam is put forth on those websites, as reflecting endless plurality and excessive differentiation with all its diversities and sects, including Sunnis versus Shiites, Hanafy versus the Shafey ideologies, and so on. On the same note, this tremendous number of Islamic websites is very minimal when compared to the sheer number of websites in general, which is estimated to be in the billions.[31]

Male preachers and other interest groups recognised the importance and utility of the Internet for promoting their popularity while communicating their messages to the Arab world and beyond. They have been attempting to target the audience that can handle and respond to the new technology.

In Egypt, nearly one fifth of the population (21 per cent) were reported to have used the Internet on a regular basis in 2009. At the same time, radio and TV channels undertook the task of communicating the teachings of Islam to nearly 44 per cent of the illiterate population.[32] By establishing a website, male preachers would be able to take their first steps toward communicating with their audience, particularly young people. It can be safely noted that using the Internet and building a website are among the key landmarks of the current stage of Islamic outreach and preaching. In addition, these websites have the potential to be expanded over time, and can interface with other websites.

Contrary to what might have been expected, most female preachers have not used the Internet in a manner comparable to how the Internet has been handled by their male counterparts. The Internet seemed to be compatible with the social circumstances of women, as well as with cultural legacies at the societal level, in a manner that could potentially allow female preachers to communicate with, and respond to, their devotees at their preferred whereabouts. Nevertheless, female preachers acknowledge the fact that the Internet has been underutilised in support of their purposes.

Engineer Suzan, an active female preacher in Cairo, states that the Internet requires effort and time that they cannot possibly afford to give at the current stage. She also demonstrated concurrence with the notion that female preachers are less likely to utilise more modern technology, particularly the Internet. Suzan adds that male preachers are less encumbered in comparison to female preachers, who have other add-on burdens, including household chores and other family commitments. Men are not expected to assume the same level of responsibility, and therefore have more luxury time, and put in less effort. As Suzan states, the single-sided onuses or responsibilities for family and household management on a day-to-day basis, lessens the access of female preachers to the Internet and modern technology that could benefit their mission.

This adds a new dimension to the interpretation of the varying levels and scales of popularity between male and female preachers. Further, female preachers who recognise and appreciate their reproductive role tend to pride themselves on their earnest commitment towards that role. In addition, part of their mission is to enhance the role of the Muslim family in society, and therefore this earnest commitment toward women's reproductive roles transcends the privacy of families, especially when it stands as a symbol of regard and respect for the Muslim community.

Nevertheless, the fact that the Internet is yet to be better utilised by female preachers does not mean that they have been completely absent from this arena. In fact, the frequent or less frequent appearance of female preachers on the Internet, and other means of mass communication, depends on the region where they operate and varies significantly from one Arab country to another. Apparently Egyptian female preachers are the least active in this arena compared with other women preachers in the Gulf area, especially those from Saudi Arabia.

In a research study examining the content areas of female-led Islamic websites, entitled, 'Hypothetical Space of Women: Content Areas of Islamic Materials', Iqbal Al-Gharby attempts to analyse the content areas of twenty female-led Islamic websites, using an analytical approach to examine the media content put forward by those websites. In addition, she also sets out to examine the *fatwas* (religious opinions) and feedback comments, as well as frequently asked questions sent by web browsers. She also tried to examine the number of female visitors per individual component for each website. As demonstrated by the research study, the identity of Islamic women is now built in an international environment that has undergone a series of crises, coupled with profound anti-Westernisation feelings.

Further, many of these websites are dominated by the views of narcissistic introverts that are seen to characterise the identity of Muslim women, and place them in a challenging and competing position with non-Muslim women. These websites tend to create a contentious relationship between the private identity and the universal character, and between what is native versus what is local. These websites portray women in their stereotypical roles, as wives and mothers, who are traditionally expected to rear their children using upright Islamic methods. Many of the female-led Islamic websites announce their allegiance to the global Islamic nation. In an attempt to go beyond the barriers of language, and in recognition of the poor Arabic language skills amongst second and third generations of immigrant families, these websites do not hesitate to provide translated versions of their content materials in targeted languages which include French, German, English and Spanish.

One common feature of these websites, whether they are male or female-led, is that they tend to address and reach out to individuals, with an emphasis on enhancing inward faith and belief. Remarkably, the websites that are run and managed by male preachers tend to use gracious language, and avoid the language of intimidation, threat and menace. On the contrary, the language of menace, the intimidation of hell and hellfire, and the repercussions of following one's whims and caprice is more explicit and direct in female-led and orientated websites that concern themselves with preaching the teachings of Islam.

The above overview of the means of mass communication utilised by Islamic preachers and activists helps us to develop a common understanding and a shared recognition of the current scene. Such a scene is characterised by the modest presence of female preachers, despite all their dedication and efforts, as opposed to the increased intensity of the presence of male preachers, across the various media of communication.

This massive variation or disparity between the media presence of male and female preachers invites further discussion and interpretation so as to understand the interrelated processes and factors that keep women lagging behind in a field that seems to allow them great space for operation and advancement. The following parts of this chapter engage in this discussion.

Limitations of Culture and Tradition

Generally speaking, the slow emergence of women on the Arab media scene is closely related to the cultural legacies that continue to have an adverse impact, particularly on the position of women in society, while identifying their expected roles and behaviours in each community.

The level of participation and representation of Arab women in public life, by and large, is still very minimal across all arenas. In 2010, the representation of Arab women in parliamentary structures accounted for 10.5 per cent only,[33] thus ranking the lowest globally. The engagement of women in economic business activities represents 29 per cent only; again the lowest globally. Further, women's economic and political participation is relatively limited. Women's engagement in the decision-making process at the national level is almost nonexistent, whether in Egypt, or in the rest of the Arab world. Although women are present intensively in the media, in Egypt this presence did not positively impact upon women. Discrimination against women persists, both implicitly and explicitly, in the language, directions, and production of televised programmes. On the religious level, women lack full access to decision-making positions in all faith-based and religious institutions.

This weak presence of female preachers in audio-visual and print media, coupled with the lack of representative groups of women in the media, including female activists, lawyers and engineers, reflects and adds to the problem. Women are almost absent, and are scarcely hosted on talk shows to share their political insight and opinions. However, women are hosted as frequent guests on televised programmes that are concerned with parenting, fashion, and make-up.

No wonder that the presence of female preachers in the media is relatively poor and awkward in a cultural setting that perpetuates the reproductive roles of women, and emphasises traditional gender stereotypes that represent the dominant culture. This uncoordinated presence of women in the media is a sentient reflection of discriminatory conditions against women in the community. On the same note, the Arab and perhaps the international community is ruled by a male-dominated and patriarchal ideology on all levels, not just in the religious field. In this masculine context, the patriarchal resources and references have been the most powerful and have caused the most impact in Islamic history. The prophets are all male, as are the companions of the Prophet, the religious jurists and the relaters, and even the religious interpretations are generated by men. Accordingly, all seems consistent with the various historic episodes and incidents, as well as with the religious and cultural parameters that instruct community members to visit male preachers to receive religious knowledge and information. In this context, visiting female preachers is seen as an option for women only, and with regard to family and women's matters only. In other words, their roles as perceived by society are merely supplemental to the core roles assumed by male preachers, who are in a position to communicate with the entire community of both men and women.

Woman's Voice as a Religious Obstacle

The presence of women in the media, particularly in the audio-visual media, is clearly related to certain strict religious interpretations concerning a woman's 'audio' and 'visual' appearance. Concerning a woman's voice, there is a controversial religious view that sees the 'voice of women as a private part', which makes it *haram* (forbidden) to be heard by a male stranger (i.e. aside from her husband, son, brother and uncles). A woman's voice, therefore, should not be exposed, exactly like the other parts of her body. While this view is not the predominant religious understanding of the matter, its impact on the visibility of women in the Islamic sphere cannot be discounted.

A woman's 'visual' appearance, particularly on TV screens, is even more controversial in many religious interpretations. Different religious channels have varying rules in this respect, which apply to hostesses or guests of their programmes and talk shows. Nabil Hammad, the former head of the Iqra' Channel, one of the most renowned Islamic channels in the Arab region, said:

We have taken many initiatives to ensure women's access to the screen, thus contradicting various trends in the Arab World. We had encountered two major trends in this issue. The first trend was that of hardliner Islamists, who forbid women's appearance on the television. The second trend was that of the entertainment group, which demeans, and degrades women; turning her into a cheap commodity.

He adds:

We allowed Muslim women to speak out and voice their opinion. This is how the Prophet Mohammed, God's prayers be upon him, approached women, when he allowed them space to express themselves.' During the days of Prophet Mohammed, women's engagement was both audio and visual. He also said, 'We have failed to avoid a few caveats. For example, some technicians have zoomed in onto the face of the female anchors or programme hostesses.[34]

Conversely, the Al-Majd Channel does not condone the appearance of women on screen, rather they only allow women's voices to be heard. By doing this, they tend to adopt the more hard-line direction, which necessitates the non-appearance of women's faces.

From this standpoint, and to avoid any act against Islamic teachings, most of the female preachers prefer to avoid appearing in the media, with the exception of a few female preachers who embrace a different view. Some Islamic female preachers who used to present televised programmes were exposed to severe attacks by well-known Sheikhs, thus leading them to succumb to or be convinced that they should avoid any appearance on screen. Some of those female preachers opted to avoid any act that might be at variance with lawful opinions, or that might be termed as *haram*: inadmissible and abhorrent. One preacher I interviewed argued that the appearance of female preachers in the media is denied from the religious perspective. Many female preachers and Islamic activists have opted to discontinue their appearance on televised programmes, especially after the *fatwa* issued by Sheikh Abu Ishak Al-Haiwani, that banned the appearance of women on screens (as explained in chapter five).

On the other hand, it was noted that this denial, coupled with the severe criticisms waged against female preachers who appeared on TV screens, was largely linked with an important factor: the relatively young age of many female preachers. Most female preachers who made an appearance on religious channels were in their thirties or forties, although there was one under the age of thirty. This is also evident by the fact that none of the older and more senior female preachers hesitate to appear on official and satellite channels, and have never been exposed to this type of attack or objection, since they have purportedly passed the age of seduction or temptation.

Women's Skills and Training

Another factor that limits female preachers and Arab women in general from attaining more media visibility and reaching audiences relates to skills and technical training. The restrictive cultural and social context, as discussed above, has indeed limited the potentialities and opportunities that can be accessed by women to develop the experience they need, such as presentation skills, and to enhance their position or status as programme anchors, hostesses and guests. Quite to the contrary, the existing culture emphasises the cultivation of 'shyness' and 'timidity' amongst women. This culture highly values women who have 'low voices', and holds in high esteem women who are 'silent.' This culture is not only adopted by the family but also by institutions, and is spurred on by the educational systems and curriculum, and through the media, as well as through the rest of the establishments of socialisation.

In the first place, such interaction with an audience and even participation *within* an audience, involves certain skills that have not been instilled in women from an early age. The restrictions imposed on women limit their opportunities to experience mass media, even in its simplest forms. Nevertheless, there are a few exceptions, which can be found in those more open and less restrictive households that are in a position to provide their girls with quality education. Only in those exceptions can girls escape this perpetuating cycle of being forced to become 'shy and timid.' On the contrary, the fact that men are more open to and can more easily interact with the outside community makes them more readily engaged with this type of mass communication and interaction, including media, sports and so on. In addition, young boys grow up with feelings of self-confidence and trust in their abilities and potentials. The interplay of these factors helps men become more responsive and less timid when they stand in front of a TV camera or a microphone. In return, this restrictive environment where the voice of a woman is perceived to be intensely private, almost intimate, and therefore should not be exposed publicly, haunts women and requires a great deal of effort on their part to free themselves from the ties imposed on them. This cannot be easily afforded to the majority of women.

Female Preachers and Media Outreach

Thus far, there has been little need felt by female preachers to reach out to their audience through the mass media; their reliance is on person-to-person preaching. The presence of female preachers in mosques and faith-based associations has not been linked with any political project, and up to the present, this group of female preachers has not constituted any part of any interest group.

Hypothetically, the current stage of activism concerning female preachers can be described as a stage of 'self-establishment' and capacity building. This stage focuses primarily on fostering a close relationship with mosques and women's groups, whether inside or outside mosques. In addition, this stage witnesses an increase in the number of female preachers, as well as in the number of mosques that are willing to receive these preachers. It is worth noting that not all mosques are designed or structured in a manner that promotes the engagement of female preachers. Mosques need certain structural and architectural adjustments; some are substantive, including allocating space inside the mosques where women can gather. In addition, the circle of activism by female preachers is expanding steadily and consistently across the various rungs of the social ladder. This state of action began consistently among women of the upper and middle classes. However, their circle of action has expanded to reach out to the less advantaged communities and mosques in poorer suburbs. Although this expansion is now happening gradually and progressively, there are no indications or signs of any expansion plan, so to speak, and neither is there any higher-level management structure acting according to a specific vision. Perhaps this issue of the expansion process merits or requires further exhaustive research, as does the course of action of female preachers, given their reluctance to utilise an effective mechanism, such as the media.

On another note, the intense presence of male preachers across the various means of mass communication is largely commended by the media itself. In light of the fact that male preachers are well received by their target audience, they represent an effective or sizeable economic opportunity for the owners of satellite channels. In addition, the fact that those preachers are linked with various interest groups and networks makes it essential for them to capitalise on the media. It is worth noting that, for the most part, many male preachers are well connected with the state-owned faith based and religious institutions, business communities, economic facilities and establishments, and/or politicised Islamic movements.

Although female preachers are not affiliated with one single group and do not operate within a specific institutional structure, there are no indications regarding the extent to which their outreach activities are evolving according to any certain vision. One substantive difference between female and male preachers is that the latter are supported by interest groups—the majority of whom are economically-orientated—that seek to manage and maintain their expanded outreach. The production firms, faith-based publishing houses, and satellite channels, as well as the male preachers themselves, feel satisfied with the large profits they make from selling their books and cassette recordings; something that has not yet been achieved at any level by female preachers.

Lastly, it is important to make a distinction between male and female preachers in terms of their courses of action and attitudes. Thus far, female preachers have been able to mobilise women from both the middle and upper classes to jointly build a social project based on the efforts of women of faith who seek to help others in pursuit of their common goal of building a Muslim community. In addition, female preachers tend to approach the entire family through the main gatekeepers, the wives and mothers. On the other hand, the endeavours of male preachers are more individually-orientated, and tend to develop religious awareness and perception at the individual level.

Even more, faith-based classes delivered by female preachers do not aim only to change the attitudes and directions of their audience, but also tend to reach out to attract the entire family to the mosque. The children of the women attending religious classes at mosques are allocated an area in the mosque. In addition, resourceful women, including those who would like to contribute, volunteer and use their skills, expertise and/or areas of speciality, or who wish to donate their money, are provided with access to various opportunities whereby they can serve their community. In some instances, female preachers have established and allocated a 'compound of resources', which is managed and run effectively.

Besides the act of preaching, female preachers tend to provide and encourage the delivery of benevolent, social outreach activities that are managed at the mosques, faith-based organisations, households of female preachers or their female devotees, and so on. These social activities extend beyond the walls of mosques, and tend to expand vertically and horizontally in the surrounding communities where they exist.

Some indicators of the female preacher's success are the rise of new social spaces in the Egyptian community, the increase in the number of female preachers in mosques, the extension of the areas allocated to females in mosques, the attendance of females from various age groups and the migration of female preachers' activities into poor and rural communities.

The lack of a relationship between female preachers and the media does not reflect their conservatism, but rather the weak presence of female professionals in the media in general. Female preachers have replaced common media tools by building a deep and direct relationship in society with their female audience.

Preaching through direct communication not only allows the preacher to ingrain their influence into the receivers, but also helps them to develop a strong network within various sectors in society, such as in economic, social and religious institutions. The poor relationship of female preachers with the media re-emphasises the deep influence of direct communication, even in our era of global technology.

Different religious streams benefit enormously from the development of the media. In the Arab-Muslim world, pioneers of the religious movements thrive on TV screens and on the world web, announcing a religious revolution supported by modern technology.

While men fully occupy the media's realm, women occasionally appear, though timidly. This is due to the religious limitations, according to conservative streams of thought, that prohibit their exposure and consider it unnecessary. On the other hand, economic groups also consider it unnecessary, seeing as men are a more profitable asset in the world of television and media in general.

Alongside the frequent appearance of male preachers, their female counterparts launched their historic presence in mosques, thus taking the first step in claiming their place in Islamic societies. Although mosques received female preachers, guides, and teachers only in the last few years, females have been accepted in mosques as an audience throughout history.

The expansion of women in mosques could be understood from various perspectives. The first sees that this expansion was a result of the growing religious trend that is supported by the media. Another perspective sees it as a development of the role of female activists in the Islamic political movement. A third perspective, however, explains the expansion as a part of the social Islamic movement. The last perspective, in contrast, is more inclined to explain the expansion as a step towards strengthening the religious presence of females in society and that in the future, females will utilise the media effectively.

Though one of these perspectives may justify women's activism in mosques, it remains that the development of women's activism in mosques throughout the Arab World, predominantly in its urban communities, and less so in its rural ones, is testament to the emergence of an active social movement for women in a religious realm that was interminably closed for them. And yet they were able to powerfully infiltrate it, even without the direct support of the media.

8

RELIGIOUS BROADCASTING
AND THE SECTARIAN DIVIDE IN IRAQ

Rafid Fadhil Ali

In the summer of 2009, the Iraqi Prime Minister Nouri Al-Maliki ordered the government-owned Al-Iraqiya Channel to stop broadcasting the *Azzan al-Zuhur* (the midday prayer call), which had previously been aired in the Shiite version. The decision was justified as an initiative of national reconciliation. The Shiite *Azzan* had been broadcast on the state channel since its establishment in 2003 but Iraqi Sunni have always viewed the state-owned channel as they might regard the state itself: as being dominated by the Shi'a. In the post-war Iraq of 2003, religion had become a divisive factor, whether in the media or elsewhere. The population, which is overwhelmingly Muslim, is divided into Shi'a and Sunni. While sectarian violence is something new to modern Iraq, sectarianism is not. One of the main reasons that people follow religious broadcasting is to observe the dates and times of their worship practices, and this lead to another controversy between Shi'a and Sunni Muslims. Shi'a usually start Ramadan and other Muslim months one day after the Sunnis. The timing of the Shiite *Azzan* is also delayed by a few minutes. These kinds of controversies reflect a deeper political and religious divide and are the driving forces for this chapter,

155

i.e. to focus on two different Iraqi TV channels, one Shi'a and one Sunni, to study religious broadcasting in Iraq.

The *Azzan* story in Iraq started in the late 1980s, when the secular but Sunni-dominated Ba'ath government of the late President Saddam Hussein started to display more religious tendencies, and soon the state channel followed suit and began to broadcast the Sunni *Azzan*. During the Persian Gulf War of 1990–91, Saddam needed to reach out to the wider Muslim world and hence the Iraqi media had to mix its historical pan-Arab nature and phraseology with more Islamic slogans and programmes. At that stage, additional prayers (*azkar*) were introduced as a follow-up to the *Azzan*. In 1994, Saddam Hussein launched what he called the 'Faith Campaign', which included more Islamic courses at schools, restrictions on alcohol consumption in public and increased Islamic broadcasting.[1]

A radio station that specialised in broadcasting the Qur'an was launched in 1992[2] and religious-focused programmes were extended across radio, TV and print journalism. Although this surge of religious media was meant to mobilise wider constituencies to support the regime, it nevertheless remained limited to Sunnis. Only a few Shi'a seemed to have been attracted to the state-controlled, Sunni broadcasting. The religious among the Shi'a followed the Arabic service on the Shiite focused Iranian Radio station. The daily religious lecture, *al-Mohadara al-Diniyah* on Radio of the Islamic Republic of Iran in particular was very popular, especially when it was conducted by Sheikh Ahmad Al-Wa'eli. Shiites also sought religious material on CDs, although this was illegal under Saddam's regime. Needless to say, Shi'as and Sunnis in Iraq did not share the same interests when it came to religious broadcasting.

The Broadcasting Landscape

In the post-war 'new Iraq' of 2003, the rising Shiite control over the state and government had reversed the Sunni–Shi'a balance of power almost completely. Shi'a dominance was increasingly felt in all areas of Iraqi society and politics, including the media. This latter area in particular has rapidly witnessed Shiite-controlled media outlets outnumbering those owned or run by Sunnis, including channels that are specifically engaged in religious broadcasting. There are at least seven Iraqi Shiite satellite channels and many local TV and radio stations broadcasting with different levels of attraction and influence. These are: Al-Furat, Al-Masar, Al-Watan, Biladi, Al-Salam, Afaq and Al-Ahad. On the Sunni side, one can only name two satellite channels that could be seen as religious: the Baghdad network and Al-Rafidain.

In the context of religious broadcasting, it should be noted that non-Iraqi Arab-speaking (religious) channels are extensively followed in Iraq. For example, the Kuwaiti Al-Anwar and the Iranian Al-Kawthar channels are popular among the Iraqi Shi'as. The Saudi Al-Majd and Iqra' networks enjoy a notable audience from the Sunni community. However, for the purposes of this study, we will be specifically looking at both sides of the Iraqi-generated broadcasting output.

Al-Rafidain

Owned by the Association of Muslim Scholars (AMS) in Iraq, Al-Rafidain has been an anti-American and pro-resistance TV channel since its launch on 10 April 2006. The AMS in Iraq is a Sunni Muslim organisation headed by Sheikh Harith al-Dhari. It was established immediately after the invasion of Iraq in an attempt to unify the Sunni clerics in the country, for a leadership bid with all Iraqi Sunnis. The AMS and its leader have rejected and opposed the political process in post-war Iraq.

Al-Rafidain demonstrates its political stance clearly in its mission statement on its website, 'To face the occupation and its helpers who name 9 April the liberation day. And to be a thorn in the eye of everyone who does not respect the feelings of the Iraqi people.'[3] The AMS has always supported the Iraqi resistance, and it is widely believed in Iraq that the AMS and its leader have a strong influence over one of the most prominent resistance groups in Iraq, the Twentieth Revolution Brigades. In late 2006, the Iraqi government accused Harith al-Dhari of supporting terrorist activities, and in 2009, seven resistance groups issued a mandate to al-Dhari to represent them and the offer was accepted.[4]

In 2007, a significant transformation took place within the Sunni community. Sunni tribal leaders from western Iraq and the American army formed an alliance against Al-Qaeda, known as *Sahwat* formations. This became a nationwide movement in the Sunni areas. Consequently, the AMS with its radical anti-American agenda was increasingly excluded from the wider Sunni direction of progress. With the crackdown by the Iraqi government on the AMS and its leader, the latter became even further removed from the prevailing climate in Iraq. The AMS has since been deprived of its network of loyal clerics in the mosques, and thus Al-Rafidain might be one of the few remaining tools of influence the AMS still have.[5]

Al-Rafidain's stated goal is, 'To call for the occupier to leave Iraq and to support the unity of Iraq and urge Iraqis to be united. To reject the occupation and its political and ideological consequences.' It is by no means a wholly religious channel, and it also broadcasts political, social and cultural programmes. Yet its religious appearance and the conservative nature of its content are clear. For example, the female presenters wear the Islamic headscarf and the channel does not broadcast songs or music. Al-Rafidain presents itself principally as an Iraqi news channel, and it states that it is concerned with economic, cultural, scientific and sporting affairs.[6]

Political issues clearly dominate the programmes of Al-Rafidain. News bulletins and political shows outnumber religious ones, with approximately half of the content about politics. There are five or six hours a day of news bulletins and the main news programme is 'Iraq Today', broadcast at 6pm and repeated after midnight. This is one of the programmes that was selected for monitoring in this study. As an Iraqi and news-focused channel, this programme represented the best focal point for studying Al-Rafidain's phraseology, and to understand not only its message, but also the way that it is delivered. The Al-Rafidain office in Iraq was closed in late 2006 following what the channel describes as attacks by the American army and the Iraqi government. This situation continues to affect Al-Rafidain's coverage on Iraq and denies it access to first-hand reporting. Al-Rafidain broadcasts from Cairo, and thus without a presence in the field, the content of the channel has been affected. It has become increasingly dependent upon user-generated content and phone reporting. In addition to the news bulletins, an average of 4–5 hours each day are occupied by political shows. Business and sport bulletins are regular, and occupy two hours of the daily broadcasting.

Despite the dominating presence of political and news programmes, the most popular show on Al-Rafidain falls within its religious broadcasting output. It is the main *fatwa* programme, *Hewar Fee al-Sharia* (Dialogue about Shari'a), presenting scholarly opinion on matters of Islamic law. It is presented by Dr. Abdu Hameed al-Obaidi, and is one of the programmes that has been chosen for monitoring in this project. By monitoring this interactive *Fatwa* show, we were able to study the religious themes, statements and perceptions of one of the most prominent Sunni scholars in Iraq. Dr Al-Obaidi is a well-respected personality among Iraqi Sunnis. His fame and popularity stem from the 1990s, when he presented and appeared on similar *fatwa* shows on official Iraqi TV during the Saddam years. Yet he has not been stained by political affiliations. As al-Obaidi is one of the founders of the Al-Rafidain channel, we were able to take a wider view of the channel's 'policy', and question that premise by analysing his programme.

As mentioned earlier, Al-Rafidain is not a channel completely focused on religion, even though it is owned by an Islamic society. Sheikh Dr. Harith Al-Dhari does not wear the traditional Muslim cleric's robe, and instead always appears in the traditional tribal Arab dress, the *abaya* (loose robe) and *egal* (head covering). Dr Abdel Hameed Al-Obeidi wears modern clothes: a suit and necktie. Unlike most of the Iraqi channels, Al-Rafidain does not broadcast American-sponsored commercials. Although most of those commercials are about supporting the Iraqi forces, the political process, and renouncing violence, Al-Rafidain views them as American propaganda. This has obviously denied Al-Rafidain the substantial revenue that many Iraqi and even pan-Arab channels have had as part of the American influence after the Iraq war.

Al-Furat

The Al-Furat satellite channel was launched in late 2004, as part of the media wing of the Islamic Supreme Council of Iraq (ISCI), one of the most powerful Shiite parties in Iraq. The ISCI was founded in Iran in 1982 during the Iraq-Iran War, as an umbrella group of Iraqi Shiite parties in exile. It was seen as part of Iranian efforts to organise the Iraqi Shiite opposition, as they had been severely suppressed by the Ba'ath government. The coalition was named The Supreme Council for Islamic Revolution in Iraq (SCIRI), and the group had the goal of toppling the late Iraqi president, Saddam Hussein. As was clear by its name, it intended to follow the Iranian pattern of the Islamic revolution. The coalition soon collapsed, leaving the sub-group headed by the late Sayyed Baqir al-Hakeem as the only party carrying the SCIRI name, but this did not mean the end of the SCIRI or its military wing, the Bader Corps, which joined the Iranian armed forces in the war against Iraq.[7] The SCIRI was one of the biggest and best-funded Iraqi opposition groups in exile. It had its own media establishment, which included a newspaper and a certain number of hours of radio and TV broadcasting facilitated by Iran.

After the fall of Saddam Hussein, Baqir Al-Hakeem returned to Iraq, ending a twenty-four year stay in Iran, but was assassinated soon after, and was succeeded by his brother Sayyed Abdul Aziz Al-Hakeem, who died in 2009. Abdul Aziz was succeeded by his son, Sayyed Ammar Al-Hakeem. Currently in his late thirties, Ammar possesses a clear passion for the media, and is believed to be the acting leader of the organisation. Ammar is directly in charge of Al-Furat, and his activities are frequently covered by the channel.

The ISCI has been a part of all of the governments formed after the war in Iraq. It is considered the biggest group in the Shiite parliamentary block, the Unified Iraqi Coalition. The group changed its name from SCIRI to ISCI in 2007, and instructed that its followers recognise the Iraq-based Grand Ayatollah Ali Al-Sistani as the supreme spiritual leader, the *Marja'a al-Taqleed*. In 2005, they won a landslide in the Shiite areas that enabled them to dominate the regional government in southern and central Iraq, including Baghdad. In the central government they are currently represented by the Vice-President Adel Abdel Mahdi, Minister of Finance Bayan Jabur al-Zubaidi (Solagh), and three other ministers. But the popularity of the ISCI has significantly deteriorated. In the regional election of January 2009, it was heavily defeated by the party of Prime

Minister Nouri Al-Maliki, and in the general election of March 2010, they could not secure more than thirty of the 325 seats in the Iraqi parliament.

In the short term, Al-Furat is unlikely to be dramatically affected by the decreasing support for the ISCI. The media output of the other rival Shiite groups still has less influence than Al-Furat. Al-Furat is based in Baghdad, with the channel facility based in the Al-Karrada district. It operates through a network of correspondents in the Shiite areas of Iraq and has offices in other countries around the world, and it is believed that Al-Furat has a back-up operation in Iran, just in case anything disturbs the central broadcasting.[8]

It is interesting to note that at a critical moment in post-war Iraqi history, Al-Furat broadcast an exclusive video of the top Shiite cleric, Ali Al-Sistani (who very rarely appears in front of the cameras), meeting with other clerics and calling for calm.

Al-Furat is a conservative channel; female presenters wear the headscarf (*hijab*) and men are mostly bearded. Although it is not a 100 per cent religion-focused station, Al-Furat is still very representative for the purpose of our project. It has more funding and resources than its peers, and it is also well organised and has higher standards of production. Political issues dominate Al-Furat broadcasting, and news bulletins and current affairs programmes occupy half of the daily broadcasting. The most followed religious show on Al-Furat is *Fiqeh al-Mustafa* (The Jurisprudence of the Prophet Muhammad). It is a *fatwa* programme presented by Sayyed Rasheed Al-Hussaini, who emerged as a TV personality after the war. He wears the traditional Shiite clerical dress: a long black robe and turban. This programme was chosen to be monitored in our study, along with the weekly Friday prayer programme.

As an Iraqi Shi'a-focused channel, Al-Furat competes mainly with other Iraqi Shi'a channels, such as Al-Masar, Beladi, Afaq, Al-Salam and Al-Watan. Al-Furat provides broadcasting of a higher quality—for example, finer audio and visual output than those channels—yet it struggles to outperform the success and influence of the better-funded non-Iraqi Shiite satellite channels such as Al-Kawthar (Iran), Al-Anwar (Kuwait), Al-Zahraa and Ahl el-Beit.

The Programmes

Fiqh Al-Mustafa on Al-Furat

This programme started in 2005, and is a thirty minute question-and-answer style show, occupying a prime-time slot on Al-Furat. It is broadcast five days a week at 7.30pm, and repeated the following afternoon. The presenter is the Shi'a cleric Sayyed Rasheed Al-Husseini, who is not a senior cleric. He appears wearing the traditional Shi'a clerical dress; black turbans are worn by those Shi'a clerics who are descended from the Prophet Mohammed, and those who are not, wear white turbans. Members of these groups are called Sayyed or Sheikh respectively. This is one of the differences between Shi'a and Sunni Islam. While almost every Sunni cleric could be called Sheikh, Shi'a categorise their clerics into two groups: the Sheikhs and the Sayyeds.

The opening segment of the programme is a Shi'a song, and the same or similar songs are played in the commercial break. Shi'a religious songs are not accompanied by music, and the lyrics always praise the Prophet Mohammed, the Shi'a Imams and the saints. Al-Husseini does not issue *fatwas* (religious rules) himself. He instead presents the *fatwas* of the supreme Shi'a spiritual leaders (*Maraji al-Taqleed*),[9] of whom there are many in the Shi'a world, but Al-Husseini gets his answers from the works and rules of only three of them: Grand Ayatollah Abul Qassim Al-Kho'i (who died in 1992), Grand Ayatollah Mohammed Baqir Al-Sadr (who was assassinated in 1999) and the present Grand Ayatollah, Ali Al-Sistani. Al-Husseini justifies his use of these three as his authorities as they are the most-followed clerics in his main target area: Iraq and the Gulf.

Telephone calls and text messages are the main method of interaction between al-Husseini and his audience, yet phone calls or texts are rarely taken or read out on air. The usual format is that the presenter announces the content of the calls and messages he received earlier—this pattern appeared in 100 per cent of the samples we chose for our study. According to Al-Husseini, he receives between 400 and 500 phone calls and text messages a day, and a team of his students help categorise the content of the communications and classify them. The calls come from the Shi'a audience in

Iraq, throughout the region, and around the world. Some non-Iraqi Sunnis contact the programme too, but Iraqi Sunnis have never directed any questions.[10] During the escalating of the Sunni-Shi'a violence in Iraq, some unknown Sunnis threatened that they would kill the presenter.[11]

Rashid Al-Husseini does not promote violence by any means. When he has received questions concerning his lack of support for *jihad* against the Americans in Iraq, he has answered, 'We should resist and launch *jihad* against the inner occupier. Our culture is occupied by Satan and selfishness. We have to refine the human being and support him against favouritism and love of power and positions.' In our sample, the word *jihad* is used only once and the content was denying that any one but the Disappeared Imam, the twelfth Shi'a Imam Mohammed Al-Mahdi, is authorised to call for *jihad*. Al-Husseini clarified, in an interview with this writer, that the senior Shi'a clerics of our time also have a similar right, but only for the defensive *jihad*, when Muslims are attacked, and under specific circumstances. He indicated that Islam is a non-violent faith.[12]

Concerning Shi'a-Sunni sectarian violence, our sample highlighted no examples. Yet Al-Husseini promoted the concepts of co-existence and fraternal spirit among Muslims. During the height of the sectarian killings in Iraq, Rashid Al-Husseini said very little about what was happening on the streets. His strategy was to stay calm and avoid sectarian messages. He also took what he called an indirect approach to resisting the sectarian violence, and was strict in his refusal to justify any act of killing.[13]

Al-Husseini sees his first priority is to fight ignorance, which he believes to be the origin of the problems. Al-Husseini rejects any calls for a religious state in Iraq as he believes that this was not successful in Iran and he supports the policies and approach of Grand Ayatollah Sistani in this context. He does not want religion and politics to be mixed, yet he calls for a civil state that respects Islam, and approved of the Iraqi constitution's way of dealing with this issue.[14]

Rashid Al-Husseini's life story is representative of a generation of Shi'a clerics and activists' families who suffered the crackdown by Saddam Hussein's government in the late 1970s. His father, a Shi'a cleric, was arrested in 1980 and was not heard from again.

The family fled to Iran, where Al-Husseini enrolled in the Shi'a University (*Hawza*) in the city of Qum.[15] He returned to Iraq after the fall of Saddam Hussein in 2003, and currently teaches junior students in the *Hawza* of Najaf. At the same time he is an occasional student in the classes of two senior Ayatollahs, Mohammed Saeed Al-Hakeem and Ishaq Al-Fayadh.[16]

'Friday Prayer' on Al-Furat

'Friday Prayer' is broadcast every Friday evening, and is usually between twenty-five and forty minutes long. It shows sections of different Friday prayers in mosques in Baghdad and around Iraq; the speeches are recorded from the prayers on the same afternoon as the broadcast. All of the mosques are Shi'a mosques and all of the speakers are Shi'a.

Politics dominates the content of the speeches, and each of the seven episodes we monitored included political messages. Approximately 66 per cent of the content of the speeches was political in nature. Shi'a Friday Imams also talk about spiritual, ethical and historical issues, but the programme highlights the parts where the preaching concerns political and current affairs. The programme does not show the whole prayer of one mosque, but rather sections of the prayers in different mosques. Usually the prayers featured clear statements about current political and security issues in Iraq, and how the speaker perceived and reacted to them, with instructions for his audience on how they should act. The nature and content of these political messages has been always in line with the policies of the ISCI. They have been mostly supportive of the Shi'a-led government and promoted anti Ba'athist propaganda, and have called on people to become involved in the political system in post-Saddam Iraq. The message is usually non-confrontational when it comes to the relationship with the Americans; in that regard it always supported the political approach of the ISCI and the Iraqi government. Mohammed al-Haydari and Jalal Al-Deen Al-Sagheer, MPs from the ISCI, appeared extensively on the show. In addition to the political messages, the two men talked about relations between the Shi'a and the Sunni in Iraq. On the anniversary of the birth of the Prophet Mohammed, Al-Haydari stated:

Mohammed is the prophet of Allah. All Muslims agree on that. This is the time of his birth; maybe this is an opportunity for Muslims all around the world to be united after the attempts to divide them. The troubles (*Fitna*) in Iraq are between the Shi'a and the Sunni but we always stress that unity among Muslims is necessary because we have the same faith, prophet, Qu'ran and Kaaba. At least in Iraq there had been no real problems between the Muslim sects until the former regime and the Takfiris (Sunni extremists) incited this conflict. But Allah saved us from the *Fitna*. We hope that there will be cooperation between the Shi'a and Sunni in the mixed neighbourhoods to fight the *Fitna*.

Al-Haydari went on to attack the Ba'ath party, and blamed it for the current troubles in Iraq.[17]

Such messages might appear friendly and positive, yet their desired effect might be prejudiced. This is because the programme does not broadcast Sunni speeches, and the continuous criticism of the Ba'ath party means that many Sunni understand from experience that it is opposing large sectors of their community. The content of al-Haydari's speeches is always present in other Friday Prayer speeches. Shi'a occasions are always observed and referred to in the speeches, and no similar treatment is given to the Sunni religious calendar. However, as this is a Shi'a programme, one would expect at most only occasional references to the parallel Sunni observances.

Hewar Fee al-Sharia *on the Al-Rafidain Channel (Sunni)*

This programme was first broadcast in 2006, the same year as the Al-Rafidain Channel went live. It is presented by Omar Khalil, and the only guest is the ever-present Dr. Abdul Hameed Al-Obeidi. The programme is broadcast live every Wednesday from 7.30 to 9 pm, and is repeated twice the next day. Every episode focuses on one single topic. Each topic is announced in advance and the audience is invited to put forth their questions via phone calls, text messages and e-mails.

Abdul Hameed Al-Obeidi is an Islamic Studies professor. He wears modern clothes, a neck tie and is clean shaven. He stated in an interview with this writer that the Prophet Mohammed instructed people not to wear the now well-known dress that differentiates clerics from other people.[18] Al-Obeidi sees himself more as a Professor than a cleric. Throughout his career he has acquired wide experience and knowledge of the different Muslim sects (*Mathahib*). He uses different sources in his *fatwas* and he typically points out the source of his *fatwa* or its justification. This includes references to the grand clerics in Sunni Islam theology, particularly the four founders of the Sunni *Mathahib*, Malik Abu Hanifa, Al-Shafa'i and Ibn Hanbal, and the prominent clerics among their followers. Al-Obeidi indicated to this writer that the real number of Muslim *Mathahib* is far greater; there are dozens, and each of them should be considered and respected, but not followed unconditionally.[19]

Al-Obeidi was born in 1941 in the city of Heet in the Al-Anbar province in the west of Iraq, the heartland of the Sunni community. In addition to his secular education, Al-Obeidi pursued theological studies in the mosques of his hometown of Heet.

He finished his Bachelor's and Master's degrees in Islamic Law and Studies from the University of Baghdad, and then worked as a teacher in high schools. In 1980, he became a tutor and then a Professor of Islamic Studies at the University of Baghdad. Between 2000 and 2005 he was the Dean of the Faculty of Islamic Law at the University of Al-Ahkaf in Hadramout in Yemen.

He enrolled at Al-Azhar University in Egypt in the late 1970s, but the Iran-Iraq War forced him to interrupt his study and return to Iraq. After the war ended, he re-enrolled at Al-Azhar in 1990. The Iraqi invasion of Kuwait, however, meant that Al-Obeidi had to return to Baghdad again, thus missing his second and last opportunity to get a degree from Al-Azhar.[20]

On the subject of relations with the Shi'a, Al-Obeidi always stresses that Shi'a Islam is a respected strand of Islam. He studied Shi'a beliefs (*fiqh*) when he specialised in comparative theology. Most of Al-Obeidi's audience and callers are Sunni, but on the rare occasions when Shi'a call, he strengthens his answers to their questions with statements and teaching from their heritage and belief.

In the 1990s, Al-Obeidi tried to get a PhD from Baghdad University. According to him, PhD students in theology in those days needed the approval of Izzat Al-Doori, Saddam's deputy. Because Al-Obeidi recognised the validity of Shi'a opinions and statements in his preaching, Al-Douri—an orthodox Sunni Muslim—kept refusing his enrolment. Yet Al-Obeidi blames Al-Doori's entourage for this exclusion, not the former Vice-President himself.

Al-Obeidi says that he regards Shi'a religious rulings as equal to all other Muslim *Mathahib*. In an interview with this writer, he indicated that some of the statements in Shi'a books and references are inaccurate, and need to be reviewed and corrected. According to Al-Obeidi, such statements would not have been approved by Ja'far Al-Sadiq, the sixth among the twelve Shi'a Imams, and the man who laid the foundation for Shi'a theology.[21] In his programme, Al-Obeidi only refers to Shi'a rulings and opinions on the rare occasion that he is asked about them directly by a Shi'a caller. The main audience for the programme are Sunni Iraqis in Iraq and the diaspora. Yet there are a considerable number of non-Iraqi Arabs who call the programme and ask Al-Obeidi questions.

With regard to Al-Obeidi's views on violence, he supports *jihad* in Iraq against the foreign forces. He classifies that as a justifiable 'Defensive *Jihad*' (*jihad al-Dafa'a*) since Iraq was invaded by foreign armies. However, he does not support the Al-Qaeda's ideology of killing and denying the faith of other Muslims, whether in Iraq or around the Muslim world.

Summary

Internal Iraqi broadcasting represents a golden opportunity for full-time, fully-fledged religious channels. There is as yet no twenty-four hour, seven days a week Iraqi satellite channel with a completely religious focus.

The programmes monitored in this study do not stress Shi'a–Sunni differences and have been cautious not to incite further sectarian violence. At the same time both parties clearly show every sign of sectarian affiliation in their products. Neither Al-Furat nor Al-Rafidain tend to engage in debate between Shi'a and Sunni over the religious beliefs of the groups they belong to. There was virtually no indication that either side was seeking to gain an audience among the other. There are no Sunni-focused programmes on the Shi'a-owned channels, nor are there ever Shi'a-focused programmes on Sunni networks. And yet, while the numbers of Shi'a callers on Sunni shows are relatively few and vice-versa, members of the rival sect calling in on both networks are treated with the utmost—if less than enthusiastic—respect, and are answered accordingly.

Both networks hold as modern an image and approach as can be consistent with their somewhat conservative religious stance, with the most prominent presenters usually dressed in modest but stylish, modern clothes. Technology is embraced as a matter of course, and while phone calls and text messages are the main means of interaction for both channels, so far neither network has ventured into exploiting the flourishing social networking media, for example Facebook or Twitter. Such media, and the vacuum in full-time, round-the-clock religious broadcasting in Iraq, present more golden opportunities for Iraqi-generated Shi'a and Sunni channels alike.

Other Shi'a Satellite Channels

Among the most watched Shi'a religious channels across the Middle East is the Iraqi Ahl Al-Beit which broadcasts from Karbala in Iraq. It is also owned by the followers of Al-Shirazi, a senior Shi'a cleric, and broadcasts the usual Shi'a rituals, speeches and other activities. Another Iraqi channel Al-Ma'arif, broadcasts the speeches and lectures of clerics close to Grand Ayatollah Ali-al-Sistani, the most senior Shi'a cleric in Iraq.

As explained before, many non-Iraqi Shi'a religious channels have a large audience in Iraq. Al-Anwar 1 and 2 are channels based in Kuwait, founded in 2004, and the good quality of the production suggests that the channels are well funded. They extensively broadcast the activities of the Shi'a clerics who follow the late Ayatollah Mohammed al-Shirazi (who was born in Karbala in 1962 and died in 2008 in Iran). The most prominent preacher on Al-Anwar is Sheikh Abdul Hameel Al-Muhajir, and the popular Shi'a religious singer, Bassim-Al-Karbala'e, also known as *Radood*, is featured regularly. Other Shi'a broadcasters with high viewing figures throughout the Middle East as well as in Iraq include: Channel 14, based in Bahrain, which concentrates more on the Shi'a morning rituals and does not have many talk shows or educational programmes; and the Al-Awhad channel, which is based in Kuwait, is headed by Abdullah Al-Hairi Al-Ahkaki, the leader of the Awhadi

Shi'a sect. Two popular Shi'a channels broadcast from Lebanon are the Al-Zahraa and Al-Thaqalain channels.

The non-Iraqi satellite channel chosen for examination in this study, however, is the Al-Kawthar station based in Iran and the oldest of the Shi'a religious channels. It is also the most well-funded.

Al-Kawthar

Al-Kawthar is a state-owned Iranian channel that broadcasts in Arabic. The channel started in 1980 under the name Sahar. About 25 per cent of its programming is religious—speeches, lecturers, talk shows, and so on, and 40 per cent are social programmes with a religious content or message, with another 25 per cent concentrating on news and politics. The programme chosen for monitoring and analysis was *Motarahat Fee al-Aqeeda* ('Debates in Belief').

Motarahat Fee al-Aqeeda (*'Debates in Belief'*) on Al-Kawthar

This programme is presented by Dr. Salim Jari, and is a platform for the prominent Shi'a cleric Kamal Al-Haydari. Al-Haydari is the sole guest of the show and appears in every episode. The role of the presenter is to direct questions to Al-Haydari and help in receiving telephone calls from the viewers. The programme discusses theological issues and each episode has a topic. During the period monitored, the issues of *imama* (leadership) dominated the topics, with Al-Haydari talking about various aspects of the concept of *imama* in Shi'ism. Notably, *imama* was the main disagreement that led to the split of Islam into Shi'a and Sunni.[22]

Sayyed Kamal Al-Haydari was born in the Shi'a holy city of Karbala in Iraq in 1956. He enrolled in the *Hawza* there and then moved to the bigger and more prestigious *Hawza* of Najaf. He attended the lessons of the prominent Shi'a clerics at that time: Ayatollah al-Kho'e, Ayatollah Mohammed Baqir Al-Sadr and Ayatollah Ali Al-Ghor'we. In the late 1970s, Al-Haydari fled to Kuwait to escape the government crackdown on Shi'a Islamists. He then went to Iran where he settled in the holy city of Qum. He finished his theological education there, and then became an Ayatollah. Al-Haydari is better known as a preacher than as a senior cleric or *Marji*, and is currently a teacher in the *Hawza* of Qum.

Al-Haydari's way of treating issues is to analyse them in light of Qur'an and Shi'a references. Although the title of the programme *Motarahat Fee al-Aqeeda* can be translated as 'Debates in Belief', it is by no means an argument between two sides. Al-Haydari never has a co-interviewee from another religion or another branch of Islam, although he sometimes discusses Shi'a belief on specific issues as contrasted with Sunni opinion. For example, when asked a direct question about why there are Shi'a and Sunni Muslims and not one single Muslim course of belief he simply answered: 'They [Sunni] chose to follow the school of thought of the Sahaba, the contemporaries of the Prophet Mohammed, while Allah chose for us to follow the school of thought of the Ahl Al-Beit, Mohammed's close family members.'[23]

Al-Haydari does not examine the difference in belief between Muslims and other religions (i.e. Christianity, Judaism, Buddhism and Hinduism). When he talks about the stories and status of the Prophets, he explains what they are from the Shi'a Muslim perspective. No comparison between Muslim and non-Muslim belief appeared in this sample. On the other hand, comparisons between Shi'a and Sunni beliefs were made in half of the episodes monitored. The overall tendency of the programme is to display and explain Shi'a beliefs in light of Muslim texts and concepts, and the comparisons mentioned came about when Al-Haydari answered questions from the viewers, not in the main body of his talks.

Al-Haydari's target constituency is Shi'a Muslims. When he talks about a Muslim consensus, for example, he means consensus among specifically Shi'a Muslims. One episode was dedicated to explaining the signs and conditions of the return of *al-Imam al-Mahdi* (The Shi'a Messiah). During this episode a caller from the audience, apparently a Sunni viewer, tried to raise questions about the different versions of the story of the *Mahdi* in both faiths. Al-Haydari said to this viewer:

My talk is with those who believe in the twelfth Imam of the Shi'a and we now live in the age of his disappearance. If the viewer believes with me in those origins let him listen to me carefully, if not then he could go to another programme on another channel and watch. I am talking now with hundreds of millions of the followers of the school of thought of Ahl al-Beit who believe that the twelfth Imam exists and was born on a certain date.[24]

Conclusion

Shi'a parties and factions have been investing extensively in the media market. This has resulted in the increasing number of satellite channels and other media organisations which have expanded the presence and influence of the Shi'a as a religious group, not only in the Middle East, but also throughout the diaspora. There have been a number of political factors that have helped the Shi'a to establish their media outlets in the Middle East, the most important of these being the fall of Saddam Hussein's ardently Sunni regime in Iraq and the subsequent rise to power of the Shi'a parties in that country, as well as the tolerant policies of the governments of Kuwait and Bahrain toward the Shi'a in those countries. Although many of the approaches and policies may differ significantly among the various Shi'a channels, they are all united in representing the Shi'a as a distinct group.

Reiterating an earlier observation, neither Sunni nor Shi'a broadcasters in Iraq shy away from using modern media and presentation to reach their distinctly separate audiences, although neither has availed themselves of the yet untapped opportunities in the ever-expanding phenomenon of social networking media. Neither has expanded on an even more simple level, with opportunities still open for a full-time, completely religion-focused broadcast channel, or channels transmitting their sectarian but, thus far, not mutually antagonistic Shi'a or Sunni messages twenty-four hours a day, seven days a week. Perhaps if Iraqi-produced TV networks take up these opportunities and others, broadcasting influences from outside Iraq's borders—particularly that of Iran's more conservative, if not revolutionary, Shi'a channel Al-Kawthar—will be weakened, creating ever more evolutionary opportunities, particularly for Iraqi-produced Shi'a media.

9

WALKING A TIGHTROPE

JEWISH RELIGIOUS BROADCASTING IN ISRAELI TELEVISION—THE CASES OF THE PUBLIC CHANNEL AND THE *HIDABROOT* CHANNEL[1]

Yoni Mandel and Ilan Manor

Introduction

The connection between religion and the state in Israel has been the subject of many academic publications and debates.[2] The nature of this relationship, and the embedded tensions it includes, influenced the political ideas of the Zionist movement, shaped the Israeli political and socio-economic arena, and—as this chapter will discuss—is also evident in the sphere of Jewish religious broadcasting in Israel. These broadcasts, as will be argued here, can serve as a source of knowledge about delicate relations rooted in Israeli society's 'secular', 'religious', and 'Jewish' characteristics, as they are an outcome of the power relations between state and religion in Israel. The analysis of programmes, therefore, focused on 'religious' but also 'national' features, and strived to understand what made specific religious content more suitable for broadcast by the Israeli mass media.

Before delving into a discussion of the content and analysis of the two channels selected—Israel's public channel (Channel 1) and a cable-television religious channel (Hidabroot)—it is necessary to contextualise the place of religion in contemporary Israel. The next section will highlight the basic tensions, and contradictions, between national and religious interpretations of the term 'Jewish.' It will briefly consider the 'religious' elements of Israeli 'secularism', and the 'national' element in Jewish-Israeli 'religiosity.'

Israeli-Jewish: The Tension between Religion and Nationalism

An understanding of the role played by Judaism—as both a religious and a political concept—in the Zionist movement and the creation of Israel, is crucial to the current discussion. The Zionist ideology was shaped in the light of European socialist and nationalist trends, and emerged as a political response to discrimination against Jews in Europe; it was intermixed from its very beginning with dominant national concepts. The founders of Zionism, who were mostly non-Orthodox Jews, emphasised Judaism as their ethnicity rather than a sacred belief, and read Jewish religion mainly through national, social and political channels. This, for example, enabled the perception of the Torah more as an historical book and not as a divine message, an interpretation which assisted justifying and encouraging the idea of Jewish immigration—or 'return'—to Palestine. This perception explains some basic Zionist ideas such as the 'redeeming of the land', 'Hebrew work in *Eretz Yisrael*', and 'the revival of Hebrew.'[3]

This inherent contradiction, through various new definitions and mechanisms, still exists in Israeli-Jewish society. For many, it is negotiated through the marking of their identity as 'secular-Jewish' persons.[4] This dissonant definition—as 'Jewish' is a reference to religion and 'secular' is associated with agnosticism—is reconciled in a national-orientated explanation. On the whole, in the Israeli case study, those who choose to classify themselves as being 'secular-Jewish' do not perceive the 'Jewish' component as religious per se, but rather as a national definition. By so identifying, this dominant social group connects itself to the Jewish majority population in Israel, and thus emphasises its inherent—political and national—difference from the Palestinian community living in the same state.

Raz-Krakotzkin stresses in his work the rooted contradiction in the Zionist-Israeli definition of the 'secular', and emphasises the mix of religious and national elements in it. According to him:

The greatest contradiction of the 'Israeli-secular'... is rooted deep in the history of the Zionist movement. From the movement's very beginning, debates between 'secular' and 'religious' have been central to defining the movement's identity, and these debates continue to accompany it. In this context, 'secular' was never a general plan, but an expression of a Jewish nationalism. The 'secular' was kept within a theological-messianic discourse, which perceives Zionism as a completion of the Jewish history, the return of the Jewish people to the 'promised land' and the implementation of Jewish yearning for redemption. The 'secular', then, is not an alternative to religion, but an interpretation of religion.[5]

When considering the Israeli mass media, this 'hybrid identity' of being both 'Jewish' and 'secular'—and thus also 'modern'—is immediately in evidence. The public channel, which is not an Orthodox station, has ended its broadcast every night for the last forty years with a reading of a religious Jewish text called *Psuku Shel Yom* ('The Daily Biblical Passage'). This ritual is followed by a picture of the flag of Israel—with the national and religious symbol of the Star of David—while in the background the Israeli national— and Jewish—anthem is played. Thus, this connection between the media and nationalism, with Jewish components—which are both religious and national—is provided in the Israeli media every night.

An important concept which needs to be stressed, and that enabled and contextualised the development of this link between 'secular' and 'religious' under a national umbrella, is *mamlakhtiyut*.[6] This term was coined by the first Israeli Prime Minister, David Ben Gurion. Deriving from the Hebrew word for 'kingdom', it refers to actions that take the needs of the state, and the various groupings within it, into consideration. In a more critical way, it might be described as a limited Zionist discourse encouraged by the establishment, which calls upon citizens to put national concerns before others (the Israeli army is one powerful example) due to the 'needs' of the 'state', thereby avoiding difficult debates about social injustices and imbedded inequalities, which might provoke instability. It is an ambivalent concept, perceived by Israeli-Jews as a 'liberal' discourse which, on one hand calls for 'coexistence with Israeli-

Arabs' (Palestinian citizens of Israel), and on the other reminds Jewish citizens to unite in their shared Jewishness and Israeliness.[7]

The concept is dominant within Israel's official authorities, and will, therefore, be observed and analysed through the case study of the Israeli Channel 1. As this research will show, this public channel, which is actually known as Israel's *mamlakhti* channel', allows—or even encourages—Jewish religious debates, but only as long as they remain within the national—or *mamlakhti*—consensus. Similar patterns, with a few differences, were monitored in the second case study—the Hidabroot channel. This channel, like Channel 1, strives to emphasise messages that are both 'Jewish' and 'religious' but also very much, or even mostly, part of the Israeli 'national' discourse.

Israeli Society: On 'Secular' and 'Religious' Communities and Media

In order to better understand the methods developed and used by the two channels, one should be familiar with the basic sub-divisions within Israeli-Jewish society, as well as the relations between these communities and the Israeli media. Compartmentalising people's levels of religiosity is probably an impossible task. Identity generally, and personal religious beliefs even more so, are fluid, changing and multi-layered concepts. It is important to acknowledge this even if this chapter defines, and so generalises, Israeli-Jewish groups as 'secular', '*Masorti*-conservative', 'Zionist-religious' and 'Ultra-Orthodox' (*Haredi*) communities.[8] This categorisation is made despite its limitations in order to enable a basic understanding of positions taken in the religious-secular debate in Israel. Moreover, it highlights the tensions, and divisions, embedded within Israeli-Jewish society, according to which one's religious affiliation is a crucial indicator of one's identity.

Focusing on the Israeli national media, a striking social insight relating to this categorisation is the dominance of 'secular-Jewish' presenters. This phenomenon is part of a broader reality, in which an even more limited social group—'secular-Jewish-Ashkenazi-men'—are better able to access prestigious and influential positions.[9] A second phenomenon related to this categorisation and crucial to an understanding of the field of Israeli religious media, is the fact that the *Haredi* community—which in itself is divided into social streams and parties—is hardly represented in the popular media, and hardly consumes it.

The different way of life that this observant community leads, demonstrated by their separate neighbourhoods and towns in Israel, is reflected also in its alienation to the 'secular' media. The *Haredi* community thus avoid, almost completely, the Israeli national media, including newspapers, television and radio, and have instead created alternative, religious-only, outlets. These are equivalent means of communication, which flourish among the different *Haredi* communities and parties in Israel. For example, *Yated Ne'eman* ('The Loyal Stake') is the daily newspaper of the Lithuanian Hassidic party *Degel Ha-Torah*, and *Ha-Modi'a* ('The Announcer') is the daily newspaper of the Hassidic *Gur* community represented by the *Agudat Israel* party. Other examples include the radio station *Kol Ba-Rama* ('A Voice in the Ramah') of the *Shas* party, and *Zman ha-Ge'ulah* ('Times of Redemption') of the Lubavitch Hassidic movement. There are also a few all-Orthodox outlets, which have no declared affiliation to a specific religious community or party, such as the radio station *Kol Hai* ('The Voice of Life') and the Internet forum *B'Hadrei Haredim* ('In the Haredi Inner Sanctum').

Religious newspapers are the most consumed media outlets within the *Haredi* community, but radio stations and Internet forums have become more and more popular. These outlets are at the centre of a heated debate among the leaders of the *Haredi* community, who are worried about the 'sinful world' that might be accessed through a computer or radio. Television is considered the most 'dangerous' device, and most *Haredi* households in Israel do not have a television set.[10]

By acknowledging this *Haredi* perception of television, one can better understand the relative shortage of religious-only channels and programmes on Israeli television. This, together with the fact that the Palestinian citizens of Israel nowadays tend to prefer to watch Arabic satellite channels,[11] suggests that the Israeli mass media is consumed largely by the following social groups: 'secular-Jewish', '*Masorti*-Conservative', and 'Zionist-religious.' It can, therefore, be posited that the Israeli mass media—like the Israeli market more generally—is produced by and for those who share their affiliation with the Zionist national stream.

This power-relation—the significant role played by 'secular-Jews' on the one hand, and the evident lack of *Haredi* viewers on the other—has resulted in the low presence of all-religious broadcasting in the Israeli mass media. Such broadcasts have been very rare on the commercial channels, and where they appear on the public channel, they are considered to be unpopular. Bearing this special situation in mind, one can better comprehend the Israeli channels—available on cable television—that have decided to broadcast only Jewish-religious content. These channels, among them, most famously, Tekhelet, Kabbalah, and Hidabroot, have all tried to walk on Israeli-Jewish society's tightropes: to broadcast religious programmes that do not aim exclusively at orthodox audiences but that also appeal to the *Masorti* Jewish and even 'secular' societies; to try and stress the combination between feeling 'nationally' Jewish and 'religiously' Jewish; to strive to connect religious content to contemporary life; to use language that incorporates 'secular' phrases, not just religious terminology; and to bring together religious and non-religious Jewish participants.

The Case of Hidabroot

Hidabroot is a relatively new Israeli all-religious channel. It began broadcasting in 2008, and is part of the Hidabroot organisation whose declared message is 'to bring religious and secular Jews closer together, through pleasant conversation, and from an attitude of openness, friendship and proximity.'[12] Hence its Hebrew name, Hidabroot, which means 'mutual talk' or 'conversation.' In order to achieve their goal, which they maintain is not solely religious, the organisation uses a variety of means, of which the Hidabroot television channel is one. Other means include a website, a monthly online newsletter, and a programme of live lectures by the organisation's Director and founder, Rabbi Zamir Cohen.[13] According to one of the board members of Hidabroot, its budget comes from 'rich donors, from outside of Israel, who are concerned about the destiny of the Jewish people, in light of some worrying phenomena such as assimilation, ignorance, and loss of values and Jewish heritage.'[14]

There are three reasons why we decided to use the Hidabroot television channel as a case study for this research. Firstly, the channel is an all-religious channel that deals with a variety of issues, and it is the most popular all-religious channel on Israeli television. Secondly, Hidabroot is the only religious channel to be broadcast via the cable network, which is totally free of charge. This means that it is constantly available to the majority of households in Israel. Thirdly, the channel straightforwardly declared its goal to bring together 'secular and religious viewers' through a unique set of programmes. All in all, we believe that an examination of this channel can shed light on some important strategies and ideas related to Israeli, national, all-religious, Jewish broadcasting.

A survey conducted in January 2009 for the Hidabroot television channel reveals some interesting figures and confirms the channel's general success. According to the survey, the channel has 156,000 viewers on a monthly basis, of which 67 per cent defined themselves as either 'religious' or *Masorti*. Interestingly, a significant percentage of people (33 per cent) who watch Hidabroot defined themselves as 'secular-Jews.'[15]

An examination of Hidabroot's weekly television listing reveals the variety of programmes aired on the channel, linked by the channel's central narrative—of bringing religious and secular Jews closer together. The schedule includes a programme of lectures given by different Rabbis, who are affiliated with Hidabroot, and who discuss various issues such as marriage relationships, stress and happiness, the place of technology in society, and so on. Other programmes deal with specific issues in relation to Jewish beliefs, such as *Shnayim be-Lev Ehad* ('Two in One Heart'), which discusses relationships in the context of Judaism, *Pesher ha-Halomot* ('The Meaning of Our Dreams'), which is presented by Rabbis who discuss spiritual and supernatural subjects, or *Sihat Nashim* (Women's Talk), in which Jewish women discuss their careers, opinions and attitudes to Jewish belief.

That Hidabroot programmes are not 'purely' religious, and that they carry themes attractive to a secular audience represents the channel's intention. Rabbi Zamir Cohen explained this, relating it to the channel's special role. According to him:

We live in an era in which the television and Internet shape and educate people, especially younger generations. These mediums are both powerful and neutral. The problem is that usually they show content which leads to a diminished sensitivity towards others and impairs the basic sense of morality. We are trying to balance this by airing a completely different kind of content, which respects all opinions ... Through the television one can reach any Jew, whether he lives in a city or in a kibbutz.[16]

A closer look into Hidabroot's programmes reveals that its agenda extends beyond the simple aims of 'reach any Jew', 'respect all opinions', or 'bring religious and secular Jews together.' The case study that was selected in order to examine these assumptions is a relatively popular interview programme called 'Linkages' (in Hebrew: *Tzerufim*), which brings together religious and secular celebrities. Through a content analysis of this programme, some light can be shed on the religious values that the channel promotes. Moreover, an analysis of this programme can suggest broader insights about religious channels' content in the Israeli context.

Linking Jewish People Together

Tzerufim ('Linkages') is a weekly recorded programme that airs during the Israeli primetime at 10 pm.[17] *Tzerufim* brings together two well known people, one secular and one religious, to discuss different issues ranging from dating to spirituality and the search for a career. Each 'couple' share interests or professional skills, e.g. two singers, two actors, two novelists, and so on. By bringing the two together and creating a friendly discussion, the programme aims to prove that a dialogue between religious and secular Jews is possible.

The selected guests on *Tzerufim* are famous within Israeli society, but it would be fair to say that the guests' popularity is limited to the community in which they perform. Most likely, these persons were selected in order to boost the programme's ratings and appeal to the channel's audience, as well as to create the desired dialogue between two figures who can act as role models for the younger generation. Of the twelve programmes monitored for this chapter, broadcast during the first half of 2009, only one hosted a pair of female guests.[18]

Tzerufim's set is designed to create an atmosphere of dialogue, openness and ease: the guests are seated on one couch next to each other and there is a coffee table in front of them. Behind them, a window is decorated with puzzle shapes, probably in reference to the programme's name and also as an indication of the full-size picture to be created by bringing together the different parts of Israeli (Jewish) society. Notably, no religious symbols or ornaments are displayed on the set. This is probably a strategic decision taken to 'lower the guards' of the potential secular viewers who are not likely to watch programmes with religious content. Instead, the viewers are made to feel that they are observing a private conversation taking place in someone's living room.

The topics discussed by the guests were an extension of this backdrop. They included issues such as the intrusion of the media into the lives of celebrities, the search for meaning in life, the role of spirituality in modern life, and humour. The more 'Jewish' subjects discussed were how to bring secular and religious Jews closer together, religious practices in contemporary 'secular' life, different ways of being Jewish, and so on. The general atmosphere was friendly and warm, and in none of the programmes did any arguments erupt. This is likely to surprise viewers who have participated in, or been witness to, the often-heated arguments between secular and religious Jewish Israelis that flare up frequently in social situations. The most heated arguments may include debates such as: service in the Israel Defence Forces (IDF) and the exemption given to *Haredi* youngsters; the budgets and allowances allocated by the government to religious colleges; the stereotypic secular view of religious life as backward, against the stereotypic religious view of secular life as sinful; contemporary political arguments such as to whose orders a religious soldier should listen— his military commander or his religious Rabbi; political debates relating to the 'democratic', 'Jewish', and 'holy' aspects of Israel; and many more.

Strikingly, in the vast majority of the programmes monitored there was no reference to any subject that might be expected to lead to confrontation between the secular and the religious guest. In the remaining programmes, the state of affairs between religious and secular Jews in Israel was raised, but without addressing any focal points of disagreement. For example, in one instance the religious singer Itzik Orlev, mentioned that the title of his record *Mitga'age'a* ('Yearning For') refers to his longing 'for a time when all Jews in Israel were united and part of one society.' However, his argument stopped there and was not followed by a critique of the current situation and cleavages between religious and secular Jewish Israelis. In another case, the 'secular' actor Nir Friedman suggested that secular and religious Jews should attend the same schools to bridge the current educational and social gaps between them. He did not elaborate on the controversial nature and sources of these gaps. The same was true when the religious comedian Ofer Halevy stated that his main mission and dream in life is to bridge the gap between groups in Israeli society. Generally, some of the guests were ready to discuss the importance of bridging, but avoided discussing the actual cleavage.[19]

In all of the examples mentioned above, the guests chose to keep their statements general and to speak vaguely about a need to 'unite', 'understand', and 'accept.' One can argue that these participants were selected because they were likely to promote messages of 'unity', and the production team may even have briefed them about it. Analysis of the discussions made between the 'religious' and 'secular' guests reveals that, in the majority of cases, they were in complete agreement on all topics discussed and did not voice different views or opinions whatsoever. The message relayed to the viewer was clear: one should forget about 'right-wing', or 'left-wing', 'secular' or 'religious' politics and disputes, and focus on the 'Jewish' common denominator. In other words: they encouraged a complete de-politicisation of the religious-secular conflict in Israel.

Interesting insights were also gained by summarising the different views raised by the 'secular' guests. Surprisingly, they tend not to represent general Israeli 'secular' sentiments and community practices, which might have been evident in a stress on their Jewish nationality or ethnicity. Instead they emphasised their Jewish religious beliefs: that they keep kosher, study Kabbalah, believe in God, have faith in the story of the creation, or avoid making a fire during Shabbat. Each of the 'secular' guests observed at least some of the religious practices, and informed their religious counterpart. For instance, in one of the programmes, the 'secular' comedian Ran Levi described himself as a 'religious Jew without a kippa.'[20] The 'secular' rapper Kobi Shimoni merged his Jewish national and religious feelings and said, 'for my secular friends I am actually religious ... since I keep kosher ... and the Star of David I have as a necklace is my motto: I am Jewish and I am also the state of Israel.'

In other cases the 'secular' participant agreed with the religious counterpart's beliefs and made statements relating to morals studied from the Torah, family or personal Jewish-*Masorti* way of life, and the role religion plays in their own 'secular' life and artistic work. On top of this, most of the 'secular' guests made a clear effort to use religious expressions in their discussions with a religious counterpart: *Toda la-El* ('Thanks God'), *Be-'Ezrat ha-Shem* ('With God's Will'), or *Yishtabah Shemo* ('The Holy One Blessed be He'), were often used, even though such terms are seldom heard when 'secular' Jews socialise together.

An additional insight that emerged out of the content analysis of this programme was a sense of apologetics coming from the 'secular' guests. When the 'secular' comedian Yuval Shem-Tov was asked if he observes the Shabbat, he reacted uncomfortably, saying, 'I do drive my car on Shabbat ... But I still love the [Jewish] religion. There are so many beautiful things in the religion, and I take what makes me feel better ... I believe that this is what the creation was all about.' When 'secular' journalist Nofar Sinai was asked about her religious knowledge she said: 'sometime I feel it is not okay... that I do not know enough about our 613 *Mitzvot*.'[21]

When the ideas raised by the religious guests were analysed, further interesting insights were gained. Strikingly, in the majority of cases, during the conversation it was revealed that the religious participants grew up in 'secular', or at least 'non-orthodox' families. One can argue that the appearance of the religious guest on the programme was designed to send a message to the 'secular' audience, according to which the religious world is not intimidating, or unfamiliar, and is actually full of former secular Jews—who believe in the state and in its army—and are now religious, happier, calmer and more satisfied.

For example, Rabbi Yuval Ashrov spoke about the 'injury in Beirut, when I was a Company Commander', that accelerated his search for meaning. 'I was always looking for something, I did yoga and other things, but until I became religious I could not rest. Till then my soul kept on searching.' Stories like this one create a feeling of closeness between the viewers and the religious guest:

the religious interlocutor was secular in his past—and therefore is more accessible to secular viewers—yet, he is religious today—and so attractive to religious viewers as well. Not surprisingly, none of the 'secular' guests on the programmes grew up in a religious house. Such a guest could have provided another perspective on the religious world and way of life, but this kind of perception was most probably not invited. This is an important indication of the programme's underlying message, regarding the actual way of bringing 'secular' and Orthodox Jews closer together: increasing the religious belief of the former.

Another insight related to the religious participants concerns their appearance. In almost all programmes analysed, the religious guest was not a *Haredi* with an Ultra-orthodox religious appearance, and instead—for example, with the male guests—wore 'secular' clothing, and not the 'expected'—or stereotypical—*Haredi* black clothes, side-locks, and beard. Most religious guests wore jeans or a suit, with a long-sleeved shirt. In most cases, the only visible difference between the religious and the 'secular' guests' outfits was the *kippa* the former wore on their heads.

Another interesting finding that came out of the analysis was the dynamic between the guests. In most cases the 'secular' guest asked the religious counterpart questions relating to the religious way of life, work and belief. However, this was not reciprocated, and viewers did not hear about 'good values' associated with being 'secular', only about the 'good values' of religious life. Indeed, the only values that the 'secular' guests put forward were related to, and emanated from, religion, but they were never competing values.

Furthermore, in most of the programmes monitored, the religious guest spoke more than the 'secular', and the latter was more commonly in the position of learner. This arguably strengthens the notion among viewers that the religious way of life has more to offer than the secular: it contains the missing piece, which would make the life of the 'secular' complete. 'I have ten children, and never had depression', said religious journalist Sarah Mali Green in one of the programmes. In another programme, 'secular' television presenter Oded Menashe said to his conversation partner: 'How come your life is so organised? You have much more meaning ... something in the air that you have.' In all of the programmes the 'secular' guests were very complimentary towards the religious way of life, and spoke about the different values they could gain from getting to know religion better. In other words, they confirmed the religious view that the secular world cannot offer anything for people who consider themselves Jewish, while the religious world holds the answers and solutions to the secular person's dilemmas.

All in all, the fact that the guests on the programme avoid referring to issues which lie at the core of the disagreement between religious and 'secular' Jews in Israel, combined with the dominance of the religious guests on the programme and the fact that most 'secular' guests describe themselves as partly religious, strengthens our conclusion that the programme has, at least to a certain extent, a missionary agenda, and that it does not really strive to create a dialogue between religious and secular Israelis, but more at making Israeli 'secular', or even *Masorti*, societies more observant. Another possible agenda could be the creation of sympathy among secular viewers for the religious society, which might help diminish secular opposition to the religious political agenda. This will be further discussed in the conclusions.

The Case of Channel 1

The decision to monitor a different religious programme broadcast on Israeli national television was made in the hope of comparing the insights gained from a religious channel with a non-religious channel, and from a cable-television channel, to a public channel. Eventually, the decision was to analyse a programme broadcast on Channel 1, Israel's public channel.

Channel 1 is part of the Israeli Broadcasting Authority (similar to the BBC in the UK). In its charter it is stated that the Israeli Broadcasting Authority must, among other things, 'reflect the state and its achievements ... promote good citizenship ... and strengthen the bond with the Jewish heritage and values.'[22] As a significant component of the IBA, Channel 1 is committed to this charter and must promote these values through the content it airs.

Channel 1 began broadcasting in 1968, and its first transmission was the IDF's annual parade, which took part during Israeli Independence Day. This fact is revealing of the channel's affiliation and positioning at the heart of Israeli Zionist discourse. At first, Channel 1 aired only three evenings a week, and later expanded to four. Between 1979 and 1983 it gradually evolved and began broadcasting in colour. Nowadays it airs programmes twenty-four hours a day, including sport, docu-dramas, news, children's shows, and talk-shows. However, it is no longer the most popular channel on Israeli television. This is due to the great success of commercial television, which gained pace during the 1990s. According to the ratings figures, Channel 1 is considered the third most popular in Israel, following commercial Channels 2 and 10.[23]

The target audience of Channel 1 is on paper 'Israeli society': as a public channel it is supposed to air content appealing to the variety of social and ethnic groups within Israel. However, when reviewing the Channel's weekly content, it is striking that it is actually aimed at a non-*Haredi* Israeli-Jewish audience. Firstly, the few Arabic programmes which Channel 1 used to broadcast were transferred to Channel 33.[24] Secondly, on weekdays there is no significant Jewish religious content aimed at the *Haredi* community.[25] The few religious programmes that are broadcast, of which we chose to focus on one, are aired on the weekend before and after the Shabbat. They involve religious content mixed with 'secular' and contemporary-national affairs and therefore cannot be considered as strictly religious programmes for religious people.[26]

Who Wants to Ask The Rabbi?

The programme selected for this study is called *She'elat Rav* ('A Question for the Rabbi') which is a recorded programme that airs weekly on Friday at three in the afternoon. The programme first aired in the summer of 2006, during the Second Lebanon War. It was an ad-hoc enterprise of Channel 1, aiming to solve religious dilemmas with which Jewish-Israelis grappled, while living in shelters in the north of Israel.[27] Following the war, the programme became permanent and remained centred on phone calls, as well as faxes, made by viewers at home willing to ask the programme's rabbi questions relating to Jewish life, tradition, and law.[28]

The set of the programme is arranged so that the host and the rabbi are situated behind a desk while two monitors behind them display the programme's logo. Callers who have a query to present to the rabbi are first greeted by the host and then they ask the rabbi their question. The latter usually responds at length (three to five minutes) and with a smile. The rabbi's attitude never seems patronising, disrespectful, or angry at the lack of religious knowledge displayed by the caller. This is arguably an important element, especially given the lack of familiarity between *Haredi* and 'secular' Jews, and the importance to the religious programme of presenting the rabbi, an ambassador for the religious world, as patient and friendly. This attitude was also evident in the rabbi's answers, which were patiently explained through Jewish legal principles, as well as common sense, with reference to contemporary life.

The target audience of the programme is most probably *Masorti* and 'secular' Jews, who are not as strictly observant as the Zionist-religious and ultra-orthodox communities. This is not a certain conclusion, but the use of television to solve religious problems seems more likely to attract people who do not have a rabbi, or live in religious surroundings, with whom, or within which, they can settle their religious questions and inquiries.

In order to better understand the context of this show, it is probably useful to look at the two people chosen to present it. The programme's host is Shlomi Goldberg. He served in the IDF as a soloist in the Military Rabbinate Orchestra, and later joined 'Voice of Israel', the country's public radio service. Currently, Goldberg serves as the Director of the Jewish Heritage Department in the IBA. The show is presented by Rabbi David Lau, the municipal rabbi of Modi'in, a new large city located between Tel Aviv and Jerusalem. He is the son of a well-known figure, Rabbi Yisrael Meir Lau, the former Israeli Chief Rabbi, and the current Chief Rabbi of Tel Aviv. Rabbi David Lau was also one of the first to answer questions on Jewish law and customs using the Internet, and is considered by Israelis to be a liberal and progressive rabbi. Lastly, Rabbi Lau served in the Israeli army, and reached the rank of Major. This military background is not a given for a *Haredi* rabbi, and in the Israeli context it is likely to help confer legitimacy and status, and it allows him to appeal to 'seculars' as an equal.

These biographical details are important to an understanding of the programme's nature, especially as Rabbi Lau's affiliation to the

Israeli establishment, supportive feelings toward the Zionist cause, and service in the Israeli army, probably made him a suitable candidate to present this programme. Being a public broadcaster, Channel 1 is likely to seek to hire rabbis who are considered to be 'liberal' and not 'extremists', and who are also willing to participate in Israeli society's activities and accept Israel's statehood. Rabbi David Lau seems to represent the concept of *mamlakhtiyut* at its best, and this no doubt contributed to the decision to have him lead the show.

Some of Rabbi Lau's comments during the show proved this point. In one programme he spoke about his latest service in the IDF reserves, and his meeting with Druze soldiers. According to him, 'these soldiers serve our country so loyally, and they deserve all of our appreciation.' In another programme he reminded viewers to follow strictly the instructions issued by the Ministry of Health. A further suggestion of his was to lessen the number of happy songs sung during a circumcision ceremony that is to take place on the Israeli National Holocaust Remembrance Day. This respectful attitude to Israel's symbols—army, governmental authorities, special commemoration days—should be contextualised with *mamlakhtiyut*, especially since the majority of the Israeli *Haredi* community is not likely to be as complimentary towards the 'secular' organisations and ceremonies of Israel.

Following the monitoring of twelve programmes in the first half of 2009, it appears that the majority of questions were not strictly religious but rather dealt with other subjects, such as social, family, and business problems with which people struggled and wanted to consult a religious authority. Only a small sub-section of the questions dealt with 'hardcore' *Halacha* (Jewish religious law) issues. A few examples of this second category include 'why is it commanded to separate six hours between eating meat and dairy?'; 'how was it decided that one's Jewish religion is dependant upon one's mother's religion and not one's father's?', and 'is it allowed to use hot water heated by the sun on Shabbat?'

Probably the more intriguing category was the first, which brought to the surface problems emanating from domestic, social and family life. A considerable portion of questions in this category involved contemporary issues, for which a religious ruling was not specified. One of them dealt with the New York Stock Exchange, when a caller wanted to inquire whether it is allowed to purchase shares in a company that works on Saturdays. Another caller inquired whether he can get the new Swine Flu vaccine, due to the rumours that it was tested on pigs. Another asked if he can turn on his new electronic hearing device in the synagogue on a Saturday, in order to hear the prayer better.

More examples from this category revealed questions related to family and social life: a mother of five said that even though her husband was a religious person, he did not treat her with respect, and wondered if the Torah allowed such treatment; another caller, who was identified as a compulsive gambler, asked whether his addiction prevented him from being a cantor in his local synagogue; an Ashkenazi caller wanted to know whether he could have prayed in a Sephardic synagogue using Ashkenazi pronunciation; another couple asked what they should have done with food given to them by a generous friend who does not keep a Kosher kitchen.

Although the callers did not reveal their religious backgrounds, it is suggested that they were not Orthodox, but rather *Masorti* or even 'secular' Jews. This is assumed since many of the queries dealt with what can be called 'big events'—birth, circumcision, death, marriage, divorce—which in Israel are supervised by the Chief Rabbinate and so require non-Orthodox Jews to receive the religious establishment's approval. Another explanation for the centrality of these kinds of questions is the great importance that these major personal events have, and the desire of many to deal with them 'correctly' from the religious point of view.

In this category were questions about youngsters who reached the age of thirteen (*Bar Mitzvah*) and wondered about religious issues (is it possible to celebrate *Bar Mitzvah* on the ninth of *Av*, which is the date on which the Jewish Temple in Jerusalem was destroyed?); questions about births and deaths (can a son who quarrelled with his brothers commemorate his father's death by himself? Is a baby who was born to a Jewish mother, and was not circumcised, still a Jew?); questions dealing with weddings and divorces (is one allowed to get married on Israeli Independence Day? Can a divorced person serve as an usher at a wedding? Can a divorced couple continue to live in the same apartment?).

Another interesting issue we considered was the questions that were not asked, and the possible significance this might have. Following an overall analysis of all the questions asked, it was revealed that one type of query was significantly absent: that which is related to social and political debates found in the midst of disputes between the religious and secular communities in Israel. These unasked questions cover issues such as the fact that *Haredi* men and women do not serve in the army, unlike their secular and national-religious counterparts; the separate curriculums of the 'secular' and religious education systems in Israel; the sensitive status quo between state and religion in Israel, and so on.

All of these questions, which sit in the secular-religious cleavage in Israel, were left out of the question-and-answer sessions in favour of questions with personal, non-political, and non-controversial cores. As a matter of fact, the programme deals with only 'neutral' topics and does not relate to points of disagreement on the national level. Perhaps this is so because the audience prefers to use the show as a service providing answers to different kinds of queries: more personal conundrums and concerns relating to Judaism rather than a forum to discuss and debate issues of disagreement amongst different groups—religious and 'secular' Jews. However, it may well be that the show deliberately wishes to air questions that do not threaten to divide Israeli society. This thesis, alongside those mentioned regarding the programme *Tzerufim*, will be discussed in the conclusions.

Conclusions

The two cases analysed in this article demonstrated different formulas for dealing with religious content in the media sphere of Israeli-Jewish society. Each channel, Hidabroot and Channel 1, has unique characteristics, but between them some interesting and telling similarities have been revealed.

One approach that was identified was highlighted through the study of Channel 1's programme *She'elat Rav*. The programme was shown to partake in the *mamlakhtiyut* discourse that characterises the channel more generally. To an extent, this is disguised by the 'neutral' and personal religious questions. However, through our content analysis, and focus on deeper, less clearly articulated themes—the questions and subjects that were not raised, the personal background of the presenters, and the 'natural' and positive way with which national institutions were treated—we have shown that it is a religious programme that is embedded deep in the Zionist national discourse, and 'guarded' by religious presenters who secure this political narrative and discourse. The Jewish religion is positioned, in this discourse, as a neutral aspect of Israel, and as if it has no competing values within the modern nation state. This is an approach that unobtrusively places the religion within the state, in its alleged 'natural' place, and so uses the religious discourse—and specifically the methodology of questions and answers—to reinforce a certain political, national and Zionist, world-view.

Another approach studied was highlighted through the analysis of *Tzerufim*, an interview programme on the Hidabroot Channel. This research has demonstrated the way this programme, which states that it attempts to 'bring religious and secular Jews closer together', actually uses religion and religious discourse as a remedy to Israel's contemporary social problems. By doing so, the programme strives to reinforce the sense of ethnic nationhood amongst Israeli Jews, thereby excluding those citizens of Israel who are not Jewish. In other words, Judaism—whether through the Israeli 'secular' or 'religious' interpretation—is used here in order to emphasise a national, political, common base. One needs to remember that this common denominator is loaded with an ability to include (Jewish-Israelis) but also exclude (Palestinian citizens of Israel). This approach to religion, as we have seen, corresponds with and links to a much broader and burning political issue: the Israeli-Arab conflict.

Moreover, by depicting religious individuals as friendly and approachable, the programme aims not to create a dialogue between religious and 'secular' people, but to push forward the missionary solution: strengthening Jewish religious belief. This is achieved by different means and, most interestingly, by bringing to the fore guests who used to live secular lives but who decided to become religious as adults. These living exemplars, who searched for the meaning of life and found it, signal to 'secular' and *Masorti* viewers that they can also live more fulfilling lives if only they search and find their answers in the 'familiar', 'welcoming', and 'accepting' Jewish religion.

We identified an interesting similarity in *She'elat Rav* and *Tzerufim*: both chose not to broadcast advanced or sophisticated religious content, and instead emphasised national, secular, and daily issues, employing national, secular and daily terminology. The Jewish religious programmes were not conversations between religious experts but, by and large, dialogues between *Masorti* or 'secular' Jews and their Orthodox counterparts, all within the Zionist discourse. This insight suggests a possible reading of Jewish religion in the more general Israeli national sphere: it needs to be clear and simple, so that a non-expert audience can participate; it needs to support the symbols of the state, and to correspond with the Jewish-Zionist limitations; and it cannot offer competing values to the political policies of the state or the prevailing discourse in Israeli-Jewish society.

Another similarity between the two programmes was the lack of female participants. In the case of *Tzerufim*, out of the twelve programmes monitored, only one included women. In *She'elat Rav*, the women who participated did so via telephone only, and the two presenters were male. Given the increasing attempts by Israeli television to include more women on screen as an act of affirmative action, it seems unlikely that this is merely coincidental. One can argue that within the Israeli-Jewish discourse, religious issues remain firmly under male authority.

The last insight is that both programmes did not genuinely reflect the socio-political reality, and instead painted a distorted picture of Israeli-Jewish society. The main and serious cleavages between religious and secular communities were ignored, and the message was that differences—if they exist—are minor in comparison to the need to unite. National and political questions, which usually tear holes in Israeli society, were not raised. Similarly, sensitive issues such as those related to state-and-religion affairs, service in the IDF, or lack of public transportation on Saturdays, were not raised in any of the programmes. The purging of these issues can be partially explained by the selection of the religious presenters and guests. They were definitely not religious anti-Zionists, but rather religious people who are part of the Zionist and Israeli national discourse. It was probably a deliberate decision made by the producers of the two programmes to paint an uncomplicated picture of the secular-religious relationship in Israel, and to ignore the well-known and obvious challenges and difficulties. This is revealing of the Israeli establishment's fear of confronting these issues publicly, and through the religious medium, as well as their penchant for idealistic solutions of 'uniting' or 'gathering' around a Jewish flag, or dream, to escape the pressing need to deal critically with the political reality.

10

CHRISTIAN BROADCASTING

A CRITICAL ASSESSMENT

Sameh Fawzy

This chapter discusses Arabic-speaking Christian satellite channels in general, and the Al Hayat and Coptic Television (CTV) Channels in particular. The topic can be tackled from various perspectives, but I have chosen to approach it from the socio-cultural and political perspectives.

The evolution of Christian Satellite channels cannot be disentangled from the surrounding socio-political challenges facing Arab Christians—such as their lack of political representation, the rise of Islamic fundamentalism, the lack of respect for Christianity in some Islamic media, the drain of Christian migration, and the inaccessibility to public media, all of which have contributed, consciously or subconsciously, to the establishment of Christian channels. However, these channels are different in shape and content, and their similar identity does not reflect similarity in approach or end goals. I selected two opposite types of Christian channels for analysis: one is unapologetically missionary, looking to proselytise Muslims, in response to the unceasing affronts on Christian faith, by launching a constant campaign on Islam; the second is completely attached to the Coptic Orthodox Church, focusing on faith, rituals, saints' festivals, masses, spiritual sermons, bible study, and so on.

The critical assessment of both of these channels opens up a discussion over the expected role of Christian broadcasting, taking into account the socio-political context in which Arab Christians live. Some recommendations will be made at the end.

An Overview

Christian religious teaching in the Arab World was, for many decades, limited to church sermons, Sunday schools, and internal publications, in addition to the religious curricula in public and private schools. The latter is a by-product of the nationalist state, which has come to be a real symbol of Arab national movements in the twentieth century.

In Arab countries, where Islam is the majority religion and Christianity is the minority, public media owned and run by governments focuses very little on Christian matters, except during important religious occasions such as Christmas and Easter. The sporadic attention to the Christian presence is sometimes seen as a 'message' to Western governments rather than to the local Christian inhabitants. Being a minority with a growing fear of marginalisation, Christians have become a monolithic group, especially in the face of growing Islamic fundamentalism. Nevertheless, the situation differs from one country to another.

In Egypt, where Christians constitute approximately 10–12 per cent of the entire population, *Copts* (Egyptian Christians) have been treated, to a large extent, as fully-fledged citizens since the nineteenth century, with the freedom to perform their own religious teaching privately, though not publicly.[1] Like any other predominately Muslim society, the generally tolerant Muslim majority still have their suspicions about Christian proselytising.[2]

In 1923, the first modern constitution in Egyptian history ensured equity for all citizens irrespective of religion, race and social status, although it stated that Islam is the religion of the state. Between 1923 and 1952, Christians were politically, economically and socially active. Nevertheless, the growing presence of the Muslim Brotherhood left Christians worried about their place in society.

The situation changed after the 1952 revolution and the economic situation of Christians was adversely affected by socialist policies. In addition, their political influence was eliminated as a result of the dissolution of the party system. Many Muslims, like Christians, were undoubtedly among the losers economically and politically. However, the policies of the 1950s and 1960s helped create a strong middle class in which all Egyptians, Muslim or Christian, benefited. As a result, a Christian technocratic elite evolved within the state apparatus, and gradually replaced the political elite and landowners, whose influence had been clearly noticed before the mid-1950s. It is worth noting that Egyptian society of the 1950s and 1960s was almost secular, and the influence of Islamic groups had been eliminated as a result of the fierce confrontation between President Nasser and the Muslim Brotherhood. However, the situation radically changed once again at the beginning of the 1970s, when President Anwar Sadat decided to build a new conservative right wing alliance between a free market economy and political Islam, to replace the socialist character of the state. Nevertheless, this alliance failed to survive or to grant President Sadat the required legitimacy, especially in the aftermath of the peace agreement between Egypt and Israel in 1979. Although the alliance proved inadequate, and was widely criticised by liberal and leftist scholars and politicians as the Islamisation of Egyptian society, it has remained a pressing social factor, even up to the present time. An outward religiosity robustly swept through the Muslim community and was accompanied by unusually conservative attitudes among the Copts, who decided or felt compelled to insulate themselves within their churches. As such, the clergy gradually became effective and outspoken representatives of the Christian community before the state, while the role of Christian secular figures began to fade.

In Lebanon, interreligious relationships have different aspects as a result of the particularity of the Lebanese political system. The proportionate power-sharing mechanism provides the eighteen officially recognised religious communities with an opportunity for their own political representation and socio-cultural presence. As such, it is normal in Lebanon to find someone who has never met or socialised with people from religious backgrounds different to their own. It could be said that most Lebanese can rely on their monolithic religious communities to develop their own identity, learn at school, find suitable employment, marry, stand before its own courts, and die and be buried in the cemetery belonging to their religious community.

In Jordan, Christians are a very tiny minority who share a special relationship with the monarchic political system. Generally speaking, they enjoy religious freedom, societal tolerance and political guardianship. A similar situation can be found, to a large extent, in occupied Palestine, where Christians enjoy freedom of expression and special social value as a result of being inhabitants of the Holy Land. However, in light of the growing Islamisation of the Palestinian-Israeli conflict, a noticeable migration of Christians, especially from Jerusalem, has been developing, and the worsening conditions of the occupied territories have all negatively impacted upon the Christian presence in Palestine.

In Iraq under the Ba'ath rule, as in Syria today, Christians were normally entitled to religious freedom in return for their unconditional support of the political regime. Usually they didn't encounter problems related to building and repairing places of worship, finding office in top-ranking positions in governmental organisations, or being able to proclaim their own cultural identity. Yet this freedom was lost in Iraq, following the removal of the Ba'ath system in 2003. Under the foreign occupation, the rights of Christians have been severely persecuted. The constant extremist assaults on their churches, houses and shops have contributed to diminishing their historical presence in Iraq, compelling thousands of them to seek religious refuge in a number of Western countries, with the same feared in Syria. Christians have been migrating in noticeable numbers to Western societies, motivated by a strong sense of fear about their future if the current regime should be toppled by Sunni political groups.[3]

In light of the above, Christian broadcasting is considered to be one of the responses by Arab Christians, consciously or unconsciously, to counter the challenges they face. Although the mushrooming Christian satellite channels are purely religious-based media, it is difficult to detach them from the previously mentioned socio-political conditions facing Arab Christians. Gripped by a growing sense of marginalisation, Christians have established these channels, in addition to an unceasing number of limited circulation publications, to explain, defend and preach their faith.

In light of this brief background of the Christian presence in the Arab World, one can underline the challenges considered to be part of the stimulus for having and developing Christian media in general and satellite channels in particular.

1. One challenge is the decreasing role of Christians at the societal level. Following the independence from foreign occupation in the 1950s and 1960s in Arab countries, Christians had a noticeable role in public life as politicians, senior public bureaucrats, ideologists, intellectuals and professionals. After almost a half century, the current scale of Christian societal presence becomes questionable. As large numbers of Christians have migrated to the West, fewer numbers of Christians have remained to assume top positions in the state apparatus. Islamic movements, which have been sweeping through Arab countries, have posed further challenges to them, most importantly concerning the pivotal question of identity and citizenship rights.

2. The rise of political Islam in Egypt, the Palestinian territories, Jordan, Lebanon and Iraq has created a more conservative and less tolerant atmosphere. The excessive use of Islamic terminology in media, social interactions, the public sphere, and political life have left Christians feeling alienated and sometimes discriminated against. In fact, one can notice two forms of the current Islamic resurgence; a politically motivated one which enthusiastically competes with other political forces to establish an Islamic society, Islamic government and the Islamic State, with the Muslim Brotherhood in Egypt and its offspring Hamas in the Palestinian territories being clear examples; the second supported by conservative Salafi groups whose goals are to return to a genuine Islam by purifying the religion from all negative practices that have been attached to it over history. Both trends create a real problem for the existence of Christians. The first excludes Christians from society and public life and treats them as second-class citizens, and the second calls on its followers to ostracise Christians for being infidels.[4]

3. There is a growing feeling of an identity crisis amongst Arab Christians. They sometimes feel, albeit with some exaggeration, that their distinct religious identity is no longer as tolerated by the Muslim majority as it was in the past. Islamic media, and sometimes state-owned media, critically discuss their own faith without giving Christians an equal chance to defend or even explain their religious beliefs. This can be largely attributed to the nature of the war on terror in the Arab world. Faced with devout Islamic militancy, the Arab governments have exerted their utmost efforts to curtail the militant aspect of the Islamic revival, while paying less attention to the impact of its extremist discourses. Sometimes Arab governments have implicitly supported the appearance of these discourses before the public to help establish their status as defenders of Islam, and to elicit public support for their crackdown on Islamic militants. As such, the Islamic militancy has been curtailed somewhat on those grounds, but the level of general religious conservatism has increased. Polemics between different religions are undoubtedly a result of the growing religious conservatism.

4. In most—if not all—Arab countries, accelerating extremism, both culturally and politically, has become a basic feature of public life. Those who are of a different religion or even adopt secular tendencies, face marginalisation from the mainstream Islamic community. As a result, Christians have been compelled to turn into a monolithic group. Although their public presence remains in some fields, such as the economy, their tendency to behave as a unified group under the banner of the Church has increased. Arab governments have clearly favoured the type of relationship with Christians in which the churches represent the Christian communities. The examples have shown that this pattern of religious representation of Christian citizens with different political and social allegiances has always provided Arab governments with required support, while often resulting in misunderstanding at the community level between different religious communities.

5. In the aftermath of what is widely known as the Arab Spring— which resulted in the ousting of autocratic regimes in Tunisia, Libya and Egypt—the situation of Christians has changed.

While they participated in the political uprising against Mubarak's regime in Egypt side-by-side with Muslims, Christians have begun to raise fears about their political and socio-economic positions in the emerging political climate following the landslide victory of Islamists in public elections in 2011 and 2012. Although some inherited fears from past periods lack proper justification, the continuation of their own religious-based problems, such as restrictions on building and repairing churches, political underrepresentation, social discrimination, etc. help to fuel their fears.[5] Christians in Syria, particularly the clergy, carry fears about the future of Christianity and Christians in the event of radical political change, particularly after the deadly attacks on churches and Christians in Iraq that left hundreds killed and injured, and forced almost half of Iraqi Christians to migrate to Western countries. It is undoubtedly too early to judge the consequences of sweeping political changes in the Arab World on its slim Christian minority, but the situation of Christians in the new Arab politics remains among the most sensitive areas in the struggle against autocratic regimes. Nevertheless there seems to be an understanding among mainstream Muslims that religious diversity should be a victim of the process of liberation of tyrannical regimes in the Arab World.[6]

6. There is undeniable influence from Arab Christian groups in the diaspora. Some of them left their own countries carrying negative impressions and confused memories. Today, they have become major defenders of citizenship rights of Arab Christians, capitalising on the contacts and networks they have created within influential Western political circles.

7. Christians themselves experience continuing turbulent denominational divisions. The slogan of 'Christian Unity' in the Middle East no longer holds much appeal to church leaders. Although the Middle East Council of Churches (MECC) was established during the early 1970s, with the aim of building Christian unity, it has witnessed throughout its lifespan obstacles, challenges, and mistrust, and has ended up with a shrinking, stagnant and bureaucratic institutional body. Today, ecumenicism is in real question, and the disputes between various churches have become among the most hotly disputed issues in the public media coverage.[7]

Models of Christian Satellite Channels

Having described the background factors that led to the establishment of Christian media, including satellite channels, it is important to look closer at the shape and content of these channels, most importantly Al Hayat and CTV. These two channels are part of a wider pool of fifteen Christian channels broadcast in Arabic to the Arab world, and to Arabic-speaking communities abroad.[8]

Generally speaking, these channels perform various multidimensional roles; educational, where they play an important role in explaining the faith; outreach, as some of these channels are obsessed with a missionary approach, either subtle or provocative; and societal, because they pay attention to the contribution of Christians in public life. This latter aspect is not paid much attention on some channels, which still concentrate on purely religious matters.

Concerning their history and emergence, the first Christian TV channel was Télé Lumière, which was established in Lebanon in 1991 at the request of some secular figures such as the late President Charel Al Helw, Antoine Saad and others. The channel has been brought under the supervision of the Council of the Catholic Patriarchs and Bishops, and proclaims an ecumenical approach, free from consumerism and politics. The terrestrial TV station evolved into a satellite channel called Nour Sat following the establishment of the first Christian satellite channel in the Middle East called Sat 7. Currently, there are numerous Christian satellite channels belonging to various denominations; Orthodox Coptic Television Channel (CTV), and Aghapy (June 2005); and Protestant channels, Malakot, Karma and Shafaa.

For the sake of discussion in this paper, Christian channels can be classified into four categories.[9] The first one is denomination, which while not a rigid category, could include three classifications: Orthodox such as Agapy and CTV, Protestant such as Sat 7, Miracle and Shafaa, and Catholic such as Nour Sat.

Aside from the two orthodox channels, Christian channels in general proclaim an ecumenical agenda, insisting that they serve the message of Jesus Christ, rather than specific denominations. However, it is important to note that the ongoing agitation between Orthodox and Protestant churches in the Middle East in general, and particularly in Egypt, negatively impact on the work in the media. Orthodox churches always warn their followers to avoid any Protestant influence, especially through the media.

The second way of categorising these channels is by their outlook. Christian channels vary in their general outlook and religious delivery. Some channels, such as Aghapy, CTV, and to some extent Nour Sat, focus on broadcasting prayers and specific programmes on faith and rituals. Others, like Sat 7, introduce religious and social matters from a Christian perspective, focusing on ways to develop the personal spiritual experience of the audience. In addition, some Protestant channels such as Shafaa have a charismatic approach, with special emphasis on how people obtain heavenly gifts, dispel their personal pains and render themselves ready for the work of the Holy Spirit.

Nevertheless, following the 25 January public uprising which launched an unceasing political mobilisation to oust the Mubarak regime, Christian satellite channels have embarked on new programs that focus on political interactions; a new trend that is also shared by Islamic satellite channels including hardline Salafi ones.

CTV, for example, started a new program called *Fe Al Nour* ('In the Light'), an evening talk show focusing on political events, which hosts debates between scholars, politicians and media persons regardless of their religion. Although the program officially started after the massacre took place in the Saints Church in Alexandria on New Year's Eve 2011 in a blast that left twenty-three persons killed and dozens injured, the program has acquired momentum after 25 January.

A third categorisation could be based on the 'missionary' inclination of these channels, or the lack of it. Most Christian channels claim to carry a message for the whole Arab world. Some, such as CTV, Aghapy, and to some extent Nour Sat, focus on Christianity, history, the Holy Book, rituals and liturgy. Others, namely Al Hayat, have a provocative approach towards Muslims, focusing on refuting Islam, and proselytising to followers. The third group, such as Al Shafaa, Miracle and to some extent Sat 7, search for reconciliation between God and people, countering evil, and reaching out to others through Christian moral and personal behaviour.

A fourth category is the media approach. Some Christian channels have highly diversified broadcasting output, such as Sat 7 and

Nour Sat, which provide their audience with multiple programmes touching on different topics and targeting different age-groups. Others, such as CTV and Aghapy, focus on church life, including prayers, saints' festivals and rituals. However, there are some channels that resemble radio broadcasting rather than TV broadcasting, whereby they introduce one guest who speaks alone for more than an hour in front of a fixed camera. In this regard, no action, change of scenery or other attractive methods are adopted. The Al Hayat channel is a good example of this kind of radio-like broadcasting.

Al Hayat Channel

The mission statement of Al Hayat, which appeared in 2003, states that it belongs:

...to the family of Jesus Christ, and its main followers have an Islamic background in addition to other Christian believers from different denominations. Its main goal is to plant the pure word of God among Arab-speaking people in Northern Africa, the Middle East, the Arab Peninsula, Europe and Australia.[10]

According to this self-definition, Al Hayat doesn't adhere to any one particular church or Christian denomination. Rather it proclaims a wider Christian agenda in which every Christian, whatever his or her denominational background, can claim ownership over its mission.

However, the main goal of the channel is to proselytise to Muslims. It believes that Muslims sink in oblivious ignorance, decadence and great loss, and true Christians play a role in enlightening them and leading them to the heavenly road of Salvation. Because of its blunt and provocative discourse on Islamic faith, Al Hayat has been subject to severe criticism across the Arab World.

Based on this perception, Al Hayat draws thought from the broad sphere of Christianity, as 'the family of Jesus' is bigger than any specific church, and its membership is open to new adherents all the time. Freeing itself from a specific organisational attachment to any church, Al Hayat adopts a very simple vision that can be summarised as follows: 'Believing in the grace of God, and the power of the Holy Spirit is the way to reach out every day to every nation, city and individual through the Word of God.' In fact, this missionary approach is the main characteristic of the channel, and makes it unique among other Christian broadcasting media.

The main strategy of the Al Hayat channel is to search for the shortcomings, deficiencies and imperfections in 'others' in order to convince them to convert to Christianity. As such, it is very provocative, and wages a direct assault on Islam, using high levels of sarcasm to render its viewers confused about their own faith. Through this continuous process, Muslims are provoked to rethink their own faith and practices, and seek a different religious identity. This is quite different from the classical style that has been often used by missionaries. In fact, Christian missionaries traditionally have taken the stance that Christianity, the religion of love, is objectively right and should be strictly followed to enjoy the gifts of salvation, and thus they never attacked Islam or other faiths in such a highly offensive manner. Al Hayat however, stresses the limitations of Islam, and the perfection of Christianity, flooding its viewers with presenters who claim to come from an Islamic background as a way to make an impact upon the audience. A Moroccan called 'Brother Rashid' is one of the most profound of these presenters.

The two most well known programmes on Al Hayat are *As'ela fi Al Iman* ('Questions in Faith') and *Sow'aal Jaree'* ('Audacious Question'). The first programme is introduced by Fr. Zakarya Boutros, a retired priest in the Coptic Orthodox church, while the second is introduced by Brother Rashid, the Muslim convert from Morocco. Both programmes introduce provocative discourses on Islamic faith and rituals.[11]

As'ela fi Al Iman has the aim, so the presenter claims, of opening a scientific and intellectual discussion on religious issues. Departing from controversial writings on Islam, the presenter, Fr. Boutros, has an offensive style when discussing Islamic faith. He always makes a comparison between Christianity and Islam in favour of the former. The following examples from some episodes of the programme illustrate this style.

In one episode, Fr. Boutros discussed the concept of the Holy Trinity in Christianity, in light of texts from the Bible, and of selected Quranic verses. He sought to prove an inconsistency in Islam regarding the Holy Trinity, illustrated in the verses he had selected from the Qur'an. In another episode, Fr. Boutros discussed the concept of 'the Son of God', which is considered to be a central tenet of Christianity, as Jesus Christ is the Son of God, who gave up His glory, taking human form for the sake of salvation. The presenter explained in detail the word 'son' in Islam and Christianity to prove the glorified position of humans in the latter, and the degradation of their position in the former. In another example, Fr. Boutros presented his view about mistakes in the Qur'an, dedicating an episode to his opinions about scientific, linguistic and historical mistakes in the text. The same assault on the Qur'an continued in yet another episode, when Fr. Boutros discussed what he believed to be contradictions in its chapters, or *Sura*, referring to different manuscripts of the Qur'an, websites containing materials on the topic, and some relevant readings. When discussing holy books, Fr. Boutros always defends the integrity and consistency of the Bible, refuting any claims of its distortion and retaliating by attacking the Qur'an. In one episode, he spoke about how to serve God through poetry, as indicated in the Old Testament, referring to Sufism and their similar manner of worshiping God. The presenter, a Muslim convert, mentioned during the episode that Sufism was not tolerated by many Muslims, and was always under constant attack from other Muslim groups. Muslims who believe in Sufism were described by other Muslim factions as infidels, the presenter added.

Fr. Boutros always appears in his traditional orthodox clothes, and discusses the topic of the episode in a dialogue with a presenter named only as 'Brother Ahmed' who is clothed in modern, fashionable clothing. The programme is broadcast nightly, focusing on religious polemic with the aim of proving the supremacy of Christianity over Islam. The presenter and speaker always use other materials to support their arguments, such as electronic messages, publications and photos in addition to interaction with the audience through telephone calls. In May 2010 the programme was removed from the channel without real explanation.[12]

Sow'aal Jaree' ('Audacious Question'), is introduced by the alleged Moroccan Muslim convert, Brother Rashid. Unlike Fr. Boutros, the presenter here adopts a more tranquil approach to tackling Islamic issues, with little sarcasm and a special focus on socio-cultural matters. The purpose of the programme is to discuss 'banned issues', which are always censored in public life. The programme, for instance, discusses the status of minorities under the rule of Islamic Law, and the extent to which this law is compatible with human rights principles. Another topic is the comparison between Christianity and Islam's understandings of the concept of God; what the similarities and disparities are. And a third example is a comparison between the Qur'an and the Bible concerning Jesus Christ. The basic characteristics of the programme are clear in the analysed data from a number of randomly chosen episodes.

In an episode entitled 'A Message to Christians before Muslims', Brother Rashid attempted to glorify the Christian perception of being 'Sons of God' rather than the Islamic understanding of being 'servants of God.' He used a recorded sermon of the famous Salafi Sheikh Mohamed Hassan, in which he equated worshipping God with humiliation. Although the Salafi Sheikh in the recording mentioned that humiliation does not mean anything except doing what is accepted before God, Rashid remained unshakable in his point of view.

In another episode entitled 'The Miraculous Nature of the Language of the Qu'ran', Brother Rashid discussed a number of sociocultural issues and their significance in the debate concerning the Arabic language. He mentioned that illiteracy is a real predicament in the Arab nations, and contradicts the Qur'an when it states that Muslims, including Arabs, are the best nation in the world. He used multiple methods of substantiating his stance. First, he showed some pictures of children repeatedly reading and reciting the Qur'an, the report ending with the conclusion that Muslims fail to understand the meanings of the Qur'an. Secondly, he discussed the issue of the language in the Qur'an, beginning with the notion that Muslims refuse to translate the Qur'an word for word, and consequently it remains ambiguous to many. Thirdly, he used some political events to back up his viewpoint, such as the proselytising approach taken by Libyan leader Mu'ammar Qaddafi in distributing some copies of the Qur'an to Italian women; the presenter contends that they couldn't read it and were not wearing 'decent clothes' at the time. The presenter also highlighted the calls for the execution of an Afghani man who announced his desire to translate the Qur'an.

In another episode, Brother Rashid continued his assault on the Qur'an, claiming that the educational systems in Arab and Muslim countries have failed due to their excessive dependence on memorising and reciting the Qur'an. The Muslims' holy book, he added, contains words that carry rudeness, affront, and lack of appreciation towards groups and individuals.

Another example comes in the episode on the 'Grand Night', the night of Al Qadr. There is a chapter, or *Sura*, in the Qur'an that is known as Al-Qadr, and according to Islam, on this night the Qur'an was revealed, and this night is better than a thousand months. In this episode, Brother Rashid described this night as pure fantasy, referring to his previous Muslim life in Morocco, when he had believed along with his fellows that Qadr was a gifted man descended from Heaven to fulfil people's desires and wishes on a particular night. This night, he continued, is a real indication of the false superiority of Muslims, who think that they are the best, and have the best religious book, while despising other faiths and prophets. It is clear, however, that the presenter conflates Islam with Muslim culture—an approach that evidently requires more study and critical assessment.

In an episode entitled 'Ethics in Islam', Brother Rashid, with a female guest, attacked Islam as an unethical religious discipline, asserting that the Prophet Mohammed was the benchmark of ethics in Islam, and all his wrongdoings are considered to be ethical behaviour. These include, they contended, invading nations, justified robbery, and polygamy. All of this conduct, they continued, was unethical, but was morally legitimate in Islam. The guest severely attacked Islam and the Prophet Mohammed, claiming that women are persecuted, raped and dehumanised in some predominately Muslim countries. Using highly provocative language, the guest described the Qur'an as inhumane. The presenter once again seems to confuse religion and individual cultures. The critics of this discourse in the Islamic World constantly ask scholars to differentiate between Islam as a religion and the conduct of its followers as human beings.

In another episode, Brother Rashid received a guest, identified by the channel as Abdel Fady, to discuss the distinction between Christianity and Islam concerning their understanding of Jesus.

The discussion focused on the contradiction of some verses of the Qur'an when describing the image of Jesus Christ.

The mentality of Muslim terrorists was the subject of another episode. Brother Rashid welcomed his guest Magdy Khaleel, a famous Egyptian Christian writer in the diaspora, and introduced the topic of Islam and its relation to suicide attacks. The presenter introduced a short documentary on the socialisation of terrorists at the hands of an Al-Qaeda branch in North Africa. In the documentary, a fifteen year-old boy learned how to produce and use explosives, to drive a car, and to blow himself up at a military site. A special festival was filmed in which armed men happily chanted jihadi songs, since one of them would soon become a martyr. The presenter and the guest put the decision to blow oneself up down to sexual fantasies—according to them the anticipation of sexual relationships with the most beautiful women in Heaven, as Islam promises them, is the overriding factor in the decision. From a critical point of view, by introducing this particular sort of approach Al Hayat sustains the stereotypical view, prevalent in some circles in the West, that Islam is a religion of terror and that all Muslims are terrorists.

A final example of this point occurred in an episode devoted to the religious polemics of Muslim Sheikhs. He showed videotapes of some of his critics, refuting their arguments and calling for a live broadcast of these polemics. If proven to be mistaken in any assertion, he continued, the Sheikhs would have to apologise publicly.

The impact of the Al Hayat channel is noticeable at many levels. First, a number of Islamic satellite channels were established specifically to counter Al Hayat, and using the same style.[13] Second, a large portion of writing published across the Arab World condemned, attacked, and warned against what was being broadcast on Al Hayat.[14] Third, the content of the programmes on Al Hayat has been hotly disputed on the Internet and in newspapers. Fourth, it has been revealed in private debates with top-level clergy of the church as well as leaders in the Islamic community that Al Hayat has negatively impacted upon the normal relationships between Muslims and Christians at the grassroots level—relationships, which have remained for centuries relatively immune to the hate-filled debates sustained at intellectual levels.[15] Fifth, although the impact of the channel in proselytising Muslims—its main goal—is too difficult to measure, one can see that the channel's influence is more obvious in the Gulf countries and Northern Africa. This could be noticed, for example, if we tracked the nationality of the audience who made telephone calls to the programme. It is worth noting that each time a public debate arises on Christian proselytising, the first entity referred to is Al Hayat, to the extent that the religious committee of the Peoples' Assembly in Egypt (the parliament) officially demanded the establishment of a channel to confront Al Hayat.[16] Sixth, in most public interviews with top clergymen in the Coptic Orthodox Church, primarily Pope Shenouda, the issue of Fr. Zakarya Boutros arises during discussions.

The Coptic Television Channel (CTV)

Unlike the Al Hayat channel, the Coptic Television Channel (CTV) is a semi-official mouthpiece of the Coptic Orthodox Church in Egypt. It was established in 2007, and its board of trustees is comprised of top-level clergymen in the Coptic Orthodox Church. The channel's owner, Sarwat Basili was a member of the highest committee of the ruling National Democratic Party (NDP), which was dissolved after the 25 January public uprising. The main goal of the channel is to introduce rituals, prayers and the church's news, and to gradually become a main Christian channel not only in Egypt, but across the Arab World and its diaspora as well.

The channel has its own orthodox style. It broadcasts live prayers and sermons, accommodates programmes on family and youth, and focuses mainly on the life of the Coptic Church. It started its broadcasting on the European satellite channel Hot Bird, and in 2009 the government allowed CTV airtime on Nile Sat along with other Christian channels such as Sat 7; a decision which was welcomed by Christians after years of official denial.

The channel has no agenda either directly or indirectly to proselytise amongst Muslims. Rather, it congratulates them on their religious festivals and receives Muslim intellectuals and dignitaries to congratulate Christians on Christmas and Easter. In addition, official visits made by Pope Shenouda and top-level clergymen in the Islamic establishments, such as the Sheikh of Al Azhar and the Minister of Islamic Endowments, are covered by the channel.

CTV has an official premise, and most of its crew originally worked in Egyptian Television. Broadcast from Egypt and organically attached to the Church, CTV carries no political agenda and rarely covers the sectarian clashes between Muslims and Christians that sporadically occur. Also, it has helped contain tensions between the two by hosting Muslim and Christian intellectuals, to discuss ways of building a more united and homogenous society.

The Channel has multiple programmes, that are mainly on faith, rituals, liturgy, saints, and Church life. Its orthodox character is clear, and sometimes it involves itself in 'denominational debates', defending the Orthodox doctrine in the face of critical views propagated by the Protestant community. In addition, the closeness of CTV to top-level clergymen upholds its relationship with the Coptic community.

Kalama la Tazol ('The Word Doesn't Fade'), is one of CTV's lead programmes, presented by the priest Bishoy Helmy, with Bishop Bishoy, the secretary of the Coptic Orthodox Synod, as the most regular guest. The programme addresses a wide audience with no specific focus on any particular age-group, and emphasises discussions on church rituals, fasting, the Holy Bible, prayers and theology. The primary goal of the programme is to explain the theology of the Coptic Orthodox Church, and to defend it against attacks from other Christian denominations. For example, one episode dealt with the prophecies in the Old Testament pointing to the coming of Jesus Christ. Another episode was about eternal life in heaven or the resurrection of Jesus Christ, and its lasting glory for Christians from one generation to the next. In summary, the channel is purely Orthodox, tranquil in its approach, focused on its mission, and never includes religious polemics with Muslims, although it has not completely given up debates with other Christian denominations.

Concerning the influence of CTV, I would argue that the channel definitely has a noticeable impact on Christians, which can be observed in various ways. First, based on personal observation and mingling with the Christian communities in Egypt, it is apparent that the channel is widely followed by Copts, especially its live broadcast of Pope Shenouda's weekly sermon. Second, its live broadcasts of Mass attract many, especially the elderly. Third, during religious occasions, CTV is considered the main media outlet, particularly its special coverage of the festivals of Coptic Saints. It is worth noting that Coptic thought is particularly focused on the Saints, such as the Virgin Mary, Saint Mark, and Saint Antounyous, the father of monastic life in the Egyptian desert. Fourth, its ability to introduce the activities of churches from every corner of Egypt in its programmes builds a constituency for CTV among Christians, who become strongly connected to their religious community. In other words, CTV has created a different religious style among Copts, who can now witness, like Muslims, their spiritual life during the day.

Based on the above discussion of the two channels considered in this chapter, representing two completely different approaches to Christian broadcasting, it would help to draw some brief comparisons between the two:

- Al Hayat's goal is to proselytise to Muslims, while CTV tries to enhance their relationship with the government and Muslims.
- Al Hayat defends Christianity by attacking other religions, namely Islam, but CTV preserves religion through explaining its theology and rituals.
- Al Hayat is very limited in its production, direction and decoration. Most of its programmes are borrowed from other Christian channels, mostly outside the Arab World, and their programmes are heavily dependent on a bilateral dialogue between a presenter and a guest. CTV, on the contrary, has a highly professional team, with sophisticated direction and presentation. Its programmes show a great level of diversity in shape and content.
- Al Hayat has no premises or studio in any Arab Country, and its broadcasting studios move from one place to another to avoid any potential threat due to its provocative programmes on Islam. In contrast, CTV has premises in Cairo, including advanced studios, and has its own production scheme.
- Al Hayat has a very ambiguous profile. Nobody clearly knows its sources of funding. It depends presumably on the Muslim converts' donations, and some funding from Western missionaries. On the contrary, CTV accepts donations and funding

from rich Coptic figures, especially from its founder Dr Basili, and also donations from the expatriate Coptic community.

- Unlike Al Hayat, CTV enjoys respect and appreciation across Egyptian society, and some Muslims reportedly say that they follow some programmes on CTV. Al Hayat has a team from different Arab countries, through which it succeeds in approaching viewers in Northern Africa and the Gulf countries. Other Channels such as Sat 7 also claim to address audiences in Northern Africa, but show considerable limitation in recruiting staff or presenting special programmes that reflect the specificity of this part of the Arab World. On the contrary, CTV is purely Egyptian, claiming no Arab agenda, and exerting no effort to reach out to communities beyond its Orthodox domain.

What Should Christian Media Do?

The Christian media came into existence for a number of reasons—educational, missionary and societal—but its current role is a little blurred. Some channels like Al Hayat are involved in religious polemics with Muslims; others like CTV are more insular. It seems to me that we need a new approach to be adopted by these Christian satellite channels. Proselytising to Muslims has resulted in misunderstanding, antagonism and popular intolerance. However, focusing mainly on theology and ritual is no longer sufficient to support the Christian existence in the Arab World. One of the main goals of Christian channels should be to support Christians as fully-fledged citizens across the Arab region, and create more positive interactions between Muslims and Christians. Inter-cultural dialogue over day-to-day life problems provides these channels with a means to fulfil this obligation. As such, I would like to conclude the chapter with some specific remarks on this issue.

My points stem from a strong belief that what is needed in the sphere of Muslim-Christian interaction, and where Christian channels (and Islamic ones as well) can strongly contribute, is in the enhancement of inter-cultural dialogue. Generally speaking, there are multiple forms of Muslim-Christian dialogue that have been practiced in various ways.[17] The first one is religious-based dialogue, where groups from both sides unilaterally or bilaterally debate religious matters in Christianity and Islam. This type of dialogue has become a symbol of the deterioration of inter-religious relationships. The second form of dialogue takes place only in times of crisis, where a number of public figures and intellectuals convene in the wake of a sectarian incident to help calm the situation down. They normally make visits to troubled areas and issue a statement calling for unity and co-existence. Experience has shown that this form of dialogue usually terminates when society overcomes the crisis. The third form of dialogue is not religious but inter-cultural, and this is what, for me, matters most. It includes intellectuals and community leaders who have committed themselves to the issue of dialogue, as it cements social cohesion on the one hand, but also nurtures respect for pluralism and difference on the other hand. Continuity and diversity are essential pre-requisites for this type of dialogue.

Inter-cultural dialogue as a concept and practice has increasingly become a matter of debate both nationally and internationally. Different arguments for this have been made. Its proponents consider dialogue between cultures as an effective tool for sustaining peace and coexistence amongst people from various religious, cultural, political and economic backgrounds. Opponents, on the contrary, raise doubts about the outcome of this type of dialogue.

However, inter-cultural dialogue has definitely borne some fruit. It helps participants from both sides to meet and debate on a regular basis, not only in times of crisis. It also encourages participants to build networks at both national and local levels. As this happens, the level of interpersonal trust will increase at the societal level as a part of the whole stock of social capital. Inter-cultural dialogue also provides room for discussing issues related to the Muslim-Christian relationship such as citizenship, religious discourses, and the role of the media in building peace, socialisation and so on. The accumulation of such work will establish traditions and norms for dialogue, which will be reinforced by both of the religious communities.

Christian satellite channels should take the lead on this track.[18] The existence of Christians in the Arab world will be consolidated and sustained if fruitful inter-cultural dialogue becomes a basic feature of public life. Open, transparent, interactive and continuous, the inter-cultural dialogue will drive Christian media away from the existing feeling of fear and the necessity of being always on the defence, or even daring to be offensive. Inter-cultural dialogue between Muslims and Christians regarding common, daily life problems will free both communities from the appalling sense of inferiority on one side, and superiority on the other.

If they want to ensure positive co-existence, Christians have to introduce a model of dialogue on their own media, and encourage Islamic media to follow a similar path. Instead of being either inflammatory or distant from society, Christian satellite channels must offer a platform for Christians and Muslims to discuss and offer remedies for pressing societal issues.

This function is overwhelmingly needed on Christian satellite channels, and on Muslim channels too if we want the media to serve the real needs of the people for harmonious relationships, peace, positive co-existence, and security.

Conclusion and Recommendations

In light of the previous discussions, some conclusions can be drawn. First of all, Christians in the Middle East face a number of challenges. One of them is the lack of ability to express their faith through the public media, especially in line with the growing fear of Christians proselytising across the Arab region. For decades, Christians have looked for influential media outlets that could enable them to explain and defend their own faith. Secondly, Christians who for almost twenty centuries have unceasingly inhabited what became the Arab world, and who have spent two hundred years struggling shoulder to shoulder with their Muslim fellows for independence and a modern state, feel, more than at other any time, that they are politically and culturally marginalised as a result of growing Islamic fundamentalism. Their mounting fear, coupled with a lack of appreciation of their presence at the community level, has led Christians to insulate themselves within churches, seeking unity in identity, and solidarity in crisis. Christian satellite channels offer them room to preserve and further their articulation within the religious community. Thirdly, Christian satellite channels differ in shape and content. They belong to different denominations: Orthodox, Catholic and Protestant. Some channels are open to more general Christian perspectives, while others are confined to the churches to which they belong. One channel, Al Hayat, has a proselytising approach towards Muslims, but others, including the Coptic Television Channel (CTV) normally show respect to other religions, and focus mainly on their Christian mission. Fourthly, the Al Hayat channel functions across the denominational divide, and has developed a unique approach towards Muslims. Missionaries, historically speaking, built their own mission by proclaiming the merits and virtues of Christianity rather than digging into the shortcomings of other faiths. Al Hayat, on the contrary, has a strident, offensive approach towards Islam, which is particularly evident in two of its programmes; the nightly programme presented by Fr. Zakaryia Boutros; and the second presented by a Moroccan Muslim convert. Al Hayat has definitely had serious consequences for the relationship between Muslims and Christians in the Arab world. Its impact can be easily seen in Muslim outrage across Arab communities, the establishment of Islamic satellite channels to confront Al Hayat, the constant religious polemics between Muslims and Christians in public and private life, and the escalation of sectarian tensions in different areas. Fifthly, the Coptic Television Channel (CTV) is an opposite model to Al Hayat. It belongs to the Coptic Orthodox Church, and focuses entirely on religious matters from an orthodox perspective, claiming no aggressive agenda either towards Muslims or other Christian communities. The channel's programmes are tailored to serve its followers through introducing prayers, Masses, and sermons, Bible study, and youth forums. Its impact is noticeable, and it has a strong following in Egypt and the diaspora. Copts follow their church life, prayers, and Pope Shenouda's sermons on CTV, and some Muslims reportedly visit the channel sporadically to get more information on Christian life.

In conclusion, Christians have established satellite channels to reach out to their communities, especially as they have lacked access to the official public media in predominately Muslim societies. This approach is tolerated to a large extent by the Muslim majority in the Arab World. Nevertheless, the Al Hayat approach to proselytising Muslims has created a different atmosphere across the Arab world in terms of interreligious relationships. It is undeniable that some Muslim channels, newspapers and websites deliberately used to attack Christianity, but Al Hayat programmes have undoubtedly accelerated the level of religious intolerance.

In Egypt, Muslims have started to think even more than before that they are a persecuted majority. Their religion is under attack by the minority, and the government is reticent and apathetic. Furthermore, some Muslims, especially political Islamic groups, believe that the church, which they mistakenly believe supports Al Hayat, has gained more strength not only in its relationship with Muslims, but also in its relationship with the state itself. On the other hand, Christians have their own concerns. They still encounter problems in building and repairing churches, getting access to high-ranking state positions, acquiring fair political representation and proclaiming their own faith. Their Christian religion is always under fire from extremist media outlets, and sometimes from fundamentalist elements penetrating state-owned media.

The situation is relatively serious. Both religious communities feel discriminated against. This translates into the acceleration of sectarian violence between Muslims and Christians, sometimes taking the shape of street-level fighting. Due to the unhealthy relationship between both communities, sometimes normal clashes over something as simple as a commercial deal turn into a sectarian problem.

11

AL-MANAR TV AND THE ISLAMIC SPHERE IN LEBANON

AN EVOLVING AGENDA

Farah Dakhlallah

This chapter examines the role of the Hizbullah-affiliated Al-Manar Television in nurturing the *Hala Islamiya* or 'Islamic Sphere' among the Shi'i community of Lebanon, and identifies the key political, social and cultural values that are promoted throughout this process. It argues that Al-Manar is one of many technologies of subjectivation employed by the Islamist party to cultivate the 'Community of the Islamic Resistance', and operates as part of a web of variegated disciplinary technologies targeting Hizbullah's (potential) constituency. Far from disseminating a monolithic set of essentialised values, Al-Manar presents a continuously evolving discourse that reflects the transformations in Hizbullah's identity and strategic positions over the past few decades. Al-Manar is not simply concerned with the transmission of certain messages, it also plays a ritual role: that of the maintenance of the 'Community of the Islamic Resistance' in time. Furthermore, Hizbullah's discourse should be seen as an 'open text' that is perpetually being inscribed and re-inscribed, read and re-read.[1] In other words, in true Shi'i form, the *'ijtihad'* or 'interpretation' is ongoing.

Introduction

The setting is a familiar one: a Sheikh addresses an audience of young people, veiled women on one side, and men on the other. They listen attentively, and speak only when invited to by the revered religious authority in the room. The topics of the programme are the usual social and personal fare articulated through a discourse of piety: love, marriage, hope, selfhood and responsibility, but the argumentation is striking. Today's episode is entitled, 'The Other, His beliefs and Me.'[2] Sheikh Akram Barakat tells his audience:

The main point is that the mind that believes in the Justice of God, believes that God will not judge people based on sect. We do not believe that only one identity, the Just one, goes to heaven and all the rest of the world goes to hell. The Qu'ran has mentioned this rationale clearly ... A person could be an atheist but may have very good human characteristics. He may help people or be generous. We believe that these good characteristics are a manifestation (*tajalli*) of certain divine qualities ... On Judgment Day there is one Truth, and this is authentic Islam as represented by the Prophet and his House. But we cannot say that everyone else is going to hell.

Upon closer inspection, the young men are all fashionably dressed in Western clothing that would allow them to blend in on the streets of any European capital. The headscarf-sporting women tend to be young, urbane and highly educated. The logo of the programme—called *Ila al-Qalb* ('To the Heart')—features a pink heart with a trail of purple envelopes. At the centre of the slick studio set rests a heart-shaped podium. This is the new face of Al-Manar Television, a more confident, more professional and, more liberal channel of the Islamic Resistance.

The Lebanese-American researcher Lara Deeb deftly captures this spirit in her ethnographic work *An Enchanted Modern: Gender and Public Piety in Shi'i Lebanon*.[3] Over a period of two years, Deeb immersed herself in community work with Hizbullah's women's organisations in Dahiya, the southern suburb of Beirut where many Hizbullah supporters live. During this time, Deeb explored 'the multiple intersections between ideas and practices of modernity and of piety in a Shi'i Muslim community in Dahiya.'[4] She observes how notions of modernity and piety are lived, debated and shaped by 'everyday Islamists', and emerges with a greater understanding of what she has termed the 'pious modern':

... the values of public piety include understanding and practicing Islam 'correctly'; sacrificing one's time, money and life to help others; and supporting the Resistance against Israeli occupation. Underlying all these values is a strong belief in the necessity of both spiritual and material progress.[5]

Deeb highlights practices of 'authentication' to establish what is perceived to be 'the true or correct meaning, understanding or method of various religious and social practices and beliefs.' It is a 'process by which those interpretations of Islam that are considered most trustworthy and legitimate are revealed.' Furthermore, '[a]uthenticated forms of Islam are intimately bound with the idea of spiritual progress, and as such, are understood by pious Shi'is as both necessary to and evidence of their modernness.'[6]

Instead of asking whether or not Islamists can be modern, Deeb unveils a Shi'i Islamist modernity, one that is both pious and modern. It involves an authentication process predicated on rationality to ascertain the nature of a God-given order. It also involves bureaucratisation and institutionalisation. Science, in this view, is compatible with Islam, as long as 'the seeker's intent lies within the bounds of Islamic morality' and as long as it will be used in the service of the community.

Another telling example of this mode of thought is the alternative to the ideal modern woman presented in this context, a model grounded in practices of public piety.

This ideal entails demonstrating knowledge and practice of authenticated Islam, being dedicated to self-improvement, and participating actively in public life and betterment of the community. Rather than an individualised self, this modern self is embedded in social relationships. In addition to the 'emancipated woman', who is imagined as selfishly abandoning her family and community, or as demanding an irrational absolute equality (understood to mean identicality) with men, this pious modern is set in opposition to other ideal types in Lebanon: the 'traditional' person, who practices religion improperly or without true comprehension and who believes that her only role is a domestic one; and the 'empty modern' and 'westernised' person, who is selfish, materialistic, and obsessed with her appearance and social status.[7]

The 'pious modern' is the particular form of *Hala Islamiya*, or the "Islamic Sphere", that is being cultivated among Hizbullah's constituency, the 'Community of the Islamic Resistance.'[8] Over the past thirty years, the Community of the Shi'i pious modern, or the 'Community of the Islamic Resistance', has emerged and been institutionalised in tandem with Shi'i political mobilisation in Lebanon. This Community is founded on two parallel notions of progress: 'progress as increased modernisation and progress as increased piety.'[9]

Public piety is articulated in the entire landscape of Dahiya—in its sights, sounds and daily rituals—through the posters of martyrs that line the streets, the banners eulogising the Resistance, the rising number of women wearing headscarves or *chadors*, the daily call to prayer and the Friday Prayers. Hizbullah's media acts to bring about the appearance of these various forms of public piety, and they also work to bring and bind together this imagined 'Community of the Islamic Resistance.'

I use the term 'imagined' community, not to question the veracity or the credibility of this community, but in the way that Benedict Anderson defined the concept. Anderson described the nation as an 'imagined political community ... It is *imagined* because the members of even the smallest nation will never know most of their fellow-members, meet them, or even hear of them, yet in the minds of each lives the image of their communion.'[10] Anderson traces the origins of national consciousness to the rise of print capitalism, which set the stage for the formation of this new imagined community that would become the nation.[11]

In a similar manner, through participating in the ritual consumption of Hizbullah's media, Al-Manar's viewers are tuning into a specific type of imagined community: that of the 'Community of the Islamic Resistance.' This community is not a static, fixed form of collective identity, but rather a moving target. Al-Manar has come to reflect the changes in Hizbullah's sense of self as a movement, evolving from a somewhat exclusivist 'Channel of the Islamic Resistance', to one that is part and parcel of, and embedded within, a diverse, multicultural Lebanese, Arab, Islamic and perhaps even global society.

The Beginnings of the 'Channel of the Islamic Resistance'

The very establishment of Al-Manar marked a shift in Hizbullah's public policy. The channel was established in 1991, a year before Lebanon's most renowned Islamist organisation announced that it would participate in the first parliamentary election in post-Taef Lebanon.[12] Until then, like most Islamist movements in the 1980s, Hizbullah spurned participation in a political process that it deemed 'unjust' and 'arrogant.' The Party of God saw itself as the vanguard of the Islamic revolution in Lebanon, and advocated the establishment of an Iranian-like Islamic state based on the concept of *wilayat al-faqih* (the guardianship of the jurisprudent). In its 'Open Letter', issued in 1985, the party introduced itself in the following manner:

We, the sons of Hizbullah's *umma*, whose vanguard God has given victory in Iran and which has established the nucleus of the world's central Islamic state, abide by the orders of a single wise and just command represented by the guardianship of the jurisprudent (*Waliyy al-Faqih*), currently embodied in the supreme Ayatullah Ruhallah al-Musawi al-Khumaini ... who has detonated the Muslim revolution, and who is bringing about the glorious Islamic renaissance.[13]

On the Lebanese political system they wrote:

It is an unjust regime in its very foundations, which is resistant to any change or reform ... We consider any opposition that manoeuvres within the specified guidelines of the regime or those specified by the oppressive world powers to be a scarecrow opposition that in the end accomplishes nothing since ultimately its interests converge with the existing regime.[14]

And their alternative was an Islamic state, though one that was chosen freely, not imposed by force:

... we do not want to impose Islam on anyone, as we do not want others to impose upon us their convictions and their political systems. We do not want Islam to govern Lebanon by force, as political Maronism is governing now.

However, we affirm our conviction in Islam as a doctrine, political system, intellectual foundation, and mode of governance. We call on all the populace to be conversant with it and its religious injunctions. We also call upon the populace to adhere to its teachings at the individual, political and social levels.

If our populace could freely choose the system of government in Lebanon, then they would definitely opt for Islam. From this standpoint, we call for the implementation of an Islamic order on the basis of direct and free choice exercised by the populace, and not on the basis of force, as others might entertain.[15]

The establishment of Al-Manar Television marked a policy of gradually opening up (*Infitah*), elsewhere described as 'Lebanonisation',[16] as a mechanism of adaptation to the post civil war context. This policy involved reaching out to the larger Shi'i community and the Lebanese public ahead of participation in the country's first post-war elections in 1992.[17] The elections were made possible after the signing of the Taef Agreement by warring Lebanese factions; the Agreement made meagre reforms to the Lebanese constitution, giving Muslims a larger share of power at the expense of Christians, a solution quite far from the 'radical' changes the authors of the Open Letter had envisaged. It is of note that Hizbullah took eight parliamentary seats, making it the largest party bloc in the 128-seat chamber that year.

The pragmatic *infitah* policy was, however, still in its infancy and, with the Lebanese South still occupied by Israeli and proxy forces, campaigning for resistance was the priority. Al-Manar regularly broadcast scenes from guerrilla operations undertaken by Hizbullah fighters in South Lebanon, music videos eulogising these fighters, TV spots threatening Israelis in Hebrew, and other such programmes.

According to one of the founders of the station, Nasser Akhdar,[18] for the first five years, Al-Manar's programmers were primarily concerned with transmitting 'the daily realities of the occupation of South Lebanon to Lebanese society' and 'the heroic acts of resistance to the occupation in an effort to bolster the resilience of the 'Community of the Resistance' in Lebanon.'[19] A variety of low-budget Islamic resistance-orientated programming was produced to campaign for the legitimacy of Hizbullah's operations in South Lebanon and the Western Beqaa; targeting a greater portion of a Lebanese society that was largely isolated from the events in those areas of the country.

By the time the Israelis withdrew from most of South Lebanon in May 2000, the network had notably matured, with higher production standards, a more diverse programming grid and a wider viewership. A satellite channel was launched, orientated towards widening the scope of its transmission of the Culture of the Islamic Resistance to a global Arab and Muslim audience. The satellite channel began emphasising the role of 'Resistance' in resolving the Arab-Israeli conflict and focused on pan-Arab and pan-Muslim issues instead of domestic Lebanese ones. These transformations would become progressively more noticeable on both the satellite and the terrestrial networks, and it soon became clear that Al-Manar was vying for its place amongst the region's leading mainstream broadcasters. With a calmer Lebanese front, the Palestinian issue began to command more airtime, and more secular soap operas and TV dramas were being purchased.

Al-Manar soon became one of the most widely watched channels by Arabic speakers worldwide, especially for news on the Arab-Israeli conflict, with some estimates citing an audience of 10 million. It broadcasts across the Arab region, as well as in Europe, Australia and the Americas, and is also available free through live streaming on the Internet. During the 2006 Israeli war on Lebanon, and despite being repeatedly targeted by the Israeli military, Al-Manar was ranked among the top ten most viewed channels in the region, even when broadcast from a secret location. Though established and run by a Shi'i Islamist party, its programming speaks to an audience well beyond its core Lebanese sectarian constituency.

Constructing al-Hala al-Islamiya

One way of assessing Al-Manar and its relationship with the trend of increased religiosity amongst its viewers (in Lebanon and abroad) is to look at its dual role in both the processes of transmission and in the ordering of social life. Al-Manar transmits certain values and messages, while bringing together and maintaining an imagined community of viewers through the ritual of communication. John Carey has described communication as 'a symbolic process whereby reality is produced, maintained, repaired and transformed.'[20] Acting as conduits for symbols—which are 'the instruments of knowledge and communication' according to Pierre Bourdieu—the media make it possible for a 'consensus' to emerge on the meaning of the social world, a consensus that contributes to the 'reproduction of social order.'[21] The values that the Islamic broadcaster transmits are those of the pious modern, which nurture a specific kind of 'Islamic Sphere' or *Hala Islamiya*; the community that it produces, maintains, repairs and transforms is the 'Community of the Islamic Resistance.'

The concept of the 'Islamic Sphere' or *Hala Islamiya*[22] was first made prominent by Ayatullah Mohammad Hussein Fadlallah, an independent Lebanese cleric (*marjaa*) who has greatly influenced the development of Hizbullah over the decades. Fadlallah argues that the *Hala Islamiya* is 'essential for the Party of God because it makes Party membership unlimited. Thus what distinguished Hizbullah from other Islamic groups is that Hizbullah regards the entire *umma* as a framework for the party, while other groups regard the party as a framework for the *umma*.'[23]

As explained by Hizbullah Deputy Secretary-General Sheikh Naim Qassim, the 'Islamic Resistance' is not just a strategic choice but a holistic worldview, a way of life:

Resistance for us is a societal view in all its aspects. It is a resistance that is military, cultural, political and mediatised. It is the resistance of the people and the *mujahideen*, the resistance of the ruler and the *umma*, the resistance of free conscience wherever it may be. That is why we have always called for the building of a *Society of the Resistance*, because the *Society of the Resistance* has the quality of endurance, while the actions of the group of the resistance are circumstantial... and whoever chases the group of the resistance will be worn out because he will have to contend with the *Society of the Resistance*.[24]

Hizbullah seeks to cultivate this 'Community of the Islamic Resistance' through the creation and maintenance of the *Hala Islamiya* or 'Islamic Sphere', an all-encompassing Islamic framework for the believer. This is pursued through the Party's infrastructure of social and cultural services that encompass a host of welfare, educational, media and other institutions such as: Jihad for Construction (*Jihad lil Binaa*), for construction and rehabilitation activities, as well as the provision of potable water and electricity in impoverished or war-torn areas; the Martyr's Foundation (*Mu'assasat al-Shahid*), to support the families of martyrs, detainees and resistance fighters; the Foundation for the Wounded (*Mu'assasat al-Jarha*), to care for wounded or disabled victims of Israeli attacks; the Khomeini Support Committee (*Lujnat Imdad al-Khomeini*), that offers general welfare services to needy families; the Islamic Health Unit (*al-Hay'a al-Suhiyah al-Islamiya*) that operates hospitals, dispensaries, dental clinics, and other health centres nationwide; and the Educational Enforcement Office (*al-Ta'bia' al-Tarbawiya*), that provides scholarships and financial aid and coordinates a network of schools, technical institutes and religious study centres nationwide. Hizbullah's Information Unit operates a television station (Al-Manar), four radio stations (Al-Nour, Al-Imam, Al-Islam and Sawt al-Mustad'afin) and five newspapers and journals (Al-Intiqad, Al-Bilad, Al-Muntalaq, Al-Sabil, and Baqiatou Allah).[25] Places of worship such as mosques and *husseiniyas*, the five times daily call to prayer, national holidays such as the celebration of the Israeli withdrawal from South Lebanon, and religious occasions such as the commemoration of Ashura or the Birth of the Prophet also provide opportunities for the reinforcement of this *Hala Islamiya*.

As mentioned by Ayatullah Fadlallah in one of his interviews, when making the distinction between Traditional Islam (*al-Islam al-Taqlidi*) and Dynamic Islam (*al-Islam al-Haraki*):

It is no secret that Dynamic Islam... is not limited to a political party. As long as there is a mosque that bellows the words "God is Great", then the Islamic movement is well.[26]

When asked about Al-Manar's role in the creation and preservation of the Islamic Sphere in Lebanon, Nassir al-Akhdar responded:

There is no doubt that Al-Manar, with the Islamic Awakening[27] in the area, has served to increase people's interest in this Awakening and has increased their conviction in the usefulness of projects that belong to this Islamic Sphere. The station has been able to influence the public to support and belong to this Islamic Sphere through increased enculturation and enlightenment, coupled with an archaeology of our enormous cultural resources, and the re-casting of Islam in a manner that accommodates it to the needs of the age... Al-Manar has a comprehensive view in re-transmitting Islamic culture in general as a framework for the project of the Resistance. So in the end, the Resistance belongs to this cultural project.[28]

Al-Manar can also be considered a product of this 'culture' that it serves to nourish, maintain and (in the case of its satellite channel) export. Al-Akhdar continues, saying:

It is a dialectical relationship but it all started with the act of resistance. With the act of resistance you can produce a media of resistance. After that it becomes a dialectical relationship and they nourish each other. But the act of resistance is the basis.[29]

Harb and Leenders[30] have described this 'Islamic Sphere' and its constituent resistance 'identity' and 'culture', as essential products of Hizbullah's institutions that 'operate today as a holistic and integrated network which produces sets of values and meanings embedded in an interrelated religious and political framework—that of *wilayat al-faqih.*'[31] Such an environment indicates that Al-Manar is but one strand in a complex web of service providers that create, maintain and reinforce the *Hala Islamiya* that nourishes the 'Community of the Islamic Resistance' and its ideal type, the 'pious modern.' Without this network of technologies of 'subjectivation' (constitution of the subject)—much of which depends on unmediated, face-to-face contact—Al-Manar's role in promoting religiosity in Lebanon would be far less effective. Members of other religious communities in Lebanon, or even Shi'is who live in mixed neighbourhoods, are less susceptible to Al-Manar's messages because in such contexts the station is operating outside of the integrated framework that cradles the Shi'i community living in areas such as Dahiya or South Lebanon or the Beqaa. Nikolas Rose describes 'human technologies' as 'hybrid assemblages of knowledges, instruments, persons, systems of judgement, buildings and spaces, underpinned at the programme level by certain presuppositions about, and objectives for, human beings.' Technologies are structured by practical rationality and governed by a conscious goal.[32]

In this context, Hizbullah's institutions, including its various media—radio stations, newspapers, magazines, websites, as well as Al-Manar—act as 'disciplinary technologies' in the Foucauldian sense, in that they structure space, time, and relations amongst individuals through 'procedures of hierarchical observation and normalising judgement, through attempts to enfold these judgements into the procedures and judgements which the individual utilises in order to construct their own conduct.'[33] In other words, the pious modern self is not constructed in the ideological texts of Shi'i *mujtahids*, but in the mundane practices of the everyday, as the self interacts with the sound of the call to prayer, the veiled community services volunteer, the words *Al-Salam Aleykum* as one turns on the evening news. The self comes to internalise and reproduce the procedures and judgements it has been subjected to through 'disciplinary technologies.'

Al-Manar Today

Since the Israeli withdrawal in 2000, Al-Manar's programming has taken on an increasingly secular character, as it tries to appeal to its wider Lebanese and Arab audience. This tendency was reinforced with Hizbullah's decision to participate in subsequent Lebanese cabinets, after the death of former Prime Minister Rafiq al-Hariri unleashed a series of tumultuous events—from the Cedar Revolution, to the Syrian withdrawal, to the Israeli onslaught on Hizbullah in 2006. Hizbullah's alliance with Christian secularist General Michel Aoun (leader of the Free Patriotic Movement) has also had a secularising impact on the channel, and indeed the Party, which has never before found itself in such close relations with a Christian-dominated group. However, this secularising tendency does not detract from the station's key messages, or indeed its role in maintaining the 'Community of the Islamic Resistance.' If anything, it demonstrates the Party's increased confidence, which allows al-Manar to open up to a more diverse viewership.

Al-Manar's morning schedule consists of the call to prayer, a programme on the Qur'an, a one-hour news bulletin, the daily morning show *Sabah al-Manar* at 8.30am and then an infomercial programme, followed by the news. The afternoon is punctuated with news talk shows and bulletins, children's programmes, and a health show. Evening shows change daily. The channel has an average of five hours of live programming per day and has more female than male presenters. International or Arab soap operas and films aired on Al-Manar are not censored, as long as they do not overtly contravene the channel's moral and political direction. Talk show guests and experts are frequently not ostensibly religious (for example unveiled women) or even Muslim, though all of Al-Manar's presenters express some form of public piety.

As observed by Anne Marie Baylouny, the growing human-interest focus of Al-Manar's programming has been largely overlooked by Hizbullah-watchers, as has the channel's more recent embrace of commercial programming targeting a wider non-Shi'i audience:

> Bombed and banned, only the news and blustering rhetoric of Al-Manar have drawn attention. Unnoticed are the numerous human-interest programs and their content. The human-interest and non-religious programming of Al-Manar signals and reinforces the organisation's embrace not merely of the multi-confessional nature of the country, but the legitimacy of alternative lifestyles, an orientation far from its origin over two decades ago, calling for an Islamic state. The change in programming, from Al-Manar's origins to today, was caused by Hizbullah's view of a future for itself among Lebanon's communities, a vision it is communicating and affirming through the station. Static depictions of Hizbullah and its media, continuing to associate Hizbullah's often-fiery foreign policy speeches with its policies and plans toward the domestic community, miss these important changes. Al-Manar reveals the far-sighted intention of Hizbullah to establish a life in Lebanon beyond its military legitimacy, promoting audiences and allowing space for discussions popular with Lebanese outside Hizbullah's core constituency.[34]

Al-Manar's Programming: An Evolving Cultural Product

Religious versus Lay Programming

Al-Manar programming can be grouped into two types: the first is its religious programming, distinguished as overtly concerned with its Islamic agenda; and the second, its lay programming, which addresses the daily concerns of its viewers. Both types arguably serve the same purpose of promoting and consolidating the Islamic Sphere and its constituent 'Community of the Islamic Resistance', by presenting both religious and lay issues through the prism of resistance. *Sabah al-Manar* and *Ila al-Qalb* present two such examples. The first programme is ostensibly secular, but highlights the channel's holistic world-view in viewing even lay matters through Islamic spectacles. The second programme is overtly religious, but presents and articulates certain issues in a manner that is both pious and modern.

Sabah Al-Manar

Sabah Al-Manar (Al-Manar's Morning) is a daily morning show broadcast between 8.30 and 10am Beirut time with a variety of segments focused on family, health, social and cultural issues. The timing of the programme suggests that its main target audience is women at home, though its producers say it is geared to the general public. The show is presented live by two veiled women in a living room-like set with subtle Islamic motifs such as an open Qur'an on a bookshelf, or a painting of Qur'anic verses. It usually features 'expert' guests, and allows for viewers to call in and ask questions. The show's guests are a mix of religious and secular characters, depending on the requirements of the topic at hand. Producer Anwar Ramadan[35] says that, as much as possible, each day of the week is dedicated to a specific theme: Mondays are focused on environmental issues, Tuesdays are unspecified, Wednesdays are educational, Thursdays are cultural, Fridays are religious, Saturdays are unspecified and Sundays cover a variety of topics.

Seven episodes observed over one week in the summer of 2009, yielded the following titles: 'Cardiac Health', 'Quranic Evenings', 'Cosmetic Dentistry', 'Preparing your Child for the Birth of a Sibling', 'In Memory of the Birth of the Three Moons',[36] 'The Victory of the Resistance in the July War', and 'Women Spending Money on the Home: Partnership or Control?' As indicated by their titles, most of the episodes tackle everyday health and family issues, but from an Islamic perspective that is predicated on a modern, progressive and scientific approach. Expert guests featured on the programme are lay and religious, Christian and Muslim, male and female.

A typical episode begins with jazzy music, overlaid onto nature scenes, (usually filmed in Lebanon). Cut to the studio, where the two female presenters begin with an Islamic greeting such as *Bi Ism Allah al-Rahman al-Rahim, Al-Salamu Aleykum wa rahmat Allah wa barakatuhu* ('In the name of God the benevolent, the merciful. Peace be upon you and God's blessings') or *As'ada Allah sabahakum* ('May God bring joy to your morning'). The presenters are dressed modestly, sporting headscarves, and both their maiden and married names are used in the captions and credits (for example Zeinab Haidar Shu'aito or Amal Ibrahim Darwish). The set is similar to those of other morning shows on Lebanese secular channels, with only a few subtle Islamic signifiers.

After introducing the theme of the episode, a 'news bulletin' is read out by the presenters featuring news relevant to the theme at hand. For example, in the episode about cosmetic dentistry, the news bulletin covered reports about a new dental anaesthetic discovered in the United States, the ability of ozone to kill bacteria that cause dental cavities, the bad effects of soft drinks and carbonated water on teeth, and a new US vaccination against dental cavities. After the bulletin, there may be a video reportage, followed by a series of interviews with experts. In an episode on 'Preparing your Child for the Birth of a Sibling', the guests included puppeteer Tamara Kildani (a francophone Christian), university lecturer Dr Dawlat Khanafat (a secular woman, with no headscarf) and education supervisor Rima Younis (a Shi'i wearing a headscarf). The episode on cosmetic dentistry featured interviews with Christian and Muslim dentists, only one of whom seemed overtly Shi'i.

The presenters tackle everyday issues from an Islamic perspective, in a manner consistent with the values espoused by the 'pious modern.' For example, the episode entitled 'Women Spending Money on the Home: Partnership or Control?' featured an interview with a female sociologist and an Islamic researcher. It highlighted Islam's views on women who work outside the home and their exclusive right to their own income, while explaining that times have changed, and there are more women in the labour market who share the financial burdens of raising a family with their husbands. Even religious topics were interpreted or authenticated in a manner that promotes the values of the 'Community of the Islamic Resistance.' The news bulletin in the episode on 'The Birth of the Three Moons', for example, focused on events that occurred during the 2006 war with Israel on this day: the environmental damage resulting from Israeli planes bombing the Jiyeh power plant south of Beirut and releasing 15,000 tonnes of oil into the sea; 510 martyrs, mainly civilians, dead and more than 100 bodies still under the rubble; the Islamic Resistance fires rockets on Israeli settlements; the Islamic Resistance battles Israeli forces in Maroun el-Ras village; dozens dead and wounded in Israeli settlements; and more than twenty Israeli attacks on the villages of Jib Sheet, Nabatieh, Batulay, Qana and Adloun. In the episode on 'The Victory of the Resistance in the July War', the presenter made reference to the intellectual and cultural values of Resistance, and its role in fighting for Justice, on the side of the oppressed. She portrayed Hizbullah's Resistance in this context as not only an Islamic but also a universal one, referring to the demonstrations in European capitals and around the world against the Israeli attacks on Lebanon.

Ila al-Qalb

Ila al-Qalb[37] ('To the Heart') is a weekly religious programme in which Sheikh Akram Barakat discusses issues that are close to the hearts of young men and women. Topics covered include: faith, hope, dress and elegance, happiness in marriage, personal *jihad*, culture of brotherhood, manners in communication, and neighbourliness. Sheikh Akram Barakat is a member of Hizbullah's Central Committee, and Head of its Culture Desk, as well as Head of the Cultural Islamic Al-Ma'aref Association (CIMA). In *Ila al-Qalb*, he gives an informal televised sermon and moderates discussion among the young men and women in the audience. He listens to their views but also corrects them, providing listeners with the 'correct' or authenticated version of Islam. His rhetoric is very much about finding solutions through religion. Sheikh Barakat regularly quotes from religious texts such as the Qu'ran, the Prophet's *Hadiths*, and the sayings of the Imams to elaborate on his ideas. The programme also features reportages and vox pops to illustrate the topic under discussion. *Ila al-Qalb* serves Al-Manar's religious-cultural agenda by dealing with personal issues such as marriage, love, friendship, social conduct and personal aspirations, reframing them within the context of the 'pious modern.'

The opening credits are set in a cityscape, with the camera zooming into the apartments of various residents. The first resident is a woman (without a headscarf) crying; the second apartment shows hands counting US dollars; the third apartment shows two men arguing. Then we see two hands, with palms open in prayer, as well as a religious verse, and the logo of the programme appears: a pink heart with a trail of purple envelopes.

In the episode 'The Other, his Beliefs and I', Sheikh Barakat presents a complex argument in favour of religiosity and tolerance in a multicultural society. While maintaining that only the People of

Justice (*Ahl al-Haq*) will surely enter the gates of Heaven, he says that God is not sectarian, and that followers of other faiths, even atheists, have a chance at forgiveness because of His benevolence. Such an argument lays the ground for increased tolerance in a multicultural society like Lebanon, because it challenges assumptions that 'The Other' is condemned to eternal damnation and that they should be treated accordingly.[38]

Despite the call for religious tolerance, in the same episode Barakat expressed damning views of what he calls Israeli and Western racism. The opening video report of the episode began by explaining that the philosophy of the rejection of 'The Other' is a form of discrimination often based on race, class, gender, age or nationality. The narrator explained that the most dangerous forms of discrimination are those based on race, colour or religion. She said that Westerners are the first to have developed a philosophy of discrimination among humans on biological grounds, and stereotypes of certain nations were nurtured in Western media through selective portrayals of their worst characteristics. The most prominent form of discrimination or racism in history is that of the Zionists, she said, as they classify people based on race and believe that Jews are superior. They believe that the souls of non-Jews are like the souls of animals, and they were only born in human form to serve them. Another severe form of discrimination was racial segregation against blacks, who were also considered sub-human. She explains that in the same manner that sidewalks were racially segregated in 1930s America, racism against Middle Easterners and Muslims had become prevalent since the events of 11 September 2001. Americans came to classify the rest of the world in terms of 'with or against us.' So in order not to have any 'Others' in your life, except for your real enemy (she said over an illustration of a fighter jet dropping bombs in the shape of a Star of David), listen well, look again, think a little, don't judge based on ignorance, and communicate in order to achieve a better understanding and build a better society. Sheikh Barakat also quoted verses from the Talmud on Jewish superiority, as well as the Protocols of the Elders of Zion, presenting it as a reliable source of Jewish thought.

In the following episode, 'The Other and I in Society', a similar discourse emerges, although focusing more on subjects of race, gender, class, tribe or clan, and social status. He gives examples of prominent female or black Muslim figures such as Fatima al-Zahraa, the Prophet's daughter, or Bilal, the Prophet's friend whom he appointed as the *muazzen* (the one who makes the Muslim call to prayer). Everyone is acceptable, whether man or woman, rich or poor, black or white, excluding the Zionist, the enemy.

Throughout, Barakat is marking the boundaries of the acceptable and the unacceptable, disciplining the viewers' way of thought. The 'Community of the Islamic Resistance' should be a tolerant community, one that does not discriminate based on race, gender, class, or even religion: even an atheist may be forgiven by God. However, members of this community should know that there are others who do discriminate against them, such as neo-conservative Americans, who perpetuate stereotypes about Muslims in the Western media, or Zionist Jews who believe that non-Jews are merely animals fit for slaughter. These values serve the ideal type of the 'pious modern': a self-styled, progressive, tolerant Islamic ideal that also emphasises Resistance against 'the oppressors.'

Conclusion

It is difficult to predict the long-term impact of Al-Manar on rising religiosity in Lebanon. The growth and persistence of public piety among the Shi'i community over the past few decades cannot, and should not, be attributed to an Islamic broadcaster, no matter how high its ratings. Hizbullah is probably the most organised political, charitable and military organisation in Lebanon today. It operates a network of services that cradle its constituency, whether in terms of healthcare, education, media, defence, construction and rehabilitation, or the provision of basic services. This is not to say that most 'pious modern' Shi'is in Lebanon benefit from these services, there are no numbers to confirm or rebut this, but I doubt it. It is rather the *Hala Islamiya* or 'Islamic Sphere' that these institutions create and reinforce, that brings people into the fold. Al-Manar is one such 'disciplinary technology', but one among many. Other factors that work in favour of the constitution of a 'Community of the Islamic Resistance' are the sectarian make up of the Lebanese state; the sectarian Lebanese mediascape; the sectarian polarisation since the assassination of former Sunni Prime Minister Rafiq al-Hariri in 2005; and the ongoing Israeli threat on the southern border. It becomes difficult in such an environment to detach oneself from one's sectarian signature identity,[39] and identify with a larger Lebanese community. Nonetheless, Al-Manar has proved to have an evolving agenda, one that has been increasingly reaching out to other non-Muslim communities in the country.

12

HAMAS BROADCASTING

AL-AQSA CHANNEL IN GAZA

Atef Alshaer

The intent of this chapter is to give an overview of the Hamas's Al-Aqsa Channel and its orientation, through representative samples from its programmes. The channel emerged within the context of the rising political power and popularity of Hamas, particularly in the Gaza Strip. In order to better situate and understand Al-Aqsa with its Hamas-embedded discourse, there is a need to contextualise, even if only briefly, the emergence of Hamas itself within the wider background of the Palestinian cause. The Gaza Strip itself, along with the West Bank and East Jerusalem, were militarily occupied by Israel in 1967. Prior to this occupation, a UN partition plan of 1947 gave the Jews in Palestine, one third of the then population, the right to have a Jewish state on 56 per cent of the land, although their ownership stood at no more than 6 per cent at the time. A year later, the Palestinians and the Arabs lost the 1948 war, which left Israel established on almost 78 per cent of the land of Palestine. From 1948–1967, Gaza was entrusted to Egypt, and the West Bank to Jordan. However, Israel occupied Gaza and the West Bank in 1967, an occupation which triggered the first Palestinian Intifada in 1987. In the late 1980s, then again at the Madrid Peace Conference in 1991 and in the Oslo Agreements of 1993, the Palestinians, under the leadership of the Palestine Liberation Organisation (PLO), made historic compromises by accepting that the Palestinian state should include only the West Bank and the Gaza Strip, with East Jerusalem as its capital, comprising about 22 per cent of the land of mandated Palestine.[1] Hamas, established in 1987 as a reformulation of its older mother organisation the Palestinian Muslim Brotherhood, founded initially in Egypt in the 1928 and in Jerusalem in early 1940s, rejected the Madrid Conference and the following Oslo Agreements with all their compromises.[2] Since then, the Palestinian polity has been marked by deep differences and severe rivalry between those who advocate peace talks with Israel (the PLO and its leading Fatah movement, and the Palestinian Authority [PA] established in accordance with the Oslo Agreements), and those who believe that the only way to end the Israeli occupation is by resistance (Hamas and other smaller factions). Hamas' profile has risen relatively quickly in the Palestinian territories. Within one and a half decades from its first communiqué in 1987, it had become a political and social force which almost every political entity in the region had to reckon with in one way or another. Its ascendance to power was paved by rising Islamic tides in the Middle Eastern region, an ascendance which augured fierce rivalry with hitherto socialist and secularist forces, most notably Fatah.[3]

Against this background, the Al-Aqsa channel was first launched as an experiment on 7 January 2006, in the same month that Hamas won elections for the legislative council with a majority. It was given the same name as the radio station Al-Aqsa. The establishment of the satellite channel was a natural development for Hamas, which has always been concerned about expanding the scope and reach of its media, particularly given the burgeoning media landscape in the Middle East, where competing media apparatuses have proliferated on a large scale in the last decade. Hamas' media presence is also a reaction to the media of the Palestinian Authority (PA), as represented by the official Palestinian TV station, which is connected to the main rival political party, Fatah.

The Al-Aqsa satellite channel constitutes part of the activities of the Ribat Media and Artistic Production Company, which was headed by the current MP and Interior Minister in the deposed government, Fathi Ahmad Hammad, who himself was a leading operative of Hamas' military wing Izz Iddin Al-Qasam, and who then became Chairman of Al-Ribat communications and Artistic productions. The company runs a string of other Hamas media apparatuses, including its bi-weekly newspaper, Al-Risalah. It launched Sawt Al-Aqsa (The Voice of Al-Aqsa) radio station in December 2003, from the third floor of the Bashir Mosque on Tal Al-Zaatar Street in Jabalya Camp, in the north of the Gaza Strip. Its first broadcasts included verses from the Qur'an, and later it was launched as a satellite channel at the peak of the Legislative election campaigns. In an interview for Al-Aqsa radio which was later televised on 10 January 2006, Khalid Mash'al, the Head of the political bureau of the Hamas movement, described the emergence of the Al-Aqsa channel as 'the blessed infant that came from the womb of Radio Al-Aqsa aims to provide an untarnished media that supports the resistance and shares with it the road of *Jihad*.'

At the time of writing, the Director of the Al-Aqsa media network was Mohammad Abu 'Un, and Mohammad Thuriya is the Director of Al-Aqsa Satellite. Both are well-known Hamas affiliates.

The different statements with which Al-Aqsa channel defines itself indicate that it is a partisan channel with an Islamic orientation. These statements include slogans—the most prominent of which is, 'towards a committed Islamic media', or 'the makers of a committed Islamic media.' Another statement posted on its website, describes Al-Aqsa as:

a channel that is Islamic in its identity, humanist in its coverage ... clear in its presentation and credible in its delivery ... it has carried the burden (concern) of the [Palestinian] cause and flown with it to the international community through the airwaves; its media is committed ... its programmes are diverse and comprehensive.[4]

In another important definition that comes under the umbrella of the question, 'who are we?' Al-Aqsa introduces itself as:

a Palestinian satellite channel, Palestinian in identity, Islamic in logic, humanist in its output and an eye on the reality of the Palestinian people inside and in the diaspora. It tries strenuously to put forward the concerns of the homeland and deals with its problems so as to keep the cause alive in all pulpits and squares. It's principled and fixed in the face of all challenges; it drives forward to preserve the Palestinian rights and principles.

It spreads Islamic thought through its various programmes. It deals with the critical issues of the umma and works hard to revive it intellectually, culturally and religiously within a message of Islamic unity.[5]

In an interview with Agence France Presse published on 13 January 2006, Ra'ed Abu Dayyir, the Director General of Al-Aqsa Radio and Television said, 'Al-Aqsa is an Islamic television channel that aims to serve the Islamic movement.' He added, 'we have a message to give and through television we can reach out to people in a better way.'[6] The same agency quoted Ibrahim Dahir, Director of News at Al-Aqsa Radio and Television, 'we do not broadcast news that contravenes our traditions and our *Shari'a* [Islamic law] and we have our own terminology.'[7]

Despite the clear identity of Al-Aqsa as a media arm of Hamas, a number of Hamas spokespersons and representatives of Al-Aqsa have preferred to portray it as an independent channel with an orientation of its own. This became particularly true when Al-Aqsa came under fire from various local, Israeli and international directions.[8]

On the local level, Al-Aqsa has been competing with the official Palestinian TV station, which has represented the position of the PLO and Fatah ever since it was founded in 1995. Prior to Hamas' takeover of Gaza on 15 June 2007, Al-Aqsa played a key role in the mobilisation of the people and in running campaigns of vilification against the PA and its security apparatuses, portraying them as in alliance with the Zionists. But its ability to function at full capacity materialised after Hamas' takeover of Gaza by force after ferocious fighting with Fatah and the PA forces. Al-Aqsa was depicted 'as a mouthpiece for the militia of Hamas', in the words of the Wafa newscaster. As criticism intensified that Al-Aqsa justified and encouraged the killing of PA and Fatah members, labelling them as infidels and collaborators with the Zionist entity, Samir Abu Muhsin, a spokesperson for Al-Aqsa, told the *Al-Sharq Al-Awsat* newspaper in London on 10 July 2007 that Al-Aqsa 'is not a party organ. It meets at times with the Fatah movement and at others with the Hamas movement and only reports what is taking place on the ground.' He added, 'we did not declare anyone to be infidel and we did not advocate the killing of anyone. Our criticisms of any person are not a call to kill that person and we are not spokespersons for any political faction.'[9]

Further criticism of Al-Aqsa came from Israel and other international agencies, including Human Rights Watch, following a series called *Ruwwad Al-Ghad* ('The Pioneers of Tomorrow'). The series is centred on a character similar to Mickey Mouse, Farfour. In this series, Farfour comes across as representing an assortment of religious, political and cultural views. The series was described as anti-Semitic, as episodes were perceived to be encouraging violence and saturating Palestinian children with hatred against Israel and the Jews. After a flurry of international and local condemnations, the series was stopped—though only after much defiance by Al-Aqsa. To distance itself from the channel, the deposed government, represented by Basem Naeem, the Minister of Health in the Gaza-based government, wrote in the *Guardian* on 12 May 2008 that the channel speaks for itself; and that it did not represent the views of the government in Gaza or of Hamas.

Al-Aqsa has faced many challenges in the course of its short history. The most severe of those came when Israel destroyed the building which housed the Al-Aqsa Channel and its equipment during its war on Gaza in 2009.[10] But Al-Aqsa continued its broadcasting from unknown places as a signal of the survival and the steadfastness of Hamas and its government in the face of the massive onslaught on Gaza. In this context, it is relevant to view Al-Aqsa as embedded within the cultural history of Hamas, a movement that emerged from 'the womb of the Muslim Brotherhood in Egypt.'[11] In the course of its history, Hamas has countered the narrative of the PLO and championed the ideology of resistance, of which the Al-Aqsa channel came to be an important faction. Its steadfastness during the aggressive Israeli assault on Gaza bolstered this image of Al-Aqsa as a channel of resistance.

The bulk of Al-Aqsa's news bulletins are concerned with the activities of Hamas and the Gaza-based government, the condemnation of the PA and Fatah in the West Bank and those who lend them any support, whether at the local or international level, and the policies and practices of the Israeli occupation.[12] These three aspects, in addition to any Islamist activities in the world that coincide with Hamas' perspective, constitute much of the channel's news treadmill. Concerning its programmes and presenters, Al-Aqsa has several religious, cultural and political programmes representing Hamas' position and culture. Some programmes are derived from news events and others are fixed in the broadcasting schedule, such as *Al Islam Wal Hayat* ('Islam and Life'), *Sada Al-Shari'* ('The Echo of the Street'), *Yasa'lounak* ('They Ask You'), and *'Ayn 'Ala Al-Watan* ('An Eye on the Homeland').

In addition, its programmes have given rise to TV personalities such as Raji Al-Hams and Islam Badr. Both are highly regarded young presenters. Raji Al-Hams, a twenty-three year old professional from the Al-Nusayrat refugee camp, is particularly noteworthy. He became a media star for his marked oratorical abilities. His oratorical gifts were noticed when he was sixteen, and ever since he has been groomed for representative roles for Hamas. With the establishment of Al-Aqsa, Raji became one of its stars. He was a staunch defender of Hamas and its politics and culture during its violent takeover of Gaza in July 2007. In phone-in programmes, Al-Aqsa presenters are often faced with an audience who complement them on their religious piety and good manners. An old woman called in on one of the live programmes 'An Eye on the Homeland', chaired by Raji Al-Hams, and told him 'every time I see you on the screen, I praise God. Forgiveness and faith emanate from your face.'[13]

The channel has a variety of religious, social and political programmes, and they all feed into each other as they cross from one genre to another. These programmes and political talk shows are often interrupted or accompanied by songs with political Islamic themes.[14] The materials that have been considered for this paper derive from programmes and political talk shows, namely *Yas'alounak* ('They Ask You'), *Al Islam Wal Hayat* ('Islam and Life'), and *Sada Al-Shari'* ('The Echoes of the Street'). They highlight themes such as the upbringing of children, the occasion of the pilgrimage, the migration of the Prophet Mohammed from Mecca to Medina in 622 AD and the twenty-second anniversary of Hamas, and others have focused on the practices of the Palestinian Authority *vis-à-vis* Hamas affiliates in the West Bank and the declaration that President Abbas would not renew his candidacy for the elections. The broadcast materials used in this paper were aired and recorded in the summer of 2009. All the programmes and political talk shows that have been mentioned used phone-ins and took comments and questions from the audience.

A recurrent theme that unites these programmes is that they all draw on the Islamic past as having relevance to the present. With regard to the political programmes and shows of Al-Aqsa, they depict Hamas as the true guardians of religion. Others are effectively depicted as intruders on 'the Islamic identity' of Palestinian society. Al-Aqsa in this respect is part of the project of Islamic revivalism with which Hamas identifies itself, a revivalism of Islam as an identity embodied in social and political practices. Hamas, unlike other secular movements, meshes religion heavily with politics, making any interpretive approach that neatly separates the two almost impossible. The force of this systematised and organised ideology is most obvious in Al-Aqsa, as it is the brainchild of a movement involved in the conflict of cultural and political values within Palestinian society, the Arab world at large and most notably against Israel as an occupying power. Yet, one can see when religion serves politics and how intensely it is brought to bear on it and when it is of less direct relevance to political contexts, as will be demonstrated in the analysis of the programmes below.[15]

Yas'alounak ('They Ask You')—Hosted by Ibrahim Al-Zaim

'The Upbringing of Children' Episode

This weekly programme is broadcast live on Sunday and repeated on Monday evening; it is an interactive programme that sheds light on social, religious and political issues through a special guest and relies on various methods of communication, most notably phone-ins. The guest is usually with the host in the studio, where they sit opposite each other, while the background is calligraphically scripted with the name of the programme.

This episode was particularly concerned with the issue of raising children, and the guest was Salman Al-Dayya, who holds a doctorate in Islamic jurisprudence from Um Durman University in Sudan. He was bearded and appeared in traditional Islamic clothing.

The programme began with the presenter, Ibrahim Al-Zaim, introducing the topic, which was 'The Upbringing of Children.'

Al-Zaim began by quoting from the canonical texts of Islam, namely the Qur'an and the *Hadith*, which is a typical practice in almost all Al-Aqsa's religious programmes and topics. The Qur'anic quote was 'O, ye who believe, save yourselves and your families from a fire whose fuel is men and stones...'[16] This was followed by the Prophet's saying, 'Each and every one of you is responsible for his people...'[17]

These two quotations introduced the premise that the upbringing of children is accorded paramount and supreme importance in Islam. They also promoted the idea that when raising children, one must follow particular principles, and that those who do not follow them can expect divine punishment. The assertion of these orientations came in the question the presenter posed to his guest, which was also introduced with a quotation from the Qur'an, in which Luqman, an ancient wise man, exhorts his son against apostasy, as it is the highest level of sinfulness in Islam. Luqman's exhortations to his son are taken as commandments. After this introduction, the presenter asked his guest, how could this 'true creed be implanted in the souls of children today?'

The guest reiterated the importance of what the presenter said and added material of his own by quoting relevant verses from the Qur'an and the sayings of the Prophet that illustrate the importance of strict adherence to God's commandments. He warned against apostasy and called upon the parents to be vigilant with the children when they are young, 'as the companions of the Prophet were', so that they are grounded in Islam, 'so that the child is normalized since a very young age on the belief and reverence of Allah.'

Then, the guest was asked to explain what Luqman said to his son in the second commandment, as recorded in the verse, 'conduct your prayer, do good and avoid bad and be patient in whatever happens to you for this is for your own good.'

The guest highlighted the order in which God's commandments came: firm belief in God in the form of the warning against apostasy, then the other Islamic commandments, including prayer, fasting, almsgiving, and so on. So far, we have seen that the framing of the issue of the upbringing of children was constituted within an Islamic framework. This framing runs throughout the interview with the gradual interpretation of, and emphasis on, various Islamic aspects concerned with the upbringing of children. The *Sura* of Luqman serves as the pivot around which the discussion revolved, since it enumerated the aspects with which parents should be concerned when raising their children.

Then the presenter asked his guest: 'who is more responsible for the praying of children, the father or the mother?' And the guest answered by saying that 'both are responsible for any shortcomings in the raising of children with regard to prayer or the obedience of God.' He elaborated, saying that the Prophet and His companions were concerned about other things, such as fasting, pilgrimage and almsgiving, than just prayers.. These commandments were clarified and elaborated upon further, so that the audience is introduced to the various Islamic dimensions concerning the raising of children, such that 'children should not be arrogant, but be humble in voice and be taught manners of eating and speaking.'

The final part of the programme consisted of questions from the audience. The programme format, as highlighted above, is interactive, and the issue is moulded within a particular framework, in this case with the intention of directing and influencing people to bring up their children in a particular way.

This is obviously a social and religious programme. It is meant to contribute to particular cultural orientations that have the Islamic canon at their centre. In this particular topic, the Sheikh highlights the importance of introducing children to the pillars of Islam and implanting those within them. Parents have a heavy responsibility to make their children Muslims. Thus, he resorted to the canon and mentioned a saying attributed to the Prophet that, 'Every person is born with an instinctive nature. Parents either make one Muslim or Christian or pagan. Fathers are responsible for the children and they will be questioned about them in the afterlife.'

In this programme, as in others, no differing points of view were presented. Rather, the Sheikh's pronouncements were presented as authoritative and were not challenged in any way. It is also noteworthy that the issue of bringing up children is of central importance in many, if not all, cultures; and Islam tackles it as a system of beliefs and practices which Al-Aqsa reinforces through many programmes which intend to influence children in accord with a particular value-laden system. But in the context of Al-Aqsa as an arm of a political movement, the issue acquires further political dimensions, since children are portrayed as the seeds from which the movement grows and prospers. Children are trained and directed in summer camps run by Hamas; they are given food and shown films by other bodies of the movement. All this happens within an ideological framework of revivalism, influence, consolidation and the formation of a generation that will grow up to strengthen the ideology of Hamas.

'The Pilgrimage' Episode

Another programme was about the pilgrimage, and it was broadcast from Mecca. Again, the programme was presented by Ibrahim Al-Zaim, and the guest of the programme was Zuheir Bin Abd Al-Hamid Al-Khayat, a local cleric in Gaza. He wore traditional dress with a head covering and had a long beard. In this interview, the Sheikh was asked about various aspects related to the pilgrimage, and began by saying that 'many of the acts that pilgrims undertake have no interpretations except that they are orders from the Almighty God, such as stoning and shaving.' This kind of statement relieved the guest of the need to ask any philosophical questions that might have questioned the rationale of the actions. Instead of asking real questions and listening to the answers, the presenter's and guest's viewpoints merely reinforce each other. Thus, the above statement, which could have been challenged, is accorded tacit acceptance. Following on from this, therefore, the presenter evoked the greatness of the day of *Arafa* (the 'day of atonement' or forgiveness, whose observance is central to the performance of pilgrimage) and the rewards that await those who observe it, and asked his guest about the meaning of *Arafa* for each Muslim.

His guest resorted to metaphorical language to highlight the sublime greatness of *Arafa*, so he offered that 'all those people watching on TV, on *Arafa*, wish that they could fly there.' He described *Arafa* as the epitome of salvation, since those who undertake it return to their homes as they were delivered from their mothers' wombs: sinless and pure. He evoked and elaborated on the image of the Muslim who submits his soul to God wholeheartedly and whom God rewards with total forgiveness. Building on this answer, the presenter asked, 'is forgiveness guaranteed straight away and should the believer not doubt it, or will it come later?' The Sheikh's response was that Muslims who undertake the pilgrimage should be hopeful and assured that God will grant them mercy and forgiveness. Referring to a verse from the Qur'an, the Sheikh highlighted that Muslims should not be in doubt over God's mercy. But he warned the pilgrims that the money that they provide for their pilgrimage should be from legitimate sources, and that they, the pilgrims, should not indulge in any sinful acts; they should pay alms, and practice kindness and piety.

The guest maintained a balance in his discourse about pilgrimage, and asserted that those who do it according to Islamic instructions will be rewarded and spiritually fulfilled, and those who transgressed in any way in the process of making their pilgrimage were warned and cautioned about the usefulness of their pilgrimage.

The presenter asks the guest about the way of the Prophet and his conduct on the day of *Arafa*. What did he do? Here the Sheikh referred to the farewell speech, *Khutbat Al-wadaa'* which the Prophet gave at Arafa. He explained that the Prophet asked the people to derive their rituals from him, 'take your rituals from me, He said.' He explained the Prophet's teachings and deeds on the day of *Arafa*, which included his afternoon prayers and other rituals. Then the Prophet sanctioned a law against backstabbing, and called for the proper treatment of women, the strengthening of social bonds based on love and respect, and emphasised avoiding disputes among Muslims, and so on. In this speech, the Sheikh explained, the Prophet 'laid the foundation of the Islamic *Umma* (Community).'

All these elaborations by the guest were meant to highlight the pure and sublime quality that the performance of the pilgrimage represents. He also connected the present with the past, a connection which we will see made more strongly in other programmes.

The last question directly linked the relevance of the past with the present. The presenter asked the Sheikh to say a few words to

Muslims in these blessed days. The Sheikh asserted that pilgrimage conveys a message of equality among people, and that this message should be reinforced among Muslims. He exhorted people to do well and be good towards one another after they have finished their pilgrimage, so that the rewards for their rituals and acts will remain intact and the values acquired during the pilgrimage will be fostered and acted upon.

In short, this programme was about the act of pilgrimage. It offered explanations of the spiritual values of the pilgrimage and the lessons that can be drawn from it. It was a religious programme which connected the past with the present, creating a spiritual continuity seen here through references to the Islamic canon and its continued validity and relevance for today's Muslims. Pilgrimage, after all, is an old Islamic ritual and the programme's overriding concern was to highlight its virtues, and its relevance and meaning in the lives of today's Muslims.

Since the materials for this paper were largely recorded during the period of pilgrimage, there was another programme on the same topic (7 November 2009). The presenter of the programme was Ibraheem Al-Zaeem and the guest was Yousef Farhat, introduced as the Director of the Public Relations Office at the Awqaf Ministry. The Director offered technical explanations about the pilgrimage, quoting along the way the relevant verses and sayings from the Qur'an and the tradition of the Prophet. The devotion of two programmes to this topic highlights the centrality of the pilgrimage as a fundamental component of Islam, with lessons for the Muslims of today. They also show the pervasiveness of what can be described as 'the airwaves spirituality', whereby there are continuous attempts to link the life of Muslims in the Golden Age of Islam with today, and to strengthen the bond between those who are conducting the actual pilgrimage in Mecca and Medina in Saudi Arabia with their co-religionists in the Arab world. Thus, the occasion has spiritual relevance to everyone, whether they are the pilgrims themselves, or the people who watch them on television.

Al-Islam Wal Hayyah ('*Islam and Life*')

This programme was modelled on the Al-Jazeera programme *Al-Shari'a wal Hayyah* ('Life and Shari'a'). The topic under consideration was the migration of the Prophet from Mecca to Medina (then Yathrib) in 622 AD. The past was visibly and more manifestly connected with the present in this programme, and thus the topic had obvious religious, cultural and political overtones.

The presenter started by highlighting the lessons that can be derived from the Prophet's migration to Mecca. The guest of the programme was a well-known Hamas leader, Ismail Radwan, who was presented as a lecturer in *Hadith* at the Islamic University in Gaza. In this programme, Ismail Radwan was presented as a scholar in the science of *Hadith*, but his political affiliation was combined, in the course of this programme, with his academic qualifications.[18]

The guest explained the context of the Prophet's migration, which resulted from the hardships he and his companions had suffered in Mecca. Here the presenter and the guest reinforced each other's statements in highlighting the difficult tests that the Prophet and his companions faced, which are not different from those that the Palestinians now face. The suggestion here was that the Palestinians can overcome their hardships the way the Prophet overcame his. But this can only happen if they stand their ground and remain steadfast in their struggle as he did. Radwan particularly highlighted the patience of the Prophet during his journey to Medina:

The Prophet taught his companions to be patient, when they were plagued with serious afflictions. And we saw those who were martyred, Sumayah, the wife of Yasir, was the first woman martyr in Islam. She was killed by the Kuffar 'infidels' of Mecca; and the companions suffered various afflictions, from torture, to being on the run and imprisonment; all for the sake of Islam. So this was a phase of patience and non-retaliation to the attacks that were launched on Muslims whatever their magnitude or nature was ... They, the companions of the Prophet, were forbidden from responding to the killing, imprisonment and torture.

He also quoted those Qur'anic verses that concurred with his explanations: 'Do men think that they will be left alone [simply] on saying, "we believe", and that they will not be tested? Those before were tested, and Allah will certainly know those who are true from those who are false.'[19]

Anyone who knows the current political circumstances in Palestine and the recent history of Hamas will understand the allusions to the present situation, where Hamas has suspended its military acts against Israel. The message here was clear to the affiliates of Hamas and to other fighters: to be patient and remain resilient in the face of adversities such as those they are facing now. His reference to the hardships the Prophet and his companions suffered and their patience and endurance suggested similarity with the Palestinian situation and the phase of struggle in which they are; the Palestinians were asked not to retaliate to the Israeli aggression against them, as it was not the right time for them to do so. Here, politics was very much wed to religion and directly so.

The narrative of the presenter interconnected with and built upon that of his guest. He asked him about the wisdom of the Prophet in not responding to the intimidation of the *Kuffars*, the infidels.

The guest highlighted that the wisdom gained from the endurance of hardships related to the fact that they constituted one phase in the way towards the realisation of an Islamic reign. When the hardships happened, they were inevitable and they constituted a test, as highlighted in the verse quoted above.

Another aspect that emerges from Radwan's discourse relates to the importance of preparation and planning for the day when the Islamic reign will take place. Using modern language, Radwan referred to the way in which the Prophet and his companions collected 'intelligence information' (*Ma'loomat Istikhabriyah*) and how they planned for their migration carefully.

Those who called the programme asked the guest to elaborate further on the migration of the Prophet and the lessons that could be derived from it. Radwan referred to two lessons and connected them with current political conditions. One related to the story of the spy Suraqa, who tracked the Prophet and his companions, to inform the people of Quraish of his whereabouts. He saw the Prophet, but his horse was immovable and he was thrown from it twice. The Prophet convinced him that he should return to Quraish without informing them of his whereabouts and he would be rewarded with the bracelets of Khosrau (a Persian King, 590–628). He returned, and through this the Prophet evaded him and the unbelievers of Quraish. In Radwan's discourse, this story is connected with those who collaborate with Israel today, those who spy on the people involved in the resistance. Thus he said:

I warn the Suraqa of today, like him and thousands, but rather hundred of thousands who, once money is put in front of them, or once they hear of gold and bronze, they become ready to sell their conscience for the sake of money and gold and bronze. This is the way our enemies work to track down our *Mujahideen* fighters and fugitives. They persuade the collaborators with money; this is particularly true in the context of imperialism, which is led by the oppressive America, where money is granted to some countries so that their sovereignty is bought off and they become clients of occupation and American decisions.[20]

Here there was a clear reference to the Palestinian Authority and other Arab countries, without them being mentioned per se, which were perceived as at the beck and call of America.

Further connections were made between the migration of the Prophet and his endurance in that situation, and the expulsion of the Palestinians from their homeland. In the discourse of Al-Aqsa in this programme, everything the Prophet did or encountered in the course of his migration from Mecca to Medina found echoes in the history and lives of the Palestinians today, whether in their eviction from Palestine in 1948, or the enmity between Fatah and Hamas, or the current political state and orientation and position of Hamas. Radwan highlighted the fact that in both of these incidents, evictions were forced and obligatory. Finally, Radwan reminded the audience that just as the Prophet was finally delivered of his woes, so will the Palestinians be delivered. He also mentioned that few remain steadfast in the face of adversities, but those who do so will be greatly rewarded. Therefore, to reiterate, in this programme strong links were made between the past and the present. The story of the Prophet's migration was connected with the forced eviction of the Palestinians from their homeland, and the hardships and tests that the Prophet faced were compared with the hardships that the Palestinians now encounter. However, movements that adhere to ideologies nourish hope and steadfastness and they are certain of victory, the way the Prophet was when he left Mecca for Medina in 622 AD. Radwan ended by declaring that 'Paradise is for those who cling to their religion and do not get involved in strife.'

Sada Al-Shari' ('The Echoes of the Street')—Hosted by Islam Badr

Sada Al-Shari' is a weekly programme presented on a Friday afternoon and repeated on Saturday evening. It defines itself as 'An open meeting with the audience, where they express their views on the latest of issues or on a subject proposed by the programme. This takes place through phone calls on our numbers from inside or outside [Palestine].'[21] The materials that have been collected from this programme for the purposes of this article, have immediate political resonance as they are directly related to Hamas and its rise to power in the Palestinian territories.

'The Twenty-Second Anniversary of Hamas' Episode

This episode was intended to celebrate the twenty-second anniversary of Hamas. The occasion was introduced in a rather grandiose manner by the presenter and then phone-ins were taken by him. Hamas was portrayed as a source of good on every front, for Palestine and for the world. Its historical beginnings were evoked before calls were received. The programme was intended not only for Palestinian followers of the movement, but those in other places as well.

The presenter asked, 'Wherever you are: how do you view the Islamic Resistance Movement Hamas, twenty-two years after its founding?' The question was followed by a description of how Hamas came into existence:

Following the beginning of the Intifada of stones by three or four days, the first Hamas communiqué was released. It went under the title of "The Intifada", and it gave the green light for Hamas to begin. Now Hamas is entrenched in Palestine and the Islamic world. This movement has branched off from the Muslim Brotherhood. That good/pious group has roots which extend back to the call of the Prophet Mohammad, Peace be Upon Him, even though it was given this name in the last century by Hassan Al-Banna. It spread gradually since then to the point where it has pervaded the world with its glorious message derived from our great religion, and until it reached occupied Palestine. It was Sheikh Ahmad Yasin, Allah's mercy be upon him, and the martyrs and the others who are still alive who have carried the burden and founded the Islamic Resistance Movement Hamas. Our honourable audience: how do you evaluate Hamas in its *jihad*, its political, social and religious dimensions?[22]

That was how the programme was introduced; Hamas was linked to an old and firm tradition of politics directly related to and connected with the tradition of the Prophet. It was inevitable that Hamas has come into existence; that is why it is called *Harakah Rabaniyya*, (the divine movement) in the popular discourse of Hamas. There was a spiritual genealogy which connected the Prophet to Hassan Al-Banna, the founder of the Muslim Brotherhood and then to Ahmad Yasin, the founder of Hamas. Qur'anic metaphors are also used in the process of this linkage: Hamas is a branch sprouting from a good tree, with its roots in the earth and branches in heaven. It is to be mentioned that this type of discourse is typical of nationalist rhetoric, where the party or the country in question seeks to legitimise and authenticate its existence through references to a pure and distant past that it purports to reclaim and safeguard.[23]

The audience was asked to evaluate Hamas, and appeared to be universally sympathetic and in agreement with what the presenter had said. Thus the first telephone respondent who called in from Egypt said, 'I ask you to remain in the resistance and to unite and fight the Zionists. God will bring you victory. We the Egyptians, if they opened the borders for us, we would come and fight alongside you to liberate the Al-Aqsa mosque and Palestine.' Another telephone call from Libya began by congratulating Hamas, saluting the Al-Aqsa channel and the members of the military wing of Hamas, the Izz Id-Din Al-Qassam Brigades, and all members of Hamas. The caller described herself as Libyan Hamas and implied that she felt Gazan. She said that she loved Hamas, and added that 'if Hamas did not exist, we would be dead by now.' So Hamas was considered to be a source of survival. Another telephone call reiterated what the presenter had mentioned about Hamas's Islamic roots. The programme was then interrupted by an on-the-street report, documenting the opinion of people on the anniversary of Hamas. This was followed by a telephone call which proceeded as follows:

I send a Hamas and Qassam salute to Al-Aqsa channel and a thousand salutes to the Palestinian people on the twenty-second anniversary of Hamas. My brother Islam Badr, (the presenter of the programme), and I would like to send a message to some scoundrels in the West Bank, those who refuse to put up the flag of Islam. I say to those scoundrels, the reign of Hamas is inevitably coming, whether you like it or not. You will be trampled on by the feet of the Qassamis ... I swear by the name of Allah that we will put the green flag everywhere throughout the West Bank.[24]

As we can see from these statements translated above, they all offered robust support to Hamas. At the same time, they tackled different aspects with which Hamas is connected, including the issue of the borders with Egypt and the tensions that this has caused. Since the caller was from Egypt, his message of support to Hamas has particular emotional resonance and appeal. He was on the side of Hamas, even though he is an Egyptian.[25] Then there was the caller from Libya who credits Hamas for her own survival. There were strong messages of devotion to Hamas from Arabs everywhere, and these reflect a wider popularity and support for Hamas than just within the Palestinian territories. Thus the programme 'The Echoes of the Streets' is not only concerned with echoes in the Palestinian street, but also in the Arab world and beyond. Hamas in this respect is more than a political movement in Palestine; it has followers and admirers throughout the Arab world, who credit it for the positions on which it prides itself.

The last caller offered the strongest and harshest words against Hamas's opponents in Ramallah. He blasted them as being disrespectful to Islam because, he claimed, they did not allow the green flag, Hamas's banner, to be put up anywhere in the West Bank. He highlighted the inevitability of Hamas's governance of the West Bank. Hamas was mentioned here as a guardian of Islam's doctrine of beliefs, and as a government.

In the course of the programme, the Palestinian Authority in the West Bank was described as being Zionist. And more than one viewer who telephoned in spoke along the following lines: 'there is no refuge except in Allah', when they mentioned the Palestinian Authority in the West Bank and its practices. They spoke of Hamas as 'The Muslims', whereas the Palestinian Authority in the West Bank was not described as Muslim. Islam here was treated as a system of governance to which only Hamas adhered. They also referred to the Palestinian Authority in the same vein as the Crusaders, and mentioned that they were faithless, as opposed to those who remained steadfast under the great leadership of people such as Abu Al-Abed, in reference to Ismail Haniya. There are many connections that can be derived from this discourse. Most obviously, Hamas was portrayed as the safeguarding force of Muslims and Islam against those who were implicitly regarded as less Muslim or non-Muslims. The Palestinian Authority was portrayed as on the side of the Zionists and the Crusaders, historical and current archenemies of Islam and the Muslims. The presenter of the programme, Islam Badr, did not interfere, so long as the people telephoning in were in agreement with the message he delivered, as will be shown later.

'The Palestinian Authority in the West Bank' Episode

This episode was devoted to discussion of the situation in the West Bank. The presenter introduced it as follows:

We will talk today about the practices of the apparatuses of Abbas-Dayton-Fayyad[26] in the West Bank which have touched and affected every Palestinian and everyone who is related to the resistance. They have arrested people and shot at them and killed them, as has happened in Qalqilya and other places. They have also tortured people from the resistance and handed them over to the occupation. Many prisoners when they are released from Israeli prisons are handed over to the Palestinian Authority who imprison them and vice versa.[27]

Whenever the Palestinian Authority was mentioned in the current discourse of Hamas, it was often connected to Zionism and America as the character of the American General who was involved in the training of Palestinian Authority personnel, General Dayton. The presenter dramatised the situation in the West Bank, and said it cannot all be covered in one programme. He then highlighted that the Al-Aqsa channel was banned from working in the West Bank. He contrasted this with the media situation in Gaza and said, 'So that we are not accused of seeing through one eye, some simple violations have happened in the Gaza Strip. But they were personal violations, which were corrected at the highest levels. Journalists work freely in Gaza and they move about as they like.'

The presenter highlighted torture in the West Bank against Hamas members and journalists and presented it as endemic and systemic, whereas he implied that in Gaza it is not. In addition, while the identities of those who carry out violations in the West Bank is revealed, it is not the same in Gaza where violations are passively rendered, obscuring the agency of the violators.

The people who called in were mostly sympathetic to what the presenter had introduced, and offered their own condemnations of events in the West Bank. Religious language was used extensively by the callers. A caller from Libya said, 'the heart weeps over what is happening to the journalists in the West Bank. What can we say? We hope that the government in the West Bank takes the right path…' The presenter then interrupted the caller, who to him was sounding soft, by asking, 'Why, in your opinion, do they attack the journalists and imprison them in the West Bank?' The answer to that was 'it is to shut their mouths.'

Another caller was more scathing towards the West Bank administration: 'The security services of Abbas have ended up executing Zionist-American plans. Under the cover of their authority, Jerusalem was completely Judaised and now they are doing the same in the West Bank.'

The programme evolved into a dramatisation of the situation in the West Bank in particular ways; it directed people into offering particular answers. The presenter asked, 'Why do these kidnappings carried out against intellectuals, journalists, women and also unfortunately children continue?'

It is noted that the presenter often spoke in the indefinite. There were no specific references and no methodical documentation when he condemned the PA for its policies against Hamas and others in the West Bank. One caller mentioned that he was shot during one of the protests in solidarity with the people of Jerusalem, and he asked the Ramallah government to cover the expenses of his treatment, but he was refused. Another caller read a poem for 'the sake of the journalists kidnapped by the authority.' Another caller asked, 'If Abbas has declared his resignation, why does he continue to imprison people?' The presenter encouraged him by asking, 'Why does he do that?'

What we really see during this programme is a choreographed concoction of rage and condemnation of the Palestinian Authority in Ramallah that represents Hamas' discourse and views against the Palestinian Authority. Religion, politics and social norms were used in a manner that showed the Palestinian Authority as being out of step with Palestinians and their cause, and on the side of their enemies. When the presenter's views seem to be challenged by a caller, who mentioned that there were arrests on both sides carried out by Hamas and Fatah, and pointed out that Palestine TV is banned in Gaza, the presenter evaded this by saying, 'We do not say that there are no mistakes in Gaza; Gaza is not a piece of Heaven. Yes, there are mistakes, but they are investigated and there are attempts by the government to put an end to these mistakes.'

Other callers toed the line. One said that 'It is not strange for those who arrest the freedom fighters and kill them, to arrest journalists as they have arrested women and others.' Another caller asked, 'What do you expect of this bandit who reigns over our brothers in the occupied West Bank and cooperates with the Zionists. This Qu'ranic verse applies to them: "whomever amongst you takes them for a friend (the Jews and the Christians), then surely he is one of them."'[28] Another caller said:

I ask all those who hear me to compare. Good is clear and bad is clear. Those who compare Gaza and the West Bank should revise their views. Why are those who make the arrests masked? They know who is on the right and that the kidnappers are in the wrong. They cover their faces so that they are never discovered. We compare those fresh, pious faces with the sulky, dark faces. We compare those enlightened faces with prostration and ablution marks on them with the ashen faced, drowned in the darkness of oppression and aggression.[29]

Another caller advised people to use reconciliatory language and not to accuse any one of idolatry or *kuffr* (mis-beliefs), because *kuffr* means that one has deserted Islam. He quoted the Prophet, 'Anyone who accuses a believer of idolatry is ranked the same.' In all these exchanges between the presenter and the callers, there was a persistent portrayal of the Palestinian Authority as an 'alien other', not Islamic, not adherent to human rights and not committed to Palestinian rights.

'The President Abbas' Episode

The Palestinian Authority and its President, Mahmoud Abbas, also known as Abu Mazen, was the subject of another programme which focused on his intention not to renew his candidature. His decision is painted by Hamas as evidence of the failed policies of Abbas and of his entire negotiation team.

The first question the presenter, Islam Badr, asked his audience was, 'Is Abbas serious? If he is serious, why did he escape?' The answers were all built around stripping Abbas and his presidency of any legitimacy. One caller said that he was elected by a few Fatah members, so his presidency was not legal to begin with. Another said, 'this is one of Abbas's plays, a piece of theatre', and when the presenter asked him approvingly, 'Why it is a play?' the caller responded, 'because Abbas wants to burnish his image among the people.' Other callers said that he had sold the Palestinian people and their cause. One of them implicated President Abbas in the death of Yasser Arafat, the Israeli war on Gaza and in the withdrawal of the Gladstone report.

In the course of the programme, pictures of political arrests in the West Bank were shown, as well as a picture of President Abbas alongside the former Israeli Prime Minister, Yahud Olmert. In short, President Abbas was portrayed as more on the side of Israel than that of his own people.

The attitudes expressed in these programmes about the Palestinian Authority and its President were even made into cartoons castigating them for pro-Israeli attitudes, and shown on the Al-Aqsa channel.

Conclusion

The discourse of the Al-Aqsa channel is populated with religious references in all types of programmes: political, religious, and others. The issues with which Hamas is concerned are covered and reiterated in its various programmes and its positions are passionately presented and ardently defended. Even when the programme is of a religious nature, such as the migration of the Prophet to Medina, the current situation of Palestine is referenced by way of lessons to be drawn from the history of Islam and by way of spiritual and predestined connections made between the past and the present.[30] Hamas here is depicted as a primordial link between that Islamic history, which is read literally, and the present in which Hamas figures prominently. Other programmes illustrate the Palestinian Authority as an extension of Zionism, and without Islamic and nationalist credentials. These methods of portraying the identity of Hamas as a natural evolution from an honourable and incorruptible Islamic doctrine and community existing in a bygone past are meant to solidify Hamas' position at the present time. Therefore, Hamas, according to Al-Aqsa, is the safeguarding force of Islam, whereas others are abusers and quisling authorities.

13

'ISLAMIC' MEDIA, DEMOCRACY
AND THE AKP RULE IN TURKEY

*Ayla Göl**

The rise of political Islam in Turkey has grabbed the attention of
the international media since the *Adalet ve Kalkınma Partisi* (Justice
and Development Party—AKP) came to power in 2002 and reaf-
firmed its rule in 2007 and 2011. The transformation of Turkey
from a secular to an Islamic state, and the fall of the former bastion
of secularism in the Middle East has set alarm bells ringing. The
media has played a crucial role during this process of change. The
AKP has been chosen to examine the relationship between the
media, good governance and democracy in the Middle East for the
following three reasons: first, the role of the media in Turkish soci-

* I would like to acknowledge the support of the Department of Interna-
tional Politics, Aberystwyth University and the Centre of Islamic Studies
at Cambridge University. An earlier version of this chapter was presented
as a paper at the Middle Eastern and Islamic Studies Seminar Series, the
University of St. Andrew's, 13 April 2010. I am particularly grateful to Dr
Michelle Burgis as well as the participants of this seminar and also Alireza
Salavati of Aberystwyth University for his efficient research assistance.
Finally, I wish to thank to the editor of this volume, Dr Khaled Hroub, for
his valuable and constructive comments.

ety has differed from its Arab counterparts due to a strong emphasis on secularism as one of the founding principles of the state;
therefore, second, media channels in Turkey have not been allowed
'religious broadcasting' (*dini yayın*) that would clash with this secularism; and third, the representations of religion and secularism
have been systematically reproduced by the state-controlled media.
However, during the ten years of AKP rule, this trend has changed
and the secular media has encountered the rise of 'Islamic media.'

Therefore, this chapter attempts to analyse the role of the media
in Turkish politics under the ruling AKP government. The methodology of the chapter is based on the possibility of establishing a
link between the theoretical debates of critical social theory and
empirical content analysis of AKP rule in Turkey. Its theoretical
framework is defined by the relationship between 'the media and
modernity' as an agent of social change, and the 'deliberative
model of democracy' as developed by Habermas.[1] The first part
summarises the power of the media as an agent of change in Turkish politics during the elections of 2002 and 2007, and the second
part explains how the state controls the media to support the principle of secularism in Turkey. The third part explains to what
extent the 'mediatisation of religion' has challenged the secular
media under AKP rule. It then offers a content analysis of one
national broadcaster—TRT—and one privately-owned TV channel—Kanal 7—to explain why the 'mediatisation of religion' has
increased the numbers of 'religious broadcasters.' The chapter
concludes by questioning the relationship between the media and
the AKP government in the context of democratisation.

Media as the Agent of Change

The AKP's time in power in 2002 was interpreted as a response to
the failure of secularism and modernity in Turkey. While the
staunch secularists at home feared that the AKP had a hidden
agenda to Islamise the state, foreign observers speculated that the
advance of a pro-Islamic identity and politics indicated Turkey's
U-turn from westernisation and modernisation. Under these
national and international expectations, an early general election
was held on 22 July 2007. Many analysts expected that the ruling

AK Party would win the election with a majority, but hardly anyone—except for one polling media agent (KONDA)—predicted a landslide victory with 46.6 per cent of the votes.[2] The 2007 election was regarded as the most important event, and a turning point, in recent Turkish political history. For AKP supporters, the election result was an unprecedented victory, but the Kemalist elite described it as a political earthquake. Some scholars interpreted the development as an increased tendency towards the 'de-secularisation' and 're-sacralisation' of modern society, in which secular tendencies are gradually being replaced or at least challenged by the resurgence of religious ones.[3] This was translated as the rise of political Islam and the new mediatised forms of religious and secular tensions in Turkey.

In 2002 and 2007, the AKP leadership used three predominant themes during the election campaigns: liberal, reformist and pluralist, in parallel with the progress of globalisation and the market economy in the world.[4] As I argued elsewhere, many voters wanted to replace the old leadership with a new one to fight against 'corruption', and two thirds of them had never voted for Islamist parties before.[5] The AKP won both general elections by bringing together the powers of democracy, an emerging small, pious bourgeoisie in Anatolia (*Anadolu burjuvazisi*), the 'green capital' (*yeşil sermaye*) and the 'Islamic media' (*Islamci medya*).[6]

The three main reasons for the AKP's success were the economy, identity and democracy. The first was the economic crisis of 2001, causing voters to try out a new party in an attempt to pay off IMF debts and loans. Therefore, it was the economy, not political Islam that brought the AKP to power. The second determining factor for the AKP's success was related to the politics of identity. The promising AKP leadership constructed a new discourse of reformist nationalism, which emphasised Turkey's Islamic identity combined with nationalism, as opposed to its secular identity.[7] The majority of AKP voters were particularly enticed by identity issues. For many 'Muslims', it was a deliberate decision to vote for the AKP, which represented their religious identity as opposed to being marginalised and excluded in the secular public sphere. Hence, the third reason was related to democratic participation and the inclusion of Muslims into the public sphere. For the majority of supporters, the AKP's programmes did not entail the Islami-sation of state institutions and society. Rather they aimed to represent a true sense of collective identity ('Muslim-selves'); to remove attention away from the state and high politics that deny the public role of Islam in society; and to include the Muslim iden-tity within the parliamentarian democracy.

In short, the AKP reclaimed the votes of the centre-right in Turk-ish politics by using a conservative, populist and nationalistic dis-course during the elections. The AKP government, like its predecessors, operated within the borders of the existing political and socio-economic structure. More importantly, the centre-right media, including liberal and secular branches, acted as the agent of socio-political change that contributed to the rise to power of the AKP. For instance, the establishment of the AKP in 2001 was pre-sented as an:

'antidote to Islamists and the shrinking political centre' by the major centre-right newspapers. The daily newspaper *Hürriyet*, 'along with like-minded media, worked systematically to legitimize not only Erdoğan and the AKP but also what came to be their trademark: 'conservative democracy".'[8]

Not only centre-right newspapers, but also other liberal papers such as *Radikal* presented the AKP as the only political agent that could integrate Turkey into a liberalising and democratising world, and above all lead it into the EU.[9] In this context, the 'fear of Islami-sation' and the alleged hidden agenda of establishing an Islamic state seemed to be exaggerated.

Since they came to power in 2002, the AKP leaders have operated through ambivalence, which allowed them to switch between Islam and modernity, and between secular and religious practices. Mean-while, the AKP's special relations with liberal democracy, the 'Islamic media', and the 'green' capital have led to a re-enchantment with religion as a source of identity and modernity in a Muslim society. The increased public visibility of Islam was an unprece-dented consequence of AKP policies. Not only in Turkey, but also in other Western countries. As Thompson argues, the increased presence of religious themes in the media may indicate a negation of the idea that secularisation is the hallmark of high modernity, and that the media is one of the key agents of enlightenment.[10]

Hence, the idea of the media as *the* agent of change is useful for understanding the complex interdependency between the AKP government, Islam, secularism and democracy in Turkey.

The power of media in Turkish politics is usually heightened during crises of secularism. For instance, on 27 April 2007, prior to the elections, the Turkish military, by way of a so-called 'press release' on the General Staff's web page, warned the government against anti-establishment activities and fundamentalist (*irticai*) developments contrary to the basic principles of the Turkish Republic. Based upon its interpretation of AKP policies, the Turkish Armed Forces declared itself part of the secularist debate as 'an absolute protector of *laiklik* (laicity)' and would take immediate action when necessary.[11] There was an 'e-memorandum' along the lines of a 'press release', referred to as the February post-modern coup of 2007. Secularists accused AKP leaders of seeking a 'silent' Islamist revolution since taking power in 2002.[12] It was evident that the secular establishment was concerned about the pro-Islamic policies of the AKP, which could bring Atatürk's legacy and his *laic* (secular) Turkish Republic to an end.[13] Subsequent key events between 2002 and 2012, such as Abdullah Gül's conspiratorial elevation to the presidency, the Ergenokon case, initiatives to remove a decades-long ban on the wearing of headscarves at universities, and tax fines for the Doğan Media group under the AKP's rule, have continued to intensify the fears of the government's sceptics. The rise of the AKP has not only led to the increasing visibility of Islam, but has also challenged the boundaries of the secular public sphere and the meaning of democracy in modern Turkey.

The Control of the Media by the Secular State

Based on the most comprehensive analysis of the available statistical data from seventy-four Western countries covering the period 1981–2001, Norris and Inglehart found a clear correlation between the modernisation of society and the decline in religious behaviour and beliefs.[14] In the age of modernity, Western societies advanced in parallel with the rise of industrial capitalism, within which the printing press became an agent of change, and the belief in rationality and scientific progress weakened religious explanations, thus supporting the individualisation of belief systems and the rise of secularism in early European history.[15]

In modern societies, the media has the power to ritualise the habits of everyday life, as well as to construct knowledge about the events of society at large. This is done by replacing the sense of belonging to smaller, traditional institutions, like family, school and church or mosque, with modern social institutions, such as the social networks of theatres, museums and art galleries, and so on.[16] Within this historical trend, the media also has the potential to take over many of the social functions that used to be performed by religious institutions. For example, attending morning prayers was commonly replaced by reading morning newspapers after the development of print capitalism in the twentieth century and, most probably, checking emails in the twenty-first century. Hence, similar social activities such as traditional rituals, worship, mourning and celebration that used to belong to institutionalised religion have been taken over by the media and transformed into more or less secular activities in the modern age. Television sets, radios, telephones and computers have gradually become an integral part of modern daily life. Historically, the initial challenge to religion came from the rise of nationalism as a modern ideology that replaced the sovereignty of God with that of a nation-state. This could not have been achieved without the channels of printing and mass media.

In early European history, the impact of printing on the Renaissance, the Protestant Reformation and the Scientific Revolution has been strongly recognised.[17] It was Benedict Anderson's *Imagined Communities* that later explained how the development of 'print capitalism' stimulated the spread of nationalism.[18] During this progress, the print media was effective not only for constructing the nation and national identity, but also for disseminating the idea of belonging to an 'imagined community' to its distant members.[19] The rise of modern Turkish nationalism neatly fits into Anderson's theory of an 'imagined community.' In particular, I have argued that the Ottoman Empire's modernisation policies led to the development of 'print capitalism', contributing to the rise of nationalism within both Muslim and non-Muslim *millets*. The imagination of a

Turkish nation was achieved via the self-other dichotomy through 'othering' Armenians.[20] As part of Turkish modernisation during the twentieth century, the media contributed to producing a national discourse and representing the 'secular face' of the new Turkish state and nation.[21] Consequently, media channels—the 'secular media'—have become creators and distributors of 'secularism' after the Turkish transition to a modern nation-state from the Islamic Ottoman Empire. In the Turkish model, the secular media was set up as part of the new state ideology to serve as a medium of 'disenchantment' with religion and sacred authority in the Turkish state and society.

In the Arab Middle East, contrary to the Turkish model, the representations of religious issues tend to originate from 'institutionalised' Islam, as discussed in various chapters of this volume. In Arab societies, institutionalised religion is mixed with the specific Arab tradition and culture of each country. In the Turkish model, Islam is synthesised within Turkey's tradition and culture between Europe and the Middle East. Religion is mediated by 'institutionalised' secularism—also referred to as 'authoritarian' secularism—that pushes Islam to the private sphere under the control of the state in Turkey.[22] In the public sphere, the representations of secularism are systematically produced by the state-controlled media and disseminated through various genres such as news, documentary, drama, comedy, entertainment, soap opera and so on. Through these genres, the state-controlled media conduits, languages, and environments, reproduced the 'secular face' of the Turkish state and society.[23]

The Turkish Radio and Television Corporation (*Türkiye Radyo ve Televizyon Kurumu*—TRT) was founded in order to achieve these specific tasks in 1964.[24] The state exercised an absolute monopoly on radio and television broadcasts, guaranteed by the Constitution (Article 133) and the 1983 Radio and Television Law (Law No. 2954). The state monopoly was interrupted when the Turkish Parliament amended Article 133 and annulled Law No. 2954 by offering the possibility of privately-owned broadcasting in 1993. However, the Turkish state found another way of asserting its control over the media after the termination of state monopoly over broadcasting.

In 1994, the Radio and Television Supreme Council (*Radyo ve Televizyon Üst Kurulu*, RTÜK) was created as a government agency to have firmer regulatory control over broadcast media in the country. Its main duties were to allocate channels, frequencies, and bands; to control the transmitting facilities of radio stations and television networks; to set up regulations concerning related audiovisual issues; to monitor all broadcasting, and also to issue warnings and assess punishments when broadcasting laws are violated.[25] In short, the RTÜK was put in charge of censorship for issues considered to be detrimental to the existence of the Turkish state. In general, any printed or broadcasting media that might have been expressing views contrary to the governmental stand on secularism, national security and peace, and/or critical of those in power, have had the possibility of being censored and shut down. The most key censorship issues have included secularism, political Islam, the military, the Kurdish question and the Armenian 'genocide.' In 2000, The RTÜK ordered more than 4,500 days of suspension on media organisations for violations of the country's broadcast principles. In 2002, 2005 and 2008, the RTÜK introduced legal changes to include monetary fines for violations of broadcast laws in the country. Its critics claim that these closures of TV and radio channels by the RTÜK create excessive self-censorship of broadcasting in Turkey.[26]

Under the censorship of the RTÜK, traditionally no 'religious broadcasting' could take place in Turkey, but the pro-Islamic AKP's policies towards multi-media groups added a new dimension to the existing dynamics. Under AKP rule, the number of TV programmes that were interested in 'religious issues' has increased. This new trend is identified as the 'mediatisation of religion' in Turkey, as I will explain next.

The 'Mediatisation of Religion' under AKP Rule

According to Danish scholar Stig Hjarvard, 'the media's impact on religion may be manifold and at times contradictory, but as a whole the media as conduits, languages and environments are responsible for the mediatisation of religion.'[27] In this understanding, 'mediatisation' is about the long-term process of changing social institutions and modes of interactions in culture and society, due to the growing importance of media in all strands of society. Hence:

Mediatisation is the process of social change that to some extent subsumes other social or cultural fields into the logic of the media. In the case of religion, the media—as conduits, languages and environments—facilitate changes in the amount, content and direction of religious messages in society, at the same time as they *transform religious representations* and challenge and replace the authority of the institutionalised religions. Through these processes, religion as a social and cultural activity has become mediatised.[28]

The three different metaphors and images of the media as conduits, languages and environments refer to the following: the first metaphor of 'media as conduits' relates to the content of media channels that transport specific symbols and messages from 'senders to receivers' across distances.[29] Specifically, researchers engage with the content analysis of media: what kinds of messages are transmitted, what topics occupy the media agenda, how much attention does one theme get compared with another and so on. According to Meyrowitz's second image of 'media as languages', the research focuses on the various ways in which the media discursively produces the messages, and frames the relationship between the 'sender, content and receiver.'[30] In particular, the choices of medium and genre influence important features such as the narrative construction, reality status and the mode of reception of particular messages. The third metaphor of 'media as environments', relates to the ways in which media systems and institutions facilitate and structure human interaction and communication. As highlighted by Hroub in the introduction, the content analysis of the Arab media is carried out to show how 'religious broadcasting' acts as a distributor of religious representations and 'anti-Western' sentiments in the Middle East; and why various kinds of messages depend on the political and cultural context of each case study, in other chapters of this volume.

In the context of Turkey, the growing importance of the media as an agent of social change that contributed towards the rise of the AKP to power has become evident, as analysed earlier, in relation to the general elections of 2002 and 2007. Furthermore, in order to examine how the media—as conduits, languages and environments—facilitated social changes in the amount, content and direction of religious messaging in Turkish society, I carried out content analysis on two TV channels—national and privately-owned.

As indicated earlier, the national broadcaster TRT had the hegemony of defining the media agenda since its establishment in 1964, and therefore it is crucial to tracing any change in religious broadcasting. The privately owned TV channel Kanal 7, was chosen because it has more programmes with 'religious' themes than other private channels, which challenges the hegemony of the TRT.

The first analysis is of the national TV broadcaster (TRT). The TRT broadcasting network consists of five national channels—TRT 1 (general), TRT 2 (culture and art), TRT 3 (youth channel with sports and music programmes and also live broadcasts from the Turkish National Grand Assembly at specific hours of the day), TRT 4 (education) and TRT-GAP (regional for the south-eastern region)—and two satellite channels (TRT-INT for Europe, USA and Australia; and TRT-AVRASYA for Central Asia and Caucasus) broadcasting internationally.[31] The state-owned TRT had the monopoly in broadcasting for almost three decades. After the AKP government came to power, it replaced the general directorate of the TRT (TRT *Genel Müdürlüğü*) in 2004. Secular sceptics of the AKP government claimed that the number of 'religious programmes' increased under their governance. In an official statement in 2006, the TRT Directorate refuted the accusation of an increasing volume of 'religious broadcasting', and provided the following comparison: there were four 'religious programmes' when the AKP took over the TRT on 12 January 2004—specifically, on TRT 1: *İnanç Dünyası* ('The World of Belief', 30 minutes); TRT 2: *İnanç ve Bilim* ('Belief and Science', 30 minutes); TRT INT: *İnanç Dünyası* ('The World of Belief', 30 minutes); TRT 4: *Diyanet Saati* ('The Hour of the Directorate of Religion', 60 minutes)—and the numbers and lengths of 'religious programmes' remained the same after 2004—that is, on TRT 1: *Yolcu* ('Traveller', 30 minutes); TRT 2: *Hayat ve Din* ('Life and Religion', 30 minutes); TRT INT: *Sonsuzluk Yolcusu* ('Traveller of Infinity', 30 minutes); TRT 4: *İslam'ın Aydınlığında* ('In the Light of Islam', 60 minutes). However, as of August 2010, the content analyses of TRT programmes indicate that the numbers of programmes with 'religious' themes had continued to increase. For instance, *Adı Güzel Kendi Güzel Muhammed* ('The Beautiful Muhammad and his Beautiful Name') is a weekly round-table discussion programme that introduces the life and exemplary habits of the Prophet Muhammad to the general public. *Kur'an Işığında* ('In the Light of Qur'an') is a daily programme that focuses on how the Qur'an can have positive effects on the daily life of the general public.

Additionally, there are more programmes with 'religious themes' on privately owned TV channels. The first privately owned commercial TV Channel, STAR 1, began broadcasting via satellite from Germany in 1990. Following STAR 1's example, more than 100 local commercial TV channels and around 500 local radio channels were established, and broadcasted without official licenses. In 1995, MED TV—a United Kingdom-based station—began satellite channel broadcasting and targeted the Kurdish audience in Turkey, the Middle East and Europe. The Turkish state immediately lobbied for its closure and often jammed its signals. In 1999, the UK's Independent Television Commission (ITC) revoked MED TV's license. Afterwards, two new satellite channels—CTV (Cultural Television) and MEDYA-TV—were set up and targeted Kurdish populations. MEDYA-TV broadcasts from mainland Europe, but is officially banned by the government because of its sympathies for the Kurdish people. In 2000, Turkey had twenty-four national, sixteen regional and 215 local television stations. None of these TV channels had openly discussed 'religious' themes, with the exception of programmes related to fasting during the holy month of Ramadan and religious festivals, until the AKP's tenure in government. In 2009, there were thirteen privately owned 'religious channels' broadcasting via the TURKSAT satellite (Cem TV, Dost TV, Flash TV, Hilal TV, STV, Ses TV, Su TV, TV 5, Kanal 7, Meltem TV, Mesaj TV, MPL TV, Mehtap TV and Batı TV).[32] Among these private channels, the content analysis of Kanal 7 and Hilal TV indicated the following findings.

Kanal 7 broadcasts a TV mini-series that explicitly engages with religious themes, usually during the holy month of Ramadan, and then repeats these programmes throughout the broadcasting schedule. The most famous ones are *Dizi Hz. Isa* ('The Prophet Christ'), *Dizi Hz. Meryem* ('Saint Mary'), *Dizi Hz Hüseyin'in Elçisi*

('The Disciple of Hussein the Prophet'), and *Islamiyet'in Doğusu* ('The Birth of Islam').[33] More interestingly, the TV series *Hz. Meryem* and *Hz Hüseyin'in Elçisi* were shot by Iranian producers outside Turkey. This proved that the TRT had established closer relations with its Iranian counterpart, IRIB, when the TRT General Director İbrahim Şahin hosted Izzetullah Zergami in Ankara. As speculated by the Iranian media, they signed a protocol to allow TRT to import Iranian soap operas and TV series' into Turkey in 2008.[34] According to sceptics of the AKP in the media, these programmes were not compatible with the broadcasting principles of TRT, and the secular tradition of Turkey.

In addition to TV broadcasting, there are over 2,000 daily newspapers circulated nationally, regionally and locally in Turkey. Of these dailies, around forty national papers have large circulations. The headquarters of all the national newspapers and broadcasting companies are situated in Istanbul and Ankara. For analytical purposes, the dailies are identified in three categories in this chapter: pro-AKP; centre-right including liberal; and anti-AKP dailies (See Figure 13.1). The following comparison shows the relationship between the Erdoğan government and the media as an agent of change, to reaffirm the AKP's place in the centre-right of Turkish politics.

In 2004, the pro-AKP media included *Zaman, Türkiye, Yeni Şafak* and *Vakit*, and their circulation was 19.9 per cent. The centre-right and liberal dailies that supported the AKP consisted of *Posta, Hürriyet, Sabah, Takvim, Milliyet, Akşam, Radikal, Dünya*, and their circulation was 49.1 per cent. The strong anti-AKP dailies were *Gözcü, Cumhuriyet* and *Star*, with a circulation of 7.1 per cent. Within four years of the Erdoğan government, these numbers had changed dramatically, as illustrated in Figure 13.1. In 2008, the pro-AKP daily papers can be identified as *Zaman, Sabah, Türkiye, Yeni Şafak, Star, A. Vakit, Taraf* and *Bugün*. It is important to note that the AKP bought the Sabah Media Group, including *Star* and *Bugün*, to control the anti-AKP media's agenda, as will be explained later. The overall circulation of the pro-AKP and centre-right media reached 40.8 per cent in 2008. The remaining liberal dailies that supported AKP policies were *Aksam* and *Radikal*, with a circulation of 5.3 per cent. The pro-AKP, centre-right and liberal newspapers all together held the largest market share, with 46.1 per cent in 2008. Mean-

Fig. 13.1: Comparison of Daily Newspapers in 2004 and 2008

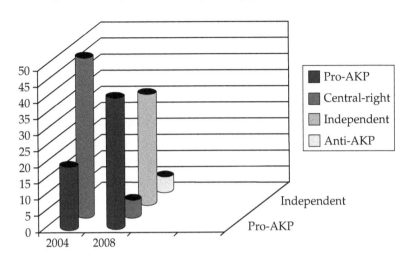

while, opposition to AKP policies created a new group of independent and sometimes critical media that included *Hürriyet, Vatan, Sözcü, Milliyet* and *Posta*. Their share in the media market was 34.1 per cent. The strong anti-AKP dailies were *Cumhuriyet, Yeniçağ, Tercüman* and *Milli Gazete*, holding the lowest market share of 4.7 per cent (See Figure 13.1).

Based on these comparisons, it is evident that there is growing control over the media by the AKP, which has established a complex interdependency between media and governance. On the one hand, the Erdoğan government has used the media as its 'ideological apparatus' to establish the AKP's hegemony in centre-right politics. On the other hand, there is a growing power struggle between the AKP government and media groups. In particular, the authoritarian ways of controlling the mass media channels—i.e. TV and newspapers—brings into question the AKP's dedication to democratic governance, to which I will now turn.

The AKP and the Deliberative Model of Democracy

In the twenty-first century, the traditional roles of the state and social institutions have lost some of their former authority and legitimacy in technologically advanced Western societies. As Castell argued, the media have to some extent taken over the traditional role of the state as providers of 'information and moral orientation' to individuals as well as to society.[35] National and international media have become society's most important storytellers, not only about each society itself but also its interaction with others. More importantly, the media has expanded to almost all areas of society, and has established pervasive networks through which most human interaction and communication must be filtered.[36] This filtering process has become more evident in the context of security and religion in Western societies since the 9/11 terrorist attacks. The media's impact on religion may be manifold and at times contradictory, but it has become even more complex since the events of 9/11 and 7/7.

Meanwhile, Turkey has found itself at the centre of a new debate, the so-called clash of civilizations between Islam and the West. The interactions between Muslim and Western societies have been framed under the shadows of terrorist events that claimed Islam's incompatibility with Western modernity, secularism and liberal democracy. Hence, the AKP's victory in Turkey was identified as one of the first examples of a democratically elected legitimate government in a Muslim society, while at the same time it was considered to be the fall of the main bastion of secularism in the Middle East. The case of the AKP in Turkey showed that the real issue at stake was not the assumed clash of civilisations, but the complex interdependency between Islam, secularism, and democratisation in a Muslim society.[37]

In Western societies, the institutional design of modern democracies combines three elements: 'equal liberties, democratic participation and government by public opinion.'[38] While the liberal tradition of democracy emphasises the importance of the liberties of private citizens, the republican and 'the deliberative traditions stress the political participation of active citizens in the democratic process and in the formation of considered public opinion, respectively.'[39] For Habermas, in the deliberative model of democracy, 'embedding the will of the electorate and the formal procedures of deliberation and decision-making in the vibrant and maximally unregulated circulation of public opinions exerts a rationalizing pressure towards improving the *quality* of decisions.'[40] This model is more concerned with the collective search for a shared solution to social problems, which takes the place of the aggregated interests of individuals or the common will of a nation.[41] Within this process, there are three 'interdependent macro-developments', which underline the political relevance of communication networks and have prompted sociologists to speak in terms of an 'information', 'network', and 'media' society, which are directly related to the complex interdependency between religion, media and democracy in this chapter. These labels refer, respectively, to the rise of the information economy; to the concentration and acceleration of information flows already alluded to; and to the revolution in information technologies.

The complex interdependency between religion, media and democracy in the twenty-first century, as Habermas argues, corresponds with changes in 'technology and education systems', which are leading to an increase in the number of well-educated individuals who are trained to absorb and process complex information:

People at all levels of society are being exposed to accelerated information flows, although access to new media and the ability to cope with the information overload are still extremely unequally distributed between the rich and the poor, men and women, and the better-educated and less well-educated classes and countries.[42]

However, these technological revolutions in the media for transmitting information and mass communication do not themselves speak for an upsurge in deliberative politics.[43] In short, the traditional institutions of states are still required in the 'mediatised' world to deliberate information between senders and receivers in a political system.

In the Habermasian deliberative model of democracy, the state, comprising the familiar complexity of institutions—parliaments, courts, executive and administrative bodies, coalition panels, committees, and so on—forms the core of the political system. The corresponding end products—laws, political programs, judicial findings, official guidelines and policies, regulations and measures—are the result of institutionalised deliberation and decision-making processes. At the periphery of the system, the public sphere is embodied in the networks of communication conducted through mass media at the bottom (See Fig. 13.2). The public sphere acquires political relevance in the first instance as a domain of published opinions, which are selected by the media for broadcast from among the contributions of various actors. The primary sources of the content are politicians and political parties, lobbyists and pressure groups and also experts and actors in civil society.[44]

As Figure 13.2 shows, there is an asymmetric structure of communication between the mass media and the state. The abstract character of the public sphere implies more or less passive public opinion and media consumers. Whereas deliberation requires reciprocity in assuming the roles of speaker and addressee, mass communication in the public sphere is best understood by drawing an analogy with the stage, which does not permit an exchange of roles between the few actors and an anonymous watching public. Furthermore, this asymmetrical structure is embodied in two types of actor who play a 'constitutive role in the dramaturgy of the public sphere: the *media experts*, in particular the journalists, who produce news bulletins, commentary, and reports; and the *politicians*, who occupy the centre of the political system and feature both as co-authors and as addressees of public opinions. Without these actors, a public sphere would not be possible in national spheres.'[45] Hence, as highlighted by Thompson, 'media institutions

Fig. 13.2: The State and the Deliberative Model of Democracy according to Habermasian Theory

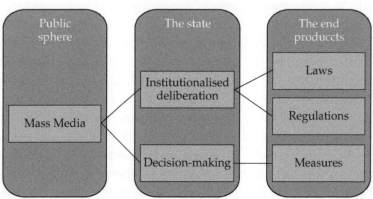

have a particularly important role to play in the development of a deliberative democracy.'[46]

When I apply this theoretical framework of the complex interdependency between media and deliberation to the case of Turkey, it highlights an interesting paradox. On the one hand, Turkey is generally regarded as a model of 'secular democracy' in a Muslim society.[47] It is historically a parliamentarian democracy and has a free press. Therefore, as identified by the Habermasian deliberative model, the two key actors of the public sphere—the politicians and the media experts—are present in Turkey. However, the interaction between the politicians and the media experts has become problematic under AKP governance. In particular, the media is an essential condition of the development of deliberative democracy as long as it cultivates 'diversity and pluralism.'[48] The media has the power to 'provide individuals with a potential mechanism for articulating views which have been marginalised or excluded from the sphere of mediated visibility.'[49] Therefore, 'deliberation thrives on the clash of competing views.'[50] In the case of the AKP, the media deliberately promoted diversity and pluralism by including the marginalised and excluded 'Muslim' voices of the AKP during the 2002, 2007 and 2011 general elections. However, in the name of promoting democracy in Turkey, the AKP in return aimed at curbing the excessive power of the military, judiciary and media.[51] As Thompson argues, 'nothing is more destructive of the process of deliberation than an orchestrated chorus of opinion which allows for no dissent.'[52] This is exactly what has been experienced under AKP governance in Turkey, because they want to destroy their opponents and replace them with new allies in the media.

I argue that the AKP government has missed an historic opportunity to progress a deliberative model of democracy in Turkey. This type of democracy had the potential to facilitate the possibility of promoting the shared purpose of finding legitimate solutions to divisive problems, and promoting 'diversity and pluralism.' In the case of Turkey, these divisive issues were Islamic identity, secularism and the so-called 'Kurdish question.' Despite a promising start, the party suffered from a deficit of democracy under Erdoğan's one-man rule and simultaneously found it difficult to move forward with its agenda. This was most evident in the AKP's relations with the media. According to Habermas, deliberation can develop a 'truth-tracking' potential between the political system at the top, and in everyday talk at the bottom via the media.[53] Hence, the deliberative model of democracy had lost its two key conditions under AKP governance: first, a self-regulating media system must maintain its independence *vis-à-vis* its environments, as explained earlier in this chapter, while connecting political communication in the public sphere with both civil society and the political centre. Second, an inclusive civil society must empower citizens to participate in and respond to a public discourse, which, in turn, must not degenerate into a 'colonising mode of communication.'[54]

In Turkey, the media traditionally has been independent. However, the independent 'self-regulating media system' was constrained by specific policies and strategies of the AKP government. As explained earlier, as the media becomes more controlled by the AKP and acts as an 'ideological apparatus' of the government, it becomes less free. Since 2004, there has been a steady deterioration of media independence as a self-regulating system, as the following three specifically-AKP policies and strategies indicate: first, the AKP launched a new strategy of changing media ownership through legal loopholes. In December 2005, the AKP took over the Sabah-ATV media group, which represented around 20 per cent of the total media market, and put it under the control of Erdoğan's son-in-law, Berat Albayrak. The AKP also bought the largest anti-government media channel STAR. Similarly, another close associate of Prime Minister Erdoğan bought KanalTürk, which was the most fiercely anti-AKP national TV channel, with large financial loans from state-owned banks.[55] This was the beginning of shifting the balance of power between the government and the media from opponents to supporters of the ruling AKP that changed the independent character of a self-regulating media system.

Second, at the same time, the AKP used the probability of an alleged coup plot against the government—most infamously in the so-called Ergenekon case—to silence its political opponents in the military, judiciary, academia and media. In particular, a large number of AKP opponents were detained on suspicion of alleged links to a small ultranationalist group known as Ergenekon. When the Ergenekon case opened in 2007, AKP supporters saw this as an opportunity for the government to clean up corruption. Unfortunately, the truth was far removed from these expectations. In a short time, hundreds were detained and arrested illegally. Some had to wait eighteen months in jail before being taken to court or seeing an indictment.[56] Third, the AKP aimed to discredit the anti-AKP media. The Turkish media is dominated by large multi-media groups such as the Doğan Media Group, Merkez Group, Çukurova Group, İhlas Group, Doğuş Group, and Feza Group. In 2008, the AKP specifically targeted the Doğan Media Group (DMG), the largest media group which owns around 50 per cent of the Turkish media. The DMG owned influential newspapers—including *Hürriyet, Milliyet, Vatan, Radikal, Referans, Hürriyet Daily News*—and widely watched TV channels—including Channel D, CNNTurk, Star TV—and many other media outlets in Turkey. Tax authorities imposed a record fine of over US$3 billion on the DMG for tax fines that stemmed from the sales of shares between group companies. The DMG claimed that the company had kept within the law concerning share transactions between group companies, and that the tax fine was 'subjective.'[57] Given the fact that this excessive fine exceeded the Doğan Media Group's total net worth, one questions the motivation behind it. There was also a history between Aydın Doğan, the owner of DMG, and the Prime Minister, Tayyip Erdoğan, since Erdoğan became the Mayor of Istanbul in the mid-1990s. This was during the 28 February, soft-coup period between 1997 and 2002, when DMG's newspapers harshly criticised Erdoğan. For instance, when Erdoğan was imprisoned after reading a nationalist poem, Doğan newspapers supported the verdict and ran headlines such as, 'Erdoğan cannot even be the Head of a village', and used victorious tones when reporting claims that the verdict had ended Erdoğan's political career.[58] During the general elections of 2002, DMG newspapers used every opportunity to undermine Erdoğan's credibility and often ran negative campaigns against Erdoğan.[59] It is evident that the harsh tax fine against the DMG was actually politically motivated.

In early 2009, the DMG case was followed by press leaks of police wire-taps and telephone calls by the AKP's opponents in pro-AKP newspapers and websites. Not surprisingly, the main aim of these leaks was to discredit the AKP's opponents, and they showed how the parties acted illegally to watch and silence the AKP. Although the publication of even legally approved wire-taps is considered a crime under Turkish law, the AKP attempted neither to identify nor punish the culprits.[60]

This brings into question why the AKP did not seek to publicly identify and punish the culprits who they had perceived to be AKP opponents. One can only speculate that the AKP in fact turned a blind eye to invading the privacy of people's telephone conversations as part of a conspiracy to destroy its opponents.

This evidence shows that the AKP has tendencies to breach the principle of the freedom of the press in Turkey, and that the government has been targeting the opposition media in order to silence its critics undemocratically. It is not surprising that Turkey has lost twenty ranking places in the Reporters Without Borders' Press Freedom Index. In the 2009 survey, Turkey's rank was reduced to 122 out of 175 countries, compared to 102 in 2008, and 100 in 2002.[61]

Moreover, Turkey has been categorised as one of the 'countries under surveillance' since the AKP government blocked several thousand websites, including the famous YouTube.[62] Hence, the AKP has destroyed the possibility of promoting the deliberative model of democracy by putting the media under the control of politics and repressing the freedom of expression in Turkey.

During the ten years of AKP rule, the national and international public perceptions of the AKP have begun to change, and the opposition parties have opened up a new front against the AKP government by accusing it of authoritarianism, abuse of power and increasing corruption. Consequently, it was not surprising that the AKP faced a defeat in the local elections in 2009. For the first time in its history, the party suffered a significant decrease in support and failed to achieve its aim to become a truly nationwide party.[63] More importantly, the 29 March local election was fought primarily on national issues—the Kurdish question—and religion played an insignificant role. It proved once again, the AKP's attempt to appeal to Islamic solidarity over ethnicity and Turkish identity was no longer politically viable. Nevertheless, the AKP was quick enough to recover from this and won the general elections for a third term in 2011.

The Next Phase of the AKP: Liberal Democracy or Authoritarianism?

The pro-Islamic AKP came to power with the support of the centre-right media, including liberal and secular branches that gave the AKP its trademark as being the 'conservative democrats' within a Muslim society in 2002. It promised much and delivered some, but has lost the support of the media in 2012. This chapter specifically analysed the relationship between the party and the media, with specific reference to democratisation in Turkey. The findings of content and data analyses in the chapter are threefold: first, the centre-right media acted as the agent of change that contributed towards bringing the AKP to power. Second, during the eight years of AKP government, the control over the media by the state to protect and promote the secular character of Turkey was challenged by the mediatisation of religion and subsequently the rise of Islamic media. The ruling AKP seized control of the key national media outlets through various undemocratic tactics and strategies. Third, the next stage of the unique AKP-media relations was based on silencing the opponents of government policies and anti-AKP media, as explained in the context of the Ergenekon case and tax fines for the Doğan Media Group.

While the AKP gradually distanced itself from the liberal values of western democracy, it has become more authoritarian and has tightened its grip on the anti-AKP media and opposition. The AKP leaders must remember key lessons from their own experience: first, they reclaimed the votes of the centre-right in Turkish politics by using a conservative, populist and nationalist discourse during the previous elections. Second, a self-regulating media system is still powerful in Turkey. If the media had the power to present the establishment of the AKP as an 'antidote to Islamists' in 2001, the media can use the same power now to reverse this perception. Third, the AKP's 'undemocratic' engagement with the Kurdish issue between 2002 and 2012 suggests that despite the AKP government's increased tendency towards the 'de-secularisation' and 'mediatisation' of religion, reflexive Turkish nationalism still overrules Islamic solidarity. Whether the AKP still has another chance to win the next general election depends upon its future policies concerning the freedom of the press, and the progress of the minority rights of Kurds as equal citizens of a democratic state, rather than their emphasis on political Islam—but this still remains uncertain.

EPILOGUE

RELIGIOUS BROADCASTING SINCE THE ARAB SPRING

The research and case studies that constitute the chapters of this book were undertaken before the Arab Spring. Their findings apply to the decade and a half prior to the recent revolutionary changes in the region. Observing the dramatic empowerment that the Arab Spring has offered the Islamist forces in the region along, with all manifestations of Islamisation, one could argue that the nature and contours of religious broadcasting have been going through a similar moral and political empowerment. In handling the new spaces of authority and influence which have opened up for them, religious channels have immediately (if not chaotically) changed, and are anticipated to remain in a state of flux, and perhaps disorientation, for the coming years. A major part of this change lies in the stronger and more apparent alliance which has surfaced between the political messages of the Islamist movements and the messages of these religious channels, in a display that was unthinkable just a few weeks before the success of the Tunisian and Egyptian revolutions in January 2011. The focus of this postscript is on three ongoing developments that stand out and deserve closer look: speedy politicisation; aggressive Islamisation; and engagement in an intra-Islamist 'war of words'.

Before discussing these three developments it is helpful to re-set the broader scene so that we can position these latest changes. Initially, the motives behind the foundation of the very first influential religious channel, Iqra', in 1998 were almost exclusively commercial, as discussed by Galal in Chapter Four. The founder and owner of the channel, Saudi billionaire Saleh Kamel, was never seen as a devout religious individual, rather a businessman with a sharp eye for profit-making enterprises. Iqra' for him was only a 'balancer' for other non-religious channels that comprised his large operation, the ART network, set up in 1993, and which mostly offered profit-making entertainment channels. The ART network transmitted music and entertainment material and provoked huge criticism from religious circles, thus Iqra' was basically established to offset that criticism. Crudely put, Iqra' was a bribe offered to religious circles, a place where they could do whatever they liked, in return for keeping quiet about other ART channels. A similar bribe-exchange practice was behind the emergence of Al-Resalah in 2006, as part of the entertainment group Rotana and channels owned by the Saudi prince Al-Waleed bin Talal. This trade-off between entertainment and religious broadcasters—between broadcasting moguls in the region and religious clergy—remained for many years one of the foundations of this 'industry'. In those long years during which enormous profit was made by Kamel and Talal from the entertainment fronts of their businesses, religious discourse was introduced into Arab audiences via the back door. These channels would try to outdo each other over who had the purest and most Islamic (and consequently stricter) stance. During those long years many Islamists gained a foothold with these channels, working their way up and becoming prominent staff and anchors. These Islamist elements, with their conscious political drive, kept pushing the messages delivered by the channels in directions that would eventually meet the objectives advocated by their Islamist movements.

Over almost a decade and a half these channels continued to claim that they had always avoided politics—an assertion that was not far from the truth. Any direct engagement in political broadcasting or advocacy would not only contradict their mandate but most dangerously would provoke harsh government measures, including the shutting down of these channels. But the impact and functioning of religious broadcasting was not very far from the boundaries of 'religious politicisation'. In fact, rising levels of religiosity in the region owed much to the years-long influence of these channels, as did rising levels of support for Islamist movements. All of this took place within a profit-making structure with state-approval. This configuration of agents and processes in the area of religious broadcasting in the Arab world has certainly helped pave the way for the Islamists' success in the political processes that took place in the Arab Spring countries.

Against the backdrop outlined above, the first change has been the speedy politicisation of matters. In the post-Arab Spring atmosphere, religious channels no longer feel the need to shy away from engaging in politics and/or taking sides. Most of the non-political Salafi religious channels—Egyptian, Saudi and others—discussed in this volume have become aggressively political. Throughout the weeks of Egypt's revolution, Egyptian Salafi channels such as Al-Nas and Al-Hikma timidly took sides in describing what was happening as *'fitneh'*—civil strife. Some Salafi scholars had even supported Mubarak as the *'walie al-amr'* (the legitimate leader whom Muslims should obey), depicting the revolutionaries as anarchists who were leading the country to disaster. Yet, immediately after the fall of Mubarak all these channels began to attack him, his un-Islamic rule, corrupt family and years of authoritarian reign. Suddenly these channels, like the non-political Salafi groups that had backed them for years, became 'revolutionary' and fully open to political discussion and politicisation.

Saudi Salafi channels have also been influenced by the Arab Spring, and politicised too, but not to the same degree as their Egyptian counterparts nor in the same internal direction of politicisation. Saudi Salafi channels have directed their religious criticism and politicisation externally, avoiding any friction with the official Saudi establishment and staying on the same page politically as the government. A partial 'political opening' has occurred for them from another angle: supporting the revolutions that have been approved by the Saudi regime, particularly in Libya and Syria. For various reasons the Gulf States, mainly Qatar and Saudi Arabia, have bluntly and materially supported the revolutions in these two countries. In parallel to the official support of these revolutions, religious channels have felt free to become 'revolutionary', praising the protests against Qaddafi and Assad. Saudi officials have been content with this support for some sinister motives, when things are seen in a broader context. The Saudis have been very nervous with growing Iranian leverage in the region, which enjoyed extraordinary expansion with the rise of a Shia-led Iraq after the toppling of Saddam Hussein. Thus, Iranian influence has spread across a 'Shia Crescent' that now includes Iraq, Syria, South Lebanon (Hizbullah) and down to the Gaza Strip of Hamas. Clearly the fall of Syria's Assad would deal a great blow to the heart of this alliance and to the Iranians in particular. One unfortunate side of this fierce rivalry between Iran and Saudi Arabia is the recourse by both of them to sectarian discourse in order to rally popular support. Thus, a political enmity and competition over influence and regional leadership has descended into Sunni/Shia polarisation. And the Salafi channels that have supported the revolution in Syria have based their support on sectarian perspectives. The conflict in Syria has been depicted in Salafi broadcasts as an exclusive Shia/Alawi fight against Sunnis. In so doing, Saudi Salafi religious channels have brought themselves in line with the new atmosphere in the region, claiming affinity to revolutions, but at the same time staying within the official discourse of the Saudi state.

The second change concerning religious broadcasting channels is the 'aggressive Islamisation' in programming and talk shows. We could define 'aggressive' as a combination of conventional social/moral Islamisation and calls to speed up this Islamisation through political mobilisation and legalisation. The Islamisation of society has always been the main goal of religious broadcasting, yet it had been confined to a traditional and 'benign' Islamist approach: a quiet bottom-up process starting from the individual and small collectives such as family and schools and reaching up to political structures and governance. To sustain such a process a conscious policy of avoiding regime provocation was adopted. This approach to active Islamisation was similar to that adopted by mainstream Islamist movements during the pre-Arab Spring years; it was a calibrated process that walked a fine line, pushing the envelope gradually yet staying within the limits of the law. In so doing, this gradual Islamisation process had been taking place despite the vigilant eye of the irritated regimes that were conflicted between the desire to stop the process or slow it down, and the lack of a convincing excuse to do so. In certain instances this Islamisation process would overstep the line, condemning this or that government for tolerating un-Islamic practices or failing to uphold Sharia law. However, it could be said that the strategy adopted by these channels was, by and large, non-confrontational with governments, exploiting the areas which were left as 'soft-politics' where conflict over power was almost nonexistent.

But this careful and timid approach has now come to an end. Religious channels have become more adamant in speaking out about the Islamisation of society. Encouraged by the new atmosphere, programmes and talk shows are now oriented towards pressuring governments to undertake constitutional and legal amendments to bring society in line with Sharia law. The quiet, apolitical Islamisation that used to take place on the ground, by movements, and on air by religious broadcasting which only attempted to exploit the margins and grey areas, has ended.

The third noteworthy change is the heavy involvement of these channels in what could be described as an 'intra-Islamist war of words'. This 'war of words' has been best exemplified in Egypt as the religious channels became the mouthpieces of rival Islamist parties competing against each other in parliamentarian and presidential elections. Despite common calls for cooperation and building a 'united front' against 'un-Islamic' forces in the elections, Salafi parties and the Muslim Brotherhood engaged in fierce competition: nominating rival candidates in same constituencies; exchanging accusations; giving pledges and revoking them; forging alliances against each other; and even indulging in smear campaigns to discredit one another. This kind of public 'intra-Islamist war of words' has been unprecedented and shocked many of their followers. Islamists appeared to their support and to the general public as mere political animals driven by desire for power, in contrast to the 'pure' and furnished image they kept projecting about themselves as clean leaders over and above the dirtiness of politics and social status of high-ranking positions. In fact, this Islamist fragmentation in the post-revolution political process cost Islamist candidates, allowing pro-ancien regime candidates to obtain surprising results. This bitter rivalry was reflected on religious channels as they repeated accusations, took the side of certain Islamist candidates and decried others. It is perhaps safe to say, based on some initial observations, that these channels have lost part of their audiences. Their claims of higher moral ground, unimpeachable honesty and 'clean mouthed' preaching have become mired in doubt.

In conclusion, a note of caution. The changes discussed above are still underway. As visible as they have been over the year that has followed the fall of regimes in Tunisia and Egypt, they are still metamorphosing and need to be examined in the longer term.

Khaled Hroub,
June 2012

NOTES

1. INTRODUCTION: RELIGIOUS BROADCASTING: BEYOND THE INNOCENCE OF POLITICAL INDIFFERENCE

1. See for example Mohamed Zayani, *The Al-Jazeera Phenomenon: Critical Perspectives on New Arab Media*, London: Pluto Press, 2005.
2. The number of Islamic religious channels varies continuously as new ones keep emerging and others are short-lived. The number of channels that could be called religious (exclusively religion-focused in definition and material broadcast) easily exceed 120, but the most influential and established number around twenty, including Sunni and Shia.
3. See Khaled Hroub, 'Identity Influence of Arab Information Channels', *Med. 2007, 2006 in the Euro-Mediterranean Space*, (Barcelona: IE-Med., 2007), pp. 251–256.
4. The Arabic-language Christian website, http://www.malikyadilan.com/general/servers/TVch.htm, provides a guide to Arabic-speaking Christian channels (and radio stations). There are around fourteen Christian channels and twenty radio stations all broadcasting religious material in Arabic.
5. See also Abdul Qader Tash, 'Islamic Satellite Channels and its Impact on Arab Societies: The Case of Iqra Channel', unpublished paper presented at conference on Arab Satellite Broadcasting in the Age of Globalisation, Cambridge Arab Media Project (CAMP), Centre of Middle Eastern and Islamic Studies, University of Cambridge, 1–3 November, 2002. Tash was one of the founders of Iqraa and its first General Director until his death in 2004. See also Chapter 4 in this volume.
6. There have been many articles and books criticising the spread of *fatwas* in Arabic. For example see: Fuad Mata, *Alf fatwa wa fatwa* [One thousand Fatwa and Fatwa], Beirut: Arab House for Sciences, 2010.
7. In February 2008 the Arabic version of *Forbes* magazine reported that the three TV preachers with the highest annual income were the Egyptian

289

Amr Khalid, the Kuwaiti Tareq Swaidan and the Saudi 'Ayed Al-Qarni at \$2.5 million, \$1 million and half a million respectively. See: http://news.bbc.co.uk/hi/arabic/business/newsid_7261000/7261877.stm
8. Marwan M. Kraidy, *Reality Television and Arab Politics: Contention in Public Life*, Cambridge: Cambridge University Press, 2010, p. 211.

2. RELIGIOUS BROADCASTING ON MAINSTREAM CHANNELS: AL JAZEERA, MBC AND DUBAI

1. Boyd, D., *Broadcasting in the Arab World: A Survey of Electronic Media in the Middle East*, Aimes, IA: Iowa State University Press, 1999.
2. Ayish, M. *Arab Television in the Age of Globalization: Emerging Trends*, Hamburg: Center for Middle Eastern and Oriental Studies, 2003.
3. See the special issue of Transnational Broadcast Studies Online, No. (16), 2006 on the new wave of Islamic televangelists in the Middle East at: http://www.tbsjournal.com/
4. Ayish, M., *The New Arab Public Sphere*, Berlin: Frank & Timme, 2008.
5. Ayish, *Arab Television in the Age of Globalization*.
6. Da Lage, O., 'The politics of al Jazeera or the diplomacy of Doha', 2005, in Zayani, M. (ed.), *The Al Jazeera Phenomenon: Critical Perspectives on New Arab Media*, New York, NY: Pluto Press, p. 56.
7. Lynch, M., 'Shattering the politics of silence: satellite television talk shows and the transformation of Arab political culture', in *Arab Reform Bulletin*, 2004, in: http://www.carnegieendowment.org/publications/index.cfm?fa=view&id=16242; Lynch, M., *Voices of the New Arab Public: Iraq, al-Jazeera, and Middle East Politics Today*, New York, NY: Columbia University Press, 2006.
8. El-Nawawi, M. and A. Iskander, *Al Jazeera: How the Free Arab News Network Scooped the World and Changed the Middle East*, Cambridge, MA: Westview Press, 2003; Zayani, M., *Al Jazeera Phenomenon: Critical Perspectives on New Arab Media*, New York, NY: Pluto Press, 2005; Ayish, *The New Arab Public Sphere*; Seib, P., *The Al Jazeera Effect: How the New Global Media are Reshaping World Politics*, New York, NY: Potomac Books, 2008.
9. Ayish, M., 'Arab Television Goes Commercial: A Case Study of the Middle East Broadcasting Center (MBC)', *Gazette*, Vol. 59, No. 6, 1997, pp. 473–494.
10. http://www.abdelkafy.com/ar/
11. http://www.islamtoday.com/
12. http://www.rissc.jo/
13. http://www.muslm.net/vb/archive/index.php/t-356928.html
14. Al Oudeh, S. 'Together Against al Qaeda Terror', Ann al Muslim Net-

work for Islamic Dialogue, http://www.muslm.net/vb/showthread.
php?t=362839, retrieved 24 October 2009.

15. http://www.youtube.com/watch?v=yWnpjYola3g&feature=relmfu
16. http://www.youtube.com/watch?v=L3EF__yB-_k
17. http://www.muslm.net/vb/archive/index.php/t-356928.html
18. Islamophobia Watch, 'Another MEMRI-inspired witch-hunt of Qaradawi', at http://www.islamophobia-watch.com/islamophobia-watch/
2009/2/7/another-memri-inspired-witch-hunt-of-qaradawi.html,
retrieved 23 November 2009.
19. Ibid.
20. Ibid.

3. 'PURE' SALAFI BROADCASTING: AL-MAJD CHANNEL (SAUDI ARABIA)

1. Gause III, Gregory F., 'Official Wahhabism and the Sanctioning of
Saudi-US Relations', *Religion and Politics in Saudi Arabia: Wahhabis and
the State*, Ayoob, M., & Kosebalaban, H., (eds) London: Lynne Rienner
Publishers, 2009, p. 135.
2. For extensive discussion and analysis on Salafism see Meijer, Roel (ed.),
Global Salafism: Islam's New Religious Movement, London: Hurst & Co,
2009.
3. Knysh, Alexander, 'Clear and present danger: "Wahhabism" as a rhetorical foil', *Die Welt Des Islams*, New Series, Vol. 44, Issue. 1, 2004,
pp. 3–26.
4. Al-Rasheed, Madawi, *Contesting the Saudi State: Islamic Voices from a
New Generation*, Cambridge: Cambridge University Press, 2007; Edens,
David, 'The Anatomy of the Saudi Revolution', *International Journal of
Middle East Studies*, Vol. 5, No. 1, 1974, pp. 50–64.
5. Ibid.
6. Al-Dakhil, Khalid, 'Wahhabism as an Ideology of State Formation', in
Ayoob, Mohammed & Kosebalaban, Hasan (eds), *Religion and Politics in
Saudi Arabia: Wahhabism and the State*, Boulder, CO: Lynne Rienner Publishers, 2009, pp. 23–38.
7. For further discussion of this issue, check Al-Rasheed, *Contesting the
Saudi State*; Wiktrowicz, Q., 'Anatomy of the Salafi Movement', *Studies
in Conflict & Terrorism*, 29, 2006, pp. 207–239
8. Wiktrowicz, 'Anatomy of the Salafi Movement.'
9. Okruhlik, G., 'State Power, Religious Privilege, and Myths About Political Reform', Ayoob & Kosebalaban (eds), *Religion and Politics in Saudi
Arabia: Wahhabis and the State*, London: Lynne Rienner Publishers, 2009,
pp. 91–107.

10. Okruhlik, 'State Power, Religious Privilege, and Myths'; Jones, T., 'Religious Revivalism and its Challenge to the Saudi regime', Ayoob & Kosebalaban (eds.), *Religion and Politics in Saudi Arabia: Wahhabis and the State*, London: Lynne Rienner Publishers, 2009, pp. 109–120; Kechichian, J., 'The Role of the *"ulama"* in the Politics of an Islamic State: The Case of Saudi Arabia', *International Journal of Middle East Studies*, Vol. 18, No. 1, Cambridge: Cambridge University Press, 1986, http://www.jstor.org/stable/162860?origin=JSTOR-pdf, pp. 53–71; Bligh, A., 'The Saudi Religious Elite *"ulama"* as Participants in the Political System of the Kingdom', *International Journal of Middle East Studies*. Vol. 17, No. 1, 1985, http://www.jstor.org/stable/163308?origin=JSTOR-pdf, pp. 53–71; Dekmejian, R. 'The Rise of Political Islamism in Saudi Arabia', *Middle East Journal*, Vol. 48, No. 4, Autumn 1994, MiddleEastInstitute.http://www.jstor.org/stable/4328744?origin=JSTOR-pdf, pp. 627–643.

11. *Saudi Gazette*, 'Council of Senior *"Ulama"* Reconstituted', http://www.saudigazette.com.sa/index.cfm?method=home.regcon&contentID=2009021529324 [Last accessed 16 Jan. 2010].

12. Wikipedia, 'Al-Majd TV Network', http://en.wikipedia.org/wiki/Almajd_TV_Network [Last accessed 25 Jan. 2009].

13. King Abdulaziz University website, 2010, http://waqf.kau.edu.sa/content.aspx?Site_ID=808&lng=EN&cid=3303&URL=www.kau.edu.sa.

14. Okruhlik, 'State Power, Religious Privilege, and Myths', p. 93.

15. Tarabich, G., *Al-Marad Bel Al-Gharb: Al-tahleel al Nafsi leusab jama'i Arabi*, Damascus: Petra Publishing, 2005.

16. Haddad, Y., 'Islamists and the "Problem of Israel": The 1967 awakening', *Middle East Journal*, Vol. 46, No. 2, Spring 1992 http://www.jstor.org/stable/4328433, pp. 266–285.

17. The author interviewed two journalists who were previously employed by the network. One interview was in Dubai Media City on 1 June 2010, and the other was a telephone interview on 5 June 2010.

18. 'Abd AlRahman, Mohammad, 'Why Mickey Mouse Must Die and Other TV Fatwas', *Manassat*, 2008, http://www.menassat.com/?q=en/news-articles/4895-fatwas-war-erupts-again-between-satellite=tv-sheikhs [Last accessed 17 Jan. 2010].

19. See Al-Riyad, 'Great role for Al-Majd satellite channel.' 25 Jul. 2008, http://www.alriyadh.com/2008/07/25/article362486.html.

20. Abd Al-Hadi, Hanan, 'The *niqāb* showing only one eye fatwa is controversial among Al-Azhar scholars in Egypt' *Aman*, 30 Jan. 2009, http://www.amanjordan.org/articles/index.php?news=2707.

21. 'Abd AlRahman, 'Why Mickey Mouse Must Die and Other TV Fatwas', *Manassat*.

22. Abu-Fadl, Magda, 'TV Fatwas: Sy Hersh Andrew vehicles dominate Arab media forum', *The Huffington Post*, 2009, http://www.huffingtonpost.com/magda-abufadil/tv-fatwas-sy-hersh-and-he_b_204277.html [Last accessed 17 Jan. 2010].

23. IPSOS,'Top 20 channels-KSA-unpublished document', 2009.

24. Dubai Press Club, *Arab Media Outlook 2008–2012 Collaborating for Growth: Forecasts and Analysis of Traditional and Digital Media in the Arab World*, Dubai: Dubai Press Club, 2009, http:// dpc.org.ae/UserFiles/AMO%20AR%20combined.pdf.

25. Interview with the author 1 June 2010, Dubai Media City.

26. IPSOS, 'Top 20 channels-KSA-unpublished document.'

27. *Al-Watan*, 'Al-Majd is the fourth TV operator in the Arab Countries', 4 May 2010, http://www.alwatan.com.sa/news/NewsText/newsdetail.asp?issueno=3043&id=88076.

28. *Ijābiyūn* ('Positive People') is a program sponsored by the STC and is broadcast at 10 pm on Sundays, beginning on 20 December 2009.

29. Wireless Federation (2009). Du & Al-Majd together offer range of Islamic Mobile Content during Ramadan (UAE). URL: http://wirelessfederation.com/news/17912-du-al-majd-together-offer-range-of-islamic-mobile-content-during-ramadan-uae/

30. According to a member of the audience in a Muslim chat room, the Al-Majd receiver even blocks other Islamic channels. He thought that this was understandable and acceptable in earlier times—meaning when it was the only Islamic network. However, it was no longer acceptable, especially since the growth in the number of similar channels.

31. Stout, D., 'Religious Media Literacy: Towards a Research Agenda', *Journal of Media and Religion*, 1534–8415, Vol. 1, Issue 1, 2002, pp. 49–60.

32. AlSnaidi hosts many other programs on Al-Majd channels, including the first ever programmes, *Chapters of My Life*, *The Forgotten Continent*, and others.

33. See http://www.islamway.com/?iw_s=Article&iw_a=view&article_id=1414.

34. Interview with Fahd Snaidi, Islam Light Network, 2006, http://www.islamlight.net/index.php?option=content&task=view&id=8605&Itemid=69.

35. It has a Facebook page and many of its episodes are available on YouTube and Shahritube.

36. Others to have taken part are Dr. Muhammad AlAwadi from

Kuwait—*Mawdat alAlhad* ('Atheism Back to Style'); Dr 'Abd Allah AlBaridi ('Salafism and the Liberalism Conflict'), Dr. Saleh bin Saba'an ('Institutionalisation and Personalisation'), Dr. Jasim AlSultan ('The Renaissance Project'), Sa'īd AlGhamidi ('The Westernisation of the Arab Countries'), and Dr. Muhammad Musa AlSharif ('The Phenomenon of Evading Religious Commitment').

37. See http://www/jawabk.com/vb/showthread.php?t=870
38. Al-Magran, 'The Adequate Answer', 15 Jan. 2010. An episode that was recorded specially for the purpose of this study.
39. Al-Magran, 'The Adequate Answer', 2009. An episode that was recorded specially for the purpose of this study.
40. AlFouzan, 'The Adequate Answer', 2009. An episode that was specially recorded for this study.
41. Okruhlik, 'State Power, Religious Privilege, and Myths', p. 95.
42. Ibid.
43. Interview with the author, Dubai Media City, 1 June 2010.
44. AP,'Saudi Fatwa on Owners of 'Immoral" TV Networks', *Emirates Business 24/7*, 2008, http://www.business24-7.ae/articles/2008/9/pages/saudifatwaonowners of%E2%80%98immoral%E2%80%99tvnetworks.aspx [Last accessed 16 Jan. 2010].
45. CJP, 'Cleric Issues Fatwa against Journalists and Writers', *Committee to Protect Journalists*, 22 Sept. 2008, http://cpj.org/2008/09/cleric-issues-fatwa-against-journalists-and-writers.php [Last accessed 16 Jan. 2010].
46. Al-Snaidi, *Dialogue Hour*, 26 Oct. 2008. An episode that was specially recorded for this study.
47. Jones, 'Religious Revivalism', p. 114.
48. Otterman, S., 'Fatwas and Feminism: Women, Religious Authority and Islamic TV', *Transnational Broadcasting Studies*, 2006, 16, http://tbs-journal.com/Otterman.html.
49. Al-Magran, Mohammad, *The Adequate Answer*, 2009. An episode that was specially recorded for this study.
50. Al-Maheni, M., 'Shabaket al Majd al-Osoolieh tuharem sowar al-nesa' we al-mousiqa we khilafat bedakhelha', *Elaph*, para. 6, 8 Jan. 2008, http://www.elaph.com/Elaphweb/Politics/2008/1/295104.htm.
51. AlHurra TV is considered the mouthpiece of the State Department. Al-Magran, *The Adequate Answer*, 16 Apr. 2006. An episode that was specially recorded for this study.
52. Al-Snaidi, *Dialogue Time*, 12 Dec. 2008. An episode that was specially recorded for this study.

4. 'MODERN' SALAFI BROADCASTING: IQRA' CHANNEL (SAUDI ARABIA)

1. Schofield Clark, Lynn (ed.), *Religion, Media, and the Marketplace*, New Jersey and London: New Brunswick, 2007; Galal, Ehab, 'Magic Spells and Recitation-competitions. Religion as Entertainment on Arab Satellite-Television', Hjarvard, S. (ed.), *Enchantment, Media and Popular Culture. The Mediatization of Religion*, Northern Lights, 2008, pp. 165–179.

2. The extent of their popularity is difficult to determine, not least in relation to viewers' priorities among different types of channels. There are only a few audience studies dealing with the religious channels. While one study by Amin suggests that Al-Majd Qur'an TV is the most popular, Al-Nas is the second and Iqra' the third most popular channel, Al-Dagher identifies Iqra' as the first, Al-Resalah as the second, and Al-Nas as the third most viewed Islamic channel (Reda Abed Al-Waged Amin, 'Attitudes of Religious Elite towards the Present and Future of the Islamic Satellite Channels: Field Study', paper presented in Arabic at *International Conference on Satellite Television and Cultural Identity. Visions for 21ˢᵗ Century Media*, College of Communication, University of Sharjah University, 11–12 Dec. 2007; Al-Dagher, Majdī Muhammad, 'Itijāhāt al-Qanawāt al-Faḍāiya al-Islāmiya fi muɛālajit qaḍāya al-Aqaliyāt wa al-Jāliyāt al-Islāmiya fi al-'ālam' ('Satellite Television Attitudes Towards Islamic Minorities in the World'), paper presented in Arabic at *International Conference on Satellite Television and Cultural Identity. Visions for 21ˢᵗ Century Media*, College of Communication, University of Sharjah University, 11–12 Dec. 2007. Shalabieh suggests that Iqra' is the most popular channel followed by Al-Majd (Shalabieh, Maĥmoud Ibrāhīm, 'Itijāhāt al-Mushāhidyyn wa arā'ihim naĥū barāmij al-Qanawāt al-Faḍāiya al-ɛarabiya wa dawarātiha al-Barāmijiya fi shahr ramadān 1427H (2006)' ['The views and attitudes of the viewers toward the programs and program schedules of the Arab satellite channels in Ramadan month 2006'], paper presented in Arabic at *International Conference on Satellite Television and Cultural Identity. Visions for 21ˢᵗ Century Media*, College of Communication, University of Sharjah University, 11–12 Dec. 2007. The popularity of Iqra' may be related to its status as the first Islamic channel but also to the fact that the channel is transmitting through different satellites (Arabsat 4B and 2B, Nilesat, Hotbird, Asiasat2) reaching a potentially wider audience. However, according to my observations more than twelve of the most famous and popular preachers left Iqra' to go to Al-Resalah after the latter was established in March 2006. Therefore, there is some probability that some viewers also shifted from Iqra' to Al-Resalah.

3. The quote is taken from the English version of the channel's website. The presentation in English is largely a translation from the presentation in Arabic which also contains a sentence that the channel aims to reach Muslims worldwide. Some of the channel's programmes have English subtitles when repeated, and it also has a weekly *fatwa* programme in English and French, as well as interviews with converts in English. http://www.Iqraa-tv.net/En/Channel.asp [Last accessed 2 May 2008]. The English part of the website is no longer available [Aug. 2009].

4. See e.g. the programmes 'Encyclopaedia of Islamic behaviour', Iqra' Aug. 2007; 'The Correct Way', Iqra' Oct. 2007; 'Good Behaviour', Iqra' Mar. 2008.

5. As noted by Sameh Fawzi in Chapter 10 in this book.

6. http://www.artonline.tv/home/ [Last accessed 5 May 2008].

7. Sakr, Naomi, *Satellite Realms. Transnational Television, Globalization & the Middle East*, London & New York: I. B. Tauris, 2001; Sakr, Naomi, 'The Impact of Commercial Interests on Arab Media Content', in *Arab Media in the Information Age*, The Emirates Center for Strategic Studies and Research, 2006, pp. 61–85; Sakr, Naomi, 'Approaches to Exploring Media-Politics Connections in the Arab World', in Sakr, Naomi (ed.), *Arab Media and Political Renewal. Community, Legitimacy and Public Life*, London & New York: I. B. Tauris, 2007, pp. 1–12.

8. Sakr, 'Approaches to Exploring Media-Politics Connections in the Arab World', pp. 6–7.

9. See Chapter 8 in this book.

10. Roy, Olivier, *Globalised Islam: The Search for a New Ummah*, London: Hurst & Co., 2004.

11. Ibid., p. 53.

12. Galal, Ehab, 'Reimagining Religious Identities in Children's Programs on Arabic Satellite-TV. Intentions and Values', Feldt, J. & P. Seeberg (eds), *New Media in the Middle East*, Odense: Centre for Contemporary Middle East Studies, 2006, pp. 104–118; Galal, Ehab, *Identiteter og livsstil på islamisk satellit-tv. En indholdsanalyse af udvalgte programmers positioneringer af muslimer* ('Identity and Lifestyle on Islamic Satellite-Television: A Content Analysis of Selected Programmes' Positioning of Muslims'), PhD-thesis, Faculty of Humanities, University of Copenhagen, 2008.

13. Roy, *Globalised Islam*.

14. See e.g. 'How we quote the Qur'an', 'Qur'an Light', 'Heaven's Medicine', 'Qur'an signs', 'Reading in the holy book', 'Qur'an and the life', 'My God's Qur'an', 'Qur'an reciting'; all broadcasted by Iqra' during the period from 2005 to 2007.

15. See e.g. 'Young people want to marry', Iqra', 2004; 'Comfort house', Iqra', 2007; 'My Paradise', Iqra', 2007.
16. 'Women's magazine', Iqra', 2001–2006.
17. See e.g. *musalsal* 'Missionary's Imam' at Iqra' March 2008.
18. See e.g. 'Those we love and money', Iqra' March 2008. This programme was often announced through short clips of a few seconds. In the advertisement for the programme a clip was always displayed in which the presenter asks the following questions: 'Did the Prophet Muhammad live in poverty all his life? Why do we often mention that the prophet was poor, did not eat, and that his house was not known for fire in the oven? Some will believe that it is the prophet who taught Muslims about poverty. Is Islam a religion for the poor? Why do some people think that poverty is one of the prophet's and saints' devoted characteristics? Is poverty the poor people's destiny or is it their laziness? Is it true that a good person is the one who is living as a monk and leaves the full life?' They are all rhetorical questions calling for a different approach to poverty.
19. See for example 'Know your diet', Iqra', Dec. 2007. The programme tells about healthy and unhealthy food and behaviour. People in the streets are interviewed about their eating habits and what they believe is healthy. See also 'Drinks in the Qur'an', Iqra', Jul. 2007. The programme presents all the drinks that are mentioned in the Qur'an and which are beneficial to humans and explains why. The recommendations are confirmed by reference to modern science and its proof of the benefits of these drinks for humans. Another example is the 'The balanced diet', Iqra' 2004.
20. See for example 'Only for adults', Iqra' June 2007.
21. See *musalsal* 'Omar ibn abd al-Aziz', Iqra' Apr. 2008.
22. Other examples are: 'Youth and Sports' and 'Youth Matters', both on Iqra.' 'Family Doctors', Iqra' 2005; 'World Culture' and 'World Economy.'
23. For example Al Jazeera broadcasts a weekly religious programme of fifty minutes. See also the monthly TV guide 'New TV Dish' (Feb. 2003) which refers to thirty-seven Arabic-language satellite channels. Most of them do not transmit any religious programmes while the remaining approximately fifteen channels broadcast on average a one hour weekly religious programme (in addition to transmission of the Friday prayer). According to the Egyptian Radio and Television Union study, from 2001 the religious programmes on the eight national television channels took up around 8 per cent of the total programming while the religious programmes on the three main Egyptian satellite channels (ESC1 and 2 and Nile International) took up around 5 per

cent of the programming and 2.4 per cent on the other thematic Egyptian satellite channels. Only 1.4 per cent of the viewers answered that the religious programmes were their favourite. See Al-Fawwāl, Nagūā, *Al-Barāmij al-Dīniya fi al-Telīfizyūn al-Maṣrī* ['Religious Programmes on Egyptian Television'], Cairo: Al-Markaz al-Qauumi lil buhuuth al-Igtimāiya wa al-Gināiya, 1994; Galal, Ehab, *Arabisk satellit-tv. Redskab til forandring?* ('Arab Satellite-Television: A Vehicle for Change?'), Masters thesis, Department of Carsten Niebuhr, University of Copenhagen, 2003.

24. Hoover, Stewart M., *Religion in the Media Age*, London and New York: Routledge, 2006.
25. 'Neo-conservatives and the End of Arrogance' (23 Apr. 2009), 'Muslims and International Justice' (28 May 2009), 'The Just Goldstone's Report Exists in the Middle of Darkness' (22 Oct. 2009).
26. The programmes: 'Rationalisation of Jurisprudence: Between Rejection and Acceptance' (7 May 2009), 'Satellite TV *Fatwas*' (14 May 2009), 'Extremism' (2009).
27. 'The Relationship Between Heads of State and the Citizens and Human Rights' (30 Apr. 2009).
28. For an analysis of the 'repentant' artists, cf. van Nieuwkerk, Karin, '"Repentant" artists in Egypt: debating gender, performing arts and religion', *Contemporary Islam*, 2, 2008, pp. 191–210.
29. Otterman, Sharon, 'Fatwas and Feminism: Women, Religious Authority, and Islamic TV', *TBS*, 16, 2006, http://www.tbsjournal.com/Otterman.html [Last accessed 31 Sept. 2007].
30. Programmes are: 'The first year of marriage' (1 June 2009), 'The girl away from her mother' (4 Feb. 2009), 'Where is the good word?' (10 Feb. 2009), 'The story of Sharif's mother-in-law' (17/2/2009), 'Does friendship prevent betrayal?' (24 Feb. 2009) 'Forbidden' (24/3/2009), 'Divorced young girls' (10 Mar. 2009).
31. 'Satellite TV fatwas' (14 May 2009).
32. Tim Cresswell, 'Introduction: Theorizing Place', G. Verstraete & T. Cresswell (eds), *Mobilizing Place, Placing Mobility: The Politics of Representation in a Globalized World*, Thamyris/Intersecting, 9, Editions Rodopi B.V., 2002, pp. 11–31.
33. Ibid., p. 21.
34. Ibid., p. 26.
35. David Croteau & William Hoynes, *Media/Society: Industries, Images, and Audiences*, London: Pine Forge Press, 1997; Hoover, *Religion in the Media Age*, p. 70.
36. Ibid., p. 16ff.
37. Ibid., p. 39.

38. Ibid., p. 55.
39. Cresswell, 'Introduction: Theorizing Place', p. 25.
40. Ibid., p. 22.

5. AL NAS SATELLITE CHANNEL: OVERVIEW, CONTENT ANALYSIS, PREACHERS

1. http://www.alnas.tv/AboutUs.aspx
2. El-Sayed, Mohammed, *Religious Islamic Satellite Channels: A Screen That Leads You to Heaven*, Reuters Institute for the Study of Journalism, University of Oxford, 2009.
3. http://www.alnas.tv/AboutUs.aspx
4. 'Al Nas Channel: Yes for Preaching, No for Politics', Interview held with Atef Abdelrashid. 5 Oct. 2006: http://www.islamonline.net/servlet/Satellite?c=ArticleA_C&pagename=Zone-Arabic-ArtCulture%2FACALayout&cid=1178724215057.
5. http://www.alnas.tv/Pages/Public/Programs/ProgramCategory-Listing.aspx
6. Website of Shereef Shehatah: www.sherif4u.com.
7. Ali Abdelal, Salafi and Annas channel, Da'wa on a screen upon request, www.readingislam.com
8. Ibid.
9. Hiba Hasanin, happens in Annas channel: http://www.almasry-alyoum.com/article2.aspx?ArticleID=28502.
10. Ali abdil'al, the Salafi and Annas channel, screen (upon request), http://www.readingislam.com.
11. Assayed Zayed, the veiled presenter, image of woman on the Salaf satellites, Naqed Forum: http://naqed.info/forums/lofiversion/index.php/t7252.html.
12. 'Interview with Atef Abed El Rasheed on islamonline.' http://www.islamonline.net/servlet/Satellite?c=ArticleA_C&pagename=Zone-Arabic-ArtCulture%2FACALayout&cid=1178724215057.
13. Mohammad Dusouqi Rushdi, 'Can we Ignore Sheiks like Yousef El Qaradawi and Khaled Al Jendy, and Intelligent and Well Educated Preachers as Amr Khaled in Favor of Those who Transmit the Tough Fatwa?', Al Youm Al Sabe3, 18 Sept. 2009, http://www.youm7.com/News.asp?NewsID=137409&SecID=162&IssueID=77.
14. Episode transmitted 7 Oct. 2010: http://www.way2allah.com/modules.php?name=Khotab&op=Details&khid=19648#UP.
15. Special episode of *Fadfadah* about *Niqab* transmitted in 14 Sept. 2009, http://www.way2allah.com/modules.php?name=Khotab&op=Details&khid=16406.

16. http://www.youtube.com/watch?v=p75IdUPDK3g&feature=related.

17. Shereef Shahata's website, http://www.sherif4u.com/index.php?do= show&cat=6&id=166.

18. 'Interview with Alarabi newspaper by Nashwa Deeb' 10 Dec., http:// al-araby.com/docs/1174//print2142182186.html.

19. Abu Ishaq Alhuweini's site, http://www.alheweny.org/new/play. php?catsmktba=661.

20. Ibid.

21. Ahmad Al Sayeh, 'The Salafi Preachers are More Dangerous than the West', 29 Nov. 2009: http://www.youm7.com/News.asp?NewsID= 150568.

22. 'How Alhuweinin Sees Sheikh Azhar', www.3arabchannel.com/ islam/view/iuXxaac3FJ4/html.

23. Alhuweini Site: http://www.alheweny.org/new/play.php?catsm ktba=663.

24. Ibid.

25. Site of Muslim Group: http://www.egyig.com/Public/articles/inter-view/11/47999487.shtml.

26. Episode of Bein Al Sotoor ('Between Lines') on Al Nas: http://www. youtube.com/watch?v=1T53bBRQlPQ.

27. Hani Yassin, 'The Islamic Satellite Channel: Between Reality and Expectations': http://www.egyig.com/Public/articles/miscellane-ous/11/61648259.shtml.

28. http://www.youtube.com/watch?v=iG9Z17P-5m4&feature=related.

6. 'MODERN' PREACHERS: STRATEGIES AND MIXED DISCOURSES

1. Saba Mahmood, *Politics of Piety, the Islamic Revival and the Feminist Subject*, Stanford University, Princeton, NJ: Princeton University Press, 2005, p. 3.

2. Clifford Geertz, 'Religion as a Cultural System', *The Interpretation of Cultures: Selected Essays*, London: Fontana Press,1993, p. 89.

3. David Demers, *History and Future of Mass Media: An Integrated Perspective*, Cresskill, NJ: Hampton Press, 2007, p. 23.

4. J. R. Beniger, *The Control Revolution: Technological and Economic Origins of the Information Society*, Cambridge, MA, Harvard University Press, 1986, p. 434.

5. Brad R. Roth, *Governmental Illegitimacy in International Law*, New York, NY: Oxford University Press, 2000, p 140.

6. Nazih N.Ayubi, *Political Islam: Religion and Politics in the Arab World*, London: Routledge, 1991, p. 62.

7. Fawal et al., *Religious Programming in Egyptian Television: The Communi-*

cators, Vol. 2, Cairo: National Center for Social and Criminal Research, the Department of Cultural and Communication Research, 1996, p. 131.

8. Al Sayed Zaid, 'Da'wa for Dollars: A New Wave of Muslim Televangelists', *Arab Insight, Bringing Middle Eastern Perspectives to Washington*,. Vol. 1, No. 3, 2008, p. 21.

9. G. Starret, *Politics, and Religious Transformation in Egypt*, Berkeley, CA: University of California Press, 1998, p. 91.

10. Al Sayed Zaid, 'Da'wa for Dollars', p. 21.

11. Fadwa El Guindi, *Veil: Modesty, Privacy and Resistance*, Oxford: Berg Publishers, 1999.

12. N. Field and A. Hamam, 'Salafi Satellite TV in Egypt', *Arab, Media and Society*, Issue 8, Spring, 2009, p. 3.

13. Salwa Ismail, *Rethinking Islamist Politics, Culture, the State, and Islamism*, London: I.B. Tauris & Co Ltd., 2006, p. 50.

14. Antonio Gramsci, *Selections from the Prison Notebooks of Antonio Gramsci*,. London: Electronic version, 2001, p. 140.

15. Ibid., p. 142

16. Aliaa Rafea, *The Students Islamic Movement: A Study of the Veil the Hijab*, A Master's degree, thesis, The American University in Cairo, 1983; Samia Al-Khashab, *Al-Shabab wa al-tayyar al-islami fi al-mujtama' al-Misri al-mu'asir: Dirasa Ijtima 'iyya midaniyya* Cairo: Dar al-thaqafa al-'arabiyya, 1988; Fadwa El Guindy, *Veil: Modesty, Privacy and Resistance*, Oxford: Berg Publishers, 1999.

17. Aliaa Rafea, 'Unraveling Different Meanings of the Veil', Sadiqi, Fatima (ed.), *Feminist Movements: Origins and Orientations, Publication of the Faculty of Art and Humanities*, Morocco: Dhar El Meharaz Fès, 2001, pp. 25–52; Arlene MacLeod, *Accommodating Protest: Working Women, the New Veiling, and Change in Cairo*, The American University in Cairo Press, 1982.

18. T.A. Van Dijk, 'Critical Discourse Analysis', D. Tannen, D. Schiffrin & H. Hamilton (eds), *Handbook of Discourse Analysis*, Oxford: Blackwell, 2001, pp. 352–37.

19. Ibid., p. 355.

20. G. Philo, 'News content studies, media group methods and discourse analysis', E. Devereux, (ed.), *Media Studies: Key Issues and Debates*, London: Sage Publications, 2007, p. 6.

21. Patrick D. Gaffney, *The Prophet's Pulpit: Islamic Preaching in Contemporary Egypt*, Berkeley, CA: University of California Press, 1994, p. 28.

22. Geertz, 'Religion as a cultural system', pp. 87–125.

23. K. Abou El Fadl, *Speaking in God's Name, Islamic law, Authority and Women*, Oxford: Oneworld Publications, 2001, p. 97.

24. Ibid., p. 54.
25. Lindsay Wise, Interview with Tareq Al Suwaidan, General Manager of Al Al-Resalah Channel, *Transnational Broadcasting Studies*, TBS16, 2006, para.1, http://www.tbsjournal.com/SuwaidanInterview.html [Last accessed 12 Dec. 2009].
26. Abu Heiba, personal communication, Jan. 2010.
27. Al Sayed Zaid, 'Da'wa for Dollars', p. 23.
28. Hadia Mostafa, 'Best of both worlds, interview with Moez Massoud', *Egypt Today*, Feb. 2003, http://moezmasoud.com/en/articles/articles37.html [Last accessed 25 Sept. 2010].
29. Naila Hamdy, 'El Mehwar The Mercurial' in *Transnational Broadcasting Studies*, TBS9, 2006, para.1,http://www.tbsjournal.com/SuwaidanInterview.html [Last accessed 12 Dec. 2009].
30. El Gondy, personal communication, 8 Jan. 2010.
31. Ibid.
32. Ma"a El Gondy, interview with Salafi preacher Mahmoud el Masry, Azhari TV channel, http://www.youtube.com/watch?v=_vWjgXm JJQE&feature=related, [Last accessed on 10 Mar. 2010].
33. Lindsay Wise, Interview with Tareq Al Suwaidan, 2006, para 2.
34. Ibid., para.18.
35. A. Bayat, 'From Amr Diab To Amr Khaled' in *Al Ahram Weekly*, Online Issue 639, 22–28 May http://weekly.ahram.org.eg/2003/639/fe1.htm [Last accessed 27 Apr. 2007].
36. Ibid.
37. Tareq Suwaidan, 'Al Rizk Episode', *A'lamatny Al hayatt programme* ('Life Lessons'), Al-Resalah TV, 2009, episode 23.
38. Tarek Suwaidan, Ta'amoulat Fi al Shari'a, *A'lamatny Al hayatt programme* ('Life Lessons'), 2009, episode 29.
39. Amr Khaled, *Bel Quran Nahya, Kasas El Quran, Part II*, Resalah TV, Aug. 2009, episode 1.
40. Lindsay Wise, 'Amr Khaled: Broadcasting the Nahda' in Transnational Broadcasting Studies, TBS13, para. 20, http://www.tbsjournal.com/Archives/Fall04/wiseamrkhaled.html [Last accessed 12 Dec. 2010].
41. Amr Khaled, *Bel Quran Nahya, Kasas El Quran, Part II*, August 2009, episode 1.
42. Ibid., episode 10.
43. Azhari Channel website, *About Us*, http://www.azharitv.net/aboutus.aspx [Last accessed 26 Sept. 2009].
44. Ma'a El Gendi, Defa'an 'an El Azhar, Azhari TV channel, Oct. 2009, http://www.youtube.com/watch?v=8Ri-r47DrHs&feature=channel [Last accessed 10 Mar. 2010].
45. Ma'a El Gendi, 'A debate with Al Habib Al Jafry', Azhari TV channel,

Oct. 2009 http://www.youtube.com/watch?v=jsrZebF4z-M&feature= related [Last accessed 10 Mar. 2010].

46. Ali Jaafar, 'Muslim preachers take to TV, Imams rebranding lessons for modern audience', *Variety.com*, 2008, http://www.variety.com/article/VR1117983548.html?categoryid=2862&cs=1[Last accessed 8 Nov. 2010].

47. Moez Masoud, 'Interview with Moez Masoud', *Wahed Min el Nas*, Dream TV, Dec. 2009, http://www.youtube.com/watch?v=kxBK jaIud2Q [Last accessed 26 Sept. 2010]

48. Moez Masoud, El Tariq El Sah, *90 Minutes Talkshow*, El Mehwar TV, episode 4, Sept. 2008, http://www.youtube.com/watch?v=0ku2Nt qwqJU [Last accessed 26 Sept. 2010].

49. Moez Masoud, *Wahed Min el Nas*, Dream TV, Dec. 2009.

50. El Gondy, personal communication, 8 Jan. 2010

51. Moez Masoud, 'Religion as a Veil', *Al Masry Al Yom Newspaper*, 9 Feb. 2010, http://www.almasry-alyoum.com/article2.aspx?ArticleID= 24336 8 [Last accessed 26 Sept. 2010].

52. Ibid.

53. Tarek Suwaidan, Ta'amoulat Fi al Shari'a, *A'lamatny Al hayatt programme* ('Life Lessons'), 2009.

54. Abu Heiba, personal communication, Jan. 2010

55. Lindsay Wise, 'Amr Khaled: Broadcasting the Nahda', TBS13, 2009, para. 16.

56. Ibid., para.7.

57. Haytham Dabour, 'The securities forces Al Da'yah Amr Khaled to leave Egypt and censors his Satellite TV Programmes' El Masry El Yom, 3 June 2009, http://www.almasry-alyoum.com/article2.aspx? ArticleID=213505, [Last accessed 26 Sept. 2006].

58. H. El Awadi, *In Pursuit of Legitimacy, The Muslim Brotherhood and Mubarak, 1982–2000*, London: Tauris Academic Studies, 2004, p. 9.

59. S. Sparre, *Muslim Youth Organisations in Egypt: Actors of Reform and Development?*, Dansk Institut for Internationale Studier, DIIS. [Electronic version], 2008, p. 1.

60. Ibid., p. 4.

61. Ibid., pp. 4–5.

62. J. Clark, *Islam, Charity, and Activism: Middle Class Networks and Social Welfare In Egypt Jordan and Yemen*. Bloomington: Indiana University Press, [Electronic version], 2004, p. 5.

63. Ibid., p. 14.

7. WOMEN PREACHERS: BROADCASTING PLATFORMS
AND EVOLVING AGENDAS

1. Thanks for Nada Helal from American university in Cairo for her help in editing this chapter.
2. Patrick D, Gaffney 'The Prophet's Pulpit: Islamic Preaching in Contemporary Egypt', Berkeley, CA: University of California Press, Dec. 1994, p. 33.
3. Ibid.
4. An interview with the researcher, 14 Sept. 2009.
5. 'Number of Mosques and Zawaya By Gov 08/2009', *Social Services*, Ministry of Religious Endowments.
6. Minister of Endowments in his speech in the graduation ceremony of male preachers, 17 May 2010.
7. An interview with Cairo Nour Institute former dean Saeed Ahmed on 7 Oct. 2009 at his office in Abu Baker Al-Seddiq mosque, Manial, Cairo.
8. An interview with Cairo Nour Institute's former dean.
9. 'The Ministry of Religious Endowment in Egypt allows women to work in mosque preaching', *Al-Sharq Al-Awsa*, 5 Nov. 2003.
10. Omaima Abdel Latif and Marina Ottaway, 'Women in the Islamic Movement: Towards an Islamic Model of Women's Activism', Washington, DC: Carnegie Institute, 2007.
11. Hoda El Saleh, 'Saudi Female Preachers: Preaching is the Right of Each Muslim and the Woman undergoes an Invisible Attack', *Al-Sharq Al-Awsat*, 11 Jan. 2007.
12. 'Female Preaching: The Features of the Future', *Qadaya w Araa'*, Islameyat online magazine.
13. Ibid.
14. Ibid.
15. Ibid.
16. Ibid.
17. Ibid.
18. Amani Saleh, 'Towards an Islamic Perspective of Feminist Epistemology', *Woman and Civilization*, Cairo, 2000, Issue 1, p. 7.
19. Omaima Abdel Latif and Marina Ottaway, *Women in the Islamist Movement: Towards an Islamic Model of Women's Activism*, Carnegie Endowment, 2007. The published paper was based on interviews conducted with women from the Lebanese Hizuallah and the Egyptian Muslim Brotherhood, in addition to some dialogues with female Islamic activists in Morocco, Kuwait, and other countries.
20. Field research conducted in 2007 in two Islamic societies of two differ-

ent socioeconomic strata. Women offering different religious and social services to the community run and work in these societies which are samples of numerous other societies that have proliferated in various Cairo districts and suburbs in the recent years.

21. Sherine Hafez, 'The Terms of Empowerment: Islamic Women Activists in Egypt', Cairo: American University in Cairo Press, 2003.

22. Diaa Rashwan, 'Social Islam and the Radical Movement', *El Ektesadeya online newspaper*, 2009.

23. Dr. Mohamed Abu Al-Fateh Al-Bayatony, 'Approach to the Science of Preaching', Al-Ressalah Institution, Beirut, 1991, p. 17.

26. Ali Bin Saleh Al-Morshid, 'Requirements of Preaching in the Present Age', Lina Library, Damanhour, 1989, p. 21.

27. Abd El Aziz AbdAllah Ben Baz, 'The call to God and Morality of Preachers', Ministry of Endowment and Islamic Affairs, Kingdom of Saudi Arabia, 1418 Hijri, pp. 20–21.

26. See chapter 6 in this book on Modern Preachers.

27. Mostafa Ashour, 'New Preachers and the Era of Image and Satellite TV', *Al Mesbar Journal*, El Mesbar Researcher Centre, Dubai, UAE, 2005.

28. Yousuf Al-Sam'aan, 'On preachers and media: from resistance to the Islam of the market', *Al-Sharq Al-Awsat*, 9 Jan. 2007.

27. 'The Internet and the Islamists and the Jihad Media', Al Jazeera, 2005. p. 28; Abd Allah Al Dahawy, 'Electronic Islamic discourse, Features and Properties', El Waa'y El Islamy Online Magazine, Issue 532, Sept. 2010. 29; Ibid.

32. 'Egypt: Internet Usage and Telecommunications Reports', Internet World Stats. Miniwatts Marketing Group, 2000.

33. 'Women in National Parliaments', Inter-Parliamentary Union.

34. Walid Salem Al Harethy, 'Ways and Forms of Women's Visibility on the Screen', *Sayd Al Fawaa'ed* online magazine, Jeddah.

8. RELIGIOUS BROADCASTING AND THE SECTARIAN DIVIDE IN IRAQ

1. See, for example, Patrick Cockburn, *Moqtada al-Sadr and the Shia inisurgency in Iraq*, London: Faber and Faber, 2008.

2. Interviews by the writer with broadcast journalists who worked in the Iraqi state-controlled media under Saddam Hussein.

3. www.alrafidain.tv

4. An arrest warrant was issued against Harith al-Dhari on terrorism charges on 16 November 2006. Al-Dhari was out of the country and has not returned since.

5. Iraqi insurgency groups announced that they gave a mandate to al-Dhari to represent them, www.alrutba.com, 1 June 2009.
6. See details on the channel's official website, www.alrafidain.tv.
7. See Adel Ra'aof, *Al-Amal al-Islami fi al-Iraq*, The Iraqi Center for Media and Studies, 2005. See also, Aziz Qadir Samanji, *Qitar al-Mowrada al-Iraqia, Dar al-Hikma*, London 2009.
8. Writer's interview with an Iraqi media expert who preferred to be anonymous.
9. The top Shi'a clerics, *Maraji al-Taqleed*, are those who are qualified to issue religious rules (*fatwa*). They are promoted to this rank after dozens of years of theological study in the *hawza* (Shi'a theological institutes). Every adult Shi'a individual has to choose one of the *Maraji al-Taqleed* and follow his rules and statements. In addition to the usual Muslim tax (*Zakat*), well-off Shi'a have to pay an additional tax (*al-Khomos-* the fifth) to the *Marji* who he follows. That is to be taken out of certain capitals and assets.
10. A sample of the episode monitored between Mar. 2009 and Oct. 2009.
11. An interview with Sayyed Rasheed al-Husseini by the writer, Jan. 2010.
12. Ibid.
13. Ibid.
14. Ibid.
15. Al-Hawza is a Shi'a college where students usually enrol for a theological education. Students usually start between the ages of fifteen and twenty. The education system consists of three main stages: (a) *al-Mokadimat* which includes the basic studies of Arabic, Qu'ran and Logic, (b) *al-Sotooh* which includes advanced religious studies for the Qu'ran and Tafseer references, (c) *al Bahth al-Kharij*, the final stage where a few senior students attend elite sessions of one of the Ayatollahs. After years some of them get the approval of this Ayatollah to become Ayatollahs themselves. There is no certain time frame for every stage. Most of the students leave the *Hawza* at some point, either to become junior clerics and preachers or leave the clergy permanently. It takes decades for those who stay to become an Ayatollah. Being a *Marj'i* is a higher status still and requires more work to earn the reputation and the followers.
16. Interview with Al-Husseini by the writer, Jan. 2010.
17. Speech broadcasted on 30 Mar. 2009.
18. Monitoring of episodes of the programme between Mar. 2009 and Dec. 2009. Also three interviews with Al-Obeidi by the writer in late 2009 and early 2010.
19. Ibid.

20. Ibid.
21. Ibid.
22. Episodes monitored of the programme between September 2009 and January 2010).
23. 25 Sept. 2009.
24. 5 Dec. 2009.

9. WALKING A TIGHTROPE: JEWISH RELIGIOUS BROADCASTING IN ISRAELI TELEVISION—THE CASES OF THE PUBLIC CHANNEL AND THE *HIDABROOT* CHANNEL

1. The authors would like to thank Dr. Tilde Rosmer from the University of Oslo for all her useful comments and feedback. She, of course, bears no responsibility for the media analysis conducted by the authors.
2. See, for example, Aviezer Ravitzky, *Religion and State in Jewish Philosophy*, Israel Democracy Institute 2002; Aviezer Ravitzky, *Zionism and Jewish Religious Radicalism*, Chicago: Chicago University Press, 1996; Gershon Shafir, and Yoav Peled, *Being Israeli: The Dynamics of Multiple Citizenships*, Cambridge: Cambridge University Press, 2002; Asher Cohen and Bernard Susser, *Israel and the Politics of Jewish Identity*, Baltimore: Johns Hopkins University Press, 2000; Efraim Karsh and Dan Urian (eds) *In Search of Identity: Jewish Aspects in Israeli Culture*, New York: Frank Cass, 1999.
3. The discussion regarding national and religious issues in Zionism is touched upon here only briefly. For further reading, see: Amnon Raz-Krakotzkin, 'There is no God, but He Promised Us the Land', *Mita'am*, Vol. 3, 2005, pp. 71–76 (in Hebrew); Baruch Kimmerling, 'Religion, Nationalism, and Democracy in Israel', *Constellations*, Vol. 6, No. 3, pp. 339–363; Tamir Sorek, 'Religiosity, National Identity and Legitimacy: Israel as an Extreme Case', *Sociology*, Vol. 43, No. 3, 2009. pp. 477–496; Yehouda Shenhav, 'Nationalism was never Modern—or Secular: On Hybridization and Purification in Bruno Latour', *Theory and Criticism*, vol. 26, 2005, pp. 75–88 (in Hebrew); Uri Ram, 'Why Secularism Fails? Secular Nationalism and Religious Revivalism in Israel', *International Journal of Politics, Culture and Society*, Vol. 21, no. 1–4, Dec. 2008, pp. 57–73.
4. According to the Israeli Central Bureau of Statistics forty-four per cent of Israeli-Jews define themselves as 'secular Jewish.' See: http://www.cbs.gov.il/hodaot2007n/19_07_104b.doc.
5. Amnon Raz-Krakozkin, 'Rabin's Legacy: On Secularism, Nationalism, and Orientalism', in: *Contested Memories—Myth, Nation and Democracy: Thoughts after Rabin's Assassination*, Lev Grinberg (ed.) Be'er Sheva,

Humphrey Institute for Social Research, Ben Gurion University, 2000, p. 97.

6. 'Statism', or even 'patriotic-statism', are the most accurate translations. This term corresponds with the concept of Israel being a 'melting-pot' of Jewish society.

7. An interesting analysis and discussion of *mamlakhtiyut* is found in Gershon Shafir, and Yoav Peled, *Being Israeli: The Dynamics of Multiple Citizenships*, pp. 1–36.

8. By *Masorti* (lit. 'traditional') Jews we include Jewish people who observe some religious practices, but who do not consider them-selves—in the Israeli context—to be 'religious.' In the American con-text, the term Conservative Judaism would probably be the best equivalent. Within 'Zionist-religious' we include the *Haredi-Leumi* ('National *Haredi*'), and the *Dati-Le'umi* ('Religious-Nationalist') move-ments. Both combine strong Zionist-national persuasions with Jewish religious faith.

9. With regards to the Israeli media see, for example, the research con-ducted in 2004 by Avraham, First and Elephant-Lefler '*The Absent and the Present in Israeli Prime-Time Television*': http://cms.education.gov. il/NR/rdonlyres/FA97A2FD-353F-4C53-AB6D-D7758885F6C9/110 187/nedarim_1.doc.

10. According to Ya'acov Isaac, from the *Haredi* advertising company Gal, 'in the *Haredi* community the radio is usually referred to as "the device"... It is not as abominable as the other device—the television—but still *Haredi* people will not speak freely about programmes they have heard over the radio.' Quoted in: Rotem, Tamar, '*Haredi* Reality in the Israeli Radio', *Ha'aretz Online*, 11 Jan. 2008 (in Hebrew): http:// www.haaretz.com/hasite/spages/943651.html. According to the *The Marker, Ha'aretz Business Magazine*: 'Even though one will not find a TV device anywhere in Bnei Brak (a *Haredi* city in the Tel Aviv area, with a population of 150,000) ... and even though listening to the radio is officially forbidden ... the leaders of the *Haredi* community were not ready for the emergence of religious Internet forums.' See: Nati Toker, 'In a Living Room in Bnei Brak You Will Not Find a TV Set, But the Emergence of the Internet Took the *Haredi* Leadership by Surprise', *The Marker Online*, 21 Dec. 2009: http://www.themarker.com/tmc/ article.jhtml?ElementId=skira20091221_1136429.

11. According to research conducted in 2006, the Palestinians in Israel have gradually shifted towards a preference for Arabic, non-Israeli, television channels. According to this research, the most popular channel among Palestinian citizens of Israel is Al-Jazeera. See: Jamal, Amal, *Media Consumption among National Minorities: The Case of the*

Arabs in Israel, I'lam: Media Centre for Arab Palestinians in Israel: 2006 (in Hebrew).

12. The official Hidabroot website: http://www.hidabroot.org/About. asp.

13. In parallel to his role in Hidabroot, Rabbi Cohen serves as the Head of the religious college (*Yeshiva*) of the settlement Beitar-'Illit in the West Bank.

14. An interview conducted with *Hidabroot*'s directors. Quoted in: *Globes Online*, 5 Mar. 2008, (in Hebrew), http://www.globes.co.il/news/ article.aspx?did=1000317520

15. The survey's results were provided by Ms. Galit Chen, from the Hidabroot channel's Marketing Department.

16. Quoted in the official Hidabroot website: http://www.hidabroot.org/ About.asp (in Hebrew).

17. Israeli primetime relates to programmes broadcast between 8.45 pm and 11 pm.

18. This issue is representative of Hidabroot channel in which most of the programmes have male presenters and guests.

19. For further reading about the religious/secular cleavage in Israel see: Cohen, Asher and Bernard Susser, *Israel and the Politics of Jewish Identity: The Secular-Religious Impasse*, Baltimore: Johns Hopkins University Press, 2000; Menachem Friedman, 'Close Yet Far: The Relations between the Religious and the Non Religious', *Meimad*, 27, Nov. 2003, pp. 16–20 (in Hebrew).

20. *Kippa*, also known as yarmulke, is a platter-shaped skullcap, worn by Jewish orthodox men.

21. 613 *Mitzvot*, or *Taryag Mitzvot*, are the 613 commandments given in the Torah and binding upon observant Jews.

22. The Israeli Broadcasting Authority Law (1965). See, the Israeli Broadcasting Authority's official website (in Hebrew): http://www.iba.org. il/doc/reshut.pdf.

23. For further reading about Israeli TV broadcasting's history, as well as the emergence of commercial television in Israel, see: Soffer Oren, 'The Eraser and the Anti-Eraser: The Battle over Colour Television in Israel', *Media Culture Society*, Vol. 30, 2008, pp. 759–775; Tasha. G. Oren, *Demon in the Box: Jews, Arabs, Politics, and Culture in the Making of Israeli Television*, Rutgers University Press, 2004; Kaspi, Dan and Yehiel Limor, *The Mediators: The Mass Media in Israel 1948–1990*, Tel Aviv: Am Oved, 1998 (in Hebrew); Gil Zvi, *House of Diamonds: The Story of Israeli Television*, Tel Aviv: Sifriyat Po'alim, 1986 (in Hebrew); Gilboa Eytan, 'The Evolution of Israeli Media', *The Middle East Review of International Affairs*, Vol. 12, No. 3, 2008; Weimann Gabriel, 'Zapping

in the Holy Land; Coping with Multi-Channel TV in Israel', *Journal of Communication*, Vol. 45, No. 1, 1995, pp. 96–102; Peri Yoram, *Telepopulism: Media and Politics in Israel*, Stanford University Press, 2004.

24. The decline of Israeli broadcasts in Arabic was a direct result of the emergence of satellite Arabic channels. They offered Palestinian citizens of Israel more comprehensive and professional, and less Zionist-oriented programmes, and became very popular. See: Jamal, Amal, *Media Consumption among National Minorities: The Case of the Arabs in Israel* (in Hebrew).

25. There is only one weekday programme called *Yesh Lekha Musag* ('Do You Have a Clue') which is broadcast once a week, and is a five minute explanation about basic Jewish practices.

26. A striking example for this is a programme titled *Mekablim Shabbat* ('Welcoming the Incoming Shabbat') presented by Dov Elboym, who used to be Orthodox but became secular. In his programme he leads critical, intellectual and scientific debates about Judaism.

27. *Ha-Tzofe* religious-Zionist newspaper wrote sarcastically that, 'If any good came out of the war in the north [Second Lebanon War] it is the TV programme *She'elat Rav* that began broadcasting.' *Ha-Tzofe* online, 11 July 2008: http://hazofe.co.il/web/katava6.asp?Modul=24&id=49 346&Word=&gilayon=2856&mador.

28. This practice, of contacting a rabbi in order to ask a question relating to the Jewish law or practices, is not new. In fact its origins go back to the sixth century and to the Jewish practice of *Responsa* (*She'elot Ve-Teshuvot*) where lay people or communities would write questions relating to Jewish law and practice to Talmudic scholars. For further reading, see: Wigoder Geoffrey, *The Encyclopaedia of Judaism*, The Jerusalem Publishing House, 1989.

10. CHRISTIAN BROADCASTING: A CRITICAL ASSESSMENT

1. The classic books on Coptic issues are: Galy Shourky, *Copts in a Changing Nation*; Abu Seif Yousseif, *Copts and Arab Nationalism*; Tarek Al Bashry, *Muslims and Copts in the Egyptian National Movement*.

2. Sameh Fawzy, 'Egypt's sectarian problem', *Daily News Egypt*, 30 June 2008.

3. For more details on socio-economic and political conditions facing Christians in the Arab World see Mohamed Abu-Nimer et al., *Unity in Diversity. Interfaith Dialogue in the Middle East*, Washington: United States Institute of Peace Press, 2007.

4. Sameh Fawzy, 'The Perspective of the Muslim Brotherhood on Citizenship', in: Amer Al Shobaki (ed.), *The Problem of the Brotherhood* (in Ara-

bic), Cairo: The Center for Political and Strategic Studies at Ahram Newspaper, 2009.

5. Sameh Fawzy, 'Copts: The Picture Is Not All Bleak', http://weekly.ahram.org.eg/2012/1082/op231.htm

6. Sameh Fawzy, the Christian Presence in the Arab World; the depth and problematic, Al Azhar Magazine, August 2011.

7. The debate between Orthodox and Protestant churches has become a fiery issue in the public media in Egypt. In 2009, the Coptic Orthodox church announced that it had obtained a fully-detailed Protestant scheme to attract its followers to Protestant churches. This charge was totally denounced by the Protestant community. However, over the last five years, the Coptic Orthodox Synod has repeated this accusation in its yearly meeting, and orthodox clergymen constantly advise their followers to avoid any kind of participation in the Protestant community.

8. These channels are: CTV, Al Hayat, Al Shafaa, Miracle, Al Malakot, Nour Sat, Agapy, Sat 7, the Truth, Al Karma, Al Tarik, Ashtar, Ashour, Aramyaa and Logos.

9. An interview with Mr. Yousseif Mansour, a producer of Christian media on 2 July 2009.

10. http://www.hayatv.tv/info/about-us/3069.html

11. Father Zakarya Boutros was born in Egypt in 1934, and was ordained as an orthodox priest in the Governorate of Monofya, and moved later to the Governorate of Al Garbya. He worked in Cairo and joined churches in Australia and the United Kingdom. He decided to resign, following disputes with his congregation in Brighton, England. The Coptic Orthodox church, to which he belongs suspended his service, and prevented him from work. He was once described in an official statement published by the Los Anglos Coptic Orthodox Diocese on 28 April, 2003 as 'a priest preaching unorthodox thoughts', referring to his Protestant approach.

12. http://www.bbc.co.uk/arabic/artandcu..._bbc_tc2.shtml

13. MTA is a model of Islamic satellite channels, which has taken the responsibility of countering Al Hayat.

14. For example: http://www.youm7.com/News.asp?NewsID=270784, www.almasry-alyoum.com/article2.aspx?ArticleID, www.saveegyptfront.org/news/?c=170&a=1154.

15. Religious polemics have become a real challenge for Muslim-Christian religions in the Arab World. A number of Coptic intellectuals have published a book warning about the negative repercussions of widespread religious debates between ordinary people. Samir Marcos et

al., *Citizens in One Nation* (in Arabic), Cairo: Egyptian Publishing House, 2010, p 22.

16. http://www.ikhwanonline.com/Article.asp?ArtID=27878&SecID=250.

17. Sameh Fawzy, 'Intercultural Dialogue: Prospects and Challenges', a paper presented at the first Egyptian-Kenyan intercultural Dialogue, Nairobi, 14–20 Nov. 2005.

18. Some Christian Channels have already contributed in this area. Sat 7 started a number of programmes to discuss societal issues, giving space to Muslim and Christian speakers.

11. AL-MANAR TV AND THE ISLAMIC SPHERE IN LEBANON: AN EVOLVING AGENDA

1. Stuart Hall, 'Introduction: Who Needs "Identity"?' in S. Hall and P. Du Gay (eds) *Questions of Cultural Identity*, London: Sage Publications, 1996, pp. 1–17.

2. *Ila al-Qalb*, episode 20, 2009.

3. Lara Deeb, *An Enchanted Modern: Gender and Public Piety in Shi'i Lebanon*, Princeton, NJ: Princeton University Press, 2006.

4. Note that Deeb refers to *a* Shi'i Muslim community, not *the* Shi'i Muslim community.

5. Ibid., p. 8.

6. Ibid., p. 20.

7. Ibid., p. 30.

8. Note that Hizbullah employs the term *Mujtama' al-Muqawama* which translates as 'Society of the Resistance.' However my preference for the word 'community' is based on Karl Deutsch's distinction between a Society and a Community. 'A *society* refers to a 'group of individuals connected by an intense division of labour, and separated from other societies by a marked drop in this intensity.' See Karl Deutsch, *Nationalism and Social Communication: An Inquiry into the Foundations of Nationality*, Cambridge, MA: The Technology Press of MIT, 1953, p. 87.

9. Ibid., p. 33.

10. Benedict Anderson, *Imagined Communities: Reflections on the Origin and Spread of Nationalism* (second edition) Verso, 2003, p. 6.

11. Ibid., pp. 37–46.

12. The Taef Agreement was signed in 1989 in Taef, Saudi Arabia. It covers political reform, the disarming of militias, the end of the civil war, special relations with Syria, and a framework for the withdrawal of Syrian troops, as well as the abolition of sectarianism. It had not been fully implemented at the time of writing. For the full text visit: http://

www.undp-pogar.org/publications/other/lebanon/taef-e.pdf [Last accessed 28 Jan. 2010].

13. Joseph Alagha, *Hizbullah's Documents: From the 1985 Open Letter to the 2009 Manifesto*, Amsterdam: Amsterdam University Press, 2011, p. 40.
14. Ibid., p. 45.
15. Ibid., pp. 44–45.
16. Judith Palmer Harik, *Hezbollah: The Changing Face of Terrorism*, London: I.B. Tauris, 2004.
17. See Annex 2 for Hizbullah's 1992 Electoral Programme.
18. Former Programming Manager for ten years and a member of Al-Manar's Administrative Council.
19. Interview with Nasser Akhdar July 2005.
20. James W. Carey, *Communication as Culture: Essays on Media and Society*, London: Routledge, 1992, p. 23.
21. Nick Couldry, *Inside Culture: Re-imagining the Method of Cultural Studies*, London: Sage Publications, 2000, p. 44.
22. Though the term is more literally translated as 'the Islamic Situation', I find 'Islamic Sphere' a more appropriate choice.
23. As'ad AbuKhalil, 'Ideology and practice of Hizbullah in Lebanon: Islamization of Leninist organizational principles', *Middle Eastern Studies*, 27:3, 1991, p. 395.
24. Naim Qassim, *Mujtama' al-Muqawama: Iradat Al-Shahada wa Sina'at al-Intisar* [Society of the Resistance: The Will for Martyrdom and the Making of Victory], Beirut: Dar Al-Maarif Al-Hakimah 2008, p. 8.
25. Nizar Hamzeh, *In the Path of Hizbullah*, Syracuse: Syracuse University Press, 2004, pp. 46–61.
26. Mohammed Hussein Fadlallah, *Trends and Milestones: Intellectual Conversations in the Affairs of Marja'iya and the Islamist Movement*, Beirut: Dar al-Malak, 2004, p. 121.
27. Elsewhere, Akhdar specifies that this 'Islamic Awakening' was instigated by the 1979 Islamic Revolution in Iran.
28. Interview with Nasser al-Akhdar, July 2005.
29. Ibid.
30. Mona Harb and Reinoud Leenders, 'Know thy enemy: Hizbullah, "terrorism" and the politics of perception', *Third World Quarterly*, 26: 1, 2005, pp. 173–197.
31. Ayatullah Khomeini's theory of Rule of the Jurist-Theologian.
32. Nikolas Rose, 'Identity, Genealogy, History', in S. Hall and P. Du Gay (eds) *Questions of Cultural Identity*, London: Sage Publications, 1996, pp. 128–150.
33. Ibid., Foucault (1977) quoted in Rose.
34. Anne-Marie Baylouny, 'Not Your Father's Islamist TV: Changing Pro-

gramming on Hizbullah's al-Manar', *Arab Media and Society*, Issue 9, Fall 2009.

35. Interview with Sabah al-Manar Producer Anwar Ramadan in January 2010, Beirut.

36. On the third, fourth and fifth days of Sha'ban (the eighth month of the Islamic calendar), Shi'is mark the birth of the three Imams known as 'The Three Moons': Imam Hussein, Imam Abbas, and Imam Zein Al-Abidin.

37. Note that this programme has been discontinued.

38. First printed in Russia in 1903, The Protocols of the Elders of Zion is a fraudulent document about a Zionist conspiracy for world domination that served as a pretext for anti-Semitism in the early twentieth century. See: http://www.britannica.com/EBchecked/topic/480269/Protocols-of-the-Learned-Elders-of-Zion, accessed 19 February 2012.

39. Iliya Harik, 'Toward a New Perspective on Secularism in Multicultural Societies' in T. Hanf and N. Salam (eds), *Lebanon In Limbo: Postwar Society and State in an Uncertain Regional Environment*. Nomos Verglagsgesellschaft Baden-Baden, 2003.

12. HAMAS BROADCASTING: AL-AQSA CHANNEL IN GAZA

1. See Victor Kattan's 2009 book on the legal status of the Palestinians and Arab/Israeli conflict in general, particularly his chapter on the partition plan, Victor Kattan, *From Coexistence to Conquest: International Law and the Origins of the Israeli-Palestinian Conflict 1819–1949*, London: Pluto Press, 2009. See also Sara Roy, *Failing Peace: Gaza and the Palestinian-Israeli Conflict*, London: Pluto Press, 2006 on the history of Gaza and its economic situation 2008; see Ilana Feldman, *Governing Gaza: Bureaucracy, Authority, and the Work of Rule, 1917–1967*, Durham, NC: Duke University Press, 2008 on the social history of Gaza 1917–1967; see Alshaer 2007, 2009 and 2010 books for reviews of these books.

2. Khalid Hroub, *Hamas: Political Thought and Practice*. Washington, DC: Institute for Palestine Studies, 2000.; Khalid Hroub, *Hamas: A Beginner's Guide*. London: Pluto Press, 2006.

3. Loren L. Lybarger, *Identity and Religion in Palestine: The Struggle between Islamism and Secularism in the Occupied Territories*, Princeton, NJ: Princeton University Press, 2007.

4. http://www.aqsatv.ps/index.php, last accessed 17 February 2012.

5. Ibid.

6. See 'Media Coverage at Palestine Television (PBC) and Al-Aqsa Satellite Channel Following Hamas's Military Takeover of Gaza. Media Monitoring Unit', *Fourth Report, Phase II*, in cooperation with the Euro-

pean Union, Ford, April 2008, p. 36. Original source: http://www. miftah.org/Doc/Reports/MKReports/TVReport010508.pdf

7. Ibid.

8. In this context, it is worth speculating that the different statements and images by which Al-Aqsa channel is portrayed by Hamas leaders and affiliates reflect diversity within the movement itself, one that suggests ideological friction and perhaps tension.

9. 'Media Coverage at Palestine Television (PBC)' and 'Al-Aqsa Satellite Channel Following Hamas' Military Takeover of Gaza', *Media Monitoring Unit, Miftah*, Apr. 2008.

10. The Israeli war against Gaza which was codenamed 'Operation Caste Lead' lasted for two weeks, starting from 27 December 2008, to 21 January 2009. It left around 1,314 Palestinian killed, 412 of them children, according to the Ministry of Health in Gaza. It also had a devastating impact on the already damaged infrastructure of Gaza.

11. See Atef Alshaer, 'Towards A Theory of Culture of Communication: The Fixed and the Dynamic in Hamas' Discourse' *The Middle East Journal of Culture and Communication*, Leiden: Brill Publications, Vol. 1, No. 2, 2008, pp. 101–121 on Hamas' discourse.

12. 'Media Coverage at Palestine Television'. *Media Monitoring Unit, Miftah*, Apr. 2008.

13. See Saba Mahmoud, *Politics of Piety: The Islamic Revival and The Feminist Subject*. Princeton, NJ: Princeton University Press, 2004. Mahmoud highlights how ethics and politics are linked and embodied within the context of Islamic movements, with particular reference to women's engagement with Islamist groups in Egypt.

14. See Atef Alshaer 'The Poetry of Hamas', *The Middle East Journal of Culture and Communication*, Brill Publications, Vol. 1, No. 2, 2009, pp. 214–230.

15. Jeroen Gunning, *Hamas in Politics: Democracy, Religion and Violence*. London: Hurst & Co., 2007, p. 129. It is worth drawing attention to Gunning's observation regarding the nexus of politics and religion in Hamas' ideology: 'Hamas appears to be largely capable of ensuring compliance through a combination of the political legitimacy derived from its representative authority structures and the authority derived from being 'representatives of God.'

16. Qur'ān, *surat at-Tahrīm*, 66/6: see http://quran.com/66.

17. Qur'ān, *surat al-'ankabūt*, 29/1–3: http://quran.com/29.

18. Ismail Radwan is a senior Hamas leader in Gaza. He is almost the only guest for the 'Islam and Life' programme on Al-Aqsa. Many Hamas leaders perform religious functions such as leading prayers in public or preaching in the mosques. Their sermons are often engaged with

the political issues of the day. Ismail Haniyya, the Prime Minister in the deposed government in Gaza, is notable in this respect; since he is regularly shown on Al-Aqsa, preaching in mosques and leading prayers, particularly during the holy month of Ramadan and Muslims' festivities. In this context, mosques serve as unique centres of power with visible effects on the socio-political dynamics of the society in question. Atef Alshaer, 'Towards A Theory of Culture of Communication: The Fixed and the Dynamic in Hamas' Discourse', *The Middle East Journal of Culture and Communication*, Leiden: Brill Publications, Vol. 1, No. 2, 2008, pp. 101–121.

19. http://www.aqsatv.ps/index.php, last accessed 17 February 2012.
20. Ibid.
21. Ibid.
22. Ibid.
23. Eric Hobsbawm, 'Ethnic Nationalism in the Late Twentieth Century', J. Hutchinson and A. Smith (eds) *Ethnicity*, Oxford: Oxford University Press, 1996, pp. 355–358.
24. Ibid.
25. The borders between Gaza and Egypt were put in place by Israel after the historic Camp David Agreement in 1978 between Egypt and Israel. Since Hamas's takeover of authority in Gaza in 2007, they had been a source of friction between Egypt and Hamas. Egypt does not recognise Hamas's authority in Gaza and is concerned about its alliances and ideological orientations which do not fit with the political stance of the Egyptian regime.
26. Salam Fayyad (b.1952) has been the Palestinian Prime Minister in President Mahmoud Abbas's Palestinian government since June 2007. He is known for his transparency. He first served as a finance minister in the government of the late Palestinian President Yasser Arafat in 2002 and served in other governments including the short-lived unity government in mid 2007, headed by the Hamas leader Ismail Haniyyah. As for Lieutenant General Keith Dayton (b.1949), he is an American general who was charged by the Bush Administration to train Palestinian security personnel in the West Bank and to coordinate security issues between the Palestinian Authority and Israel.
27. Ibid.
28. Qur'ān, *surat al-ma'idah*, 5/51: http://quran.com/5
29. http://www.aqsatv.ps/index.php?section=media, last accessed on 17 February 2012.
30. Mohammad Arkoun's view on the use of what he calls 'imaginary Islam' comes to mind. Such an Islam, he opined, 'involves systematic references to an Islam that is isolated from the most elementary his-

torical reasoning, linguistic analysis or anthropological decoding, operating as a psychological, cultural and intellectual obstacle to a serious approach to the major twin themes of rule of law and civil society.' Mohammad Arkoun *Islam: To Reform Or To Subvert*, London: Saqi Books, 2001, p. 345.

13. 'ISLAMIC' MEDIA, DEMOCRACY AND THE AKP RULE IN TURKEY

1. J. B. Thompson, *The Media and Modernity: A Social Theory of the Media*, Palo Alto, CA: Stanford University Press, 1995; Jurgen Habermas, *Europe: The Faltering Project*, Cambridge: Polity, 2009.
2. See 'AKP % 48'e dayandı CHP % 20'nin Altında', *Radikal*, Istanbul, 19 Jul. 2007. It is worth emphasising that in 2002 the AKP had 34.2 per cent of votes but 65 per cent of the parliament (363 MPs) due to the current political system, which has a 10 per cent electoral threshold for representation in the Turkish Parliament. In 2007, the AKP had 46.6 per cent of votes but less MPs (340) due to the same threshold rule. Despite the rise of ultra-nationalism in 2007, the Nationalist Movement Party (*Milliyetci Hareket Partisi*—MHP) barely passed the threshold with 14.3 per cent of votes. In 2002, it had 8.3 per cent of votes. 'A Turning Point for Turkey?', *The Economist*, London, 21 Jul. 2007.
3. Peter Berger and et al., *The Desecularization of the World: Resurgent Religion and World Politics*, Washington D.C., The Ethics and Public Policy Centre, 1999.; N. J. Demerath, *Crossing the Gods: World Religions and Worldly Politics*, Washington: Rutgers University Press, 2003.
4. Y. Akdoğan, *Muhafazakar Demokrasi* [Conservative Democracy], Ankara: AK Parti Yayini, 2004. This publication is regarded to be the party's ideological manifesto.
5. Ayla Göl, 'The identity of Turkey: Muslim and Secular', *Third World Quarterly*, 30: 4, 2009, pp. 795–812.
6. Derya Sazak, 'AKP and Medya', *Milliyet*, 27 Feb. 2007. [Last accessed 31 Aug. 2010]. http://www.milliyet.com.tr/2007/02/27/yazar/sazak.html.
7. Nur Vergin, 'Monday Talk with Nur Vergin', *Today's Zaman*, 23 Jul. 2007.
8. Cihan Tugal, 'NATO's Islamists: Hegemony and Americanisation in Turkey', *New Left Review*, 44, Mar-Apr. 2007, p. 19.
9. Ibid.
10. J. B. Thompson, *The Media and Modernity: A Social Theory of the Media*, Stanford, CA: Stanford University Press, 1995, pp. 3–4.

11. TSK Press Release, Turk Silahli Kuvvetleri (Turkish Armed Forces), *Genel Kurmay Başkanlığı Basın Acıklaması* (Turkish General Staff Press Release), Ankara: TSK, 27 Apr. 2007. For details of the press release see Göl, 'The Identity of Turkey', p. 797.

12. M. J. Gerson, 'An Islamic Test for Turkey', *The Washington Post*, Washington D. C.: Council on Foreign Relations, 6 June 2007, Publication No. 1356.

13. S. Rainsford, 'Turkey Awaits AKP's next Steps', 23 Jul. 2007.

14. P. Norris and Inglehart, R., *Sacred and Secular: Religion and Politics Worldwide*, Cambridge: Cambridge University Press, 2004.

15. Elizabeth L., Eisenstein, *The Printing Press as an Agent of Change: Communications and Cultural Transformations in Early-modern Europe*, Cambridge: Cambridge University Press, 1979.

16. D. Dayan and E. Katz, *Media Events: The Live Broadcasting of History*, Cambridge, MA: Harvard University Press, 1992.

17. Eisenstein, *The Printing Press*.

18. Benedict Anderson, *Imagined Communities: Reflections on the Origin and the Spread of Nationalism*, London: Verso, 1991.

19. Ibid.

20. Göl, Ayla 'Imagining the Turkish Nation through "othering" Armenians', *Nations and Nationalism*, 11(1), Jan. 2005, pp. 121–140.

21. Yael Navaro-Yashin, *Faces of the State: Secularism and Public life in Turkey*, Princeton, NJ: Princeton University Press, 2002.

22. Göl, 'The Identity of Turkey.'

23. Navaro-Yashin, *Faces of the State*.

24. www.trt.net.tred [Last accessed on 1 Sept. 2010].

25. http://www.pressreference.com/Sw-Ur/Turkey.html [Last accessed on 1 Sept. 2010]

26. Hayirli, Dilek, 'New RTÜK bill to raise foreign media ownership ceiling to 50 pct', *Today's Zaman*, 6 Apr. 2010.

27. Hjarvard, Stig 'The Mediatisation of Religion: A Theory of the Media as Agents of Religious Change', *Northern Lights*, 6, 2008, p. 13.

28. Ibid., p. 14, (Emphasis is mine).

29. Joshua Meyrowitz, 'Images of Media: Hidden Ferment—and Harmony—in the Field', *Journal of Communication*, 43(3), 1993.

30. Ibid.

31. Turkey Press, Media, TV, Radio, Newspapers—newspaper, television, number, freedom, online, broadcasting, role, government, censorship 30 Jan. 2010 01:44. http://www.pressreference.com/Sw-Ur/Turkey.html [Last accessed 1 Sept. 2010].

32. *Dini Kanallar frekanslarini ogrenebilir miyim?* (Turksat), 7 June 2009.

http://www.uydu.info/soru-sorun-cevaplayalim/dini-kanallar-fre-kanslarini-ogrene-bilir-miyim-turksat/ [Last accessed on 1 Sept. 2010].

33. http://www.kanal7.com/index.php [Last accessed on 1 Sept. 2010].
34. *TRT İran'dan dini bütün diziler ithal ediyor*, http://www.medyafaresi. com/haber/17397/medya-trt-irandan-dini-butun-diziler-ithal-ediyor-iste-o-diziler.html [Last accessed on 1 Sept. 2010].
35. M. Castell, *The Information Age: Economy, Society and Culture*, 3 vols., London: Blackwell, 1996.
36. Ibid.
37. Göl, 'The Identity of Turkey.'
38. Habermas, *Europe: The Faltering Project*, p. 141.
39. Ibid.
40. Ibid., p. 143.
41. Ibid., p. 144.
42. Ibid., p. 153.
43. Ibid., p. 154.
44. Ibid., p. 161.
45. Ibid., pp. 156–7.
46. Thompson, *The Media and Modernity*, p. 257.
47. E. Fuat Keyman, 'Modernisation, Globalisation and Democratisation in Turkey: The AKP Experience and its Limits', *Constellations*, 12(2), 2010, p. 322.
48. Thompson, *The Media and Modernity*, p. 257.
49. Ibid.
50. Ibid.
51. Henri J. Barkey, 'Turkey's Moment of Inflection', *Survival*, 52(3), 2010, p. 46.
52. Thompson, *The Media and Modernity*, p. 257.
53. Habermas, *Europe: The Faltering Project*, p. 173.
54. Ibid.
55. Gareth Jenkins, 'Turkey: AKP Pays the Price', *International Relations and Security Network*, 1 Apr. 2009.
56. Soner Cagatay, 'Turkey lost Turkey', *The Wall Street Journal*, 12 Jul. 2010.
57. *Hürriyet* Daily Newspaper, Istanbul, 8 Sept. 2008.
58. *Radikal* Daily Newspaper, Istanbul, 24 Sept. 1998.
59. *Milliyet* Daily Newspaper, Istanbul, 11 June 2002; *Sabah* Daily News, Istanbul, 24 Oct. 2001.
60. Gareth Jenkins, 'Turkey: AKP Pays the Price', *International Relations and Security Network*, 1 Apr. 2009.
61. http://en.rsf.org/press-freedom-index-2009,1001.html; http://en.rsf.

org/press-freedom-index-2008,33.html http://en.rsf.org/press-free-
dom-index-2002,297.html [Last accessed 11 Sept. 2010].
62. http://en.rsf.org/surveillance-turkey,36675.html [Last accessed 11
Sept. 2010].
63. Jenkins, 'Turkey: AKP Pays the Price.'

BIBLIOGRAPHY

AbdAllah Ben Baz, Abd El Aziz, 'The Call to God and Morality of Preachers', Ministry of Endowment and Islamic Affairs, Kingdom of Saudi Arabia, 1418 Hijri.

'Abd Al-Hadi, Hanan, 'The *niqāb* showing only one eye fatwa is controversial among Al-Azhar scholars in Egypt', *Aman*, 30 Jan. 2009: http://www.amanjordan.org/articles/index.php?news=2707.

'Al-Majd is the fourth TV operator in the Arab Countries', *Al-Watan*, 4 May 2010, http://www.alwatan.com.sa/news/NewsText/newsdetail. asp?issueno=3043&id=88076.

'Al Nas Channel: Yes for Preaching, No for Politics', Interview held with Atef Abdelrashid. 5 Oct. 2006: http://www.islamonline.net/servlet/Sat ellite?c=ArticleA_C&pagename=Zone-Arabic-ArtCulture%2FACALay out&cid=1178724215057.

'Abd AlRahman, Mohammad, 'Why Mickey Mouse Must Die and Other TV Fatwas', *Manassat*, 2008, http://www.menassat.com/?q=en/news-articles/4895-fatwas-war-erupts-again-between-satellite=tv-sheikhs [Last accessed 17 Jan. 2010].

Abed Al-Waged Amin, Reda, 'Attitudes of Religious Elite towards the Present and Future of the Islamic Satellite Channels: Field Study', Paper presented in Arabic at *International Conference on Satellite Television and Cultural Identity. Visions for 21ˢᵗ Century Media*, College of Communication, University of Sharjah University, 11–12 Dec. 2007.

Abu Ishaq Alhuweini's site, http://www.alheweny.org/new/play. php?catsmktba=661.

Abu-Fadl, Magda, 'TV Fatwas: Sy Hersh Andrew vehicles dominate Arab media forum' *The Huffington Post*, 2009, http://www.huffingtonpost. com/magda-abufadil/tv-fatwas-sy-hersh-and-he_b_204277.html, [Last accessed 17 Jan. 2010].

Abu-Nimer, Mohamed et al., *Unity in Diversity. Interfaith Dialogue in the Middle East*, Washington: United States Institute of Peace Press, 2007.

AbuKhalil, As'ad, 'Ideology and practice of Hizbullah in Lebanon: Islamization of Leninist organizational principles', *Middle Eastern Studies*, 27:3, 1991.

Akdoğan, Y., *Muhafazakar Demokrasi* [Conservative Democracy], Ankara: AK Parti Yayini, 2004.

AlAluka, The Scientific Council Forum, 2008, http://majles.alukah.net/showthread.php?t=32438.

Al Bashry, Tarek, *Muslims and Copts in the Egyptian National Movement*.

Al Dahawy, AbdAllah, 'Electronic Islamic discourse. Features and Properties', *El Waa'y El Islamy*, Issue 532, Sept. 2010, http://alwaei.com/topics/view/article.php?sdd=2284&issue=520.

Al Harethy, Walid Salem, 'Ways and Forms of Women's Visibility on the Screen', *Sayd Al Fawaa'ed*, Jeddah.

Al Sayeh, Ahmad, 'The Salafi Preachers are More Dangerous than the West', 29 Nov. 2009: http://www.youm7.com/News.asp?NewsID=150568.

Al-Bayatony, Dr. Mohamed Abu Al-Fateh, 'Approach to the Science of Preaching', Al-Ressalah Institution, Beirut, 1991.

Al-Dakhil, K., 'Wahhabism as an ideology of state formation', Ayoob, Mohammed & Kosebalaban, Hasan (eds), *Religion and Politics in Saudi Arabia: Wahhabism and the State*. Boulder, CO: Lynne Rienner, 2009.

Al-Fawwāl, Nagūā, *Al-Barāmij al-Dīniya fi al-Telīfizyūn al-Maṣrī* [The religious Programmes on Egyptian television], Cairo: Al-Markaz al-Qauumi lil buhuuth al-Igtimāiya wa al-Gināiya, 1994.

Al-Maheni, M., 'Shabaket al Majd al-Osoolieh tuharem sowar al-nesa' we al-mousiqa we khilafat bedakhelha', *Elaph*, 8 Jan. 2008, http://www.elaph.com/Elaphweb/Politics/2008/1/295104.htm.

Al-Rasheed, Madawi, *Contesting the Saudi State: Islamic Voices from a New Generation*, Cambridge: Cambridge University Press, 2007

Al-Riyad, 'Great role for Al-Majd satellite channel', *Al-Riyad*. 25 Jul. 2008, http://www.alriyadh.com/2008/07/25/article362486.html.

Al-Sam'aan, Yousuf, 'On preachers and media: from resistance to the Islam of the market', *Al-Sharq Al-Awsat* newspaper, 9 Jan. 2007.

Al-Snaidi, F., 'Hewar ma' e'lami', *Islamweb*, 2006, http://www.islamway.com/?iw_s=Article&iw_a=view&article_id=1414.

———, 'Interview with Fahd', *Islam Light Network*, 2006, http://www.islamlight.net/index.php?option=content&task=view&id=8605&Ite mid=69.

Alhuweini Site: http://www.alheweny.org/new/play.php?catsmktba=663.

Ali Abdelal, Salafi and Annas channel, Da'wa on a screen upon request, www.readingislam.com.

Ali Bin Saleh Al-Morshid, 'Requirements of Preaching in the Present Age', Lina Library, Damanhour, 1989.

Alshaer, Atef, 'Towards A Theory of Culture of Communication: The Fixed and the Dynamic in Hamas' Communicated Discourse'.

Amin, Hussein, 'The Arab States Charter for Satellite Television: A Quest for Regulation', in *Arab Media & Society*, Cairo: Kamal Adham Center for Journalism Training and Research (Religious Channels), 2008.

Anderson, Benedict, *Imagined Communities: Reflections on the Origin and Spread of Nationalism* (second edition) Verso, 2003.

———, *Imagined Communities: Reflections on the Origin and the Spread of Nationalism*, London: Verso, 1991.

AP, 'Saudi Fatwa on Owners of "Immoral" TV Networks', *Emirates Business 24/7*, 2008, http://www.business24-7.ae/articles/2008/9/pages/saudifatwaonowners.of%E2%80%98immoral%E2%80%99tvnetworks. aspx [Last accessed 16 Jan. 2010].

Arkoun, Mohammad, *Islam: To Reform Or To Subvert*, London: Al-Saqi Books, 2002.

Art Online http://www.artonline.tv/home/

Ashour, Mostafa, 'New Preachers and the Era of Image and Satellite TV', *Al Mesbar Journal*, El Mesbar Researcher Centre, Dubai, UAE, 2005.

Assayed Zayed, the veiled presenter, image of woman on the Salaf satellites, Naqed Forum: http://naqed.info/forums/lofiversion/index.php/t7252.html.

Avraham, E., First A. and N. Elephant-Lefler, *The Absent and the Present in Prime-Time: Multi-Cultural Diversity in TV Commercial Broadcasting in Israel*, Jerusalem: The Second Authority for Television and Local Radio, 2004 (in Hebrew).

Awadi, H. El, *In Pursuit of Legitimacy, The Muslim Brotherhood and Mubarak, 1982–2000*, London: Tauris Academic Studies, 2004.

Ayish, M., 'Arab Television Goes Commercial: A Case Study of the Middle East Broadcasting Center (MBC)', *Gazette*, Vol. 59, No. 6, 1997.

———, *Arab Television in the Age of Globalization: Emerging Trends*, Hamburg: Centre for Middle Eastern and Oriental Studies, 2003.

———, *The New Arab Public Sphere*, Berlin: Frank & Timme, 2008.

Ayubi, Nazih N., *Political Islam: Religion and Politics in the Arab World*, London: Routledge, 1991.

Azhari Channel website, *About Us*, http://www.azharitv.net/aboutus. aspx [Last accessed 26 Sept. 2009].

Barış, Ruken, *Media Landscape—Turkey*, http://www.ejc.net/media_landscape/article/turkey/, 2001.

Barkey, Henri J., 'Turkey's Moment of Inflection', *Survival*, 52(3), 2010.

Bayat, A., 'From Amr Diab To Amr Khaled' in *Al Ahram Weekly*, Online

Issue 639, 22–28 May http://weekly.ahram.org.eg/2003/639/fe1.htm [Last accessed 27 Apr. 2007].

Beniger, J. R., *The Control Revolution: Technological and Economic Origins of the Information Society*, Cambridge, MA: Harvard University Press, 1986.

Berger, Peter and et al., *The Desecularization of the World: Resurgent Religion and World Politics*, Washington D.C.: The Ethics and Public Policy Centre, 1999.

Bligh, A., 'The Saudi religious elite "*ulama*" as participants in the political system of the kingdom. *International Journal of Middle East Studies*. Vol. 17, No. 1. pp. 37–50, 1985, http://www.jstor.org/stable/163308? origin=JSTOR-pdf.

Boyd, D., *Broadcasting in the Arab World: A Survey of Electronic Media in the Middle East*, Aimes, IA: Iowa State University Press, 1999.

Cagatay, Soner, 'Turkey lost Turkey', *The Wall Street Journal*, 12 Jul. 2010.

Carey, James W., *Communication as Culture: Essays on Media and Society*, London: Routledge, 1992.

Castell, M., *The Information Age: Economy, Society and Culture*, 3 Vols., London: Blackwell, 1996.

CJP, 'Cleric Issues Fatwa against Journalists and Writers', *Committee to Protect Journalists*, 2008, http://cpj.org/2008/09/cleric-issues-fatwa-against-journalists-and-writers.php [Last accessed 16 Jan. 2010].

Clark, Lynn Schofield (ed.), *Religion, Media, and the Marketplace*, New Jersey, and London: New Brunswick, 2007.

Clark. J., *Islam, Charity, and Activism: Middle Class Networks and Social Welfare In Egypt Jordan and Yemen*. Bloomington: Indiana University Press, [Electronic version], 2004.

Cohen, Asher and Bernard Susser, *Israel and the Politics of Jewish Identity: The Secular-Religious Impasse*, Johns Hopkins University Press, 2000.

Couldry, Nick, Inside Culture: Re-imagining the Method of Cultural Studies, London: Sage Publications, 2000.

Cresswell, Tim, 'Introduction: Theorizing Place', G. Verstraete & T. Cresswell (eds), *Mobilizing Place, Placing Mobility: The Politics of Representation in a Globalized World*, Thamyris/Intersecting, 9, Editions Rodopi B.V., 2002.

Croteau, David & William Hoynes, *Media/Society: Industries, Images, and Audiences*, London: Pine Forge Press, 1997.

Da Lage, O., 'The politics of al Jazeera or the diplomacy of Doha', in Zayani, M. (ed.), *The Al Jazeera Phenomenon: Critical Perspectives on New Arab Media*, New York, NY: Pluto Press, 2005.

Dabour, Haytham, 'The securities forces Al Da'yah Amr Khaled to leave Egypt and censors his Satellite TV Programmes' *El Masry El Yom*, 3 June

2009, http://www.almasry-alyoum.com/article2.aspx?ArticleID=213 505, [Last accessed 26 Sept. 2006].

Dayan, D. and Katz, E., *Media Events: The Live Broadcasting History*, Cambridge, MA: Harvard University Press, 1992.

Deeb, Lara, *An Enchanted Modern: Gender and Public Piety in Shi'i Lebanon*, Princeton, NJ: Princeton University Press, 2006.

Dekmejian, R., 'Saudi Arabia's Consultative Council, *Middle East Journal*, Vol. 52. No. 2, Spring, 1998, Middle East Institute, http://www.jstor.org/stable/4329186?origin=JSTOR-pdf.

———, 'The Rise of Political Islamism in Saudi Arabia', *Middle East Journal*, Vol. 48, No. 4, Autumn 1994, Middle East Institute, http://www.jstor.org/stable/4328744?origin=JSTOR-pdf. pp. 627–643.

Demerath, N. J., *Crossing the Gods: World Religions and Worldly Politics*. Washington: Rutgers University Press, 2003.

Demers, David, *History and Future of Mass Media: An Integrated Perspective*, Cresskill, NJ: Hampton Press, 2007.

Denoeux, G., 'The Forgotten Swamp: Navigating political Islam', *Middle East Policy*, Vol. 9, No. 2, 2002.

Deutsch, Karl, *Nationalism and Social Communication: An Inquiry into the Foundations of Nationality*, Cambridge, MA: The Technology Press of MIT, 1953.

Dubai Press Club, *Arab Media Outlook 2008–2012 Collaborating for Growth: Forecasts and Analysis of Traditional and Digital Media in the Arab World*, Dubai: Dubai Press Club, 2009, http:// dpc.org.ae/UserFiles/AMO%20AR%20combined.pdf.

Dynamic in Hamas' Discourse' *The Middle East Journal of Culture and Communication*. Brill Publications, Vol. 1, No. 2, 2008.

Edens, D., 'The Anatomy of the Saudi Revolution', International Journal of Middle East Studies. Vol. 5, No. 1, Jan. 1974.

'Egypt: Internet Usage and Telecommunications Reports', Internet World Stats. Miniwatts Marketing Group, 2000, http://www.internetworld-stats.com/af/eg.htm.

Eisenstein, Elizabeth L., *The Printing Press as an Agent of Change: Communications and Cultural Transformations in Early-modern Europe*, Cambridge: Cambridge University Press, 1979.

El Fadl, K. Abou, *Speaking in God's Name, Islamic law, Authority and Women*, Oxford: Oneworld Publications, 2001.

El Gondy, Ma"a, interview with Salafi preacher Mahmoud el Masry, Azhari TV channel,

El Guindi, Fadwa, *Veil: Modesty, Privacy and Resistance*, Oxford: Berg Publishers, 1999.

El Saleh, Hoda, 'Saudi Female Preachers: Preaching is the Right of Each

Muslim and the Woman undergoes an Invisible Attack', *Al-Sharq Al-Awsat*, 11 Jan. 2007, http://www.aawsat.com/details.asp?section=17&issueno=10271&article=401131&feature=1.

El-Nawawi, M. and A. Iskander, *Al Jazeera: How the Free Arab News Network Scooped the World and Changed the Middle East*, Cambridge, MA: Westview Press, 2003.

Episode of Bein Al Sotoor ('Between Lines') on Al Nas: http://www.youtube.com/watch?v=1T53bBRQlPQ.

Fawal et al., *Religious Programming in Egyptian Television: The Communicators*, Vol. 2, Cairo: National Center for Social and Criminal Research, the Department of Cultural and Communication Research, 1996.

Fawzeh, Samy 'Intercultural Dialogue: Prospects and Challenges', a paper presented at the first Egyptian-Kenyan intercultural Dialogue, Nairobi, 14–20 Nov. 2005.

Fawzy, Sameh, 'Egypt's sectarian problem', *Daily News Egypt*, 30 June 2008.

Feldman, Ilana, *Governing Gaza: Bureaucracy, Authority, and the Work of Rule, 1917–1967*, Durham, NC: Duke University Press, 2008.

'Female Preaching: The Features of the Future', *Qadaya w Araa'*, *Islameyat*.

Field, N. and A. Hamam, 'Salafi Satellite TV in Egypt', *Arab, Media and Society*, Issue 8, Spring, 2009.

Friedman, Menachem, 'Close Yet Far: The Relations between the Religious and the Non Religious', *Meimad*, 27, Nov. 2003 (in Hebrew).

Göl, Ayla 'Imagining the Turkish Nation through 'othering' Armenians', *Nations and Nationalism*, 11(1), Jan. 2005.

Gaffney, Patrick D., 'The Prophet's Pulpit: Islamic Preaching in Contemporary Egypt', Berkeley: University of California Press, pp. 33 Dec. 1994.

———, *The Prophet's Pulpit: Islamic Preaching in Contemporary Egypt*, Berkeley, CA: University of California Press, 1994.

Galal, Ehab, 'Magic Spells and Recitation-competitions. Religion as Entertainment on Arab Satellite-Television', S. Hjarvard (ed.), *Enchantment, Media and Popular Culture. The Mediatization of Religion*, Northern Lights, 2008.

———, 'Reimagining Religious Identities in Children's Programs on Arabic Satellite-TV. Intentions and Values', J. Feldt & P. Seeberg (eds), *New Media in the Middle East*, Odense: Centre for Contemporary Middle East Studies, 2006.

———, *Arabisk satellit-tv. Redskab til forandring?* ('Arab Satellite-Television: A Vehicle for Change?'), Master's thesis, Department of Carsten Niebuhr, University of Copenhagen, 2003.

———, *Identiteter og livsstil på islamisk satellit-tv. En indholdsanalyse af udvalgte programmers positioneringer af muslimer* ('Identity and Lifestyle on

Islamic Satellite-Television: A Content Analysis of Selected Programmes' Positioning of Muslims'), PhD-thesis, Faculty of Humanities, University of Copenhagen, 2008.

Gause III, Gregory F., 'Official Wahhabism and the Sanctioning of Saudi-US Relations', in Ayoob, M. & Kosebalaban, H., *Religion and Politics in Saudi Arabia: Wahhabis and the State*, (eds), London: Lynne Rienner Publishers, 2009.

Geertz, Clifford, 'Religion as a Cultural System', *The Interpretation of Cultures: Selected Essays*, London: Fontana Press, 1993.

Gendi, Ma'a El, 'A debate with Al Habib Al Jafry', Azhari TV channel, Oct. 2009 http://www.youtube.com/watch?v=jsrZebF4z-M&feature=related [Last accessed 10 Mar. 2010].

————, Defa'an 'an El Azhar, Azhari TV channel, Oct. 2009, http://www.youtube.com/watch?v=8Ri-r47DrHs&feature=channel [Last accessed 10 Mar. 2010].

Gerson, M. J., 'An Islamic Test for Turkey', *The Washington Post*, Washington D. C., 6 June 2007, *Council on Foreign Relations*, publication no. 1356.

Gil, Zvi, *House of Diamonds: The Story of Israeli Television*, Tel Aviv: Sifriyat Po'alim, 1986 (in Hebrew).

Gilboa, Eytan, 'The Evolution of Israeli Media', *The Middle East Review of International Affairs*, Vol. 12, No. 3, 2008.

Gräf, B. and Skovgaard-Petersen, J., *The Global Mufti: The Phenomenon of Yusuf al-Qaradawi*. New York, NY: Columbia University Press, 2008.

Gunning, Jeroen, *Hamas in Politics: Democracy, Religion and Violence*. London: Hurst & Co., 2007.

Hürriyet Daily Newspaper, Istanbul, 8 Sept. 2008.

Habermas, Jurgen, *Europe: The Faltering Project*, Cambridge: Polity, 2009.

Haddad, Y., 'Islamists and the "Problem of Israel": The 1967 Awakening', *Middle East Journal*, Vol. 46, No. 2, Spring 1992, http://www.jstor.org/stable/4328433, pp. 266–285.

Hafez, Sherine, 'The Terms of Empowerment: Islamic Women Activists in Egypt' American University in Cairo Press, 2003.

Hall, Stuart, 'Introduction: Who Needs 'Identity'?' in S. Hall and P. Du Gay (eds.) *Questions of Cultural Identity*, London: Sage Publications, 1996.

Hamas: A Beginner's Guide. London, Ann Arbor: Pluto Press, 2006.

Hamdy, Naila, 'El Mehwar The Mercurial' in *Transnational Broadcasting Studies*, TBS9, 2006, para.1,http://www.tbsjournal.com/SuwaidanInterview.html [Last accessed 12 Dec. 2009].

Hamzeh, Nizar, *In the Path of Hizbullah*, Syracuse: Syracuse University Press, 2004.

Harb, Mona and Reinoud Leenders, 'Know thy enemy: Hizbullah, "terrorism" and the politics of perception', *Third World Quarterly*, 26: 1, 2005.

Harik, Iliya, 'Toward a New Perspective on Secularism in Multicultural Societies' in T. Hanf and N. Salam (eds), *Lebanon In Limbo: Postwar Society and State in an Uncertain Regional Environment*. Nomos Verglagsgesellschaft Baden-Baden, 2003.

Harik, Judith Palmer, *Hezbollah: The Changing Face of Terrorism*, London: Tauris, 2004.

Hayirli, Dilek, 'New RTÜK bill to raise foreign media ownership ceiling to 50 pct', *Today's Zaman*, 6 Apr. 2010, http://www.todayszaman.com/tz-web/news-206526–105-new-rtuk-bill-to-raise-foreign-media-ownership-ceiling-to-50-pct.html.

Hiba Hasanin, happens in Annas channel: http://www.almasry-alyoum.com/article2.aspx?ArticleID=28502.

Hjarvard, Stig, 'The Mediatisation of Religion: A Theory of the Media as Agents of Religious Change', *Northern Lights*, 6, 2008.

Hobsbawm, Eric, 'Ethnic Nationalism in the Late Twentieth Century', J. Hutchinson and A. Smith (eds) *Ethnicity*. Oxford: Oxford University Press, 1996.

Hoover, Stewart M., *Religion in the Media Age*, London and New York: Routledge, 2006.

Hroub, Khalid, *Hamas: Political Thought and Practice*. Washington, DC: Institute for Palestine Studies, 2000.

Ibrāhīm Shalabieh, Maĥmoud, 'Itijāhāt al-Mushāhidyyn wa arā'ihim naĥū barāmij al-Qanawāt al-Faḍāiya al-ɛarabiya wa dawarātiha al-Barāmijiya fi shahr ramadān 1427H (2006)' ('The views and attitudes of the viewers toward the programs and program schedules of the Arab satellite channels in Ramadan month 2006'), Paper presented in Arabic at *International Conference on Satellite Television and Cultural Identity. Visions for 21ˢᵗ Century Media*, College of Communication, University of Sharjah University, 11–12 Dec. 2007.

Interview with Tareq Al Suwaidan, General manager of Al Al-Resalah Channel, *Transnational Broadcasting Studies*, TBS16, 2006, http://www.tbsjournal.com/SuwaidanInterview.html [Last accessed 12 Dec. 2009].

'Interview with Alarabi Newspaper by Nashwa Deeb' 10 Dec., http://al-araby.com/docs/1174//print2142182186.html.

'Interview with Atef Abed El Rasheed on Islamonline.' http://www.islamonline.net/servlet/Satellite?c=ArticleA_C&pagename=Zone-Arabic-ArtCulture%2FACALayout&cid=1178724215057.

Iqra' http://www.Iqraa-tv.net/En/Channel.asp

Islam for Everyone Forum, http://vb.islam2all.com/showthread.php?t=5635, 2009.

Ismail, Salwa, *Rethinking Islamist Politics, Culture, the State, and Islamism*, London: I.B. Tauris & Co Ltd., 2006.

Jaafar, Ali, 'Muslim preachers take to TV, Imams rebranding lessons for modern audience', *Variety.com*, 2008, http://www.variety.com/article/ VR1117983548.html?categoryid=2862&cs=1[Last accessed 8 Nov. 2010].

Jamal, Amal, *Media Consumption among National Minorities: The Case of the Arabs in Israel*, Nazareth: I'lam Media Centre for Arab Palestinians in Israel, 2006 (in Hebrew).

Jenkins, Gareth, 'Turkey: AKP Pays the Price', *International Relations and Security Network*, 1 Apr. 2009.

Jones, T., 'Religious revivalism and its challenge to the Saudi regime', *Religion and Politics in Saudi Arabia: Wahhabis and the State*, Ayoob, M., & Kosebalaban, H. (eds), London: Lynne Rienner Publishers, 2009.

Karsh, Efraim and Dan Urian (eds) *In Search of Identity: Jewish Aspects in Israeli Culture*, London: Frank Cass, 1999.

Kaspi, Dan and Yehiel Limor, *The Mediators: The Mass Media in Israel 1948–1990*, Tel Aviv: Am Oved, 1998 (in Hebrew).

Kattan, Victor, *From Coexistence to Conquest: International Law and the Origins of the Israeli-Palestinian Conflict 1819–1949*, London: Pluto Press, 2009.

Kechichian, J., 'The Role of the *'ulama'* in the Politics of an Islamic State: The Case of Saudi Arabia', *International Journal of Middle East Studies*, Vol. 18, No. 1, Cambridge: Cambridge University Press, 1986, http:// www.jstor.org/stable/162860?origin=JSTOR-pdf.

Keyman, E. Fuat, 'Modernisation, Globalisation and Democratisation in Turkey: The AKP Experience and its Limits', *Constellations*, 12(2), 2010.

Khaled, Amr, *Bel Quran Nahya, Kasas El Quran, Part II*, 2009.

Kimmerling, Baruch, 'Religion, Nationalism, and Democracy in Israel', *Constellations*, Vol. 6, No. 3.

King Abdulaziz University website, 2010, http://waqf.kau.edu.sa/content.aspx?Site_ID=808&lng=EN&cid=3303&URL=www.kau.edu.sa.

Knysh, Alexander,'A Clear and Present Danger: "Wahhabism" as a Rhetorical Foil', *Die Welt Des Islam*, New Series, Vol. 44, Issue 1, 2004, pp. 3–26.

Latif, Omaima Abdel and Marina Ottaway, 'Women in the Islamic Movement: Towards an Islamic Model of Women's Activism', Carnegie Institute, Washington, 2007.

Lybarger, Loren L., *Identity and Religion in Palestine: The Struggle between Islamism and Secularism in the Occupied Territories*, Princeton, NJ: Princeton University Press, 2007.

Lynch, M., 'Shattering the Politics of Silence: Satellite Television Talk Shows and the Transformation of Arab Political Culture', *Arab Reform*

Bulletin, 2004,: http://www.carnegieendowment.org/publications/ index.cfm?fa=view&id=16242

———, *Voices of the New Arab Public: Iraq, al-Jazeera, and Middle East Politics Today*, New York, NY: Columbia University Press, 2006.

Mahmood, Saba, *Politics of Piety, the Islamic Revival and the Feminist Subject*, Stanford University, Princeton, NJ: Princeton University Press, 2005.

Mahmoud, Saba, *Politics of Piety: The Islamic Revival and The Feminist Subject*. Princeton, NJ: Princeton University Press, 2004.

Marcos, Samir et al., *Citizens in one Nation* (in Arabic), Cairo: Egyptian Publishing House, 2010.

Masoud, Moez, El Tariq El Sah, 'Interview with Moez Masoud', *Wahed Min el Nas*, Dream TV, Dec. 2009, http://www.youtube.com/ watch?v=kxBKjaIud2Q [Last accessed 26 Sept. 2010].

———, 'Religion as a Veil', *Al Masry Al Yom Newspaper*, 9 Feb. 2010, http://www.almasry-alyoum.com/article2.aspx?ArticleID=24336 8 [Last accessed 26 Sept. 2010].

———, *90 Minutes Talkshow*, El Mehwar TV, episode 4, Sept. 2008, http:// www.youtube.com/watch?v=0ku2NtqwqJU [Last accessed 26 Sept. 2010].

———, *Wahed Min el Nas*, Dream TV, Dec. 2009.

Meijer, Roel (ed.), *Global Salafism: Islam's New Religious Movement*, London: Hurst & Co., 2009.

Meyrowitz, Joshua, 'Images of Media: Hidden Ferment—and Harmony— in the Field', *Journal of Communication, 43*(3), 1993.

Miftah, 'Media Coverage at Palestine Television (PBC)' and 'Al-Aqsa Satellite Channel Following Hamas' Military Takeover of Gaza'. *Media Monitoing Unit, Miftah*, Apr. 2008.

Milliyet Daily Newspaper, Istanbul, 11 June 2002.

Mostafa, Hadia, 'Best of both worlds, interview with Moez Massoud', *Egypt Today*, Feb. 2003, http://moezmasoud.com/en/articles/articles37.html [Last accessed 25 Sept. 2010].

Muhammad Al-Dagher, Majdī, 'Itijāhāt al-Qanawāt al-Faḍāiya al-Islāmiya fi muɛālajit qaḍāya al-Aqaliyāt wa al-Jāliyāt al-Islāmiya fi al-'ālam' ('Satellite Television Attitudes Towards Islamic Minorities in the World'), Paper presented in Arabic at *International Conference on Satellite Television and Cultural Identity. Visions for 21ˢᵗ Century Media*, College of Communication, University of Sharjah University, 11–12 Dec. 2007.

Naeem, Basem, 'Hamas Condemns the Holocaust', *The Guardian*, 12 May 2008.

Navaro-Yashin, Yael, *Faces of the State: Secularism and Public life in Turkey*, Princeton: Princeton University Press, 2002.

Norris, P. and Inglehart, R., *Sacred and Secular: Religion and Politics Worldwide*, Cambridge: Cambridge University Press, 2004.

'Number of Mosques and Zawaya By Gov 08/2009', Social Services, Ministry of Religious Endowments, http://www.msrintranet.capmas.gov.eg/ows-img2/htms/pdf/social/137.pdf.

Okruhlik, G., 'State Power, Religious Privilege, and Myths About Political Reform', *Religion and Politics in Saudi Arabia: Wahhabis and the State*, Ayoob, M., & Kosebalaban, H. (eds) London: Lynne Rienner Publishers, 2009, pp. 91–107.

Otterman, S., 'Fatwas and Feminism: Women, Religious Authority and Islamic TV' *Transnational Broadcasting Studies*, 16, 2006, http://tbsjournal.com/Otterman.html.

Otterman, Sharon, 'Fatwas and Feminism: Women, Religious Authority, and Islamic TV', *TBS*, 16, 2006, http://www.tbsjournal.com/Otterman.html [Last accessed 31 Sept. 2007].

Peri, Yoram, *Telepopulism: Media and Politics in Israel*, Stanford, CA: Stanford University Press, 2004.

Qassim, Naim, *Mujtama' al-Muqawama: Iradat Al-Shahada wa Sina'at al-Intisar* [Society of the Resistance: The Will for Martyrdom and the Making of Victory], Beirut: Dar Al-Maarif Al-Hakimah, 2008.

Radikal Daily Newspaper, Istanbul, 24 Sept. 1998.

Rainsford, S., 'Turkey Awaits AKP's next Step', *BBC News*, 23 Jul. 2007.

Ram, Uri, 'Why Secularism Fails? Secular Nationalism and Religious Revivalism in Israel', *International Journal of Politics, Culture and Society*, Vol. 21, No. 1–4, Dec. 2008.

Rashwan, Diaa, 'Social Islam and the Radical Movement', *El Ektesadeya*, 2009, http://www.aleqt.com/2009/02/06/article_192928.html.

Ravitzky, Aviezer, *Religion and State in Jewish Philosophy*, Jerusalem: Israel Democracy Institute, 2002.

———, *Zionism and Jewish Religious Radicalism*, Chicago, IL: Chicago University Press, 1996.

Raz-Krakotzkin, Amnon, 'There is no God, but He Promised Us the Land', *Mita'am*, Vol. 3, 2005 (in Hebrew).

———, 'Rabin's Legacy: On Secularism, Nationalism, and Orientalism', *Contested Memories—Myth, Nation and Democracy: Thoughts after Rabin's Assassination*, Lev Grinberg (ed.). Be'er Sheva, Humphrey Institute for Social Research, Ben Gurion University, 2000.

Rose, Nikolas, 'Identity, Genealogy, History', in S. Hall and P. Du Gay (eds.) *Questions of Cultural Identity*, London: Sage Publications, 1996.

Roth, Brad R., *Governmental Illegitimacy in International Law*, New York, NY: Oxford University Press, 2000.

Roy, Olivier, *Globalised Islam: The Search for a New Ummah*, London: Hurst & Co., 2004.

Roy, Sara, *Failing Peace: Gaza and the Palestinian-Israeli Conflict*, London: Pluto Press, 2006.

Rubin, M. 'Green Money, Islamist Politics in Turkey', *Middle East Quarterly*, 12(1), 2005.

Rushdi, Mohammad Dosouqi, 'Can we Ignore Sheiks like Yousef El Qaradawi and Khaled Al Jendy, and Intelligent and Well Educated Preachers as Amro Khaled in Favour of Those who Transmit the Tough Fatwa?', Al Youm Al Sabe3, 18 Sept. 2009, http://www.youm7.com/News.asp?NewsID=137409&SecID=162&IssueID=77.

Sabah Daily News, Istanbul, 24 Oct. 2001.

Sakr, Naomi, 'Approaches to Exploring Media-Politics Connections in the Arab World', Naomi Sakr (ed.), *Arab Media and Political Renewal: Community, Legitimacy and Public Life*, London & New York: I. B. Tauris, 2007.

———, 'The Impact of Commercial Interests on Arab Media Content', *Arab Media in the Information Age*, The Emirates Center for Strategic Studies and Research, 2006.

———, *Satellite Realms. Transnational Television, Globalization & the Middle East*, London & New York: I. B. Tauris Publishers, 2001.

Saleh, Amani, 'Towards an Islamic Perspective of Feminist Epistemology', *Woman and Civilization*, Cairo, 2000, Issue 1.

Saudi Gazette, 'Council of Senior "ulama" Reconstituted', *Saudi Gazette*, 2010, http://www.saudigazette.com.sa/index.cfm?method=home.regcon&contentID=2009021529324 [Last accessed 16 Jan. 2010].

Sazak, Derya, 'AKP and Medya', *Milliyet*, 27 Feb. 2007. http://www.milliyet.com.tr/2007/02/27/yazar/sazak.html.

Seib, P., *The Al Jazeera Effect: How the New Global Media are Reshaping World Politics*, New York, NY: Potomac Books, 2008.

Shafir, Gershon, and Yoav Peled, *Being Israeli: The Dynamics of Multiple Citizenships*, Cambridge: Cambridge University Press, 2002.

Shenhav, Yehouda, 'Nationalism was never Modern—or Secular: On Hybridization and Purification in Bruno Latour', *Theory and Criticism*, Vol. 26, 2005 (in Hebrew).

Shereef Shahata's website: http://www.sherif4u.com/index.php?do=show&cat=6&id=166.

Shobaki (ed.), *The Problem of the Brotherhood* (in Arabic), Cairo: The Center for Political and Strategic Studies at Ahram Newspaper, 2009.

Shourky, Galy, *Copts in a Changing Nation*; Abu Seif Yousseif, *Copts and Arab Nationalism*.

Site of Muslim Group: http://www.egyig.com/Public/articles/interview/11/47999487.shtml.

Soffer, Oren, 'The Eraser and the Anti-Eraser: The Battle over Colour Television in Israel', *Media Culture Society*, Vol. 30, 2008.

Sorek, Tamir, 'Religiosity, National Identity and Legitimacy: Israel as an Extreme Case', *Sociology*, Vol. 43, No. 3, 2009.

Sparre, S., *Muslim Youth Organisations in Egypt: Actors of Reform and Development?*, Dansk Institut for Internationale Studier, DIIS. [Electronic version], 2008.

Starret, G., *Politics, and Religious Transformation in Egypt*, Berkeley, CA: University of California Press, 1998.

Stout, D., 'Religious Media Literacy: Towards a Research Agenda', *Journal of Media and Religion*, 1534–8415, Volume 1, Issue 1, 2002, pp. 49—60; p. 50.

Suwaidan, Tarek, Ta'amoulat Fi al Shari'a, *A'lamatny Al hayatt programme* ('Life Lessons'), 2009.

Tarabich, G., *Al-Marad Bel Al-Gharb: Al-tahleel al Nafsi leusab jama'i Arabi*, Damascus: Petra Publishing, 2005.

Tasha. G., Oren, *Demon in the Box: Jews, Arabs, Politics, and Culture in the Making of Israeli Television*, Chapel Hill, NC: Rutgers University Press, 2004.

'The identity of Turkey: Muslim and Secular', *Third World Quarterly*, 30: 4, 2009.

'The Internet and the Islamists and the Jihad Media', Al Jazeera, 2005, http://www.aljazeera.net/Mob/Templates/Postings/ChannelDetailedPage.aspx?GUID=E1C44B9A-EDCE-43F4–8221–76941EBABDE4.

'The Ministry of Religious Endowment in Egypt allows women to work in mosque preaching', *Al-Sharq Al-Awsa*, 5 Nov. 2003.

'The Perspective of the Muslim Brotherhood on Citizenship', in Amer Al.

'The Poetry of Hamas', *The Middle East Journal of Culture and Communication*, Brill Publications, Vol. 1, No. 2, 2009.

Thompson, J. B., *The Media and Modernity: A Social Theory of the Media*, Stanford, CA: Stanford University Press, 1995.

TRT Press Release (2006) *TRT'den açıklama: Dini yayın artmadı*, 9 June 2006, http://www.uydu.info/trt'den-aciklama-dini-yayin-artmadi/.

TSK Press Release, Turk Silahli Kuvvetleri (Turkish Armed Forces), *Genel Kurmay Başkanlığı Basın Açıklaması* (Turkish General Staff Press Release), Ankara: TSK, 27 Apr. 2007.

Tugal, Cihan, 'NATO's Islamists: Hegemony and Americanisation in Turkey', *New Left Review*, 44, Mar.-Apr. 2007.

Van Dijk, T.A., 'Critical Discourse Analysis', D. Tannen, D. Schiffrin & H. Hamilton (eds), *Handbook of Discourse Analysis*, Oxford: Blackwell, 2001.

van Nieuwkerk, Karin, '"Repentant" artists in Egypt: debating gender, performing arts and religion', *Contemporary Islam*, 2, 2008.

Vergin, Nur, 'Monday Talk with Nur Vergin', *Today's Zaman*, 23 Jul. 2007.

Weimann, Gabriel, 'Zapping in the Holy Land; Coping with Multi-Channel TV in Israel', *Journal of Communication*, Vol. 45, No. 1, 1995.

Wigoder, Geoffrey, *The Encyclopedia of Judaism*, Jerusalem Publishing House, 1989.

Wikipedia, Al-Majd TV Network, http://en.wikipedia.org/wiki/Almajd_TV_Network [Last accessed 25 Jan. 2009].

Wiktrowicz, Q. (2006), 'Anatomy of the Salafi movement', *Studies in Conflict & Terrorism*, 29, 2006, pp. 207–239.

Wireless Federation, 'du & Al-Majd together offer range of Islamic Mobile Content during Ramadan (UAE)', 2009, http://wirelessfederation.com/news/17912-du-al-majd-together-offer-range-of-islamic-mobile-content-during-ramadan-uae/.

Wise, Lindsay, 'Amr Khaled: Broadcasting the Nahda' in Transnational Broadcasting Studies, TBS13, http://www.tbsjournal.com/Archives/Fall04/wiseamrkhaled.html [Last accessed 12 Dec. 2010].

'Women in National Parliaments', Inter-Parlimentary Union, http://www.ipu.org/english/home.htm.

Yassin, Hani, 'The Islamic Satellite Channel: Between Reality and Expectations': http://www.egyig.com/Public/articles/miscellaneous/11/616 48259.shtml. http://www.youtube.com/watch?v=iG9Z17P-5m4&feature=related. http://www.youtube.com/watch?v=p75IdUPDK3g&feature=related.

Zaid, Al Sayed, 'Da'wa for Dollars: A New Wave of Muslim Televangelists', *Arab Insight, Bringing Middle Eastern Perspectives to Washington*, Vol. 1, No. 3, 2008.

Zayani, M., *Al Jazeera Phenomenon: Critical Perspectives on New Arab Media*, New York, NY: Pluto Press, 2005.

Internet Sources

'About *Hidabroot*', *Hidabroot's Official Website*, http://www.hidabroot.org/About.asp [Last accessed 5 Jan. 2010].

Netanyahu, Yir'am, "A Proper Answer: A Television Review", *Ha-Tzofe Online*, 11 Jul. 2008 (in Hebrew), http://hazofe.co.il/web/katava6.asp?Modul=24&id=49346&Word=&gilayon=2856&mador [Last accessed 5 Jan. 2010].

Rotem, Tamar, '*Haredi* Reality in the Israeli Radio', *Ha'aretz Online*, 11 Jan.

2008 (in Hebrew), http://www.haaretz.com/hasite/spages/943651. html, [Last accessed: 5 Jan. 2010].

Shiram, Matan, 'Yes Launches a Channel with Missionary Content', *Globes Online*, 5 Mar. 2008 (in Hebrew), http://www.globes.co.il/news/article. aspx?did=1000317520 [Last accessed 5 Jan. 2010].

'The Israeli Broadcasting Authority Law—1965', *Israeli Broadcasting Authority Official Website* (in Hebrew), http://www.iba.org.il/doc/ reshut.pdf [Last accessed 5 Jan. 2010].

'The Social Survey 2006', *Israeli Central Bureau of Statistics' Official Website*, 12 June 2007 (in Hebrew), http://www.cbs.gov.il/hodaot2007n/19_ 07_104b.doc, [Last accessed 5 Jan. 2010].

Toker, Nati, 'In a Living Room in Bnei Brak You Will Not Find a TV Set, But the Emergence of the Internet Took the *Haredi* Leadership by Surprise', *The Marker Online, Ha'aretz Business Magazine*, 21 Dec. 2009 (in Hebrew), http://www.themarker.com/tmc/article.jhtml?ElementId=s kira20091221_1136429 [Last accessed 5 Jan. 2010].

Websites

http://www.aqsatv.ps/ar/?action=allprog&day=Fri
http://www.h-net.org/reviews/showrev.php?id=24825
http://www.alquds.co.uk/index.asp?fname=data/2010/09/09–17/17qpt73.htm
http://www.youtube.com/watch?v=_vWjgXmJJQE&feature=related, [Last accessed on 10 Mar. 2010].

INDEX

Al-Kawthar: 170; 'Debates in
Belief' (*Motarahat Fee al-Aqeeda*),
169–70; founding of (1980), 169
Al-Majd network: 6–7, 37, 40,
47–8, 50–1, 53, 58, 148; channels
of, 41–3; 'Dialogue Time' (*Sa'at
Hiwar*), 39, 41, 44, 52–4; financial income of, 40; Open Islamic
Academy, 44; origins of, 38;
personnel of, 39, 41–2; satellites
used for broadcast by, 62; 'The
Adequate Answer' (*Al Jawab Al
Kafi*), 39; *ulama*, 37, 48, 52, 55
Al-Manar: 219, 222, 225, 227–9,
235–6; Al-Manar's Morning (*Sa-
bah al-Manar*), 229–30; founding
of (1991), 223–4; 'To the Heart'
(*Ila al-Qalb*), 220, 230, 233
Al-Nas TV: 58, 83, 87–8, 91;
founding of (2006), 81; 'Fathers
and Sons' (*Aba' Wa Abna'*), 100;
'Heart to Heart' (*Fadfadah*),
82–4, 97; personnel of, 88, 100–1;
'We'll Live it Right!' (*Han'ishha
Sah*), 82–3, 85–7, 89, 93, 95
Al-Qaeda: 158; branches of, 209;
ideology of, 19–20
Al-Rafidain: 167; 'Dialogue about
Shari'a' (*Hewar Fee al-Sharia*),
159, 165; owned by AMS, 157–8;
website of, 157
Al-Risaleh: 6–7, 12, 52, 62, 114,
123; 'Call of Faith', 19; founding
of (2006), 110
Al-Thaqalain: 169
Al-Zahraa: 169
Albayrak, Berat: head of Sabah-
ATV media group, 278
Algeria: 12
Alhafez TV: personnel of, 90
Alhuweini, Abu Ishaq: 83, 87–8,
91–2, 99; background of, 96;
ideology of, 96–8

Allah bin Maneia, 'Abd: 37
Anani, Malika Al-bu: representa-
tive of Unification and Refor-
mation Movement, 133
Anderson, Benedict: *Imagined
Communities*, 266
Aoun, General Michel: alliance
with Hizbullah, 229; leader of
Free Patriotic Movement, 229
ARA Group: owner of MBC, 16
Arab Radio & Television (ART):
58, 60, 118; channels owned by,
57, 65
Arab Spring: Egyptian Revolu-
tion (2011–12), 200; Libyan
Civil War (2011), 200; Tunisian
Revolution (2010–11), 200
Arafat, Yasser: death of (2004),
258
Association of Muslim Scholars
(AMS): ideology of, 158; owner
of Al-Rafidain, 157–8; personnel
of, 157
Atatürk, Mustafa Kemal: 263;
legacy of, 265
Australia: 225
Azan: relaying via media broad-
cast, 5
Al Azem, Sadiq Jalal: seen as
agent of Westernisation, 46

Badr, Islam: 242, 255, 257
Bahrain: 168, 170
Al-Banna, Hassan: founder of
Muslim Brotherhood, 253
Barakat, Sheikh Akram: head of
CIMA, 233; member of Hizbul-
lah's Central Committee and
Culture Desk, 233; referencing
of Protocols of Elders of Zion,
234
Basili, Sarwat: member of NDP,
210; owner of CTV, 210

Dubai Television (DTV): 32;
founding of (1974), 15, 17; part
of DMI, 17; 'Safe Homes' (*Al
Boyout Al Amena*), 14, 19, 23–4,
26, 29–30
Dylan, Bob: 'Masters of War', 112

Egypt: 33, 41, 51–2, 81, 104, 109,
123, 134, 141, 146, 152, 199,
237, 241; Alexandria, 130, 203;
Cairo, 40, 44, 83, 85, 94, 96, 106,
111, 113, 127, 130, 143, 158,
212; Christian community of,
91, 196–7, 210–11; constitution
of (1923), 196; Free Officers
Revolution (1952), 197; Gaza,
130; government of, 111; impact
of Six-Day War (1967) on, 39;
Ministry of Islamic Affairs,
98, 128; Ministry of Religious
Endowments (WAQF), 130, 210;
People's Assembly, 210; Revolution (2011–12), 200; Zaqazeeq, 99
Erdoğan, Recep Tayyip: family
of, 278; Mayor of Istanbul, 279;
Turkish Prime Minister, 272,
278–9
Ergenekon: 278–9, 281
European Union (EU): 264

Al Fadl, Abou: view of traditions
of Islamist juristic interpretive
community, 109
Fadlallah, Ayatullah Mohammad
Hussein: 227; concept of *Hala
Islamiya*, 226
Fahmi, Ahmad: News Editor at
Al-Majd network, 39
Fareed, Naser: 95
Farhat, Yousef: Director of Public
Relations Office at Awqaf Min-
istry, 248

Fatah: 238, 256; ideology of, 240;
members of, 240, 258
fatwa: 10, 30, 40, 64, 66, 73, 82, 89,
92, 161–2; concept of, 9; delivery
via media broadcast, 9–10, 25,
47, 96; examples of, 40, 51, 98,
148; media discussions of, 20,
49, 63, 78, 84, 158
Al-Fayadh, Ishaq: students of, 164
feminism: Islamic, 135; Western,
135–6
fikr: growth of, 46
Fiqh Al Waqei ('Jurisprudence of
Reality'): influential figures in,
18
France: Revolution (1789–99), 70
Free Patriotic Movement: allies of,
229; members of, 229

Gabriel, Archangel: revelation of
Qur'an to, 57
Al Gamas, Sheikh Hamad: Chair-
man of Board of Directors of
Ola Al-Majd Company, 41–2
Geertz, Clifford: 109; definition of
religion as cultural institution,
104
Germany: 271
Al-Gharby, Iqbal: 'Hypothetical
Space of Women: Content Areas
of Islamic Materials', 144
al-Ghazali, Mohammed: 106
Al-Ghor'we, Ayatollah Ali: 169
Al-Gindi, Nivin: 71; host of 'Af-
fection and Mercy', 70
van Gogh, Theo: *Submission*
(2004), 31
Goldberg, Shlomi: background of,
187; Director of Jewish Heritage
Department of IBA, 187
Gomaa, Sheikh Ali: Mufti of
Egypt, 118

INDEX

Hussein, Saddam: Faith Campaign, 156; fall of (2003), 6, 160;
regime of, 156, 163–4, 170
Huweini, Abu Ishaq: 83

Ibrahim, Sa'ad Al Din: seen as
agent of Westernisation, 46
Al Ibrahim, Waleed: Owner of
ARA Group, 16
Independent Television Commis-
sion (ITC): revocation of MED
TV's license (1999), 271
International Monetary Fund
(IMF): debts and loans, 263
Iqra' Channel: 7, 12, 52, 58, 63, 67,
71, 75, 78, 110; ''Abdin's Famly'
(*Ilet 'Abdīn*), 65; 'Affection and
Mercy' (*Mauadah wa Rahma*),
58, 68, 70–2, 75–7, 79; 'Arab
Inventions' (*Iktishāfāt 'arabiya*),
65; 'Evidence' (*Al-Bayynah*), 58,
68–9, 72–3, 75, 77–9; founding
of (1998), 6, 57; 'Life is Good'
(*al-Dunia bi Khair*), 65; part of
ART package, 57, 65; 'People's
History' (*Ḥakāya al-Nas*), 64;
personnel of, 147; 'Problems
from Life' (*Mushkilāt min al-
Hayat*), 66; satellites used for
broadcast by, 62; 'Science with
Arabs' (*al-'ulūm 'ind al'arab*),
65; 'Today's Events' (*Ahdath
al-Youm*), 65; 'Treasure Hunt'
(*Bahth 'an Knuz*), 65; website of,
59–60
Iran: 156, 160, 164, 272; Islamic
Revolution (1979), 160; Qum,
164, 169
Iran-Iraq War (1980–8): 160, 166
Iraq: 6, 163; Ba'ath Party, 160,
164–5, 198; Baghdad, 160–1, 164,
166; Christian community of,

198, 201; government of, 155,
157–8, 164; Heet, 166; Karbala,
168–9; Najaf, 164, 169; Operation Iraqi Freedom (2003–11),
54–5, 156, 163, 198; parliament
of, 161; satellite channels of,
157, 161; Shiite population
of, 155–7, 160–1, 163–5; Sunni
population of, 155–8, 163–5,
170; Twentieth Revolution Brigades, 157
Islam: 9, 13, 22, 32, 37, 42, 53–4,
58, 67, 69, 73, 77, 95, 100, 110,
125, 128, 143, 145, 199, 203, 205,
207–8, 212–15, 233, 244, 248, 259,
265, 274; *Arafa*, 246–7; conver-
sion to, 206; media broadcasting, 3; moderate, 59, 75, 120;
political, 2–3, 38, 62, 199, 261,
282; radical, 62; Ramadan, 5,
42, 111, 115–16, 155, 271; *shari'a*,
23–4, 27, 116, 120, 132; social,
138; *zakat*, 47
Islam Today Group Establishment:
personnel of, 19
Islamic Call: concept of, 139
Islamic Cultural Society: 132
Islamic Group (*Al-Jamaah Al-Islamiah*): website of, 142
Islamic Supreme Council of Iraq
(ISCI): electoral performance of
(2009), 160–1; formerly SCIRI,
160; founding of (1982), 160;
ideology of, 164; member of
Unified Iraqi Coalition, 160;
owner of Al-Furat, 159
Islamism: 3–6, 8, 10–11, 22, 36, 62,
124, 128, 201, 241; activism, 9;
conservative, 106; contemporary, 106; extremist, 36; feminist, 131, 134, 142; impact of Six-
Day War (1967) on, 39; Shi'a,
221, 225; social, 138

'Un, Mohammad Abu: Director of Al-Aqsa, 239

Unification and Reformation Movement: members of, 133

Unified Iraqi Coalition: members of, 160

United Arab Emirates (UAE): 17; Dubai, 2, 17, 40, 44; Dubai Media City, 16

United Kingdom (UK): 35, 271; 7/7 bombings, 274; education system of, 30; House of Commons Media Select Committee, 31; London, 15–16, 57, 123, 130, 240

United Nations (UN): Conference for Women (1995), 131; Partition Plan for Palestine (1947), 237; Population and Development Conference (1994), 131

United States of America (USA): 35, 68, 76, 114, 251; 9/11 attacks, 14, 20, 32, 36, 234, 274; military of, 158; Washington DC, 54

Al-Wahhab, Muhammad bin Abd: founder of Wahhabism, 36

Wahhabism: 36, 96; *ulama*, 49

Waqf: concept of, 111

World Forum of Islamic Youth: first conference of *da'eyats* (2007), 132

World Islamic Scholars Federation: members of, 19

Yaqoub, Mohammad Hussein: 83, 87–9, 91

Yasin, Ahmad: founder of Hamas, 253

Yemen: 41, 119; Hadramout, 166

al-Zahraa, Fatima: family of, 235

Al-Zaim, Ibrahim: host of 'They Ask You', 243–4, 246, 248

Zionism: 134, 173, 175, 191, 193, 235, 240, 253, 255, 258; Israeli, 186, 188; opposition to, 192; origins of, 174

al-Zubaidi, Bayan Jabur: Iraqi Finance Minister, 160

Milton Keynes UK
Ingram Content Group UK Ltd.
UKHW012123030424
440541UK00005B/169